ECHOES OF THE TAMBARAN

**Masculinity, history and the subject in the work
of Donald F. Tuzin**

ECHOES OF THE TAMBARAN

**Masculinity, history and the subject in the work
of Donald F. Tuzin**

Edited by David Lipset and Paul Roscoe

ANU
THE AUSTRALIAN NATIONAL UNIVERSITY

E PRESS

ANU
E PRESS

Published by ANU E Press
The Australian National University
Canberra ACT 0200, Australia
Email: anuepress@anu.edu.au
This title is also available online at: http://epress.anu.edu.au

National Library of Australia Cataloguing-in-Publication entry

Title: Echoes of the Tambaran : masculinity, history and the subject in the work of
                Donald F. Tuzin / edited by David Lipset and Paul Roscoe.

ISBN: 9781921862458 (pbk.) 9781921862465 (ebook)

Notes: Includes bibliographical references.

Subjects: Tuzin, Donald F.
                Ethnologists.
                Ethnology--Papua New Guinea--Sepik River Region.
                Essays.

Other Authors/Contributors:
                Roscoe, Paul Bernard, 1948-
                Lipset, David, 1951-

Dewey Number: 305.8009957

Cover design and layout by ANU E Press

Contents

Section One: History, Masculinity and Melanesia

Section Two: Culture, the Agent and Tuzin's Methodological Individualism

Section Three: Comparativism, Psychoanalysis and the Subject

Section Four: Style

Preface

In the Sepik Basin, which was the ethnographic crucible for everything Donald F. Tuzin wrote, ritual culture was dominated by what became known in Tokpisin as the *Tambaran*—a (male) tutelary spirit that anchors the ritual life of many lowland New Guinea societies. Incarnated in a particular location, geographic feature or item of ritual patrimony, its voice might be heard in the cry of bamboo flutes or the boom of water trumpets. In return for gifts, the *Tambaran* spirit would serve as the guardian or patron upon whom groups of people under his aegis might rely as they made their way through life. To those of us who knew him, Donald Tuzin was a decidedly generous—rather than a punitive or misogynistic—*Tambaran* and this book can be seen as a ritual prestation, or at least a piece of one, to his abiding spirit and voice.

Tuzin passed away unexpectedly in 2007 (see Chapter 1), so our gift is a mortuary-related prestation. It is a commemorative volume rather than a *festschrift* in honour of a living scholar. Although the essays commissioned for and collected herein are partly intended to answer our grief, we do not offer them by way of ending our mourning and so return to daily life. Nor are they a symptom of melancholia by which we cling ambivalently to the memory of our colleague, teacher and friend in order to avoid doing so. We recognise this kind of project cannot replace the man, intellectually or personally. Indeed, though the volume responds creatively to central ethnographic and theoretical themes as well as to stylistic motifs in Tuzin's work—to masculinity in Melanesia, to the relationship of culture to the subject, to his ethos *qua* author and fieldworker—we readily concede that it does not address the entire career of his interests.

At the same time that the gaps in this volume must signify his irrevocable absence (particularly to we who knew him), it does succeed in another way. It responds to the implicit threat that premature death poses to our sense of mortality and intellectual vitality by asserting that coherent, critical dialogue and collegiality not only remain possible in the face of shocking loss, but also perhaps become more precious.

With regard to this latter sentiment, we are grateful to acknowledge the biographical help we received from Beverly Tuzin, his widow; a reading of our introductory essay by Melford Spiro, his senior colleague in the Anthropology Department at the University of California, San Diego; the support provided by Kathryn Creely, the librarian who worked with him in the Melanesian Archive there; advice from Elfriede Hermann, Wolfgang Kempf and Margaret Jolly, who pointed us to the ANU E Press as an ideal outlet for the volume; and excellent comments on a previous draught from two anonymous reviewers.

Introduction: Donald F. Tuzin, An Anthropologist's Anthropologist

David Lipset and Paul Roscoe

In 2007, Donald Francis (Don) Tuzin died at the age of sixty-one. We who knew him as students and colleagues or simply admired his work from afar lost an anthropologist's anthropologist—a kind that has gone out of fashion, to say the least. He combined the interests of a generalist with the skills of an experienced field ethnographer. His work drew from and contributed to archaeology as well as reflexive anthropology. Driven by methodological individualism and a strong commitment to comparativism, he focused on social control, dreams, politics and art, cannibalism, food symbolism, the psychodynamics of masculinity, the origins of religion, sexuality and childhood. At the same time as the depth of expertise and sheer creativity he brought to these and a great variety of other subjects broke new ground and won him publication in distinguished disciplinary venues, he influenced large swathes of subsequent research. He was among a wave of international ethnographers who in the late 1960s began to focus belated attention on the Sepik Basin of Papua New Guinea, and he emerged as their dean. In this introductory essay, we sketch out Tuzin's life and discuss the main themes in the essays that make up this commemorative volume.

Background

Tuzin's maternal ancestry had deep American roots. His mother, Thelma Louise Smith (b. 1920), grew up in rural southern Illinois, where her father, George Wesley Smith (1895–1949), owned a small vegetable farm in West Vienna. Although she never attended university, Thelma grew up dreaming of higher pursuits and read incessantly. For many years, she worked on a historical American novel involving Native Americans, and this interest might have later drawn Don to anthropology. Thelma had three brothers, one of whom, Donald, was killed in Japan in 1944, the year before Don, her son, was born. She died at the age of fifty-four.

Tuzin's patrilineage was made up of working-class immigrants. His father's father, Fanzieshek Tuzinkiewics (later Francis [Frank] Tuzin), came to the United States from Poland in the first decade of the twentieth century. In Poland, the men in his family had worked as bakers ('*tuzin*' is Polish for 'dozen'), and Frank owned a bakery on East Fourteenth Street on the Lower East Side of New York until his death in 1951. His son, Constantine (Con) Francis Tuzin (b. 1917), grew up as an apprentice in the bakery, before enlisting in the army in 1942. He was stationed in Springfield, Illinois, where he met and married Thelma in October 1943. Subsequently, he was posted as an instructor in the Quartermaster Subsistence School in Chicago, and it was there that Don Tuzin was born on 14 June 1945.

Tuzin's initial acquaintance with Chicago was brief. His father was moved to an army base in California, and, following demobilisation in 1947, the family moved to the river town of Winona, Minnesota, where Con began work as a manager in the Federal Bakery and where Don, as he would later recall, enjoyed Huck Finn-esque childhood adventures on the banks of the Mississippi. In 1959, his father was hired by the Kitchens of Sara Lee Incorporated, and the family returned to Chicago—first to the suburb of Norridge and then eight months later to Sauganash, in the city itself. Here, Tuzin attended Von Steuben High School and met his future wife, Beverly Chodd, who lived just two houses away. In Chicago, the Tuzin family's prospects took a marked turn. Con invented several of Sarah Lee's best-known recipes, including layer cakes and brownies, and eventually rose to become vice-president in charge of overseas corporate expansion. He retired from Sara Lee in 1977 and died just two years later at the age of sixty-one—the same age as would his son almost 30 years later.

Becoming an Anthropologist

Tuzin attended and received his BA from Western Reserve University in 1967, shortly before its merger with Case Institute of Technology. It was here he became interested in anthropology and participated in the excavation of Native American archaeological sites left by the Mound Builders. Olaf Prufer, a Harvard-trained archaeologist at the Cleveland Museum of Natural History, had an adjunct lectureship at Case and recalled coming to know Tuzin well as an undergraduate:

> I think it was I who made him decide on becoming an anthropologist (although he was not fond of dirt, dust and heat)…Don was with my operations during the summers of 1964 and 1965…in the hills of southern Ohio, where he valiantly sought a professional identity. He shared, in 1965, our rage at [President Lyndon] Johnson's destructive decision to go whole hog in Vietnam by committing the army to this hopeless venture…During the…regular academic year, he opted for some coursework with me at Case…His work was excellent. I still must have his paper on the kinship structure of rural Ross County. (Prufer 2007; see also Prufer 1965)

In 1967, after receiving an MA from Case Western Reserve, Tuzin boarded the *Queen Elizabeth II* and went for postgraduate studies at the University of London with the intention of doing research in East Africa. Mary Douglas became intellectually important there (Robbins and Leavitt 2008), and, although he would later reject her theoretical vision, Tuzin recalled her keen intellect and early mentoring with fondness. While in London, Tuzin also met the Australian social anthropologist Phyllis Kaberry, who nurtured his interest in the Sepik region of Papua New Guinea. 'Kaberry's...vivid descriptions of the Abelam [were]...captivating, and [they]...drove Africa quite out of my mind...I was irrevocably attracted not only to Melanesia, but to the Sepik region' (Tuzin 2001:x). At the suggestion of Anthony Forge, Tuzin decided to do fieldwork in Ilahita, a village of Arapesh speakers in the East Sepik District in what was still the Australian Territory of New Guinea (Tuzin 2001:xi). Reo Fortune tutored him in Arapesh language in Cambridge, UK, and Margaret Mead, who had worked with Fortune among the Mountain Arapesh to the east, also supported his work, visiting him in the field and later writing the foreword for his first book. Beverly Tuzin recalled two details of Mead's 1971 visit to Ilahita. First, she was certain that the people 'felt' palpably Arapesh. And second: 'she brought us whiskey—as etiquette-informed visitors to anthropologists-in-the-field should—and told us stories under the pounding rain on our tin roof, while tossing back shots. Then she fell asleep in the middle of Don's response. Don and I were befuddled about what to do—keep talking or not, keep drinking or not, wake her up, go to bed, etc. Finally, we just sat there until she woke up. Then we all went to sleep.' (Beverly Tuzin, Personal communication, 13 September 2009.)

The following year, Tuzin transferred to the doctoral program in the Anthropology Department of the Research School for Pacific Studies at The Australian National University (ANU) in Canberra, which was 'to New Guinea anthropology what the University of London was to African anthropology' (Tuzin 2001:xi). It is perhaps an early indication of Tuzin's social capacities that, despite his emerging relationship with Margaret Mead, Derek Freeman agreed to become his advisor. The two developed a close working relationship that lasted until Freeman's death in 2001. Freeman's influence shaped Tuzin's longstanding interests in criticism and scientific method, the subject and individual choice in culture, and the integration of biological and social anthropology. In the near term, of course, Freeman supervised Tuzin's doctoral fieldwork, which began in September 1969, and Beverly Tuzin recalled that Freeman 'was extremely supportive during and after fieldwork. In addition to anthropological counselling during fieldwork, he sent Don books to read at his leisure (outdoor adventures of guys achieving great feats—mountain climbing, conquering the Antarctic, etc).'

Tuzin's research focused on issues of social organisation, law, ritual and symbolism. A resourceful fieldworker, he collected fine-grained material on many topics. In March 1970, taking a field break after six months in Ilahita, Tuzin went to Sydney and married Beverly Chodd, his high-school sweetheart. Beverly recalled that the wedding

> was arranged by the missionaries Don had befriended in Ilahita, due to the fact that our original plans to be married on a ship had been foiled. The bridesmaids were elderly missionaries. Don's father was the next youngest person there (other than Don and me). He happened to be there, supervising the building of a Sara Lee factory, but he was the only family/friend in attendance.

Shortly thereafter, the newlyweds left for New Guinea. Or, as Tuzin once put it, without any trace of guile: 'Right after we got married, I jumped straight into the bush.'

Figure 1 Don and Beverly Tuzin in Ilahita after being married in Sydney. 'When we returned to Ilahita,' Beverly recalled, 'the small-plane pilot dipped his wing as we passed over the village. The people of Ilahita decorated the path to our house and our house with colorful crotons, etc. They also lined the path and welcomed us.'

After a good Malinowskian period of 22 months in the field, Tuzin returned to Canberra in 1972 and started to write up his dissertation. Michele Stephen remembered the impressive figures he and Beverly cut in those days:

> Very tall and straight, over 6'4", he never allowed even a trace of an academic slouch to lessen his imposing stature, always carrying himself with a kind of nonchalant elegance. His black hair, brilliant blue eyes, olive complexion and classical features added up to movie-star good looks, which he perhaps tried to disguise, but failed, with a heavy beard. Soft spoken with just the hint of an appealing diffidence of manner, he nevertheless could be firm and even intimidating for all his charm. Don and his tall, equally elegant wife, Beverly, made a stunning couple... on the campus of the ANU, two tall, almost impossibly beautiful young Americans. Both might have been Hollywood actors playing the role of the dashing anthropologist and his lovely companion.

Tuzin saw his time as a graduate student at ANU as 'idyllic', Beverly recalled. 'His office window opened onto an enclosed courtyard with trees and grey and pink galahs...He valued his...animated discussions during the regular morning/afternoon teas [and in] departmental seminars, which often included...heated arguments.' Edenic as Canberra might have been in the early 1970s, Tuzin now had to think about getting his first job. He recalled a crucial role that the South Asianist Paul Alexander, who was part of his cohort at ANU, played in this process:

> Around September 1972, we were both a few draft chapters into our theses...Paul ...[had] a copy of the *American Anthropological Association Guide to Graduate Departments* in his hand. He had found just the department for me. UC San Diego had all the scholars I admired. I must write to them, Paul demanded. 'But I don't know if they're even hiring,' I responded. 'Never mind!' Paul said, in terms that were probably a little more colorful than that. Thereupon, he REFUSED TO LEAVE MY OFFICE until, then and there, I wrote to the department to introduce myself. One thing led to another, and now, thirty-three years later, *I'm* still at UC San Diego. I literally do not know where I would be, without Paul. (Quoted in Feil 2005:233)

In 1973, Tuzin left Australia for a job interview in San Diego. While getting dressed at the hotel to meet faculty, he put on a tie for the first time in several years and felt several lumps in his neck. Upon returning to Canberra, he declined to go for a check-up and biopsy, his wife recalled, until he had finished his dissertation. Once he did submit it to his committee, he got the diagnosis. He had contracted Hodgkin's Lymphoma, although the stage of its development was not immediately determined. Now, he refused treatment until after the thesis defence. He defended successfully, and he and Beverly proceeded that very same afternoon to hospital. Tuzin underwent a splenectomy, and the disease was then staged at 2a, meaning all the cancer was above the diaphragm. He received one month of radiation treatments in Sydney, before leaving Australia for southern California to take up an assistant professorship at the University of California, San Diego (UCSD). He was twenty-eight.

La Jolla Years

Tuzin began to undergo weekly doses of chemotherapy at the UCSD Medical Center in Hillcrest and had to wrestle with their side effects as he began his new job. In addition to nausea, he became anaemic, weak and paranoid. Beverly recalled how certain he was that his colleagues hated him and how convinced he became that his teaching was going poorly. Marc Swartz, the political anthropologist who was then chair of the UCSD department, remembered holding quite the contrary view. He recalled Tuzin 'lecturing on kinship. I thought I knew about kinship, but I didn't know as much as Don did. He was absolutely brilliant' (quoted in Kinsman 2007). The treatments left him in remission and perhaps with a Johnsonian sense of urgency and concentration. During these first years in La Jolla, his sons, Gregory (b. 1976) and Alexander (b. 1980), were born and in quick succession his Ilahita material began to burst out.

In the early 1970s, Ilahita village, where Tuzin conducted the bulk of his fieldwork, had a population of nearly 1500 people, making it one of the largest villages in Papua New Guinea. Given that Ilahita society was acephalous, Tuzin raised a classic structural-functional problem that would have made Meyer Fortes proud: how could the village hold together in the absence of formal leadership? His first book, *The Ilahita Arapesh: Dimensions of Unity* (1976), sought to answer this question and raised issues that would intrigue him for the rest of his career. Ilahita village society was divided into a dual organisation in which 'moieties, sub-moieties, initiation classes and age-sets' crosscut and overlapped one another to produce an 'intricate web' of solidarity among villagers (Tuzin 1976:xxiv–xxv). Derek Freeman had interested Tuzin in the project of combining Popper's (1950) version of methodological individualism (cf. Hayek 1952; Weber 1968) with historical explanation: how did the elaborate sociology that held Ilahita village together come about? Arguing against Levi-Strauss's (1963) claims that dual organisation arose from the structure of the human mind, Tuzin claimed that it derived instead from individuals making mundane choices in the face of recurring situational demands. The book applied this analytical framework to a historical reconstruction of how this complex social organisation might have arisen.

A companion volume, *The Voice of the Tambaran*, which appeared four years later (1980), went in a different theoretical direction. The ethnographic goal was to portray rituals of initiation into the Ilahita male cult. During fieldwork, Tuzin himself had observed several stages of this complex rite, and with his considerable literary skills he was able to convey the vitality of its ethos with a nuance that few in the Melanesian literature had achieved. In addition, the book sought to interpret the symbolism of a wide range of phenomena: myth imagery and cult-house construction—from anchor posts to bark painting facades. As a whole, Tuzin argued, the cult defined moral order for Ilahita men, although its influence upon women remained obscure.

While influenced by Derek Freeman's strong bio-cultural vision, Tuzin's interest in cultural theory in relation to emotion and other psychological capacities was also guided by the distinguished Freudian Melford Spiro, the founder of the UCSD Anthropology Department, and another psychoanalytically oriented colleague there, Robert Levy. For example, in his article 'The Breath of a Ghost: Dreams and the Fear of the Dead' (Tuzin 1975), he examined how Arapesh dreams, and their interpretations, draw upon individuals' relationships with loved ones. Dreaded dream visits from the ghosts of deceased parents were said to resonate with ambivalent feelings of mourning. Similarly, a subsequent contribution to Herdt's (1982) well-known anthology *Rituals of Manhood* explored how individual men reacted to having to sponsor their sons' subjection to terrifying ordeals in male-cult rituals. In another quite original piece, entitled 'Miraculous Voices: The Auditory Experience of Numinous Objects' (1984), Tuzin argued that 'numinous' or 'religious' feelings that have often been documented as preceding an epileptic seizure might illustrate how patterns of brain activity could produce an existential response that might be culturally appropriated as 'religious'. The resonating sounds of the Arapesh 'voice' of the *Tambaran* cult spirit produced by bamboo flutes being blown into the base of wooden drums could, through simple acoustics, produce brain-wave patterns and 'numinous feelings' that individuals would then interpret as religious awe. Similar dynamics might be related to sounds produced in religious contexts more generally. Through these and other essays drawing from his Ilahita material, Tuzin developed his own thoroughly bio-psychosocial perspective on culture.

He remained interested in Ilahita's historical experience. In 1983, he co-edited a collection with the social anthropologist Paula Brown Glick, *The Ethnography of Cannibalism* (Brown and Tuzin 1983). His piece in the volume analysed vivid stories told by Ilahitans about the desperation of Japanese soldiers who were said to have cannibalised villagers in the last days of the New Guinea campaign. By this time, too, events were moving him towards a return to Ilahita. Following the lead of Bateson and Mead in the 1930s, Tuzin had thought to undertake a second project to be located somewhere in rural Indonesia. In 1979, he spent six weeks exploring Bali, Java and Sulawesi looking for an appropriate field site. Unhappily, he could not win grant support for this research project. Three graduate students at UCSD, Karen Brison, Stephen Eyre and Steven Leavitt, had decided to do doctoral fieldwork in Papua New Guinea, and Tuzin wrote and submitted a grant in support of a comparative project that was to be focused on middle childhood in contiguous cultures in the vicinity of Ilahita (Leavitt, Personal communication). In 1985, he received National Science Foundation funding for the project.

Tuzin, Beverly and their two sons returned to Ilahita for 11 months in 1985–86. There, he found a community in disarray, at least from a culturally conservative point of view. A year earlier, many villagers had converted to evangelical Christianity and during church service confessionals had revealed the secrets of the male cult to women and children in the community, exposing the knowledge that flutes were not the voices of the spirits but were 'actually' men blowing them.

Figure 2 Tuzin's informant Tomi insisted that his two boys plant coconuts on his land so that they would have a conditional link to him. Ilahita, 1986.

Photo: B. Tuzin

On the basis of his research into the meaning and consequences of these events, Tuzin published an ethnographic masterpiece, *The Cassowary's Revenge: The Life and Death of Masculinity in a New Guinea Society* (1997). The centrepiece of the book was the destruction of the Ilahita male cult at the hands of the very men who once had treated it as axial in their lives. In the opening chapter, Tuzin wrestled candidly with the angst he felt about what had happened, and he reflected on how he had himself figured in people's thinking. At the centre of his inquiry was a clever argument that the myth of the cassowary had come to be understood as having foretold the death of the male cult, the end of which was enabled by its having been culturally exogenous to Ilahita in the first place. The male cult of the *Tambaran*, he argued, had been adopted from the neighbouring Abelam as a result of the latter's military superiority. The misogyny that accompanied it, Tuzin argued, had never sat well with traditional Ilahita notions of male–female relations (relations that indeed recalled Mead's famous characterisation of gender among the Mountain Arapesh as uniformly nurturant (Mead 1935; cf. Fortune 1939; Roscoe 2003). The coming of evangelical Christianity provided a constituency of Ilahita men with an excuse to do away with the cult, the cult whose values they had not endorsed. What resulted, Tuzin believed, was a masculine tragedy. Tuzin's book is a portrait of sad betrayal, domestic violence and ritual confusion as well as other more material afflictions. *The Cassowary's Revenge* quickly became a modern classic in Melanesian ethnography as well as in the study of masculinity amid cultural change.

In the aftermath of the mid-1980s Ilahita fieldwork, Tuzin occupied himself in a series of smaller projects. He wrote two energetic papers on sexuality. In one, he traced anthropological interest in the topic back to Malinowski (Tuzin 1994); in the other, he argued that the study of sexuality would benefit both conceptually and empirically from a focus on what he called the 'excluded middle' that was constituted by the interaction of practice and cultural discourse (Tuzin 1991:872).

Together with Thomas Gregor, he also organised a major Wenner-Gren symposium that resulted in *Gender in Amazonia and Melanesia: An Exploration of the Comparative Method* (Gregor and Tuzin 2001). This volume used gender in these two distinct geographical areas as a focus for reconsidering the utility of the comparative method in anthropology—a method that Tuzin refused to surrender despite growing hostility in mainstream cultural anthropology. In their co-authored piece, Tuzin and Gregor compared male cults in Ilahita and Mehinaku, not as an assertion of patriarchy or even male–female interdependency but rather as an anguished attempt to sustain the integrity of an otherwise ambivalent, frail masculine subject. Tuzin also published *Social Complexity in the Making: A Case Study Among the Arapesh of New Guinea* (2001), which was written to augment a sequence of courses in which he participated at UCSD called 'The Making of the Modern World'. In this book, he returned to and expanded notions of cultural evolution and change that had run through earlier work. At the time of his death in 2007, Tuzin was full of enthusiasm for a biography of Derek Freeman on which he was working with Peter Hempenstall, the emeritus Pacific historian. The project was to be called 'Truth's Fool: Derek Freeman and the Future of Anthropology'.

In addition to his scholarship, Tuzin's further legacy to the Melanesianist community is large. He founded the University of California Press series *Studies in Melanesian Anthropology* and served as a senior editor of the series from 1984 to 1994. He was also on the boards of the journal *Oceania* and the allied *Oceania Monographs*. But perhaps his greatest contribution to Melanesian scholarship lay in his role as co-founder, long-time academic advisor and honorary curator of the Melanesian Archive, housed in the Geisel Library at UCSD. Fitz John Porter Poole and Tuzin started the archive in 1982. Working with UCSD librarians, they secured two large Title IIC grants for the project from the US Department of Education. Created to staunch 'Ethnographic Loss and Scatter', the archive collects fieldnotes and other unpublished materials of anthropologists who work or have worked in Melanesia, together with patrol reports and other government documents from the region (Tuzin 1995:24). Along with dissertations, MA theses, microform sets of archival materials held by other institutions, and book and journal holdings related to the region, the archive Tuzin and Poole founded—and which Tuzin worked hard to maintain— made it the world's largest depository of materials on the cultures of Melanesia and made UCSD an outstanding resource for research. As Kathryn Creely, the Melanesian Studies Librarian at UCSD, commented:

> [T]he Archive could not exist without Don's contributions—intellectual and personal. His vision for building the collection, his intellectual curiosity, his wonderful relations with colleagues internationally in the field of Melanesian anthropology, and above all, his own kindness, courtesy and humor were all essential ingredients in the our endeavor. (Quoted by JaCoby 2007)

In addition, the archive provides copies of materials to libraries in the Pacific—a feature of which Tuzin was proud. In honour of his commitment to Melanesian scholarship, the archive has recently been renamed for him.

Figure 3 Don Tuzin, 2005, La Jolla

Photo: B. Tuzin

In addition to a productive scholarly career, Tuzin was active in administration at UCSD. Joel Robbins, one of his colleagues in the Anthropology Department there, recalled how Tuzin 'believed that UCSD was the most exciting university in the world, and he gave his time and heart to it accordingly' (quoted by JaCoby 2007). He twice served as chair of the Anthropology Department, helping it through a politically difficult period of expansion into a prominent four-field department. From 1990 to 1993, he served as Associate Chancellor of the university under Richard Atkinson. Atkinson recalled asking Tuzin to move with him when he became President of the University of California system, hoping to groom him as a chancellor or university president himself. Citing his commitment to scholarship and teaching, however, Tuzin declined to leave San Diego. In 2004–05, he served as the elected Chair of the UCSD Academic Senate. In these administrative roles, he proved able, and had an ability to listen with patience and make decisions that were deemed fair. At UCSD, he is and will be remembered as a substantial figure in the history of what is still a young university.

Because it conveys something about the austerity and selfless dedication that possessed him, we want to end this biographical section (which recalls his initial cancer treatment) with a word about the process of his passing. In 2001, Tuzin was visiting Machu Picchu during a family vacation in Peru, when he suffered a bout of nausea and shortness of breath that he imagined to be altitude sickness (his wife later suspected it was a blood clot that had broken). From that time on, his health slowly deteriorated, his energy declined, and his doctors were unable immediately to diagnose why. Over the following year, he again suffered acute shortness of breath. Upon return to La Jolla, he began to receive various treatments. An unnecessary pacemaker was implanted in his heart. He suffered thyroid damage. Beverly recalled this period of their lives as involving 'a lot of waiting for test results'. During the summer of 2006, however, he was promoted to Distinguished Professor in the UC system—its highest rank. That autumn, he received a diagnosis of pulmonary hypertension, which his doctors thought was related to scatter effects from the cruder, less pinpointed form of radiation he had received 33 years earlier, in 1973. By early winter, he was no longer able to walk to the library, and, in November, he went on oxygen 24 hours a day, which depressed and scared him. Until then, he had carried on with everyday life, working as normally as possible and complaining to no-one. Indeed, most people had not even realised he was ill. 'Basically,' Beverly said, 'he was able to fake it pretty well.' Donald Tuzin died on 15 April 2007, intending to undergo preliminary evaluation so as to become eligible to join a waiting list for a heart–lung transplant.

The Essays

In the aftermath of Tuzin's unexpected and decidedly premature death, our instructions to contributors were sparse: engage an aspect of his work. The chapters in the resulting volume thus engage a variety of topics, differing also in ethnographic texture and, of course, methodological orientation, but they all respond to Tuzin's principal interests in the Sepik: masculinity and epistemology. In addition, some authors, such as Birth, Knauft and Robbins, while making a theoretical point, adopt a somewhat more personal tone. Others, including Lipset, Roscoe and Stephens, write more formally as they focus on a particular analytical topic. We note these rhetorical differences and let them stand. They are, we think, useful expressions of the loss from which this volume emanates. In all, we have grouped the chapters according to the following four themes: 1) Sepik prehistory, history and contemporary Melanesian masculinities; 2) culture, the agent and methodological individualism; 3) comparativism; and lastly, as might be appropriate to a commemorative project of this kind, 4) Tuzin's style as a fieldworker and author.

History, Masculinity and Melanesia

A major project in Tuzin's first volume, *The Ilahita Arapesh* (1976), was the reconstruction of village prehistory, and he returned to archaeological issues in his last book, *Social Complexity in the Making* (2001). Lamenting anthropology's continuing contempt for social-evolutionary inquiry, Tuzin held up the value to archaeologists of communities such as Ilahita for understanding processes of social transformation (2001:5–10). Drawing from several types of data, Tuzin argued that, beginning in the late 1800s, Ilahita exploded from a community of 100–200 people to almost 1300 under the pressure of large-scale migrations northwards from the Sepik River of dense populations of Abelam people. This process of expansion was eventually halted by the 'pacification' of the region in the 1940s, but by then the village had already become one of the largest in New Guinea. The conceit of an Abelam 'invasion' is a longstanding one in Sepik anthropology, but in his contribution, Paul Roscoe counters that it never occurred, or at least not as it is usually represented. The characteristics of the Abelam–Arapesh region commonly taken as evidence for such a mass migration, he argues, are better explained as the product of localised ecological conditions. The formation of Ilahita village was no different to standard processes of village formation elsewhere in the area, and the unusual size to which it grew is better attributable to the village's unusual topography rather than to prehistoric immigration. This being the case, Roscoe concludes, Tuzin's description and analysis of the strategies that Ilahitans adopted for coping with their conurbation assume a far greater relevance than he might have imagined. Rather than being *sui generis*, as Tuzin thought, they are applicable to village formation and maintenance processes throughout the Sepik region.

Whether or not warfare was a major factor in the rise of Ilahita village, the male cult, or the *Tambaran*, became an axis of interest in subsequent work, which culminated in his account of the 'death' of the *Tambaran*—for example, its collapse in 1984 amid millenarian expectations fomented by a 'Christian revival', and fostered by Ilahitan interpretations of Tuzin's own 1969–72 fieldwork there, and the promise of his return. With the public exposure of cult secrets to women and children, male domination—the very meaning of ritual masculinity—collapsed, as Ilahita sought to pivot towards a new, globalised future. Among the Abelam—eastern neighbours to the Ilahita Arapesh—and about the same time as Tuzin, Brigitta Hauser-Schäublin experienced a series of developments that marked a similar, radical cultural transformation and ultimately led her to surrender her Abelam field site.

As Tuzin did in *The Cassowary's Revenge*, Hauser-Schäublin seeks to understand the processes that effected this transformation. She does so with an elegant analysis of the Abelam string bag, a seemingly mundane artefact that actually illuminates two conjoined, systemic principles upon which Abelam culture appears to be based. On the one hand, there is the structure of these bags— manufactured by a looping technique from a single piece of twine. On the other, there is their semi-transparent surface—an artefact that both conceals and reveals what is inside. Abelam men's knowledge in the 'pre-modern' era, Hauser-Schäublin proposes, was organised on the same two principles. Referring to a reality beyond the world of everyday life, of routine processes and practices controlled by human agents, this hierarchically structured knowledge and the manner in which it was disbursed involved an interplay between revealing and concealing and an inter-looping of the two modes. In a new era shaped by colonialism, Christian proselytisation, political independence and the advance of a capitalist economy and globalisation, the 'death' of the Abelam *Tambaran*, as we might call it, involved a determination to put an end to the 'pre-modern' era and the principles represented in the string bag of the *Tambaran*. The values fostered by and embodied in the bag, with its continual loops of concealing and revealing, no longer sufficed as a model for identity.

David Lipset and Bruce Knauft also focus on Tuzin's interest in masculinities in contemporary Papua New Guinea but suggest that their transitions do not necessarily conform to the tragedy that befell the Ilahita male cult in the mid-1980s. Lipset deploys Lacanian semiotics to do so. For Lacan, the subject's position in culture is based in eternal desire, which is attracted by metaphorical substitutions for, rather than negations of, past loss. The phallus, moreover, is the privileged signifier of both desire and loss. Lipset therefore opines that

Tuzin's view of Ilahita masculinity in the mid-1980s was one-dimensional. Instead of tragedy, ritual masculinity was observed making multiple kinds of substitutions that combine the presence and the absence of the phallus into an equivocal register.

Knauft, relying on a historical methodology, arrives at a similar conclusion. Among the Gebusi of the Highlands fringe, he argues that the trajectory of ritual masculinity is unpredictable, rather than uniformly negative or disparaging as in Ilahita or Abelam. In 2008, he found Gebusi men less violent than they had been during earlier years. What is more, in the wake of post-colonial devolution, they had revived central masculine institutions: the longhouse, male initiation and traditional dancing. It is too easy, Knauft avers, to misjudge the future of Melanesian men.

Culture, the Agent and Tuzin's Methodological Individualism

The basis of Tuzin's dynamic view of Ilahita as well as his tragic view of ritual masculinity lay in a Popperian conception of the actor in society. The four chapters in this section all respond to aspects of this interest in culture, the agent and the recursive relationship between the two. Drawing on vernacular reactions to 'strange' occurrences he observed during research in Trinidad in 1996, Kevin Birth elegantly discusses the uncanny through the Vichean approach that Tuzin adopted towards it. As Birth points out, the uncanny disrupts Cartesian dualism—the division between the mental and the material world that undergirds the more naive epistemologies of science. Although it is founded on observed particulars, the uncanny evokes the *mysterium*—a sense of something behind the world of perception. To avoid this dilemma, Birth informs us, Tuzin invoked Vico's critique of Descartes' dualism and his distinction between *verum* (truth: that which is created by the human mind and which, for this reason, we *can* know) and *certum* (certainty: our acquaintance with and beliefs about the physical world). Along with Langer's approach to aesthetics and Morris's pragmatism, the concept of *verum* galvanised Tuzin's study of such phenomena as the Ilahita *Tambaran* cult, directing him towards the active process of meaning creation. For Tuzin, the uncanny was a vital component in this process. By focusing on ('subjective') apperception rather than on ('objective') perception, Tuzin appreciated that the 'strange' coincidence—the symbol apperceived to have intrinsic import—acted as a socially creative force, prompting the collective imagination and creation of truth and playing a vital role in religious experience. The Vichean approach that Tuzin adopted towards the uncanny, Birth suggests, has wide-ranging use for the study of post-colonialism and modernity, for ethnographic enterprise, and for anthropological epistemology.

If Vico, Langer and Morris influenced Tuzin's theoretical approach to symbolism, Popper's methodological individualism provided him with theoretical inspiration for understanding society. In a trenchant examination of the entire sweep of Tuzin's work—from his first to his last book—Don Gardner finds that a sense of the complexity of the total human person rather than any conceptual privilege attached to the individual was what drove his analysis. In light of the daunting metaphysical issues that lurk in the wings of methodological individualism, Gardner suggests, Tuzin might have been better served if he had set his Popperian prescriptions aside. His interests in an interactionalist approach to social life and his concern with comparison would be better advanced, Gardner continues, by the considerations evident in Weberian analytical practice or by Philip Pettit's 'explanatory ecumenism'.

Drawing from Tuzin's view that culture should be seen as arising from the contingencies of individual action and subjectivity, Stephen Leavitt finds reminiscences about childhood told by a Bumbita Arapesh man to be an empirically useful expression of the rhetorical relationship between narrator, as actor, and cultural norms. He carefully analyses a case in which an informant recalled incidents that involved childhood adventures with classificatory siblings who would rather not have shared the fruits of their foraging exploits in the rainforest. Insisting that they do so, he threatened to tell on them. As his father had died prematurely by the time he spoke to Leavitt, the informant was expressing anxiety about achieving full status in the patrilineal community.

In his contribution, Joel Robbins offers an elegant assessment of the convergence of his own holist, or realist, concept of society with Tuzin's methodological individualism, to which, he suggests, Tuzin became less of an adherent in later years. Following up a point made by Derrida, Robbins distinguishes between what he calls the 'messianic promise' (a hint of a new time) and messianism (a wide-ranging belief in a specific future) and goes on to reflect upon an incident in which the Urapmin people of Papua New Guinea showed a willingness to acknowledge the former while going on with their day-to-day lives. That is, action and temporal order are shown to coexist in complicated ways. As if to express his own grief, Robbins laments, in a poignant conclusion, how cultural anthropology as a discipline has closed itself off from this kind of subjectivity. The allure of the other, which interested Tuzin and himself, has diminished in favour of the allure of universals, of human rights, capitalism, science and the postmodern subject.

Comparativism, Psychoanalysis and the Subject

Robbins' nostalgia returns us to the subtitle of this introductory essay. While hardly narrow, pedantic, unimaginative or incurious, Tuzin was not theoretically chic. Tuzin was a strong proponent throughout his career of comparativism, particularly with a psychological bent, notwithstanding the severe attacks it began to sustain in the late 1980s from mainstream anthropology and most especially its postmodern critics. The core of his position was to be found in the introduction he co-wrote with Tom Gregor in their edited volume on gender in Amazonia and Melanesia: 'Without comparison, we risk miring our work in exotica and in the description of the particular…For, without comparison— without systematic observation, classification, and generalization— anthropology will become nothing at all' (Gregor and Tuzin 2001:7–8).

This section includes four comparativist essays that follow this methodological persuasion. Tuzin's pursuit of an interactionalist paradigm, so Gardner points out, led him into the burgeoning literatures of developmental psychology and cognitive science in the latter part of his career, and he came to share a sense of incredulity with such scholars as Sperber and Boyer at mainstream anthropology's lack of interest in widely dispersed or universal psychological characteristics.

Michelle Stephen, picking up on the thread of a discussion she once had with Tuzin, argues for the value of Melanie Klein's psychoanalysis in comprehending these parallels and themes. A younger contemporary of Freud, Klein viewed emotional life in terms of the mother rather than the father. For Klein, prior to the unconscious Freudian guilt attached to a fantasised patricide were envy and paranoid fears aroused by a fantasised matricide. In her approach, masculinity and femininity are shaped against a mother image of such terrible power that both genders feel themselves damaged by the struggle. The results, Stephen demonstrates, are particularly evident in the terrible images of the Balinese and Hindu Durga, as well as in other fantasies of violent mothers.

Although Tuzin was well read in the psychoanalytic literature, his notion of psychological development was neither Kleinian nor Freudian but harked back to his adherence to methodological individualism. As we mentioned above, in the mid-1980s he won a National Science Foundation grant to do comparative research on middle childhood based on the view that socialisation into culture takes place in and through experience with peers rather than with adults, and that this experience is creative not rote. In her contribution, Karen Brison, who was a member of that project, argues that rural preschoolers in Fiji play in mixed-age groups that are informed by hierarchical norms of superiority and inferiority. In urban Fiji, in contrast, kindergarteners are taught by powerful teachers in same-age groups. The play of the groups, as she observed them, differed. The former played in terms of hierarchical relations. The latter made up fantasies of monsters and superheroes, as well as about consumption, and, as they did, were learning to be autonomous individuals who would have to devise and use strategies to deal with the inequalities they would encounter in adult life.

The final pair of essays in this section returns us to Melanesian ethnography. Thomas Gregor and Gilbert Herdt take up the issue of ritual masculinity, and subject it to a comparative framework, albeit of quite different kinds. In a meditation about ritual violence against male initiates that relies on Herdt's Sambia work and Tuzin's Ilahita Arapesh studies, Gregor goes back to the question of why good people might do bad things to each other. After reviewing some of the more egregious practices—which he likens to torture—that were staged against male youth, together with the misogynist ideology that justified them, he goes on to ask whether there are any data to suggest that what boys had to endure was resisted by any or all of the stakeholders, such as the boys themselves, the initiators, their fathers, or the boys' mothers. There is, Gregor finds, and he cites evidence of defiance, which he locates in the disconnection between domestic and ritual values in these societies.

Herdt contrasts the repression of discourse about sexuality in Sambia culture with a Freudian model and the Foucaultian notion of state-based power/ knowledge/norm. Among Sambia, secrecy about desire and pleasure was functionally integrated with the maintenance of the male cult but also with conjugal relations and the body. Boys could not become successful men if they betrayed elders' secrets about ritual intimacies that had gone on. They must never talk either about having been an object of desire or about desiring others. These kinds of issues, Herdt concludes, have been difficult to study because ethnographers carry the biases and categories of their backgrounds to the field, which also restricts discourse about sexuality.

Tuzin's Style

Having begun this volume and this essay with biography, this final section comes back to qualities of Tuzin's style as a fieldworker and author. Among his many other personal virtues, observes Alexander Bolyanitz, Tuzin was unerringly gracious and polished. He was gentle in the way he corrected those in error and generous in deflecting indignity from deserving targets. Tuzin epitomised, Bolyanitz observes, the courtesy that is the hallmark of anthropological method in the field, and he uses this insight to reflect on an issue that has been rather neglected in anthropology's postmodern turn and its reflexive attention to the morally charged dynamics of fieldwork: the implications—for the fieldworker and the 'fieldworked'—of returning to the same group of people.

To be an ethnographer, Bolyanitz points out, fieldwork method demands that one be polite (in local terms). If data are to be gathered, one can ill afford to disparage what one is told. When Tuzin showed interest in the story of Nambweapa'w during his first fieldwork, for example, he did not of course believe it, but 'courtesy and method' discouraged him from expressing doubt about the tale. Methodological interest, in other words, dictated courtesy. The more often ethnographers return to the field, however, the more they become implicated (or complicit) in local affairs, and the more this connection between courtesy and method undergoes metamorphosis. As they become better known as a person in the local community, as they come to know better what it is to be a person in local terms, their behaviour becomes more polite and civil—method contributing more to courtesy than courtesy contributes to method. In Tuzin's case, his uncritical acceptance of the foundational mythology of the *Tambaran* was to help bring about its downfall 15 years later. For Bolyanitz, the results might have been less ironic, but no less personally profound in comprehending the effects of repeated returns to the field on his persona.

In her contribution, Diane Losche focuses on Tuzin's rhetorical talents to draw attention to a broader and neglected issue in the analysis of ethnographic representation. Debate about construction, she points out, has concerned itself principally with issues of truth value—how faithfully ethnographic 'facts' represent what is 'really' going on—and, subsequently, with the rhetorical narrative modes by which ethnographers constitute themselves in their texts as 'authorities'. But what also deserves commentary is a more nuanced interpretation of the voice of the anthropologist, of tone that colours the many different types of cultural forms that an ethnographic work describes, and the manner in which this voice varies from one ethnographer to another and, sometimes, between texts by the same author.

In most of his work, Losche notes, Tuzin's voice is magisterial, authoritative and dramatic—a tone that creates the sense of a grand narrative of great historical moment. In this respect, the voice is similar to that of Margaret Mead's in her earliest work on the Mountain Arapesh—cultural congeners of the Ilahita Arapesh. This is a most effective voice for creating a canonical text about a cultural system—one that sweeps away the confusions and ambiguities of a cultural life observed and truncates methodological doubt about the accuracy of what is represented. In her later work on the Mountain Arapesh, however, Mead uses a very different voice—one of hesitation and uncertainty—to which Tuzin also resorted in *The Cassowary's Revenge*.

* * *

By design, the essays that make up the four parts of this book address the issues and methodologies with which Tuzin worked during his career. While they neither adhere to nor necessarily advocate his theoretical positions, they do reflect upon the majority of his topical interests and accurately portray, we think, the distinguished, if rarefied, disciplinary lineage to which Tuzin belonged. Notwithstanding the rise of post-structuralism, textual cultural concepts and the focus on cultural difference, his work remained more or less rooted in British social anthropology on the one hand, and in North American bio-psychological anthropology on the other. The present volume is meant to show that both carry on—in part because of Tuzin's gifts.

References

Brown, Paula and Donald Tuzin (eds) 1983. *The Ethnography of Cannibalism*. Society for Psychological Anthropology, Special Publication. Washington, DC: Society for Psychological Anthropology.

Feil, D. K. 2005. Obituary, R. (Riodon) Paul Alexander, 1942–2004. *The Australian Journal of Anthropology* 16:232–6.

Fortune, Reo F. 1939. Arapesh Warfare. *American Anthropologist* 41:22–41.

Gregor, Thomas and Donald Tuzin (eds) 2001. *Gender in Amazonia and Melanesia: An Exploration of the Comparative Method*. Berkeley: University of California Press.

Hayek, J. W. N. 1952. The Principle of Methodological Individualism. *The British Journal for the Philosophy of Science* 3:186–9.

Herdt, Gilbert (ed.) 1982. *Rituals of Manhood: Male Initiation in Papua New Guinea*. Berkeley: University of California Press.

JaCoby, Pat 2007. *Tributes to UCSD Faculty Leader Don Tuzin Follow His April 15 Death*. La Jolla: Communications Office, University of California, San Diego.

Kinsman, Michael 2007. Donald Tuzin 61; Anthropology Professor at UCSD. *San Diego Union-Tribune*, 20 April 2007.

Lévi-Strauss, Claude 1963. *Structural Anthropology*. New York: Basic Books.

Mead, Margaret 1935. *Sex and Temperament in Three Primitive Societies*. New York: Morrow.

Popper, Karl 1950. *The Open Society and Its Enemies*. Princeton, NJ: Princeton University Press.

Prufer, Olaf H. 1965. The McGraw Site: A Study in Hopewellian Dynamics. *Cleveland Museum of Natural History, Scientific Publications* (NS)4:1–144.

Prufer, Olaf H. 2007. Donald Tuzin: Tributes from Friends and Colleagues. Unpublished ms. Minneapolis, Minn.: Files of the Author.

Robbins, Joel and Stephen Leavitt 2008. Donald Francis Tuzin (1945–2007). *American Anthropologist* 110:277–9.

Roscoe, Paul 2003. Margaret Mead, Reo Fortune, and Mountain Arapesh Warfare. *American Anthropologist* 105:581–91.

Tuzin, Donald 1975. The Breath of a Ghost: Dreams and the Fear of the Dead. *Ethos* 3:555–78.

Tuzin, Donald 1976. *The Ilahita Arapesh: Dimensions of Unity*. Berkeley: University of California Press.

Tuzin, Donald 1980. *The Voice of the Tambaran: Truth and Illusion in Ilahita Arapesh Religion*. Berkeley: University of California Press.

Tuzin, Donald 1982. Ritual Violence Among the Ilahita Arapesh: The Dynamics of Moral and Religious Uncertainty. In G. Herdt (ed.) *Rituals of Manhood: Male Initiation in Melanesia*, pp. 321–55. Berkeley: University of California Press.

Tuzin, Donald 1984. Miraculous Voices: The Auditory Experience of Numinous Objects. *Current Anthropology* 25:579–96.

Tuzin, Donald 1991. Sex, Culture and the Anthropologist. *Social Science and Medicine* 33:867–74.

Tuzin, Donald 1994. The Forgotten Passion: Sexuality and Anthropology in the Ages of Victoria and Bronislaw. *Journal of the History of the Behavioral Sciences* 30:114–37.

Tuzin, Donald 1995. The Melanesian Archive. In S. Silverman and N. J. Parezo (eds) *Preserving the Anthropological Record*, pp. 23–34. Second edition. New York: Wenner-Gren Foundation for Anthropological Research.

Tuzin, Donald 1997. *The Cassowary's Revenge: The Life and Death of Masculinity in a New Guinea Society*. Chicago: University of Chicago Press.

Tuzin, Donald 2001. *Social Complexity in the Making: A Case Study Among the Arapesh of New Guinea*. London: Routledge.

Weber, Max 1968. *Economy and Society*. Guenther Roth and Claus Wittich (eds). Berkeley: University of California Press.

Section One: History, Masculinity and Melanesia

1. The Abelam 'Invasion' and the Rise of Ilahita Revisited[1]

Paul Roscoe

Introduction

With a 1959 population of not quite 1300, the Arapesh-speaking village of Ilahita in the East Sepik Province was by no means the largest of New Guinea's villages. This honour belonged instead to several coastal fisher-forager groups. The Kawenak Asmat village of Ayam was found to have 1409 inhabitants in its first reliable census, in 1960; in 1930, 1702 inhabitants were counted in the census in the Waropen village of Nubuai; and the two village complexes that made up the Koriki 'tribe' in the early 1920s had 3960 inhabitants between them (Roscoe 2006:40). Even in the Sepik, Ilahita was only marginally larger than the fisher-forager, Kambot-speaking village of Kambaramba, which had a mid-1950s population of about 1100 people (Roscoe 2006).

What set Ilahita apart from its rivals, however, was its subsistence base: it was by far the largest village of any cultivating society in New Guinea. By Tuzin's own account, it was Ilahita's size that induced him to make it his field destination and the analytical focus of his first major book, *The Ilahita Arapesh: Dimensions of Unity* (1976).[2] *The Ilahita Arapesh* was a remarkable work, not least because, to explain Ilahita's rise and continued functioning, it adumbrated practice theory several years before practice theory became current in English-speaking social science. Tuzin himself claimed to have adopted methodological individualism as his approach, but close readers of his text noticed that he was at pains to emphasise what methodological individualism (and its anthropological counterparts, action theory and interactionism) commonly took for granted or, worse, cast as nothing but patterns emergent from the actions of individuals (see Evens 1977): the social and cultural context that constituted the grounds of an agent's action. Tuzin perceived that a focus on the individual as a motivated and strategising agent had to be tempered with attention to the cultural context in which that agent is enculturated and must operate and which he or she

---

1 For comments on previous versions of this chapter, I am extremely grateful to Terence Hays and two anonymous reviewers.
2 Subsequently summarised and integrated with the findings of his second volume, *The Voice of the Tambaran* (1980), as *Social Complexity in the Making* (2001).

reproduces or transforms—the recursive linkages that became the heart of practice theory (Bourdieu 1977; Giddens 1984; Ortner 1984; Sahlins 1981; see also Gardner, this volume).

The main purpose of *The Ilahita Arapesh*, however, was to deploy this framework to account for the rise of an extraordinarily large village of cultivators and to investigate the strategies that its members had developed to cope with the resulting problems of scale. In this chapter, I want to critique the former explanation in order to bolster the importance of the latter. Drawing on an argument that still holds force in Sepik anthropology, Tuzin attributed the rise of Ilahita to the northwards migration from the Sepik River of dense populations of Abelam-speaking people—a demographic momentum that provoked intensified fighting to Ilahita's south, a flight of refugees northwards to Ilahita, and the consequent explosive rise in Ilahita's size. This proposition is untenable, however; given the facts that Tuzin reported, immigration from the south is an implausible explanation for Ilahita's growth; as I shall try to show, the Abelam 'invasion' never occurred, at least as it is commonly represented; and the dense Abelam populations to the south of Ilahita were the product instead of unusually favourable local ecological conditions. Why then was Ilahita so large? Far from a historical accident, I shall argue, the village simply represented an unusually large exemplar of standard village formation processes in the area. The consequence of these conclusions is that the second, major aspect of Tuzin's argument—his investigation of the strategies that enabled Ilahita to function—should be taken not as a sociology of a unique village but as a generalisable theory of how villages in the Ilahita/Abelam region adapted to the demands of large-scale social organisation.

The Abelam Invasion and the Rise of Ilahita

The hypothesis that the Abelam represented a southern group intrusive on Torricelli-speaking peoples to their north derives from two sources. The first was Donald Laycock's (1965) pioneering linguistic work on the Ndu language family, of which the Abelam are members. From his survey of languages in the region, their lexicostatistical relations and the manner in which they were distributed across the landscape, Laycock had deduced that speakers of the Ndu language family must have migrated northwards from the Sepik River region many centuries before contact, eventually intruding on the Torricelli peoples of the Prince Alexander and Torricelli mountains and their foothills. At contact, the Abelam had reached no further than these foothills (Figure 1.1), but to their east, Laycock's linguistic data indicated, the Ndu-speaking Boiken had managed to push their way even further northwards, across the foothills and mountains to the coast of the Bismarck Sea. Laycock also drew attention to another feature of the linguistic distributions in this area, what we might call the Maprik 'bulge'—the aneurism-like protuberance of Abelam speakers around Maprik Government Station into Arapesh-speaking, Torricelli lands (partly visible, top right of Figure 1.1), which suggested that migrational pressure exerted from the south by Abelam people had created a localised 'blow-out' into Arapesh territory.

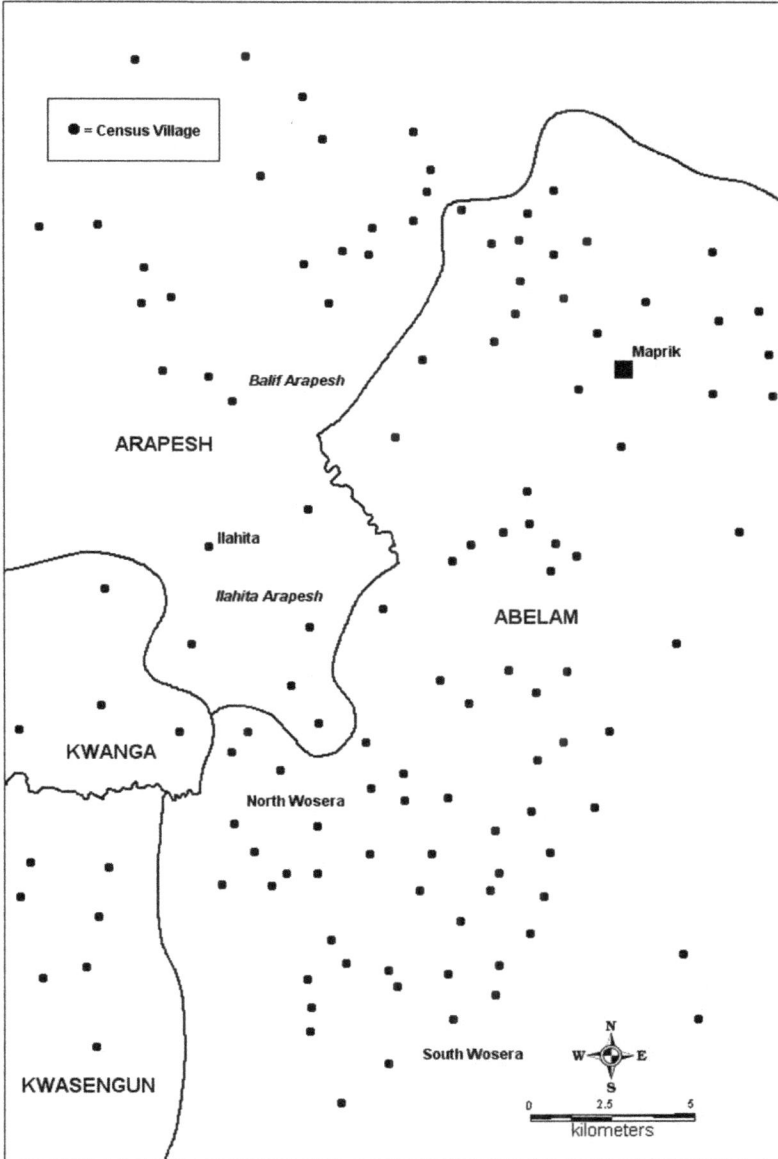

Figure 1.1 Ilahita village and the Abelam–Arapesh region

The second body of evidence used to advance the notion of an Abelam 'invasion' was the region's ecology—specifically, the juxtaposition of the rolling grasslands of the Sepik Plains, which stretch from the Sepik River to the foothills of the coastal mountain chain, and the forested foothills themselves. Whereas the grass plains are thinly populated by the Ndu-speaking Sawos languages, the foothills are thickly populated with Ndu-speaking Abelam and Boiken populations. To explain this unusual situation, Haantjens et al. (1965) proposed that the grasslands had once been forested but had then been over-cultivated, leaving an exhausted, terminal-succession grassland. Anthony Forge, Tuzin's doctoral advisor, voiced the logical conclusion that tied the two bodies of evidence— linguistic and ecological—together (Forge 1965). Dense populations of Ndu speakers had moved northwards from the Sepik River, propelled forward by their over-cultivation of the land, leaving the grasslands in their wake. As far as the Abelam were concerned, Forge (1965:24) suggested there had been a

> jostling together of large, fairly densely packed Abelam villages, fighting each other and gradually moving as a whole in a northerly and later westerly direction…[U]p till the imposition of government control this process was still going on, especially in the west of the Abelam area, where the Abelam of the Wosera were pushing back the [Ilahita] Arapesh to the north and the Gawanga [that is, Kwanga] to the west [Figure 1.1].

It was to this scenario that Tuzin contributed a chronology of the Abelam 'invasion' of the North Wosera–Arapesh region and a hypothesis concerning its social consequences for Ilahita. In Tuzin's telling, the *ur*–Torricelli-speaking inhabitants of the Wosera–Arapesh area had started out as small-scale communities similar to those that Margaret Mead had described in the 1930s among the Mountain Arapesh to the east.

> There seems little doubt that these people were once distributed sparsely across the face of the Torricelli and Prince Alexander foothills. They lived in movable communities of not more than 100 to 200 persons, subsisting on sago and the products of hunting and gathering. What horticulture they may have practiced would have been rudimentary and marginally productive by today's standards. In fact, groups of precisely this description still inhabit large areas of the Torricelli Mountains and also the hills south of the Sepik River in its upper reaches. (Tuzin 1976:82–3)

In the Ilahita region, according to Tuzin, this situation prevailed until about 1880, when the impact of the Abelam incursions into the North Wosera began to make itself felt. Pressing northwards against the Torricelli speakers, the wave of Abelam newcomers began to intensify competition and warfare over land in the North Wosera. The Abelam held the advantage in this fighting. As a predatory, *village*-based people, supported by intensive yam cultivation, they easily prevailed over the small, mobile, hamlet-based communities of the Arapesh. Those of the latter who were not exterminated in these confrontations had little alternative but to flee north to areas of lower population pressure and less intense fighting.

In these hapless refugees, Tuzin detected the grounds of Ilahita's extraordinary size and the transformation of social organisation in the region. Ilahita's size stemmed from the military interest that speakers of the Ilahita dialect of Arapesh had in the refugees fleeing from the fighting in the North Wosera: by incorporating them into their villages, they could add to their military ability to resist the encroaching Abelam threat to their south. As a result, population densities and group sizes among the Ilahita Arapesh increased rapidly. Ilahita village was especially favoured by these migrations and incorporations, however, because it had an abundance of land in its gift. As Arapesh villages to the south of Ilahita grew larger, they reached a point at which they were unable to accept more immigrants and were obliged to pass them on northwards to Ilahita. With resources to spare, Ilahita could afford to wax ever larger to their rear until, about 60 years after the onset of the Abelam encroachment, it had reached some 1200 in size.

To contain and control these increases of scale, Ilahita dialect speakers were obliged to transform their social organisation. They did so by consolidating their hamlet-based society into the village-based organisation of their Abelam enemies and adopting Abelam cultural devices for integration such as the *Tambaran* cult. The ironic result was an eventual stalemate: the Abelam intrusion into the North Wosera was eventually brought to a standstill by communities of a scale and organisation that 'were indirectly the creation of the Abelam themselves' (Tuzin 1976:74). No group was forced to transform itself more extensively than the Ilahita giant, however, and after 'pacification' had frozen the system in place, these social and cultural innovations were to become the other focus of Tuzin's inquiries.

The Rise of Ilahita

Perhaps the most pressing difficulty with Tuzin's scenario for the rise of Ilahita is the extreme brevity of its chronology. By absorbing successive refugees, according to Tuzin, Ilahita had gone from a population of 'not more than 100 to 200' (Tuzin 1976:82) people to a population of 1200 or more in the space of just 60 years (1880–1940). In support of this conjecture, his inquiries in Ilahita identified a significant immigrant population. Three clans (of a total of 39) and two wards (of a total of six) identified themselves as immigrants (Tuzin 1976:72, 92, 162), indicating that some 41 per cent (7.7 per cent plus 33.3 per cent) of Ilahita's population were immigrants or descended from immigrants. To be generous, let us say that half of Ilahita's population in 1940 were immigrants from fighting further south—yielding a ratio of one 'immigrant' for every one 'indigenous' resident.

A moment's reflection will reveal how low a ratio this is to explain such a large population expansion in so short a time if it was indeed driven by immigration. If immigration was the principal cause of Ilahita's unusual size then we should expect a ratio more in the neighbourhood of 1:5 or 1:11 (depending on whether Ilahita's original population was 100 or 200).[3] What the actual ratio of 1:1 tells us is that about 50 per cent of Ilahita's growth must have come from natural increase, not immigration. To complicate things further, one of the two wards that Tuzin listed as immigrants, Ilifalemb, was descended from refugees from fighting not in the North Wosera to the south but among the Bumbita Arapesh to the *north-west* of Ilahita (Tuzin 1976:72, Table 3, 77, fn. 2). Accordingly, if we remove Ilifalemb—about 17 per cent of Ilahita's population and about 40 per cent of its immigrant population—from the calculation, the ratio of immigrants to aboriginal Ilahita population falls to about one in three. In this scenario, about two-thirds of Ilahita's expansion has to be attributed to natural growth rather than immigration.

What makes these calculations so problematic for Tuzin's argument is the conclusion to which they lead: whether we remove the Ilifalemb immigrants from the calculation or retain them, natural growth over the period 1880–1940 must in itself have contributed markedly to Ilahita's size. Indeed, to take the analysis one step further, we need hardly invoke immigration at all to explain Ilahita's size! Under Tuzin's scenario, to achieve a ratio of 1:1 for the immigrant and autochthonous inhabitants of Ilahita, natural growth rates would need to lie between 2 per cent and 3 per cent, depending on whether the 1880 population was 100 or 200.[4] And here is the problem: at these rates, an aboriginal population of 100–200 would reach 1200 within just 80–90 years. (If we remove Ilifalemb from the calculations then the ratio of immigrants to indigenes falls to 1:3. To achieve this ratio, natural growth would need to be 2.5–3.75 per cent—rates that by themselves could achieve an end population of 1200 in just 65–70 years.) Given Tuzin's description of the immigrant/autochthonous composition of Ilahita in 1940, in other words, it would take an original population of 100–

3 If the original population was 200, then roughly 1000 members of the end population—that is, one in five—would have to originate from immigrants. If the starting population was 100 then roughly 1100 members of the end population—one in 11—would have to be descended from immigrants.
4 The relevant equation for the precise ratio, R, by which immigrants should outnumber Ilahitans is given by: $R = (1200 - P_o \times e^{60r})/(P_o \times e^{60r})$, in which P_o is the population of Ilahita in 1880 ('no more than 100 to 200') and r is the natural rate at which this population grew in the 60 years from 1880 to 1940.

200 people between just five years longer and no more than 30 years longer to reach 1200 *through reproduction alone* than if its growth also incorporated the proportion of immigrants that Tuzin documented in Ilahita.

If Tuzin's figures for the composition of Ilahita village in 1940 are correct, in sum, his explanation and chronology for the rise of the village are trapped in a vicious circle. There is no way to attribute Ilahita's rapid growth to immigrants fleeing fighting induced by an Abelam intrusion without also requiring that Ilahita's natural growth rate be so high as to make immigration almost irrelevant as an explanation for Ilahita's growth!

Perhaps, then, the chronology is wrong? It might be significant that Tuzin deduced from his informants that Ilahita's growth began in 1880. In the late 1960s, when he conducted the fieldwork for *The Ilahita Arapesh*, this would have been the generational period just beyond the memory of the oldest of Ilahita's living denizens—a potential fracture line that facilitates 'telescoping' in orally transmitted chronologies. Among the Yangoru Boiken, 45 km to the east, I found this same period—between the penultimate (*woranga*) and ultimate (*andeka*) generations of the kinship terminology—to be a temporal dumping ground for all sorts of legendary events, some of which, on historical evidence, could have occurred only scores if not hundreds of years earlier. Perhaps, then, the Abelam invasion, the fighting in and flights from the Wosera, and the growth of Ilahita all occurred as Tuzin claimed, but instead of beginning about 1880 they were in train an unknown number of generations earlier?

On current evidence, there is nothing to gainsay this scenario. The problem is that the more we push the beginnings of Ilahita's growth back into prehistory, the more plausible it becomes to attribute that growth to reproduction alone rather than immigration. If we suppose that the process started in 1800 instead of 1880, for example, Ilahita could have grown from 100–200 to 1200 people under natural growth rates of between 1.2 per cent and 1.7 per cent. If we suppose the process started 200 years before it terminated then natural growth rates of just 0.9–1.2 per cent would have been sufficient. Growth rates such as these, though, are so typical of 'tribal' societies that we should then be surprised if Ilahita's emergence were *not* the result of natural growth. So perhaps there is no reason to invoke an Abelam 'invasion' to explain Ilahita's size? Perhaps there was no dense jostling of Abelam villages fighting their way northwards? But how then are we to explain the distributions of languages and the variation in population density in the region that suggest otherwise? It is to this issue that I now turn.

Rethinking the Abelam 'Invasion'

There is considerable evidence that a population speaking one or more proto-Ndu languages once lived in the region of the Middle Sepik River and, at some point in the past, spun off migrants who did indeed begin to move northwards, eventually intruding into territory controlled by speakers of Torricelli-phylum languages. In addition to Laycock's lexicostatistical evidence (cited above), settlement histories from villages throughout Abelam, Boiken and Sawos-speaking territories relate movements from the southern parts of the Sepik Plains northwards into the Torricelli and Prince Alexander foothills (Roscoe 1994:56–61). Subsequent to the publication of *The Ilahita Arapesh*, in fact, geo-archaeological evidence suggested a possible explanation for these migrations. Some 6000 years ago, the Middle Sepik and the swamplands to its south were covered by a large inland sea that extended at least as far west as the Chambri region, due south of Maprik. Subsequently, this shoreline began to progress eastwards due to sediment infilling from the Sepik River, eventually reaching its modern position some 1000 years ago (Swadling 1997; Swadling et al. 1989).

If modern environments and social systems are any guide, many of the populations living along the shores of this ocean embayment would have been fisher-foragers with densities in the region of 3–7 people/sq km and settlement sizes in the hundreds (Roscoe 2005). As the shoreline retreated to the east, however, these populations would have experienced significant transformations in their ecological relationships as open ocean became lakes, then marshlands, and finally dryland. In the initial phases of this transformation, the environment might have become temporarily more productive rather than less, since tidal lakes and marshes are commonly more food rich than salt or freshwater alone (Roscoe 2006). As these changes progressed, however, and the land began to dry out even more, subsistence likely became more difficult, and it is not difficult to imagine migrants occasionally spinning off in search of better fortune elsewhere (Roscoe 1989).

All of this accords with Forge's and Tuzin's hypotheses of an Abelam intrusion into the Torricelli populations north of the Sepik Plains. What we should doubt, however, is that the refugees spun off by the environmental transformation of the Middle Sepik advanced northwards at anything like the densities that Tuzin and Forge envisaged. The idea that the Abelam advance involved a dense population seems to have originated, at least in part, from a desire to explain the extraordinary densities of Abelam populations in the Maprik and Wosera areas. From at least the 1960s, commentators have designated these densities as the highest in New Guinea outside the Highlands. If my calculations from census registers are any guide, in fact, the densities of some Abelam communities might have been the highest *anywhere* in New Guinea, reaching well more than

200 people/sq km (Figure 1.2). Be that as it may, a mass intrusion of migrant populations from the south was one way of accounting for the region's unusual demography. It is not, however, the only way to account for the situation, nor is it without its problems.

To begin with there is the ecology of the Sepik Plains themselves. These days, the plains are covered with little but *kunai* sword grass—a vegetational cover that Haantjens, Forge, Tuzin and others have taken as evidence that the plains were once home to populations so dense as to exhaust their soils (see above). What this overlooks, however, is evidence that the plains were *always* relatively infertile. To begin with, they are sparsely watered. On the standard topographic map, watercourses are absent from scores of their square kilometres. This compares with the heavily populated foothills to the north, where barely a square kilometre of mapped land is not transected by a stream or river. Compared with the foothills, in other words, populations, crops and vegetation on the plains would have encountered significantly greater difficulty procuring water. Tellingly, perhaps, the few contemporary settlements that exist in the plains are all to be found in narrow bands of gallery forest along the rivers that bisect the plains. Nor is it clear that the soils of the plains could ever have supported intensive cultivation. Today, they constitute clay soils, and there is no reason to believe they were ever otherwise. Rather than having been farmed to exhaustion, in sum, the plains to the north of the Middle Sepik might have been no different from those of the Sandaun Province to the west. To the best of our knowledge, the Sandaun Plains have never had to support dense farming populations, yet their grassland and gallery forest ecology is remarkably similar to that of today's Middle Sepik Plains.

As for the distribution of languages in the Abelam–Arapesh region, this is certainly congruent with a hypothesis that Abelam is intrusive on the Torricelli languages, but it provides no reason to suppose any large-scale 'invasion'. For one thing, it is unsafe to interpret the Maprik 'bulge' as some kind of linguistic aneurism caused by the pressure of Abelam migrants bursting through into Arapesh populations (cf. Laycock, see earlier). Rather, it appears to be an artefact of topography: the foothills of the Torricelli Mountains, which generally lie on an east–west axis, swing sharply to the north-west in this particular region. What appears to be a bulge on the linguistic map is simply a band of Abelam settlement following the curve of the foothills until it meets southern Arapesh territory.

Migration, moreover, is not the only—nor even, perhaps, the prime mechanism— that determines the distribution and spread of language boundaries. People can maintain their residences and yet import speech forms from their neighbours through relationships of exchange, trade, religious movements, and so on. People can also move and yet leave their speech forms behind; in the small-scale, patri-local communities that characterise much of New Guinea, wives are the classic example—moving to the settlements of their husbands and, if their husbands speak a different language, assimilating it. Wives who are linguistic immigrants can also serve as potent vectors of linguistic change because, as the primary enculturators of their children, they might mix their natal language with that of their husbands', thereby transforming it. Thus, as I have argued elsewhere, differences in marriage rules might be as important as migration in explaining the distribution of the Ndu languages (Roscoe 1994).

In sum, the Abelam might have intruded on the Torricelli languages of the southern foothills, but there is nothing in the available evidence to compel a conclusion that they did so *en masse*, as a 'migration'. What proponents of an Abelam intrusion seem to have overlooked, in fact, is that, under favourable ecological conditions, humans can achieve high population densities in a surprisingly short time purely through *natural* population increase. The important question, then, is this: were conditions in the Abelam–Arapesh region sufficiently favourable to natural population growth to account for their high densities? A comprehensive response to this question is difficult given the limited ecological data currently available, but there is good reason to believe they were.

The general distribution of population in the hinterlands of the Sepik coast is one of moderate densities along the coast, low densities in the peaklands of the coastal ranges, and comparatively high densities along the southern foothills of the chain. This population distribution is quite consistent, in fact, with how we would expect the density of cultivating peoples on this kind of gross geomorphology to vary. To consider the peaklands first, there are two reasons their slopes are less fertile—and hence less densely populated—than those at their base. First, they are steeper; second, rainfall erosion continually carries soils from higher elevations to lower altitudes. Thus, along the Prince Alexander–Torricelli mountain chains, the soils of the peaklands are thin and difficult to farm, subject to rapid erosion, and largely unreplenished with sediment from elsewhere. As a result, population densities in the mountains themselves are low; indeed, several extensive sections are effectively unpopulated.

In contrast with peaklands, the lower flanks of mountain chains are more favourably positioned to support population: their slopes are more moderate, and they are dissected by multiple waterways carrying eroded sediments out of the mountains. The most favourable environments of all, in fact, are those at the immediate base of the ranges. Here, as the steep slopes of the mountains transition to flatter lands, the sudden change in the angle of outflow causes waterways from the mountains to deposit especially heavy loads of their suspended sediments, creating a band of exceptionally rich, shallow-sloping alluvial soils. On the ocean side of the Sepik's coastal range, this transition is very abrupt and the band of rich soil is comparatively narrow; on the southern flanks, however, the transition extends over several kilometres and the band of rich soils is considerably broader.

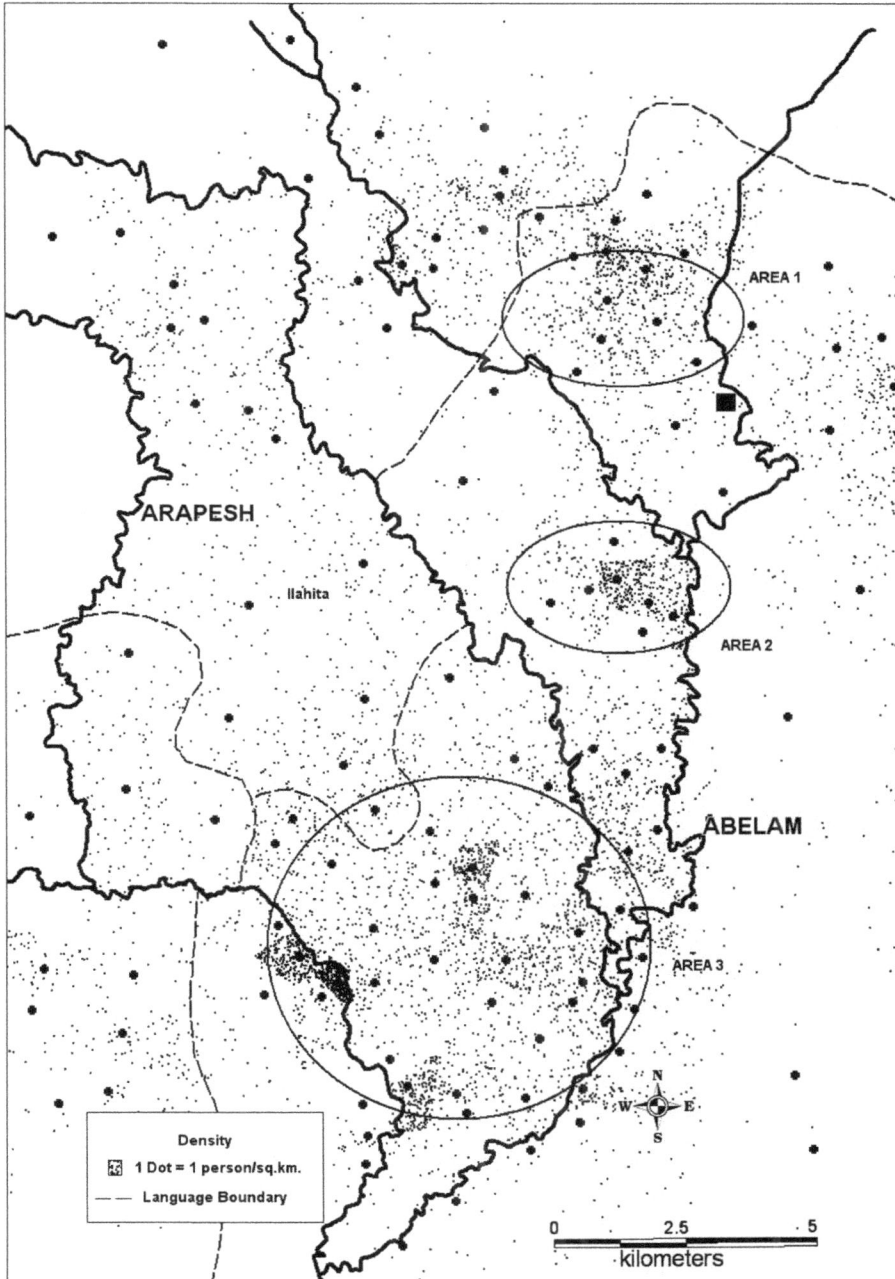

Figure 1.2 Population densities in the Arapesh–Abelam region

The consequence of this geomorphology can be seen in the top right-hand quadrant of Figure 1.2, which plots the distribution of population in the Arapesh–Abelam region shown in Figure 1.1. The band of higher population running diagonally across this quadrant from upper left to lower right marks the region where the mountains to the north flatten out towards the lower foothills and plains to the south. Within this band, the area of especially high population density marked as Area 1 nicely illustrates the link between geomorphology and density (Figure 1.3). Villages in the high foothills and mountains (for example, Nungalimb, Maputma, Sahali), where slopes are steep, support comparatively low population densities (9–39 people/sq km). Villages in the low foothills removed from the mountains (for example, Apangai, Bongiora, Yamelikum, Neligum and Cheragum) have similar to somewhat higher densities (10–60 people/sq km). The highest densities, however—between 87 and 124 people/sq km—are found in several of the villages located right at the immediate base of the mountains (for example, Kuminibus, Kukwal, Gwoingwoin and Wamsak), where the mountain slopes break sharply into the lower foothills depositing rich loads of sediment.

What this suggests is that Abelam populations in the southern foothills of the coastal mountains are dense, first and foremost, because they happen to inhabit a band of rich environmental resources. There is no reason, in other words, to evoke some massed immigration in the past to account for their density; they would be just as high if a sparse aboriginal population had a couple of centuries or so to increase through natural growth alone.

The same line of argument can be applied to the high densities of the Wosera region, which Tuzin saw as critical to explaining Ilahita's size. Here, though, the ecological advantage derived from the three major rivers: the Amuk, Screw and Nanu, the largest in the entire region between Yangoru and Dreikikir. The lower quadrants of Figure 1.2 show the distribution of population density in relation to the Abelam–Arapesh border (dotted lines; cf. Figure 1.1). The first thing to note from Figure 1.2 is that the distribution of population does not fit well with a hypothesis that the Abelam were 'bulldozing' Torricelli speakers northwards. If this were the case, we should expect the highest densities to lie along the Abelam–Arapesh border, where the 'bulldozing' was actually taking place. In fact, they lie from 2 to 7 km south of it. What Figure 1.2 suggests instead is that the high densities in the Wosera are related to its ecology. As can be seen, the core of the Wosera—demarcated in Figure 1.2 as Area 3—lies where the Amuk, Nanuk and Screw rivers converge. Tumbling from their headwaters in the Torricelli Mountains, these waterways course through the foothills along incised channels, and then debouch into the Wosera core. At this point, their gradients become shallower and their banks lower, allowing large sediment loads to be deposited over substantial areas, especially during wet-season flooding, to produce rich alluvial soils and significant stretches of productive wetland. Not surprisingly, the Maprik Agricultural Surveys of the 1960s found these to be the most agriculturally productive soils in the entire survey area (TPNG 1965).

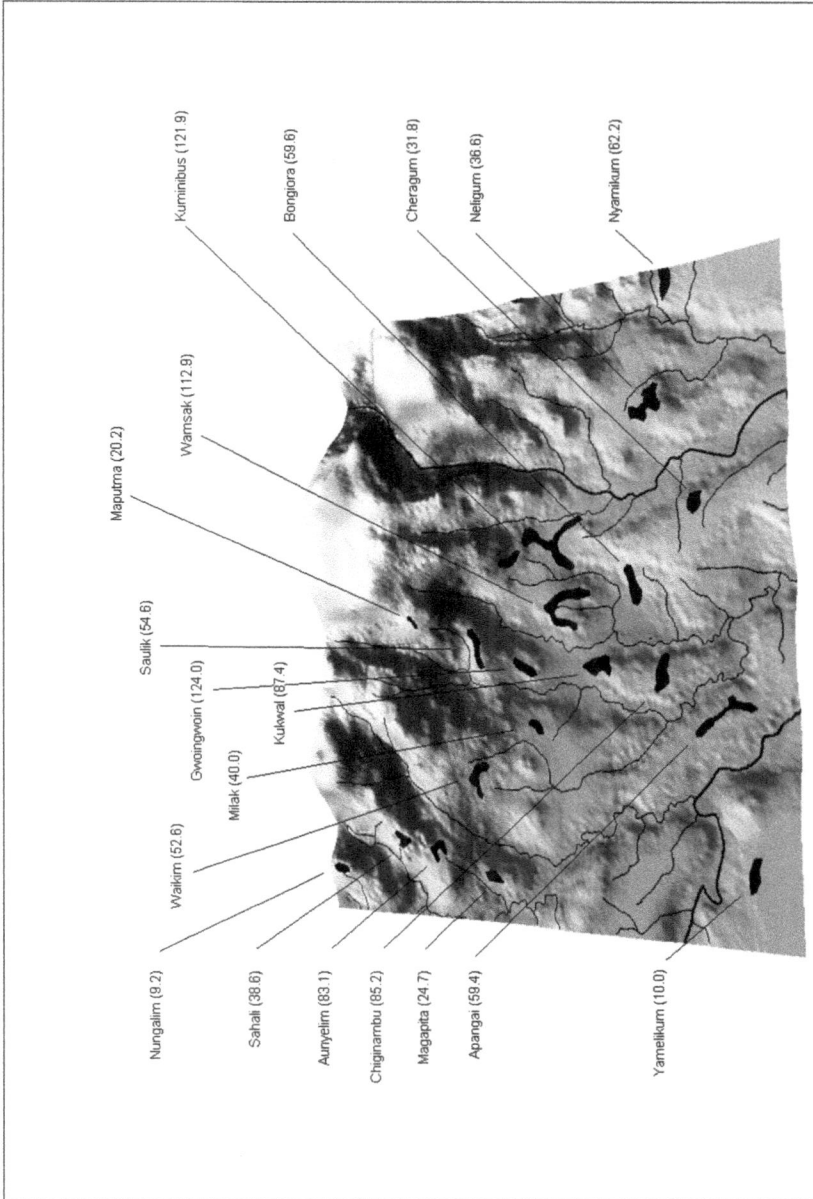

Figure 1.3 Foothill contours in Area 1

Note: Figures in parentheses are village densities as people/sq km.

Areas of exceptionally high density on Figure 1.2 are possibly artefactual, but they occur where local ecological peculiarities would lead us to expect them: where river gradients change suddenly or where wetlands occur that can be exploited with high-yield yam varieties. Area 2, for example, marks a set of villages located at the base of the foothills where the Ninab and Screw rivers join before immediately debouching onto flatter land. The arc of higher density population running from approximately 12 to 3 o'clock in Area 3 represents several villages that overlook an extensive area of wetland to their east. The exceptionally high-density area at 9 o'clock in Area 3—the Stapigum–Gulakim–Sarakim region—is at the base of the low foothills and overlooks an expanse of wetland to its south. And the area of higher density at 7 o'clock borders the same wetlands.

Rethinking the Growth of Ilahita Village

Where does all of this leave the question that motivated *The Ilahita Arapesh*? If, as I am suggesting, there was no Abelam 'invasion', if ecology rather than migration accounts for the distribution of population in this region, and if the growth of Ilahita village had little to do with the historical contingencies of immigration and emigration then what does explain the variations we observe in the size of Abelam and Arapesh villages, and in particular the inordinate size of Ilahita? To address these questions, we need first to consider a more fundamental question. What *is* a village? This issue has largely been overlooked in anthropology; the fact that humans create spheres of sociality tends to be taken as a given, as self-evident, when in fact it needs to be explained. It is here, I believe, that the real value of *The Ilahita Arapesh* lies. Whatever the merits of his migrational hypothesis for the rise of villages in this region, Tuzin's crucial insight was to link warfare to the development of *social groups*. Specifically, he cast these villages as defensive responses to particularly intense warfare. Now, his particular interests were the communities of the Abelam–Arapesh border region. But it is possible radically to generalise his proposition. At contact, warfare was endemic throughout the Sepik. Consequently, it is but a small step to suggest that defensive responses to war were responsible for the formation not just of especially *large* villages, but of *villages everywhere* in New Guinea.

As I have argued elsewhere at much greater length (Roscoe 1996, 2009), the formation and reproduction of Sepik villages were motivated primarily by defensive concerns with the threat posed by surprise attacks. According to Tuzin, this was the case for Ilahita Arapesh villages, and in the case of Ilahita village itself defence was the *only* occasion when its members 'unanimously convened' (Tuzin 1976:56, 59). Likewise among the Abelam: 'strong forces work towards village cohesion…In pre-contact times there was the mutual need to defend the village against aggression and even now the village lands have to be defended against rival claims in the [law] courts' (Lea 1964:48). The Abelam village, according to Forge (1990:162) was 'a defensive but not necessarily an offensive unit'. 'Western Abelam villages are clear-cut political units with boundaries defended by all the villagers' (Scaglion 1976:82).

This role of village groups as defensive units was not limited to the Abelam–Arapesh region but was found throughout the Sepik. Among the Yangoru Boiken (Roscoe 1996, 2009), the village was a mutual defence unit against the threat of attack at night. Likewise among the Iwam of the Upper Sepik, 'the main function of the village as a whole is defense against an attack from outside' (Rehburg 1974:221). According to Harrison (1993:6), the component descent groups of Middle Sepik River villages could, and often did, act quite independently of one another in launching war, but 'a village acted as a unit only for defence'. For the Anggor, 'the ultimate manifestation of village solidarity is encountered in warfare, when co-villagers stand together to defend their community against violence and destruction' (Huber 1974:214). Villages were the important defensive units in other parts of New Guinea as well, but in many places different kinds of units emerged that constituted the security group. In the Central Highlands, the clan (and in a couple of places perhaps also the 'tribe') appears to have been the defensive organisation; in south-west New Guinea, it was sometimes the men's-house group; and in yet other areas it was a longhouse or hilltop hamlet (Roscoe 2009:80–8).

The threat of attack not only motivated the formation of villages as mutual defence units, it also exerted pressures to enhance their military strength by increasing their size. The physical properties of space and time coupled with particular subsistence and topographic circumstances, however, exerted countervailing tendencies that differentially constrained the compass of village boundaries. And in these circumstances lie the explanation for the varying sizes of villages in the Abelam–Arapesh region and elsewhere. For a mutual-defence group to function, its members must live sufficiently closely together to be able to render one another effective military aid in the event of an attack. There is little point in forging defensive relationships with people who live so far distant that, by the time they arrive to render military aid, the attack is over and done with. One factor affecting how many people can live in close enough proximity to render mutual military aid is population density. The more people that subsistence productivity can support per unit area of land, the more people can live sufficiently closely together to provide effective military support. As noted already, population densities in the Abelam–Arapesh region were among the highest in New Guinea, providing a ready explanation for the large mean village sizes that Tuzin remarked upon and attempted to explain. My best estimate of contact-era density in the environs of Ilahita Village, for instance, is about 44.2

people/sq km. Density in the Stapigum region—one of densest in the North Wosera—was about 89.6 people/sq km. These figures are far above those for most of the Sepik beyond Maprik.

In foothill regions such as those of the Abelam–Arapesh area, however, topography is a second determinant of village size—one that is especially important in imposing variability about the general mean. In rugged terrain, dwellings located on the same ridge complex are better able to render one another military aid than settlements located equally closely together but separated by deep valleys that impede a speedy response. Ilahita vividly demonstrates the point. Ilahita's topography differed significantly from that of its smaller neighbours, and Tuzin himself pointed out the implications:

> In addition to its unusually large size, Ilahita is also somewhat atypical in its physical configuration. Most villages in the region are, following the north–south grain of the foothills, arranged linearly with hamlets strung out end-to-end for the entire length of the village. Other villages are formed on horseshoe-shaped ridges or are divided between parallel ridges. Ilahita, on the contrary is sprawled over a star-shaped system of ridges, with the several wards radiating out from a central hub. The effect of this is that…the village can grow large and *yet remain relatively self-contained geographically*. (Tuzin 1976:87, emphasis added)

Ilahita was so large, I suggest, not because of intense, migration-induced warfare but because of the defensive implications of this topographic peculiarity. With the exception of three outlier hamlets, the contact-era village occupied some 4.5 km of a single, continuous ridge-top complex. Were this population strung out along a linear ridge, it would be far too elongated to constitute a discrete sphere of mutual defensive interest; only about 40 per cent of the inhabitants would live within 1 km of its geographical centre. Ilahita's unusual star-shaped topography, however, concertinaed this length in such a way that about 80 per cent of the population lived within 1 km of its geographical centre, along ridge-top paths (Tuzin 1976:57, 91). With so many warriors able to live so closely together, Ilahita was able to grow to an enormous size while still retaining its defensive *raison d'être*.

Conclusion

The Ilahita Arapesh: Dimensions of Unity amply demonstrated the elegance of Don Tuzin's thought; it foreshadowed the influence his work would have within and beyond Sepik anthropology; and it is a bitter reminder of what we have lost with his passing. More than 30 years later, I continue to return to this volume, not just in admiration of the breadth and depth of its propositions and insights but also to assess and retest what is perhaps the most remarkable sociological work that Melanesian anthropology has ever produced. In this chapter, I have tried to show that the first component of the book's argument— the explanation for Ilahita's emergence—is difficult to sustain. Rather than the emergent product of historical contingency, Ilahita more likely arose from natural population growth in favourable ecological conditions, its atypical size reflecting the military implications of its unusual topography.

Rather than diminishing the value of *The Ilahita Arapesh*, however, my intent has been to elevate it. The main body of Tuzin's volume was devoted not to Ilahita's rise but to an exquisitely delicate dissection of the strategies that Ilahitans had developed to cope with the rivalries and conflicts engendered by life in such a gigantic conglomerate. Tuzin's presentation of Ilahita as the product of historical contingency had the effect of limiting the applicability of this analysis; it implied that these coping strategies were associated with a social entity that, if not unique, was at least highly unusual. If, in contrast, and as I contend in this chapter, Ilahita represented but one tail in a distribution of social units in the Sepik, different in degree from other village groups but not in kind, *The Ilahita Arapesh* becomes a trenchant analysis not of one unusual Sepik village but of them all. The dual organisation that accommodated Ilahita's putative growth by progressive structural subdivision and ritual integration—a system of mechanical solidarity that contrived interdependency among the parts of the community while simultaneously dissipating the hostilities between individuals and subgroups that otherwise might destroy the village—was one that we should look for in many other communities in the Sepik, if not perhaps in all small-scale societies (Roscoe 2009:89–101).

References

Bourdieu, Pierre 1977. *Outline of A Theory of Practice*. R. Nice (trans.). Cambridge: Cambridge University Press.

Evens, T. M. S. 1977. The Predication of the Individual in Anthropological Interactionism. *American Anthropologist* 79:579–97.

Forge, Anthony 1965. Art and Environment in the Sepik. *Proceedings of the Royal Anthropological Institute of Great Britain and Ireland* 1965:23–31.

Forge, Anthony 1990. The Power of Culture and the Culture of Power. In Nancy Lutkehaus, Christian Kaufmann, William E. Mitchell, Douglas Newton, Lita Osmundsen and Meinhard Schuster (eds), *Sepik Heritage: Tradition and Change in Papua New Guinea*, pp. 160–70. Durham, NC: Carolina Academic Press.

Giddens, Anthony 1984. *The Constitution of Society*. Berkeley and Los Angeles: University of California Press.

Haantjens, H. A., J. A. Mabbutt and R. Pullen 1965. Anthropogenic Grasslands in the Sepik Plains, New Guinea. *Pacific Viewpoint* 6:215–20.

Harrison, Simon 1993. *The Mask of War: Violence, Ritual and the Self in Melanesia*. Manchester: Manchester University Press.

Huber, Peter Birkett 1974. Identity and Exchange: Kinship and Social Order Among the Anggor of New Guinea. Unpublished PhD Dissertation, Duke University, Raleigh, NC.

Laycock, D. C. 1965. *The Ndu Language Family (Sepik District, New Guinea)*. Pacific Linguistics, Series C, No. 1. Canberra: The Australian National University.

Lea, David A. M. 1964. Abelam Land and Sustenance: Swidden Horticulture in an Area of High Population Density, Maprik, New Guinea. Unpublished PhD Dissertation, The Australian National University, Canberra.

Ortner, Sherry 1984. Theory in Anthropology Since the Sixties. *Comparative Studies in Society and History* 26:126–66.

Rehburg, Judith 1974. Social Structure of the Sepik Iwam. In R. Daniel Shaw (ed.) *Kinship Studies in Papua New Guinea*, pp. 211–22. Ukarumpa, PNG: Summer Institute of Linguistics.

Roscoe, Paul B. 1989. The Flight from the Fen: The Prehistoric Migrations of the Boiken of the East Sepik Province, Papua New Guinea. *Oceania* 60:139–54.

Roscoe, Paul B. 1994. Who Are the Ndu? Ecology, Migration, and Linguistic and Cultural Change in the Sepik Basin. In Andrew J. Strathern and Gabriele Stürzenhofecker (eds) *Migration and Transformations: Regional Perspectives on New Guinea*, pp. 49–84. Pittsburgh: University of Pittsburgh Press.

Roscoe, Paul B. 1996. War and Society in Sepik New Guinea. *Journal of the Royal Anthropological Institute* (NS)2:645–66.

Roscoe, Paul B. 2005. Foraging, Ethnographic Analogy, and Papuan Pasts: Contemporary Models for the Sepik-Ramu Past. In Andrew Pawley, Robert Attenborough, Jack Golson and Robin Hide (eds) *Papuan Pasts: Cultural, Linguistic and Biological Histories of Papuan-Speaking Peoples*, pp. 555–84. Canberra: Research School of Pacific and Asian Studies, Pacific Linguistics, Australian National University.

Roscoe, Paul B. 2006. Fish, Game, and the Foundations of Complexity in Forager Society: The Evidence from New Guinea. *Cross-Cultural Research: The Journal of Comparative Social Science* 40:29–46.

Roscoe, Paul B. 2009. Social Signaling and the Organization of Small-Scale Society: The Case of Contact-Era New Guinea. *Journal of Archaeological Method and Theory* 16:69–116.

Sahlins, Marshall 1981. *Historical Metaphors and Mythical Realities: Structure in the Early History of the Sandwich Islands Kingdom*. Ann Arbor: University of Michigan Press.

Scaglion, Richard Bruce 1976. Seasonal Patterns in Western Abelam Conflict Management Practices: The Ethnography of Law in the Maprik Sub-Province, East Sepik Province, Papua New Guinea. Unpublished PhD Dissertation, University of Pittsburgh, Pennsylvania.

Swadling, Pamela 1997. Changing Shorelines and Cultural Orientations in the Sepik-Ramu, Papua New Guinea: Implications for Pacific Prehistory. *World Archaeology* 29:1–14.

Swadling, Pamela, John Chappell, Geoff Francis, Nick Araho and Baivu Ivuyo 1989. A Late Quaternary Inland Sea and Early Pottery in Papua New Guinea. *Archaeology in Oceania* 24:106–9.

Territory of Papua and New Guinea (TPNG) 1965. Report on Intensive Agricultural Surveys in the Maprik Sub-District, 1961–4. Unpublished ms. Konedobu, PNG: Bureau of Statistics.

Tuzin, Donald F. 1976. *The Ilahita Arapesh: Dimensions of Unity*. Berkeley: University of California Press.

Tuzin, Donald F. 1980. *The Voice of the Tambaran: Truth and Illusion in Ilahita Arapesh Religion*. Berkeley: University of California Press.

Tuzin, Donald F. 2001. *Social Complexity in the Making: A Case Study Among the Arapesh of New Guinea*. London and New York: Routledge.

2. The String Bag of the *Tambaran*: The fragile loops of concealing and revealing in Abelam culture

Brigitta Hauser-Schäublin

Introduction

Some things only become clear with hindsight. This goes for my own fieldwork in the Sepik area (between 1972 and 1983), and it is probably true of other anthropologists as well, many of whom, as I gather from their writings, went through the same difficulties as I did. When I set out for Papua New Guinea, I took with me a pre-postmodern conception of 'culture', fuelled by the fascination for other, preferably still 'autochthonous' world views and agency in faraway societies. This predisposition often made it difficult to grasp what appeared to me in my understanding of 'culture' as seemingly precipitate and unexpected actions by the people I was living with, and to reflect on them and class them in terms of scientific concepts.

I was reminded of this when reading Don Tuzin's *The Cassowary's Revenge* (1997); it brought back memories of events during my fieldwork among the Abelam (between 1978 and 1983), which at the time had shocked and scared me. I came to realise that a new era had begun in Papua New Guinea, an era and setting in which I no longer wished to conduct fieldwork—nor was I any longer willing to take the risk.

Against the background of the socially disruptive events that Tuzin describes for the Ilahita Arapesh, complemented by three personal experiences of my own, I set out in this contribution to develop and describe a systemic principle upon which I believe Abelam culture is based. At the risk of falling prey to a 'lurking functionalism' (Roscoe 1995:4) or, even worse, a furtive structuralism, I shall address the issue of cultural aesthetics—similar to what Anthony Forge (1966, 1970, 1973) attempted for the field of art. I focus on the *Tambaran* cult[1] as still

---

1   By *Tambaran* (Tok Pisin), the Ilahita Arapesh describe everything 'that men do'. Tuzin calls the *Tambaran* cult a 'cult of war and human sacrifice' with a 'misogynistic ("woman hating") rhetoric'. *Tambaran* refers to all initiation grades and the ritual paraphernalia used as well as the spirits associated with the cult (Tuzin 2001:11–15). In contrast with the Ilahita Arapesh, the Abelam use the term '*maira*' to cover everything mysterious, secretive and sacred. I shall use *Tambaran* in this contribution in the sense of a lingua franca term common in the Maprik area.

practised by the Ilahita Arapesh and the Abelam in the 1960s and 1970s from an eccentric perspective, concentrating mainly on the structural foundation of these male cults, which hinge on the notion of secrecy and concealment. The starting point of my analysis is the string bag (Abelam: *wut*, Tok Pisin: *bilum*), a 'typical' Abelam product that is manufactured by women. I go on to show that the string bag conjoins two systemic principles: on the one hand, its structure, involving a looping technique that relies on the use of a single twine; on the other, its texture, with its transparent character that reveals only a partial view of the inside—that is, of the string bag's contents. I argue that Abelam men's knowledge, which, at the core, is founded on secrecy and concealment, is organised on the same two principles. The interplay between revealing and concealing and the inter-looping of the two modes characterise the hierarchically structured body of social knowledge; at the same time, they relate to a reality that lies beyond the world of everyday life with its routine processes and practices that are, by and large, controlled by human agents.

In making this argument, I see many similarities with the contributions by both Birth and Herdt (this volume), though these authors argue from a different theoretical perspective. The *Tambaran's* string bag is located in male ritual secrecy, when men collectively create objects—string bags of a different quality—that are presented to the uninitiated as *mysterium* or, as Birth puts it, the 'uncanny'. Thus, men create something new from that which exists out there in the real world (string bags manufactured by women), thereby producing their own truth and their own cultural reality. With the *Tambaran's* string bag, men also aim at attracting or impressing women and, at the same time, keeping them out of their ritual domain (see Herdt, this volume). Whether they succeed is another question, with which I cannot deal in this chapter.

As I hope to show, the string bag of the *Tambaran* bundles the socially hierarchically structured knowledge and governs social access to it. I argue further that the mode of handling knowledge—probably typical for the Maprik area as a whole—and the way the keepers of this knowledge revealed it to specific groups, step by step, were linked to the specific social and historical conditions of Maprik cultures that I define as the 'pre-modern'. This situation was superseded by a new era shaped by colonialism, Christian proselytisation, political independence and the advance of a capitalist economy and globalisation. As Tuzin describes so well in *The Cassowary's Revenge*, the people of the Maprik area were determined to put an end to the 'pre-modern' and to usher in a new, completely different era, which was to be played by new rules and in which the old string bag of the *Tambaran* had run its course.[2]

---

2 Where not noted otherwise, I rely on ethnographic data that I collected mainly in Kalabu (Hauser-Schäublin 1989a).

The Shock of Other Modernities

Essentially, there were three separate episodes that left me shattered in my self-understanding as an anthropologist and prevented me from conducting further fieldwork in Papua New Guinea once I had finished my research among the Abelam. I was simply no longer prepared to take the risk. The first episode refers to an evening-long discussion with a young man (from the hamlet we were living in) who came to visit us at our house. In the course of our talk, he described in full detail—but retaining an utterly friendly, chatty tone—how he and a group of young men, all of them out of work at the time, had once killed a man and, on a second occasion, a woman during a stay in one of the coastal towns, for absolutely no reason, and not in anger, simply because they felt bored. The murders were never solved. The young man whom we knew otherwise as a gentle-minded young Abelam man showed absolutely no remorse; he was simply telling us his *stori* ('story'), albeit a little different to the accounts we otherwise heard from old men about the 'earlier days' (Tok Pisin: *taim bipo*).

But why was he telling us all this? Was there a faint touch of threat in his words? Would he be capable of murdering us too one night, again for no apparent reason? In the other two episodes, we were involved directly.

In 1979 we went with two old men to a neighbouring village that we had visited several times before. The people there were planning to stage a bride-price ceremony, and I wanted to document the event that was being held at the ceremonial ground. I was sitting on the floor, concentrating on what was going on, making sound recordings and taking photographs, when, suddenly, I found a group of young men standing in front of me. Their leader addressed me in English. He ordered me to pack up my tape recorder and all my other equipment and leave immediately. I found myself surrounded by about a dozen young men whom I had not noticed before because I had been concentrating on the adult men and the elders who were responsible for the ceremony. The speaker of the group was wearing boots, long trousers and a white long-sleeved shirt and stood before me, threateningly. There was no doubt: the situation was serious. None of the others understood what he was saying, but from his harsh tone they must have realised what was going on. After many months of speaking Tok Pisin only, I found it hard to switch to English, but in stuttering words I tried to explain to him why I was here and what I was doing. He did not, however, accept the argument that I was documenting traditional knowledge and oral traditions still known to the old people in order to safeguard it for future generations. 'We need roads, economic development, the opportunities to earn money, to grow cash crops,' he answered coarsely. 'We know how the old folks used to live, and what they know we have known for a long time. What are you doing for us?' he asked provocatively. 'Your work will be full of lies just like that of that English woman and that German man who were here before you,[3] and it is not going to help us in any way. We don't need you Whites! Piss off! Pack your things or otherwise we'll destroy them!' He took a threatening step towards me in his heavy boots.

It was a close shave but the situation was resolved when I called for the village councillor who had the power to decide whether a person should leave the village or was allowed to stay. He told me to stay, after which the group of angry young men dispersed (see also Hauser-Schäublin 2002).

In the second episode, together with a group of artists from Kalabu, we were on our way to the Arapesh village of Yamel to visit a location in the mountains that was one of the main sources of the white pigment (*sabyo*) used by Abelam artists. The Abelam had obtained the pigment there since times beyond memory, and the arrangement was part of the reciprocal relationships between the two villages. When we arrived in Yamel, a few old men waved to us, nodding in agreement when the Kalabu men told them what we had come for. A few younger men got up from the group and accompanied us to the location we were heading for. We finally arrived at the steep mountain slope and, after the painter and his helpers had selected a few chunks of raw, white earth-pigment, the young men from Yamel suddenly confronted us, demanding money. When one of the Kalabu elders objected, maintaining that this was going against an age-old agreement between the two villages, one of the young men rebuked him, saying that the age of the old men was over and that now was the 'time of money' ('*taim bilong ol lapun i pinis, nau mani i tok*'). From now on, the men would have to pay for the pigment. The young men from Yamel owed no duty of respect to the Abelam elders, so none of them dared to object. There was a long moment of silence. Finally, my husband got out his wallet and paid the demanded fee. We returned to Kalabu immediately without stopping off for the usual polite exchange of compliments.

In both episodes, young men had unmistakably demonstrated rejection, resistance and renunciation: rejection of white people, resistance against the rule of the old men, and renunciation of the traditional ways. These were clear signs of a profound cultural change and the beginning of a new, post-colonial era in which young people (especially young men) looked to the future with high hopes and bright expectations. The traditional Abelam beliefs and practices that had governed the relationships with the old powers and the forces that had, until then, shaped people's lives and doings, including exchange with the ancestors and other supernatural spirits, no longer met the demands of life

---

3 He was referring to the British-Australian anthropologist Phyllis Kaberry, the first researcher to do fieldwork among the Abelam, in 1939–40, and the German ethnologist Gerd Koch, who undertook a collecting and documentation expedition through the Maprik area in 1966.

in a young nation-state and fell far short of what young people associated with it. High on the agenda now were economic and political goals that could be achieved only through Western concepts of education and development (see also Sahlins 2005 on this issue). New identities were in demand, and these called for new points of reference.

It is only with hindsight and through drawing on the more recent, general anthropological discourse—the global/local issue, identity and modernities— that I came to realise that these young men were caught up in the difficult process of acquiring a new identity and shaping their own view of modernity (see also Gewertz and Errington 2004; Goankar 1999).[4] There was no room left for traditions and their keepers (see also Jourdan 1996); these were simply blocking the road to the future.

Don Tuzin was not a man to shy away from the challenges that cultural change engendered even though at times he found it difficult to bear, having experienced the fascination of the *Tambaran* culture during his first fieldwork among the Ilahita Arapesh. In *The Cassowary's Revenge*, he wrote about Ilahita's renunciation of the *Tambaran*, with which he had been confronted during his second stay, from 1985 to 1986. He describes how the Ilahita Arapesh 'killed' the *Tambaran* cult in a public display. It was on the occasion of a Christian revivalist church service on a Sunday in 1984 that the men publicly gave away the secrets of the *Tambaran* to the women and other non-initiated people, telling them that the male cult had been based on deceit and that the only secret was that there actually was no secret at all (Tuzin 1997:1). Tuzin discusses what social and psychological disruptions this, in his opinion, deliberate and planned public execution, carried out in an atmosphere of millenarian expectations, had on the people. What impressed me about his book, apart from its thick description, was the way in which the author questioned and reflected on his own involvement in this 'Greek tragedy' (Tuzin 1997:64) and on what role his American foreignness, his long, first sojourn in Ilahita between 1969 and 1972, his departure, but also his promise to return had possibly had on the irreversible events. Tuzin not only admitted his indirect involvement, he was also prepared to take over co-responsibility for what happened; at the same time, the book clearly expresses the anthropologist's sorrow and dismay about the loss of culture.

According to Tuzin, one of the gravest consequences this killing and radical abolishment of the *Tambaran* had was that the men had robbed themselves of the foundations of their masculinity (Tuzin 1997:26,181). With the *Tambaran* gone, they had lost their means to exert power over women and keep them in check. They had toppled themselves from the throne and were now facing their

---

4   In his first two monographs, Tuzin did not use the term 'modernity'. Hirsch (2001) rightly asks: 'When was modernity in Melanesia?'

own vulnerability at the hands of the previously powerless: 'We now know in some detail what happened during the ensuing months, with the *Tambaran* dead, custom repealed, and the women ecstatically seizing control' (Tuzin 1997:161). The myth of the cassowary woman (Tuzin 1980:11) tells the story of how once a man stole the feather coat of a cassowary woman who was bathing naked in a nearby pool, thus bringing her under his control. Many years later, the woman discovered her feather coat hidden away and was able to escape—back in her shape as a cassowary. Tuzin (1997:176) equates the betrayal of the *Tambaran* to the women with the return of the feather coat to the cassowary woman—in other words, the setting free of primordial female power and the gaining of independence from male domination. This regained autonomy, which found expression in various new forms of women's behaviour towards men, Tuzin interprets—as the title of his book tells—as the 'Cassowary's Revenge'.[5] As Tuzin goes on to show, however, this newly won freedom has not made the male–female relationship any easier or better. On the contrary, it has merely led to increasing brutality and more domestic violence (Tuzin 1997:177); at the same time, mothers still treat their sons with harshness.

According to Tuzin, Ilahita village and its culture grew from the interaction between various Abelam and Kwangga groups that successively moved into the area and mingled with the resident Arapesh people, influencing their culture lastingly (see Roscoe, this volume). The *Tambaran* cult as such, or at least its higher initiation grades, and the ideals of manhood associated with it originated among the Abelam people (Tuzin 1997:4, 84), who began moving into the area about 1870 (Tuzin 2001:15). In fact, the Ilahita initiations as well as the associated *Tambaran* spirit beings and ritual artefacts (including the ceremonial house) correspond with Abelam ceremonial practice in many respects. In the following, I take my own Abelam data as specific variant of a general Maprik culture that overlaps ethnic groups and languages, with the aim of offering a comparative description. I do not know whether comparable public 'executions' of the *Tambaran* occurred in other villages of the Maprik area; there are certain clues that suggest similar actions, but maybe not in such radical form.[6] Between 1995 and 1999, the Maprik Council, the assembly of village councillors—that is, the elected village representatives (Tok Pisin: *kaunsel*)—decided

> that wild pigs should be hunted down and either exterminated or driven away from the village to the back of the mountains. Semi-domestic pigs were to be put behind fences and could no longer be left wandering around the village or in semi-liberation, or they would be killed too. (Coupaye 2004:150–1)

---

5   Apparently, and to the dismay of the men, the women were not surprised by the men's 'revelations'.
6   To this, Scaglion (1999:211) says: 'From the Abelam perspective, real change can only occur cataclysmically via a total restructuring of the world.' The Ilahita Arapesh appear to have fully shared his view.

In 2001, Coupaye did not see one garden that was fenced in as had been the custom in the old days to keep the pigs out and away from the crops. The ban on pigs was explained on hygienic and safety grounds (aggressive boars) and with the argument that the pigs were reducing productivity by ravaging gardens. This form of utilitarian reasoning ignores the pivotal significance that pigs had in ceremonial life as ritual gifts and sacrificial animals. Coupaye reports that in Nyelikum, his fieldwork site, all the people had become practising Christians[7] and there was no trace left of traditional ceremonial life, and no ceremonial house.[8] In Kalabu and in all the other villages of the Maprik area that I used to visit during fieldwork, the sacrifice of pigs used to be a prerequisite for the building of a new ceremonial house and preceded all rituals associated with the cultivation of long yams and/or with initiations.[9] Even though the *Tambaran* had not been eradicated as dramatically in other parts of the Maprik area as it had been in Ilahita, the ban on pigs brought an end to all forms of *Tambaran* activity, since one of the main ceremonial requisites—the sacrifice of pigs— could no longer be fulfilled.

The Technology of the String Bag

As described elsewhere (Hauser-Schäublin 1996), the Abelam are a typical representative of a 'non-cloth culture' in Oceania.[10] Line, streak, string and frond are the constituent elements in all forms of artistic expression, be it painting or the adornment of human beings, yams, pigs or string bags of various shapes and sizes. In their form-giving and form-defining capacities, the line and string respectively are of central significance (see also Ingold 2007). In Abelam, they go by the same term: *maindshe*. *Maindshe* is white, or at least light, if we wish to apply our Western colour criteria to the beige-coloured thread used for making string bags. String is made from the bast fibre (Tok Pisin: *mangas*; Abelam: *sibe*) of various plants, preferably from the bark of the *yitinbin* tree. The bark goes through a number of processing steps until the fibres are twined into string. The Abelam were not familiar with textile techniques other than string bags and plaited mats.[11] String bags are produced by a looping technique relying

---

7   Ludowic Coupaye, Personal communication, 2007.

8   Google Earth reveals only two or three ceremonial houses left in the entire Maprik area (July 2008).

9   During Coupaye's fieldwork, ceremonial (long) yams were still being grown in Kalabu; for some of the men, they provided an opportunity to gain prestige.

10   Despite the cultural change described briefly above, I shall stick to the ethnographic present when referring to the period between 1978 and 1983. I chose not to use the past tense because I do not know which aspects of the issues I describe are really 'past and gone' and which are still relevant. The ethnographic present reflects a snapshot of things.

11   Abelam men also produce plaited ceremonial mats (these decorate the lower part of the front of the ceremonial house and the projecting roof). Plaiting is based on a different technique (vertical and horizontal elements that are interwoven) to looping; one should therefore distinguish between the two techniques (for example, Coupaye 2004:Ch. 7).

on so-called hourglass looping. Only one string, or thread, is used, to which 'extensions' are attached continuously (see MacKenzie 1991:75–80). Loops are added one by one until the entire fabric, the string bag, is completed.[12] In contrast with other textile techniques, the string bag displays the following features:

> The structure of a looped string bag is differentiated from that of a basket in that it is flexible and laterally expansive. It differs from a woven textile because it requires only one element, simply interworked with itself, to form the fabric, whereas all woven textiles are constructed from two component parts, a warp interlaced with a weft. (MacKenzie 1991:209)

An empty string bag is of almost two-dimensional, trapezoidal shape to which a carrier strap of differing length is attached. When suspended from the apex of the strap—women carry their string bags with the strap passing over the forehead, while men carry their small personal bags over the shoulder—a string takes on an almost triangular shape. But when filled, a string bag becomes an impressively bulgy container that covers its contents like a skin (see also MacKenzie 1991:Plate 89). The term *'wut'* describes repositories of different size and fineness, all depending on what they are used for. String bags are always based on the same technology: string looping; this gives the bags their distinctive texture—they are soft, pliable and extremely sturdy. Women carry their babies in string bags, just as they do piglets that have been freshly weaned and which women carry around on their backs in order to accustom them to their new, human environment as a first step in domestication. The large string bags used for carrying firewood and field crops are made of more coarse material and are left undecorated. The finest and most artistic pieces serve to hold the more personal items that men and women carry on them (such as betel-nuts and betel pepper and small lime containers). They are decorated on the front side with the help of red and black-dyed strings displaying patterns of horizontal lines, squares or triangles, and trapezoids respectively, connected by diagonal lines.[13]

The Paradigmatic Character of the String Bag

A special technological feature of string bags is that they are translucent, providing a partial view of their contents. Men also produce artefacts in the

---

12   Decoration is added by the simultaneous use of differently coloured threads or by twining such a thread onto the main 'white' thread (Schuster 1989:375).
13   On string-bag patterns from the Iatmul, Kwoma, Sawos and probably also Abelam areas, see Schuster (1989:376–8).

looping technique (mainly insignia and decorations such as *kara-ut*, boar-tusk pectorals, and headbands), but they use a needle (made of cassowary bone), which allows them to thread the plied string through very tight meshing. The distinctive texture of the different objects—open versus closed loops—is based on the same technique but follows a gender-specific division of labour (see also MacKenzie 1991:Plates 34 and 35). One also finds this type of 'closure' on the small plaited bags that older men make for themselves, which are also opaque. They use them for their personal belongings; at the same time, they serve as male insignia indicating that the owner has almost completed the full initiation cycle.

In everyday life, the Abelam frequently take advantage of the transparency of string bags. For instance, it shows who presently is in possession of betel-nuts—a much sought-after natural stimulant, which are chewed with betel pepper and lime powder. Among kin and friends, it is absolutely normal to 'feel' a person's string bag to see whether he or she is carrying any betel-nuts. Should this be the case one can ask for one—a request that may hardly be turned down. This means that carrying around a string bag always implies having to be prepared for inquisitive looks and demands.

As Forge (1966, 1971, 1972) and Losche (1995) have shown, *wut* is also the term used to designate the painted initiation chamber that is constructed within the ceremonial house and into which initiates are taken during initiation ceremonies. The commonplace term for painted palm-leaf sheaths (Tok Pisin: *panggal*), outside any sacred context, is *'mbai'*. The same term—*mbai* literally refers to the actual palm-leaf material—is also used to designate the large triangular painting facing the public meeting ground on the facade of ceremonial houses. These facade paintings are never called *wut* even though they always include images of string bags and string-bag patterns.

Wut is used as the term for the painted, triangular palm-leaf head decorations that, according to contexts, either the initiates or the novices wear for dances on the ceremonial ground. Here, *wut* is an allusion to the initiation chamber within the ceremonial house where the novices are kept prior to their public appearance. *Wut* conjoins several different meanings and contexts. The string bag is the 'prototype' of all things visible and female and references what men keep concealed and secret; the two aspects—open and hidden—are co-present. Non-initiates, however, also know that each initiation grade has its own specific string-bag pattern that serves as its emblem. Women who enjoy making string bags know all these patterns and manufacture string bags for their husbands (occasionally for a brother) and for themselves, according to their husband's current initiation grade.

With regard to technique, string bags and paintings have one thing in common, and that is *maindshe*, the 'string' or 'white line', respectively. The facade painting on a ceremonial house, for example, is based on an interconnected network of white lines. The head artist starts drawing a white line at the apex of the triangular-shaped facade, which has been primed with black paint and is lying flat on the ground. In the process of painting, further similarities to string-bag production become apparent: the white line is drawn unbroken from top to bottom so that in the end the surface is covered, and thereby structured, by a network of white lines (Hauser-Schäublin 1989b).[14] The actual painting of the facade is done in horizontal bands equivalent to those formed by the looping technique used in making string bags.[15] The bands have no centre point and no sides; actually, they are bands of ornament-style painting (see Stevens 1996). One of the main differences between string bags and painting is that, in painting, the large-sized motifs show figurative representations while on string bags the patterns consist exclusively of lines and geometric shapes (Hauser-Schäublin 1989b). Furthermore, painting is the work of specialists—that is, male artists—and is always kept secret from women and non-initiates, while string bags are manufactured by women, anywhere and at any time.

It is on the technological level—the creation of a network with the help of a line or a twine—that the analogy between painting and string bags becomes evident, but the two differ in terms of conditions of production and nomenclature; and this in turn references the significance of concealing and revealing in men's knowledge management.

The term *wut* also designates the womb—in other words, the 'bag' that contains the foetus (see also MacKenzie 1991:143–4). What all the concepts of *wut* have in common is that they represent containers of some form or another: string bags, a woman's 'bag' (in the sense of womb) and the initiation chamber. In its capacity as container, *wut* has the singular power to transform its contents (see also Losche 1997): a fetus grows to become a child in its mother's womb; an untamed piglet becomes a domesticated pig; in initiations, living men catch glimpses of the wondrous world of the ancestors and return 'impregnated with the beyond', while novices are transformed into knowledgeable men. None of these creatures comes out of *wut* the same as they went in; they all go through a condensed process of irreversible maturation and change. *Wut* possesses an agency, a generative power that transforms all creatures. In the secret male rituals staged in the ceremonial house, *wut* is again associated with femaleness. The association between the most important male spirits, *nggwalndu*, which are

---

14   The helpers contribute the red and yellow contours to the white lines, or fill them in.
15   The difference between the string bags of the Iatmul and those of the Abelam is that the former manufacture them by producing closed rings to which a new ring is then added, while the Abelam manufacture them in a continuous, spiral-shaped process (Schuster 1989:374).

shown to the initiates in the painted initiation chamber, *wut*, and the string bag in the sense of womb—in Tok Pisin, both concepts go by the term '*bilum*'—is also made by the Ilahita Arapesh (Tuzin 1980:244–5). There it is even stated explicitly that the *bilum* of the *nggwal* 'contains the children of all creatures, crying to be born' (Tuzin 1980:244).

In summary, one could say that the power of *wut* lies in the magic of transformation, the capacity to change irreversibly. This power is definitely female (see also Forge 1966:26); this also applies to the initiation chamber within which the novices transcend to a higher level of knowledge and attain a new social status; among other things, this transformation finds expression in the new name that the initiates receive when re-entering the secular realm of the village. What the adult men retain is, however, the social control over the whole process; this is shown in mythology, but, above all, it becomes evident in the incessant play of concealment and revelation.

The Language of Concealing and Revealing

The looping technique and the visual penetrability it produces—typical features of the string bag—create opportunities for the play of concealment and revelation. The two principles are also played out in a different field of Abelam culture—namely, in language and speech. Speaking in metaphors is a practice that enables people to keep ritual secrets concealed but hint at them all the same. In Tok Pisin, metaphorical speech is referred to as '*tok piksa*'; in Abelam, as '*andsha-kundi*'. *Andsha-kundi* is a ritualised form of speech that men use during ritual events held on the ceremonial ground (for example, mortuary feats, feasts held in the context of the yam cycle or during the construction of a new ceremonial house). Speakers revert to a wide range of metaphors to reference events and persons, but which only those informed are able to fathom.

As a speech form in its own right, *andsha-kundi* displays a specific structure. Similar to the looping technique in string-bag production, here 'loose ends' are twined and then looped into consecutive speech figures. Without announcement, the speaker begins with a seemingly meaningless sentence, hooks the next one on to it that makes just as little sense as the first, and so forth. It is only when these separate pieces are linked together that a meaningful speech figure begins to take shape. Here is an example of a song-speech performed by men (M) and women (F):[16]

---

16   Performed during a wake on 10 February 1979 at the ceremonial ground of Ndusaki in Kalabu. It is the song of Lake (Numbunggen hamlet, Kalabu). When these songs are performed, the women often contribute only the refrain; here they actually actively participate in creating the speech figure.

M: You tell me to tie it up, and I tie it up.

F: You tell me to carry it, and I carry it.

M: These men are called Katu and Imagwate. They tie up a pig and carry it away.

F: These men Katu and Imagwate catch a cassowary and tie it up.

M: I have lucky hands.

F: Katu and Imagwate often catch pigs and cassowaries. They have lucky hands.

(Hauser-Schäublin 1989a:157)

The verse begins with an action—tying up—that someone has given orders for. In the following line, a second action—carrying an unnamed object—is added to the first. In the third line, the names of the actors are given; they refer to a pair of male ancestors (*nggwal*; in Tok Pisin: *tambaran*). By revealing their names, the speaker-singer discloses his identity as a member of the ritual ward associated with the two *nggwal*. At the same time, the listener hears what has been tied up and carried away: first a pig, and then a cassowary. The singer-speaker describes himself as a good hunter ('lucky hands'). In the two final lines, the singer reflects this self-portrayal onto his two *nggwalndu*, thus bringing to expression that the last were well disposed to him. At the same time, he is conveying the message that he is acting as the *nggwal*'s proxy.[17] Next to its specific texture, the constant back and forth between inside and outside and between concealing and revealing (see also Hauser-Schäublin 1992) plays a major role in this speech form.

In *tok piksa*, the metaphor of the string bag is a recurrent theme; it not only references a 'thing' or an 'object', it also actually refers to a complex interlinkage of actions. Let me explain this with a further example. On the occasion of the opening of a new ceremonial house in Kalabu in 1978, the men, in alternation with the women,[18] struck up a song (*nggwal mindsha*) in honour of the most prominent *nggwalndu* of Kalabu, called Sagulas, in which they used the metaphor of *wut* to tell of his deeds.

M: I am under the water on earth. You may beat the slit-drum and call me. Then I shall set out to come and see you.

F: You must beat the slit-drum, then I shall appear in the village.

---

17 With this song-speech, the singer is promising the deceased that he will sacrifice a pig to honour him.
18 The men performed inside the ceremonial house while the women who sang the refrain stood outside, at the foot of the house's roof (Hauser-Schäublin 1989a:237–40).

M: Sagulas is making a string bag.

F: I know, Sagulas is making a string bag with which one can catch the fishes *kavi* and *mara*.

M: When he is making the string bag, many men come to watch him at work. When he has finished the string bag, all are welcome to come and see it and rejoice in it.

(Hauser-Schäublin 1989a:237)

The song begins at the home of the *nggwal* Sagulas: a pool in the bush where he rests at the bottom.[19] When the men start beating the slit-drums in the village (to start a ritual), he awakens and follows their call to the settlement. This is more or less the standard opening to all songs of this kind. Following this, two strands of action are inter-looped: the men sing of the *nggwal* who is making a string bag, which is then picked up and continued by the women who sing of manufacturing nets for catching fish. What the men really mean with the metaphor of making string bags is that Sagulas—that is, the men themselves—is busy producing secret things; in other words, painting ritual objects in preparation for an initiation. The women pick up this motif but give it a different turn, as men do not 'produce' string bags in the literal sense of the term. They describe the string bag as a fishing net. But, as one man explained, this phrasing actually means catching fish with one's bare hands and is a hidden reference to the final act in an initiation where the men indeed have to catch fish without the help of a net in a dammed stream. To what extent this reflects the men's interpretation of the wordage and in how far the women deduce the fish catch from the fact that Sagulas resides in water, I am unable to say with certainty. The constant back and forth between hinting at and then concealing again goes hand in hand with the reciprocal enactment of knowledge and not knowing between men and women.

The Loops of the *Tambaran* and his String Bag

In this section, I go on to show how the principle of concealment and revelation is enacted in the ritual life of men. I shall also address the problem once raised by Anthony Forge (1966) of the unresolved relationship between visual form, the names of single motifs in painting and their meaning in initiations, which I discuss from the perspective of the systemic qualities of the string bag. Forge's respondents gave him three different designations for the motif of the spiral:

---

19   As in the case of the other spirits, *wale*, the *nggwalndu* are said to reside in hidden pools and waterholes deep in the bush; these pools are regarded as passages to the world beyond, where the sun shines when it is night in the human realm.

swirl in the water, leg of pork and fern frond. What Forge wanted to find out was: what did this heterogeneous terminology mean in the context of initiations? Why have three so completely different meanings, and, raising the question to the next level, is it actually possible to translate the visual into language, and what is the relationship between the two forms of communication (Forge 1970:289; see also Losche 1995, 1996, 2001)?

In a figurative sense, this type of partial visual penetrability that one encounters in string bags—the 'empty spaces' between the looped string—is also found on the facade painting, actually on the entire front of a ceremonial house. In a sense, the face of a ceremonial house, too, is not 'opaque'; it contains 'empty spaces' that allow 'glimpses' as well, thus reflecting one of the basic principles of the *Tambaran* cult among the Abelam. By this I mean, in analogy to the translucency of the string bag, the interplay between outside and inside. The elements shown on the front of a ceremonial house (including the motifs of the actual facade painting) function as hidden references to the various initiation stages and the secrets they incorporate, and thus operate in a similar manner to *tok piksa*, the metaphorical speech I described above.

In order to make this interplay between concealing and revealing clearer to the reader, I shall briefly outline the various initiation stages and the rituals that go with them—actually the only ritual events that are staged inside the cult house. At the time of my fieldwork in Kalabu, initiation among the Abelam consisted of an entire cycle of ranked grades; the completion of a full cycle could last up to several decades.[20] Initiations always go hand in hand with the cultivation of long, ceremonial yams, the festive display of the finest tubers and the sacrifice of pigs. The first initiation grade is for young boys; the final stage is attained only by very few old men. Each initiation grade includes (apart from a series of rituals that the novices go through and, at times, week-long periods of seclusion) a cult scene that the initiators create inside the ceremonial house. The first grade is called *nggumaira* (*nggu*: 'stagnant water', *maira*: 'miracle', 'secret', often translated in Tok Pisin as *tambaran*). The created imagery consists of a hole that the men dig inside the ceremonial house and fill with water.[21] The waterhole is covered with a layer of white foam (produced by triturating a special plant) on which the artists create a concentrically shaped picture with flowers and strips of leaves.[22] The novices—all young boys—are escorted to the *nggumaira* in single file; after taking a brief glimpse at it, they are led away again and told to turn their backs on the 'miracle'. In the meantime, the men

---

20 At the time of my fieldwork, some initiation grades had not been staged for many years. My husband and I were able to witness some in neighbouring villages to which Kalabu men had been invited as guests. I shall continue to use the present tense when describing the different cult scenes although, as mentioned, these initiations are no longer performed.

21 The scene is based on the notion that the spirits reside in pools.

22 The strips are also referred to as *maindshe*, 'string' or 'streak'.

cover up the image by throwing earth on it, making it look as if the ground has 'swallowed' the picture. Then the boys are told to turn round and look—the miracle has vanished!

For the second grade (*ulke*), double-sided carvings called *ulke* are lined up flanked by standing anthropomorphic male and female carved figures (*wapinyan*). *Ulke* is the term for predominantly female spirit beings, which are also associated with pools in the bush. The material secrets of *nau*, the third stage, consist of bizarre-shaped bamboo roots that are displayed upside down. The root ends often have the shape of birds' heads; the figures are frequently embellished by painting and adding feathers to them. *Nau* are considered to be female beings and are often decorated with women's adornments. Bamboo flutes (transverse flutes) represent the voices of the *nau* and are called *nautagwa* (*nau*: women). The female *nau* spirit beings live in treetops and have power over game animals (wild pigs, cassowaries), either driving them into or leading them away from the men hunting them.

Both grades—*ulke* and *nau* (by the time of my fieldwork they had been conflated into one single grade)—deal with female spirit beings associated with the 'wild' forest. The wood used for their representative carvings is taken from the lower ends and roots of plants, respectively.

The next two initiation grades are subsumed under the term '*nggwalndu*';[23] their constituent parts are called *nggilenggwal* ('black' *nggwal*) and *naranggwal* ('decorated' *nggwal*). *Nggwalndu* are male ancestor spirits. Although each *nggwal* has a name of his own, individuality is of no significance; they are not distinguished in terms of outer image or behaviour. A *nggwalndu* initiation demands the staging of a feast with long ceremonial yams—namely, with the type called *mambutap*. Yam and *nggwalndu* stand in close relationship to each other. The yam tubers that are put on display each receive the name of a specific *nggwalndu*. The long yam is one of the many embodiments of these powerful spirit beings.

The *nggwalndu* initiation scenes are highly elaborate. The spirits are represented by massive carvings. In *nggilenggwal*, these consist of large faces to which occasionally a chest part is added. The carvings are placed upright and have tent-shaped backs attached to them, which are covered with plaited and painted mats. *Nggilenggwal* have neither arms nor legs. The figures are covered above by a mat-roofing called *nggilut* ('black string bag'). In front of the figure (occasionally there are several figures), the men lay out shell rings in a semicircle and stick bone daggers in the ground (both items are associated with stars). The semicircle is referred to as 'hole in the ground' so that, in fact, each *nggilenggwal*

---

23 *Nggwalndu* refers to ancestral spirits associated with the village as well as with a specific ceremonial ground and clan. The same term is used for 'grandfather' and 'stomach'.

is shown sitting before, or even in, a waterhole. The voices of the *nggilenggwal* are sounded by singing into bamboo tubes sticking in a wooden cylinder (*kundi ure*). *Naranggwal* focuses on huge male figures cut from tree trunks. They are placed next to each other in the ceremonial house, reclining on a rack that has been erected parallel with the longitudinal axis. Above them is a painted canopy made of palm leaves sewn together. Above the canopy there is a hidden floor where the initiators take up position. The walls are also made of painted palm leaves, thus creating a fully decorated initiation chamber. It is called *narut* ('decorated string bag'). As in the case of *nggilenggwal*, here, shell rings are laid out in a semicircle in front of the figures; here, too, they indicate stars.

The name of the last initiation grade is *puti*. At the time of fieldwork, this grade had not been performed for something like 30 years. It is also called *bikna*, which is the name of a bird that lives and nests predominantly on the ground. In the past, this level was reached by only a few old men—partly for demographic reasons, but also because of the tremendous amount of pigs required for sacrifice. A man who had passed this grade enjoyed special status in his ritual moiety and his clan as well as in his ward and the village as a whole; he became a so-called *numandu* ('big-man'). The cult scene for this grade consists of a single figure that is placed—again, in the longitudinal axis—at the centre of the ceremonial house. Like *nggilenggwal*, it has a carved face; its body is made of a tent-like frame over which a finely plaited mat is laid and painted red, black, yellow and white. The outer surface of the tetrahedron-shaped body, which has the same shape as the ceremonial house itself, is decorated completely with shining white shell rings and likened to a bright, starlit sky.

The front side of the seated *puti* figure is fitted out with angled and raised arms and bent legs, made of banana stems. In its hands it holds spears, while its feet are equipped with the hoof-shaped claws of a cassowary. In front of the figure, again, shell rings are laid out in a semicircle. In contrast with the *nggwalndu* stages, here, there is no initiation chamber since now the interior of the ceremonial house as such is looked upon as *puti*'s house—his *wut*. The term *puti* means effectively the 'empty one', 'he who has given everything'. The figure is compared with an old man sitting near a fire warming his skin in the ashes (see also Stöcklin 2004:Cover plate).

An experienced old man once commented on the initiation cycle with the words: '*nggumaira* opens the door, *puti* closes it.' What he was saying was that, with *puti*, the world of mysteries and secrets has come to an end;[24] there is no knowledge of what lies beyond; what is left at the end of the journey is simply the void.

---

24 In his three monographs (1980, 1997, 2001), Tuzin describes and discusses the beings and their innate properties that the Ilahita Arapesh subsume under the term *Tambaran*, mainly with reference to myths.

The principle upon which the succession of the various stages and the relationship between the different grades are based always follows the same structure: the initiating members of one ceremonial moiety dramatically enact and visualise knowledge about the mysteries and terrors of existence for the initiates of the opposite moiety. After subjecting the novices to a series of often-painful procedures and tests, the true nature of these mysteries and terrors are then revealed to them. In each stage, they are made to believe that this time they are going to encounter the real secrets and that they are about to take a next step into the intriguing world of the spirit beings who make the world go round and shape the fate of human beings. Consequently, with each stage, the scenes and ritual procedures become more complex—up to the end where a few men reach *puti* and encounter the void, the realm where all human knowledge ends.

The System of Relating the Outside to the Inside

Concealing and revealing are founded on the principle of ambiguity and implication—a system of signs that offers a broad range of interpretation. The signs themselves are not random in any way, and what applies to the Sagulas song-speech described above also goes for the constituent motifs of sacred imagery.

Many of the highly meaningful objects used in imagery are human-made and hand-shaped artefacts. These artefacts are ambiguous in the sense that they possess a public and a secret dimension—an 'outside' and an 'inside'. I discovered the loops between the 'outside' and the 'inside'—meaning the initiation grades—only when I began going through photographs of the Abelam collection from the Basel Ethnographic Museum whilst still in the field. After having worked for months with several old Abelam men—namely, artists—on the terminology and the meaning of the various objects, I suddenly realised that I had often recorded two terms. These terminological discrepancies first had me muddled. One of my closest co-workers, the artist (*maira yagwandu*) Kwandshendu, led me onto the right track when he explained: 'When you have a carving on the outside of the ceremonial house it has a special term, but when you use it inside the house for an initiation scene, it has a different name.' What Kwandshendu was describing was actually the visualised version of *andsha-kundi* (hidden speech); in other words, depending on the situation, the objects were referring to different action and meaning contexts and thus carried different names and significations. In fact, what Kwandshendu had explained to

---

What the Abelam call *maira*—literally, secret and mysterious—actually refers more to what lies behind the *Tambaran*. Of *nggwalndu* (ancestors, ancestor spirits), they say they are *maira*; however, the term *maira* does not denote a category of beings as such but rather their innate properties, the features that human beings are unable to fathom.

me here—almost casually, in undramatic terms—was the relationship between the esoteric and the exoteric that becomes fused in the motifs of the facade painting and the various three-dimensional objects that adorn the face of a ceremonial house. This interconnection between the 'outside' and the 'inside' is known foremost to the *maira yagwandu*, the artists.

What surprised me about this explanation was the fact that the Abelam conceptualise the principle of concealing and revealing as a system in which all the visible, outside elements of a ceremonial house actually refer to secret, 'inside' contexts; and they put the system into practice knowingly. Until now, Melanesia specialists have usually assumed that it is up to the anthropologist to 'uncover' such a system and its working order, 'but [that it] does not involve the conscious corroboration by or intent of the users of the system' (Losche 2001:158). Kwandshendu's explanation clearly shows that—notwithstanding anthropological qualms and speculations—the indigenous artists (and other 'big-men') are fully aware of the linkage between motif and object, and between term and function. With this, he also provided an answer to Anthony Forge's question. Meaning is defined by context, and terminology is therefore not determined by the object or the motif, but by the circumstances. When Kwandshendu went through the visible signs on the ceremonial house with us, it became clear that Abelam men 'read' the front of a cult house as a system of signs, which, at the same time, serves as a mnemonic device to register the single grades in initiation.

Painting is a self-contained part of this system. The single bands and the motifs shown on the facade serve as signs that have distinctive names and allow room for differing interpretations. In its total structure, a facade painting reflects the sequential order of the initiation grades and the way they are interrelated. A facade painting is created from top to bottom and this is also the way it is viewed and read: the topmost rows of motifs refer to cult scenes that are centred on the forest as the abode of mysterious creatures and spirit beings that live in pools or in treetops. The apex of the painting shows a flying fox (*matmboi*); it is classified as a female being that lives in the tops of trees and tries to confuse hunters below; *matmboi* serve as references to the *nau* initiation grades. Beneath the flying fox there follows a variegated array of spirals. This is the motif for which Anthony Forge noted the three differing terms (see above) and which had him rather confused and, later, inspired Diane Losche (1995) to venture new interpretations. In Kalabu, and in the context of initiations, the spirals are interpreted as the traces of water spiders scurrying over the surface of a pool or as 'rippled water surface' and 'foam', respectively. They reference the first initiation grade, *nggumaira*, where a foamy image is created on the surface of a waterhole, as well as *ulke* spirits and the pools where these female beings are said to reside. The next band of motifs shows female bats (*kwandshe*) with their young (*kumbui*) clinging to their breasts. These bats refer to female spirits that glide silently through the bush, not unlike witches, the people say; they represent the central figures in the cult scene of the *ulke* initiation grade. The band showing the black–red fruits and the pair-wise grouped spirals are also associated with the mysterious realm of the forest and its inhabitants; the latter represent birds (of the *maintshe* or *baintship* species, respectively). The band displaying the splendidly decorated dancers (the motif is called *ndudama*) is a reference to what the Abelam believe to be the most significant and greatest *maira* of all—that is, men in full ceremonial adornment. The dancers who have their eyes shut are described as having just returned from the mysterious and splendid world of the beyond, still mesmerised by the beauty and the miracles they saw there. Finally, the eye comes to the bottom row with its huge faces and the minute zigzagging bands that depict the figures' arms and legs (the motif is called *nggwalnggwal*); the figures represent the *nggwalndu* class of ancestral spirits. The string bag patterns encompassing them are emblems of the *nggwalndu* initiation grade and thus also signify the painted initiation chamber in the *naranggwal* grade, called *narut*.

The facade painting is like a kaleidoscopic image consisting of rows of motif bands that can be conflated to create different images, all depending on who the viewers are, what their level of knowledge is, and what perspective they are viewing it from. Accordingly, the motifs refer to different things with alternative meanings to different viewers.

Unlike the two-dimensionality of conventional painting, which relies on the consistent medium of colour, the visible face of a ceremonial house with all its ambiguous elements of different shapes and material constitutes a three-dimensional work of art that intricately enacts the esoteric and the exoteric. As described above, the first initiation grade, *nggumaira*, involves only perishable material and is therefore not expressed by a permanent image on the outside representation. The only reference to this ephemeral cult scene is a narrow, waved band showing small, colourful fruits and leaves (*mindshakuso*) located below the carved crossbeam on the lower exterior. The same type of band encompasses the actual *nggumaira* image created over the artificial pool inside the ceremonial house.

All the other initiation grades that rely on comparably durable objects for their specific cult scenes are represented on the visible face of the ceremonial house as follows. The *ulke* initiation, including the homonymous carvings, is represented by the carved crossbeam located beneath the facade painting and described in this context as *tikik*. The *nau* initiation is signified by the birds' heads made of bamboo roots and located on the inside of the protruding side walls—that is, the roof of the house; here they are designated *vi warya*. The tunnel-shaped entrance (*korekore*) to the ceremonial house references the entry to the initiation chamber inside (*atapine*), while the carved pythons (*ndua*), which are usually located above the *korekore*, indicate the places of origin of spirit beings (*wale*) that play a role in several, different initiation scenes.

Nggilenggwal, or to be more precise, the plaited initiation chamber (*nggilut*), is represented by the plaited mat (*kimbi*) located at the lower end of the face of the cult house. The spears (*vi*) stuck into the projecting roof are also a reference to this grade. Inside the house, similar spears are placed over the corridor that leads to the initiation chamber, with their pointed ends aimed at the novices.

Naranggwal, in which the colourfully painted initiation chamber (*narut*) plays an important role, is first and foremost referenced by the large facade painting (*mbai*) itself. During the *naranggwal* initiation, a raised—that is, suspended—floor, actually the roof of the initiation chamber, is constructed where the initiators position themselves and imitate spirit voices (with the help of musical instruments). For its construction, the men use thick vines, which they refer to as *samban* in this specific context—that is, in the interior of the ceremonial house. Similar vines can be found on the outside of the cult house—to be more specific, winding themselves up on the inside of the extended walls and ending high up under the protruding roof peak. Here the vines are referred to as *narkassa*.

The last initiation stage, *puti*, described as an old man whose back is formed by the star-covered sky, the cosmos, is signified by the ceremonial house (*korambo*) as a whole. As such the ceremonial house also stands for the entity that contains all the secrets and miracles that the novices have come to see in kaleidoscopic imagery in the course of the initiation cycle over the past years. When a new ceremonial house is inaugurated, the front, matted, lower section of the house is decorated with shell rings; above them is exhibited a selection of the most beautiful string bags made especially for the occasion by the women. *Puti* and the ceremonial house stand in a microcosm/macrocosm relationship to each other. One should also add here that the ceremonial house with its sloping ridge (designated simultaneously as *nyit*, 'sky', and *yapa*, 'father') bears reference to the western realm of the cosmos and is aligned to the course of the setting sun.[25]

---

25 To describe the complex semantics and the cross-referencing between cult house and ceremonial ground and their specific decorative elements would be beyond the scope of this chapter (but see Hauser-Schäublin 1989a:285–302).

Concealing and Revealing as Hallmarks of the Unexplainable

The secrets that men conceal and then reveal in rituals relate to a transcendental mode of perception and understanding of phenomena that cannot be explained in any other way. The impressive images created by the assemblage of variegated objects and artefacts reference notions and concepts that lie beyond the boundaries of their own innate logic; they bear on matters that lie hidden away and will, in essence, always remain inaccessible and enigmatic. They address issues such as the diversity of existence in the world, the origins of this existence, life and death, as well as modes of regeneration to overcome death.

Concealment and revelation constitute an idiom of intimations, a form of communication that does not offer explanations, but instead provides glimpses of ever-changing combinations of single elements and phenomena in kaleidoscopic fashion. For the Abelam, the unexplainable has always been a part of everyday life: unexpected encounters in the garden, down at a stream or deep in the bush; a wild pig suddenly dashing out of the dense undergrowth a few feet in front of the hunter; a flying fox with outstretched wings gliding soundlessly over somebody returning from the garden in the twilight; a snake vanishing stealthily into an overgrown pool; shooting stars falling from the sky but never hitting the ground; small yam cuttings, almost withered away, growing to become magnificent tubers; a wife no longer issuing menstrual blood, and instead a child grows in her belly. Such and many similar phenomena are experienced as facets of a reality that, in the end, is not fathomable and will always remain a mystery. The people look upon it as a transcendental reality that shows itself only in bright but brief glimpses. Prism-like, the pieces join together to reveal a kaleidoscopic picture, an image, however, that keeps changing according to its innate properties as well as to the perspective of the viewer.

Men sometimes dream of unexplainable phenomena and discuss them with others in meetings at the ceremonial ground in a joint search for answers to matters that do not immediately reveal themselves. They are looked upon as signs that point to hidden realms of being.

Ritual life and the ceremonial house represent specific forms of organising and shaping the relationship between humans and their transcendental reality. On this stage, the living play the part of the 'non-initiated' who are barred from discovering the ultimate secret, just as the women and children are excluded from the secrets of men, and, vice versa, the men are banished from the female realm of menstruation and giving birth (see Hauser-Schäublin 1995). This secluded world with its own logic and powers reveals itself only through signs and clues, which the old men try to catch hold of in cult scenes. What characterises the relationship between the concealed and the revealed is the co-presence of both 'worlds': the visible and the invisible. What lies concealed and reveals itself in fleeting glimpses and ephemeral images does not exist in a time frame that is separate from the here, now and then. Concealing and revealing constitute a mode of dealing with, and mediating, co-presence (Hauser-Schäublin 1997). In spatial terms, the cult house and the ceremonial ground create an interface between the realms of the visible and the invisible (Hauser-Schäublin 2003). This junction is a powerful and dangerous place and demands special modes of conduct. If people misbehave, no matter whether they are men, women or youths, the 'old folk' (*golepa*) impose sanctions; at least this is the way that men commonly explain unexpected blows of fate.

Conclusion

During initiation rituals, the initiating men from the one ritual moiety often terrorised the novices of the opposite moiety, or at least put fear into them by threatening them with terrible ordeals; it was part of the 'game'. In conjunction with the interplay of concealing and revealing, the knowledgeable were able to retain power over the unknowledgeable. The use of power and terror did not, however, split the world of men into durable categories of superiors and inferiors; instead, here again we encounter the principle of continuous looping—social looping, this time—since the novices of the one moiety later became the initiators of the neophytes of the other ritual half, and so forth, in an ongoing process of interchanging roles.[26] The two ritual halves stood in a continuous, competitive exchange relationship that found expression through various channels such as yam and pig feasts, initiations and the construction of ceremonial houses. The representations that were created and enacted in initiations were not made for their own sake nor was the concept of concealment and revelation merely an instrument of social control based on multiple forms of 'deception'—hoodwinking the non-initiates—as the confession by the men of Ilahita might suggest. This would be taking a very short view of things.

Moreover, the mode by which the enigmatic was organised and mediated also served as the basis of the social system, relying on structures and processes—so far, my initial hypothesis—that were also modelled on the principle of concealment and revelation. We have here a segmentary concept that creates nested divisions of knowledgeable and unknowledgeable on the basis of exclusion, integration and inclusion: the men were ignorant of the secrets of women; children and women had no knowledge of the secrets of men; and young

---

26 See Losche (2001) on the interlocked ritual exchange relationships between the initiators of one ceremonial moiety and the novices of the opposite half.

men—graded according to initiation level—were nescient of the knowledge of the older, enlightened men, with the enactment and mediation of knowledge oscillating between the two ritual moieties.

The relationship between human beings and the world beyond, and the mode in which the Abelam conceptualised and shaped this bond, created the screen on which the interplay between concealing and revealing was enacted as a means to create hierarchies of knowledge in society, while at the same time it formed the loops that held all the segments together.

I doubt whether Ilahita Arapesh men were ardent nihilists or merely great theatrical actors attempting to keep the ignorant unwitting and under control, as a reader might infer from Tuzin's (1997) description. When the men declared that the *Tambaran* had been nothing but lies and deception, they were in fact addressing only one aspect of representation—namely, the notion of concealment (and revelation) vis-a-vis women and children. In view of the findings presented here, one should really reassess the 'killing of the *Tambaran*' as recounted by Tuzin and also reconsider the two episodes described above where some young Abelam men voiced their protest against the 'law of the past'. What the Christian revivalists described with hindsight as the 'old men's sleight of hand' was only half the truth. In fact, the conceptual background upon which the principle of concealment and revelation was founded—the netherworld beyond that revealed itself in bright flashes and brief episodes—had simply run its course in the eyes of the revivalists (and others in the Maprik area), replaced with promises that the Holy Spirit was ready to deliver to believers instant salvation and riches. What yet stood in the way of Salvation was the old, ever co-present world of spirits that was considered evil (see also Reithofer 2006:Ch. 4; Strong 2007), and for this 'the *Tambaran* had to die' (Tuzin 1997:64). The prophecies heralded an end to all toils and the advent of a paradisiacal world, not in distant days to come, but now, in the immediate future. The rituals staged by the Christian revivalists were geared to transforming the future into the present. Tuzin tells of a

> tiny repertoire of maddeningly repetitive, largely tuneless hymns… The blaring incessancy of the hymns quickly became for us a kind of torture…Continuing long into the night and resuming at first light, these hymns were sounding when we went to bed, sounding when we woke up, churning whatever sleep we achieved during the long hours of the service. (Tuzin 1997:222–3)

It seems that the 'second coming' had to be sung into existence, that the tomorrow should become today.

The group of believers included both men and women, headed by prophetic service leaders. The revivalists distanced themselves from non-believers or members of other denominations in a more general sense of the term, but drew a strict dividing line between themselves and the so-called 'traditionalists'. The Holy Spirit's cornucopia would not come in the shape of a string bag; instead it was to contain trucks and aircrafts (Tuzin 1997:149–50). The riches were to come as money and cargo, not as fertility and regeneration.

This new world of belief and thought rested on a completely different foundation; it was embedded in global relations and transactions, in ideas of progress, development and Western capitalism, and demanded from the people a completely new orientation and perspective (Sahlins 2005). The 'confessions' made by the revivalists in Ilahita and the demands that the young Abelam men confronted me with during my fieldwork actually show that people had begun to alter their orientation and to adjust to the demands of a changed and changing world. The values fostered by the old men and embodied by the string bag of the *Tambaran* with its incessant and systemic loops of concealing and revealing no longer sufficed as a canon on which people could model their identity.

The string bag had become riddled with holes; its loops had come apart. It was no longer able to contain what it had held before—neither the two co-present 'worlds' nor the social order that relied on the segmentary principle of exclusion and inclusion and which was fuelled by concealment and revelation. The groups over which the agents of the *Tambaran* in earlier days had wielded power through the string bag—the young men and the women—firmly took possession of their newly gained freedom (as the opening passages of this chapter showed), moving into new fields of action, well beyond the reach and the 'revenge' of the cassowary.

References

Coupaye, Ludowic 2004. Growing Artefacts, Displaying Relationships: Outlining the Technical System of Long Yam Cultivation and Display among the Abelam of Nyamikum village (East Sepik Province, Papua New Guinea). Unpublished Ph.D. dissertation. Norwich, UK: University of East Anglia.

Forge, Anthony 1966. Art and Environment in the Sepik. *Proceedings of the Royal Anthropological Institute of Great Britain and Ireland* 1965:23–31.

Forge, Anthony 1970. Learning to See in New Guinea. *In* P. Mayer, (ed.) *Socialisation: The Approach from Social Anthropology*, pp. 269–91. New York: Tavistock.

Forge, Anthony 1971. Marriage and Environment in the Sepik: Comments on Francis Korn's Analysis of Iatmul Society. In R. Needham (ed.) *Rethinking Kinship and Marriage*, pp. 133–44. London: Tavistock.

Forge, Anthony 1972. The Golden Fleece. *Man* 7:527–40.

Forge, Anthony 1973. Style and Meaning in Sepik Art. In Anthony Forge (ed.) *Primitive Art and Society*, pp. 169–92. London: Oxford University Press.

Gewertz, Deborah and Frederick Errington 2004. Toward an Ethnographically Grounded Study of Modernity in Papua New Guinea. In Victoria S. Lockwood (ed.) *Globalization and Culture Change in the Pacific Islands*, pp. 273–84. Upper Saddle River, NJ: Pearson Prentice Hall.

Goankar, Dilip Parameshwar 1999. On Alternative Modernities. *Public Culture* 11:1–18.

Hauser-Schäublin, Brigitta 1989a. *Kulthäuser in Nordneuguinea*. Berlin: Akademie-Verlag.

Hauser-Schäublin, Brigitta 1989b. *Leben in Linie, Muster und Farbe. Einführung in die Betrachtung außereuropäischer Kunst am Beispiel der Abelam*. Basel: Birkhäuser.

Hauser-Schäublin, Brigitta 1992. Der verhüllte Schrein. Sakralarchitektur und ihre Umhüllungen in Bali. *Ethnologica Helvetica* 16:171–200.

Hauser-Schäublin, Brigitta 1995. Puberty Rites, Women's Naven, and Initiation. In Nancy Lutkehaus and Paul Roscoe (eds) *Gender Rituals: Female Initiation in Melanesia*, pp. 33–53. New York and London: Routledge.

Hauser-Schäublin, Brigitta 1996. The Thrill of the Line, the String, and the Frond, or Why the Abelam Are a Non-cloth Culture. *Oceania* 67:81–106.

Hauser-Schäublin, Brigitta 1997. Die Vergangenheit in der Gegenwart: Zeitkonzeptionen und ihre Handlungskontexte bei den Abelam in Papua-Neuguinea. *Baessler-Archiv* (NS)45:409–29.

Hauser-Schäublin, Brigitta 2002. Gender: Verkörperte Feldforschung. In Hans Fischer (ed.) *Feldforschungen: Erfahrungsberichte zur Einführung*, pp. 73–99. Berlin: Reimer.

Hauser-Schäublin, Brigitta 2003. Raum, Ritual und Gesellschaft: Religiöse Zentren und Sozio-religiöse Verdichtungen im Ritual. In B. Hauser-Schäublin and M. Dickhardt (eds) *Kulturelle Räume—Räumliche Kultur: Zur Neubestimmung des Verhältnisses zweier fundamentaler Kategorien menschlicher Praxis*, pp. 43–87. Münster: LIT.

Hirsch, Eric 2001. When Was Modernity in Melanesia? *Social Anthropology* 9:131–46.

Ingold, Tim 2007. *Lines: A Brief History*. London: Routledge.

Jourdan, Christine 1996. Where Have All the Cultures Gone?: Sociocultural Creolisation in the Solomon Islands. In Jonathan Friedman and James G. Carrier (eds) *Melanesian Modernities*, pp. 34–52. Lund, Sweden: Lund University Press.

Losche, Diane 1995. The Sepik Gaze: Iconographic Interpretation of Abelam Form. *Social Analysis* 38:47–60.

Losche, Diane 1996. The Impossible Aesthetic: The Abelam, the Moa Bird and Me. *Oceania* 66(4):305–10.

Losche, Diane 1997. What Do Abelam Images Want from Us?: Plato's Cave and Kwatbil's Belly. *The Australian Journal of Anthropology* 8:35–49.

Losche, Diane 2001. Anthony's Feast: The Gift in Abelam Aesthetics. *The Australian Journal of Anthropology* 12:155–65.

MacKenzie, Maureen 1991. *Androgynous Objects: String Bags and Gender in Central New Guinea*. Chur, Switzerland: Harwood Academic.

Reithofer, Hans 2006. *The Python Spirit and the Cross: Becoming Christian in a Highland Community of Papua New Guinea*. Göttinger Studien zur Ethnologie 16. Münster, Germany: LIT.

Roscoe, Paul B. 1995. Of Power and Menace: Sepik Art as an Affecting Presence. *Journal of the Royal Anthropological Institute* (NS)1:1–22.

Sahlins, Marshall 2005. The Economics of Develop-man in the Pacific. In Joel Robbins and Holly Wardlow (eds) *The Making of Global and Local Modernities in Melanesia*, pp. 23–42. Hampshire, UK: Ashgate.

Scaglion, Richard 1999. Yam Cycles and Timeless Time in Melanesia. *Ethnology* 38:211–25.

Schuster, Gisela 1989. Netztaschen der Zentral-Iatmul im Museum für Völkerkunde Basel. In Beate Engelbrecht and Bernhard Gardi (eds) *Man Does Not Go Naked. Textilien und Handwerk aus afrikanischen und anderen Ländern*, pp. 335–89. Basel, Switzerland: Wepf.

Stevens, Peter S. 1996. *Handbook of Regular Patterns: An Introduction to Symmetry in Two Dimensions*. Cambridge, Mass.: MIT Press.

Stöcklin, Werner 2004. *Toktok: Am Rande der Steinzeit auf Neuguinea*. Basel, Switzerland: Friedrich Reinhardt.

Strong, Thomas 2007. 'Dying Culture' and Decaying Bodies. In Sandra Bamford (ed.), *Embodying Modernity and Post-Modernity: Ritual, Praxis, and Social Change in Melanesia*, pp. 105–23. Durham, NC: Carolina Academic Press.

Tuzin, Donald 1980. *The Voice of the Tambaran: Truth and Illusion in Ilahita Arapesh Religion*. Berkeley: University of California Press.

Tuzin, Donald 1997. *The Cassowary's Revenge: The Life and Death of Masculinity in a New Guinea Society*. Chicago: University of Chicago Press.

Tuzin, Donald 2001. *Social Complexity in the Making*. London: Routledge.

3. 'Skirts–Money–Masks', and Other Chains of Masculine Signification in Post-Colonial Papua New Guinea

David Lipset

> This is our starting point: through his relationship to the signifier, the subject is deprived of something of himself, of his very life, which has assumed the value of that which binds him to the signifier. The phallus is our term for the signifier of his alienation in signification. (Lacan 1977a:28)

Introduction: The Lacanian phallus in a post-colonial setting

With revision, the Lacanian phallus—*qua* concept of the subject in culture as based on a void of meaning—might also serve as a starting point for this chapter. Here, however, I do not intend to theorise the emptiness of the subject in an abstract, psychoanalytic sense. Instead, my conceptual and empirical focus is on a particular group of rural, post-colonial men. Specifically, this chapter concerns shifting signifiers of masculinity in the Sepik region in Melanesia, this being the issue and region that so vexed Tuzin (1997) in his magisterial account of the demise of the male cult in Ilahita village. To begin, I must briefly explain why, among all the decentred concepts of personhood and gender in society (see, for example, Dumont 1986; Durkheim 1933–97; Leenhardt 1979), I prize the Lacanian phallus.

First of all, notwithstanding its masculine register, the Lacanian phallus does not stand for itself in any simple kind of way. It is, yet it is not, the male organ. Instead, the phallus is a symbol of symbols—a master signifier that nevertheless does not define reality/discourse in and of itself, as patriarchy might be said to do. It is a trope established by 'desire of the other, not so much because the other holds the key to the object desired, as because the first object of desire is to be recognized by the other' (Lacan 1977b:58). Initially, the phallus, *qua* signifier, comes into being as the object of maternal desire. 'If the desire of the mother *is* the phallus, the child wishes to be the phallus in order to satisfy that desire' (Lacan 1977b:289). In other words, the Lacanian phallus is defined relationally (see also Strathern 1988) and its relationality is based on an impossible, unfulfillable desire. For Lacan, the lack of the other leaves an indelible trace in the subject, a trace that constitutes yet subverts subsequent chains of signification in which persons and objects are substituted for, or superimposed upon, her absence and missing desire for her desire that motivates their meaning.

The entry into culture—for example, the domain Lacan calls the Symbolic—basically arises from an oedipal injunction; a taboo, to be sure, but one that does not result from the intervention of the father himself. It results, according to Lacan, from what amounts to a semiotic substitution, a substitution of the 'name of the father' (1977b:67) for the love and desire of the mother. This substitution both is and opens up the world of language, law and social action. The Name-of-the-Father, that is, is discursive rather than literal. With the symbolic lack of the imaginary object—the mother's desire—the phallus is 'castrated' (1977b:289). The absence of the other makes signification possible, signification in which, like the male cult, the phallus might misrecognise itself, and be misrecognised, as a powerful and self-sufficient subject or as an illusory kind of gift, albeit one that can never be repaid, much less unilaterally possessed. The 'function of the phallus is to pass for the signifier of the desire of the other' (Nobus 1999:113).

While its relational construction, its gender, detachability and ambiguous position as master-signifier make the Lacanian phallus a useful template for a reconsideration of masculinity in Melanesia, its most trenchant attribute is its irretrievable, yet ambivalent, dispossession from desire, its absent centre. The phallus is associated with the loss of pleasure. But the register in which Lacan casts this alienation is not single toned. The phallus is signified in people and things that represent both presence and absence at once. Again, like male cult spirits, the phallus is an emptiness that appears as a force in society, thus to divide, or subtract, women from men by virtue of its illusions. Its modality is one of combination, mixture and incongruity consisting of rupture and continuity, melancholy and optimism. 'The phallic signifier', as Žižek phrased this contradictory quality, is 'an index of its own impossibility. In its very positivity it is the signifier of "castration"—that is, of its own lack…In the phallus, loss as such attains a positive existence' (1989:157).

Post-colonialism, however—the condition of authority in societies emerging from the experience of colonisation (Mbembe 1992)—as distinct from post-colonial critiques of hegemonic discourse (Said 1978; Young 2001), requires modification of the Lacanian phallus. Amid post-colonialism, everything—every illusory signifier of legitimacy—is pluralised. Instead of a singular Name-of-the-Father, multiple languages, names, cosmologies, laws, medical systems, currencies, and so forth coexist, perhaps in competition with each other, as rival signs of equivocal intervention. So instead of one Symbolic into which the phallus is castrated and exiled, I posit two Symbolics, both of which take their cut from the 'very life' of the subject, thus to 'bind him to the signifier'. Two

Names-of-the-Father—that is, two discursive bodies—'symbolically castrate' the phallus, thus to doubly bind him to very different sorts of signifiers of his alienation. Together, the two Symbolics—the many pre-state, pre-capitalist ones, and that of modernity—give rise to unpredictable, complicated chains of signification. In my view, the former are not eliminated by the latter. Instead, the register of these chains is not just tragic, joyless and dismembered. However impossible or inaccessible they might be, the post-colonial scene remains full of objects of desire for the subject. Their circuit of meanings is positive and productive as well as empty. Of course, this is not quite how Tuzin viewed the fate of the male cult in Ilahita (and see also Knauft, this volume).

Wither Masculinity in Ilahita?

Recall the ingenious trope at the centre of Tuzin's argument in *The Cassowary's Revenge* (1997): the myth of Nambweapa'w foretold the retaliation of (fundamentalist Christian) women against the deceit of the male cult! The voice, in other words, with which Tuzin identified was that of culturally conservative masculinity, rather than that of the Christians or with their particular male and female constituencies. For Tuzin, the deliberate revelation of the secrets of the *Tambaran* cult by millenarian evangelicals in 1984 devastated its members and led to anomie in society at large. Among the many consequences, the male cult lost its position as the object of desire in society. Men stopped planting long yams for competitive ceremonial exchange. They stopped building cult houses. They stopped initiating male youth. The quality of their oratory declined. With men deprived of their sacred rationale for solidarity, domestic violence between husbands and wives increased. No longer under the authority of cult elders, male youth entered into other forms of criminal behaviour as well. Meanwhile, female prophets accused men of being polluted by sexual infidelities. Expectations of how much money was appropriate in mortuary exchanges to honour the dead, and especially men, became ambiguous. Food production dropped. Disease spread through the community.

A grim, melancholy picture, to be sure, but *The Cassowary's Revenge* might also serve as an account of the relationship of the phallus to the two Symbolics I discussed above. If the *Name-of-the-Father* never totally severs the phallus from the other, but leaves him in an impossible state of desire in which objects create more desire to the extent that they inevitably fail to fulfil desire, perhaps the injunction against the *Tambaran* that modernity—represented by Christian revivalism—managed to occasion, might be interpreted in a less catastrophic register. A discussion of what subsequently took place would vindicate me— for example, the revival of the male cult, in whole or in part. But I do not know what has happened in Ilahita since 1985. So instead of reanalysing *The*

Cassowary's Revenge, I turn to the fate of ritual masculinity in another Sepik setting: the Murik Lakes in the estuary of the great river, where I have done research since 1981.[1] In Murik, modernity has not 'killed' the male cult. Rather, men improvise improbable, unforeseen chains of substitution.

So as to develop this rather abstract point ethnographically, I proceed as follows. I will first sketch Murik concepts of personhood. I then introduce the Gaingiin Society, a public, age-graded society in which rights to senior masks used to be exchanged in return for wives' sexual services. In the next section, I go on to analyse a moment in 1988 when money was substituted for sexual intercourse during a grade taking. In conclusion, I argue that this substitution took place in a broader context in which the pre-state phallus is *combining* metaphorically with the modern, rationalised phallus in several ways rather than just the single, tragic modality that Tuzin reported in Ilahita.[2]

The Embodiment of Murik Personhood

Domestic community consists of multiple cognatic lineages domiciled in clusters of households of siblings and their extended families. While persons define themselves and are identified in terms of and through kinship (see Lipset and Stritecky 1994), embodiment and the relationship of personhood to the body are distinctive and need to be spelled out in a little detail.

Embodiment is based on three assumptions. One differentiates it through acts of nurture. Parents give food to children (Barlow 2010). They are then understood not to grow 'big' or 'strong' for having eaten but to become indebted to them both sentimentally and ritually for having benefited from their 'hard work' (Barlow 1985). A second indication of embodied identity is aesthetic. Gifts of ancestral insignia (*sumon*) are ritually bestowed. The body is recognised as possessing several important internal sites: its blood, stomach, semen for men, and the womb and breast milk for women. Rather than fixed at birth, however, the jural person is defined by an ensemble of shell and teeth ornaments, as well as other accessories, that decorates the body. Rank in the lineage is signified by conferral of an outfit of individually named *sacra*, one of which might serve as a metonym for the whole, usually its basket (*sumon suun*) and/or a medallion made of boars' tusks and bird-of-paradise plumage. These insignia are entrusted to firstborn members of their senior sibling groups who bestow them upon kin during rites of passage and are otherwise obliged to protect them from exposure

---

1   Tuzin himself had suggested that my ex-wife, Kathleen Barlow, and I might find the Murik Lakes an interesting setting to research.

2   It is commonplace to view post-colonial masculinity in Papua New Guinea as a historical tragedy (Brison 1995; Knauft 2002; Robbins 2002; Wardlow 2006; Zimmer-Tamakoshi 1997).

to conflict, which pollutes the paraphernalia. The key point here is that the rank and identity are viewed as having to be *presented* to the bodies of kin. Of course, they are not given at random. They are transacted in return for the ritual work donors received from previous generations, which reciprocity defines the jural body (Lipset 1990).

If its exterior is an object upon which personhood is bestowed, *qua* food and sacred ornamentation, then, to a certain extent, its interior is understood as a *vehicle*. The subject, in this latter sense, is said to be a spirit (*nabran*) in a canoe-body (*gai'iin*) carrying or transporting insignia. The entailed sequence of boarding, departing, passing through a kin or ancestor-based channel, travelling over the water, arriving, or coming ashore at the appropriate, kin-based dock, and disembarking from a vehicle all foreground the spatial mobility of the spirit-subject, but also its separability or detachability from the body—again, to invoke Marilyn Strathern's (1988) phrasing of Melanesian embodiment. In daily life, when human spirits (*nor*) paddle across the Murik Lakes, or travel up the coast to Wewak, the town market, they put this schema—of movement, but also of their being in society—into practice.

This concept of vehicular embodiment reaches beyond ordinary, daily life and is applied cosmologically. At the same time as people voyage, ancestor spirits venture through the lacustrine/marine space in their own zoomorphic canoe-bodies, such as fish-canoes (*tand gai'iin*) or bird-canoes (*pise gai'iin*), among many others—canoe-bodies that they may board and then disembark upon reaching their destinations so as to return to their humanoid canoe-bodies (Lipset 2009:63). Similarly, when human spirits dream, they leave their canoe-bodies to move about in other canoe-bodies with the spirits of other kin—mostly dead—before returning to their human vehicles, say, at dawn when they get up from under their mosquito nets. That is, dream life is another instance of canoeing. In these and other ways, the Murik subject is viewed as composed of multiple canoe-bodies that people get into and out of for the purposes of travelling to and from kin and the market.

There is another, occult meaning of the canoe-body. From a masculine point of view, but not necessarily a feminine one (see Barlow and Lipset 1997), the canoe-body is associated with the phallus. Outrigger-canoe logs are ritually transformed from female to male when they are cut down. Carving requires chastity that mystically empowers the canoe-bodies of the carpenters at work. Their chastity also safeguards the integrity of the wooden hull from sexual pollution by women. Canoe prows are intricately adorned with phallus-like motifs (see Lipset 2005). Overseas voyages of outrigger canoes were protected by the chastity of the helmsman's wife (Barlow 1985). And, in the aftermath of a phase of male initiation, when a father learned that his son had stoically withstood the pain of having a sharp blade of a palm of sword grass inserted into and yanked out of his urethra (to show him how to expel the impure feminine blood contacted during intercourse), he might exclaim: 'Oh! My canoe has come shore!' (Lipset 1997:280).

The embodiment of the person/subject in general, and the phallus in particular, is thus imbued with vehicular, spatial and transactional meanings; and, vice versa, canoes are informed with phallic embodiment. These ideas coalesce into a single image. When a son is born, kin are said to observe with relief, 'he will take his father's place' (*yan kaban osangait*). The image of 'taking his place' acknowledges that youth may and should succeed age in occupation of, or claim to, the latter's status, rights and obligations. But it also acknowledges that this succession is contingent upon reciprocal agency: it must be given and taken. This view of reproduction as generational substitution is not, however, understood as reincarnation or biological regeneration. It is rather imagined in an idiom of kin-based expectation that further action will result in 'replacement' (cf. Weiner 1980). This idea has widespread application. The point is that the three images—of generational succession as 'taking the place of', the canoe–body–phallus association and the bestowal of rank—combine to form a concept of action as the replacement of passengers travelling in decorated canoe-bodies through hereditary channels. A son or daughter thus becomes a metaphor in the social structure for his or her same-sex parent as actor and node of relationships for the parent. In Murik terms, a heir is sometimes said to be her mother's or his father's 'canoe'. In this pre-state concept of personhood, the metaphor of reproduction is simultaneously the reproduction of a metaphor, of a heir who should take over steering a canoe-body. Simultaneously, it is a cultural assertion that substitution is not only possible, but is a solace.

From a Lacanian viewpoint, of course, such an unequivocal view of reproduction is just half the story. In addition to relief, the appearance of a heir should also give rise to an expression of *Non*! by which the *Name-of-the-Father* metaphorically expels the phallus into the Symbolic or culture. For Lacan, culture cuts the phallus off from the desire of the other—a symbolic castration that motivates the subject's commitment to language, convention and law, on the one hand, but also recreates this originary oedipal intervention and the eternal gap between the pleasure of maternal acknowledgment and the impossibility of its retrieval, on the other. We shall now see that the Murik do indeed value reproduction, which is to say, 'replacement', as both a consolation and a loss of the other. To document this contradiction, I turn to the public masquerade I call the Gaingiin Society.

The Gaingiin Society, or 'The Name of the Father' in the Post-Colonial Moment

The Gaingiin Society is an initiatory association (Bernardi 1985). It is a system of names, masks and rules that affords its members veiled agency in society. It is made up of seven age grades, and the membership of each consists of one or several cohorts (*orub*) of men who are said to have been born about the same time. Every grade is collectively named after the group of spirit masks (*gaingiin*) it holds. Adjacent grades are related through matrilateral kin ties. Mothers' brothers have junior partners who are classificatory sisters' sons. They refer to themselves, however, as 'fathers' of the latter whom they call 'sons'. In pre-colonial times, the ethos of which the masks still manifest, 'the right to give battle…[was] retained…in severalty' (Sahlins 1972:171). Intertribal relations were then self-governed, and each village was defended by its male cult. The Gaingiin Society, then, served the male cult and the community. It trained youth in the skills and defensive postures appropriate to the ethos of *warre* when 'every man is Enemy to every man' (Hobbes 1972:223), prepared them for the rigours of initiation, and instructed them in its organisation. At the same time, its masks asserted authority in certain circumstances in order to facilitate the accomplishment of specific ritual goals. In the past 100 years or so, the Gaingiin Society has persisted, but it has come to serve different functions, the community having long since conceded its reliance upon the military services of the male cult to the state and having been thoroughly influenced by petty capitalism and missionary Christianity.

In 1981–2001, the seven grades in the Gaingiin Society still possessed their masks. Each one had the right to make and don masks that concealed its wearer's domestic identity, at least pseudo-anonymously.[3] The masks went on being imagined as warrior spirits. As spirits, they are mute and bearers speak not a word while appearing in them. As warriors, they may attack anyone junior in grade to themselves. Young men in the entry-level grade, whose masks are called *Gaingiin* (see Figure 3.1), constantly stalked village avenues and plazas chasing and menacing uninitiated children with throwing sticks. Children would flee (in delight). Gaingiin is a well-loved, but earnest and scary, bogey who associates the public square, at least among children, to the aforementioned Hobbesian posture, made into an intense game of chase. Once in a while, a parent might hand over a toddler to the monster, who might be seen holding it up over its head, as the child screams in terror, struggling to be given back to its mother or

---

3   The masks, however, run barefoot through the tidal flats and leave footprints that are said to be universally recognisable.

father. When Gaingiin does so, the toddler will cling to the parent as if for dear life. Public space is alive with threatening spirits whose names mothers and fathers yell to bring children to heel when they do not listen.

Figure 3.1 A proud, newly initiated Gaingiin grade

Photo: David Lipset, 2001

The Dimbwan and Bananain masks (Figures 3.2 and 3.3) belong to two of the top grades in the Gaingiin Society. As bearers of its senior authority, who oversee a measure of *civitas*, they have a right to install a community-wide taboo against the harvesting of coconuts. That is, the two spirits may (temporarily) supersede corporate property rights—a nontrivial privilege in pre-state terms. During the run-up to major feasts, such as end-of-mourning rites or initiations, ritual sponsors may oblige Dimbwan and Bananain to make property markers (*jaba'iin*) out of the midribs of sago fronds (*saidug*). Grade members beat them so that yellow streamers, which are 90 cm or more long, dangle from the stiff part of the midrib that is left. The two masks will then erect the *jaba'iin* at the openings of channels and footpaths leading to coconut groves, which are then said to become 'their property'. If someone steals coconuts, the Dimbwan and Bananain maskers may chop down the coconut groves in which the theft has taken place and attack the village at large with spears. In addition, the two masks provide 'security'. In 1993, for example, I saw Dimbwan 'escort' a group of women through the coconut groves to a waterhole and then bring them home. 'He' did so, it was said, to make certain that no coconuts were stolen along the way. The two masks also have the right to suspend their taboo temporarily and allow the gathering of coconuts, should a contingency arise, such as a drought or a funeral. When the Dimbwan grade agrees that sufficient coconuts have accumulated in 'their groves' to supply a pending feast, they will secretly adorn themselves with flowers in the bush and return to the village to declare by their appearance that final preparations for the feast should start.

Figure 3.2 Bananain

Photo: David Lipset, 1993

Figure 3.3 Dimbwan

Photo: David Lipset, 1993

The taboo the senior masks install exerts a supra-social, yet indirect, kind of authority over the whole community in a flexible register that is named and masculine, but masked and numinous rather than human. The question is: authority over what? Over property represented as *coconuts*. Coconuts are property, to be sure. In Murik terms, however, they are also associated with the breast. That is, coconuts evoke the desire of the other prior to the intervention of the *Name-of-the-Father*. This connection is surely visible (and audible) in the way Murik people literally suckle coconut milk (*dapag arum*) out of them. It is made explicit in the effigy of a spirit woman called Namiit, who appears in a phase of male-cult initiation, her breasts then being represented by coconut half-shells attached to her torso. The reference is also made with grotesque inflection during a rite of reversal called *noganoga'sarii*. Following the death of a successful lineage head, women and men attack each other, armed with coconut half-shells filled with a fetid mixture of animal faeces and mud that they try to stuff in the mouths of affines (see Lipset and Silverman 2005). More data could be adduced about the maternal symbolism of coconuts (see Lipset 1997:279). Suffice to say that the taboo forbidding their harvest begins to suggest an authority that might be likened to a Lacanian injunction tabooing the desire of the other revised in terms of a Melanesian semiotic—for example, the ethic of reciprocity and interdependency of a culturally particular variety. The compensation in return for promotion into the most senior grade confirms this interpretation.

'The Snake Caught Me!'

Until the 1960s, taking the Dimbwan mask demanded a 'total prestation' (Mauss 1973:3) from the Bananain maskers. As I indicated above, each member of the senior grades has a junior partner in the adjacent grade who is his classificatory sister's son, but who is ritually addressed as a 'son'. The senior man's 'son' eventually is granted rights to the mask. In order to compensate his ritual 'father' for grade taking, the leading 'son' had to permit his 'mother'—for example, his wife[4]—to 'marry' his 'father' in the Dimbwan cohort. The provision of a wife's sexual services was called 'sending [lit. doing a] his skirt' (*dago'timariin*) to his counterpart. That is, a husband would ask his wife to offer to engage in sexual intercourse with his senior masking partner. Should she agree, her expression of desire for the 'father' set further ritual exchanges in train that would culminate in the grade taking of the whole cohort.[5] In 1981, the late Murakau Wino sketched out the sequence to me.

---

4   A wife may be addressed or referred to as 'mother' in Murik kin terminology.
5   See Thurnwald (1916) and Fortune (1939) for two other accounts of the exchange of sexual intercourse in the context of warfare and male-cult ritual in the Sepik region. And see also Lipset (1997) for a discussion of wife lending in the context of the Murik male cult.

Husbands and wives belonging to the Bananain grade would paddle across the lakes to collect sago frond midribs. Upon returning to the village, they would pile them up in an isolated, private spot in the coconut groves. That night, the leading member of the junior grade would 'send his skirt' to his 'father' (his classificatory mother's brother). The provision of sexual intercourse by the junior partner's 'mother' was said to 'pick out the thorns of the sago frond caught in his feet'. The woman would go to him carrying a sago frond over her shoulder. Placing the base of the frond on his shoulder, the husband's 'father' acknowledged her desire.

The couple would go off together to the pile of sago fronds that were to be used to make the raffia-like cloaks of the new Dimbwan masks. The couple would have intercourse there. The woman would then return to her husband and declare: 'The snake caught me!' (*Ma wakun tenangakum*). The leader of the junior grade—that is, the man who had just sent his wife—would then gather the rest of the couples in the cohort together to prepare a feast for the whole senior grade who were to instruct them how to assemble the Dimbwan costumes.

The phallus, or 'the snake', as I say, was not meant to inseminate the wife of the junior masker. That is, it was not meant to impregnate the woman; it was rather offered as a phallic pleasure given in return for the work he and the senior grade would do to prepare the masks for the initiates. Its reproductive significance was, rather, afforded transactional meaning. The wife's/mother's sexuality was imputed reciprocal use value; its pleasure, as well as the husband's implicit resentment at temporarily having to relinquish (rights to) her, were compensation. By having intercourse with the junior woman, the senior masker became obliged to yield his and his grade's paramount status in the Gaingiin Society. They would initiate the junior cohort and retire. Now symbolism in the grade-taking rite does indeed evoke birthing imagery, as we shall momentarily see, so in this sense, the formulation of sexuality as exchange, and the metaphor of replacement, becomes a culturally specific formulation of reproduction, which of course recalls the great Trobriand ethnography of Annette Weiner (1978, 1979, 1980).

Weiner was concerned with expanding the temporal and material purview of cycles of reciprocal exchange. Her central point, however, stressed the importance of incorporating local concepts of exchange, wherein the Trobriand concept of reproduction as 'replacement' became her exemplar—'replacement' being their gloss for the elaborate and extensive transactions that result in sociological succession (Weiner 1980:78f). My interest in the Murik notion of 'replacement' in the Gaingiin Society in post-colonial Papua New Guinea obviously differs from Weiner's focus on exchange theory. I am interested in the relationship, and the connections, between pre-state and post-colonial meanings of masculinity that I compare and contrast with the Lacanian phallus.

So as to petition entree into the senior signifiers in the Gaingiin Society, instead of being cut off from the desire of the other by the *Name-of-the-Father*, a junior masker would voluntarily give in to symbolic castration by conceding 'his mother's desire'. What is more, the senior man would *not* permanently taboo his ritual 'son' from maternal desire, but would rather return her desire to him. She goes back to her husband, happily celebrating his partner's phallus; 'The snake caught me!' she would exclaim, the announcement of which brought with it the prestige and authority of her husband's partner's mask. The temporary transfer of conjugal rights opened the door of initiation to the junior grade. The dependency of the phallus upon their 'mother's desire' could not have been made any more plain in this scenario. But instead of being colonised by her loss into the emptiness of the Symbolic, the door led elsewhere. It led to another phallus.

1988: Installing a coconut taboo

Giving 'skirts' for the purposes of compensating initiators ended in the Gaingiin Society when a new gift—money—was substituted. In order to argue that money became a signifier of the pre-state phallus in this context, and eventually that this substitution belongs to a larger itinerary of the signified, I now return to the late 1980s, only a few years after Tuzin found Ilahita in the throes of a messianic revolution that had left cultic masculinity in ruin. At that time, Lissant Bolton, Kathleen Barlow and I had undertaken the Sepik Documentation Project, for which we were buying contemporary objects for, and documenting existing collections in, the Australian Museum (Lipset and Barlow 1987). As our concomitant theoretical aim was to investigate changing concepts of value in intertribal trade, we called on selected villages along the north coast and on the Lower Sepik and interviewed people about historical and contemporary exchanges, in addition to marketing and eliciting data about photographs of museum objects. When we got to the Murik Lakes in August 1988, we bought a Yangoron costume in Darapap village, the Yangoron masks being a family of spirits that belongs to a mid-level grade in the Gaingiin Society, which had been imported from Mushu Island up the coast to the west of the Murik Lakes. They appear in public from time to time dressed in coconut-bark capes and overalls. 'Father' and 'son' masks are distinguished (from their 'mother') by big, erect phalluses that bounce up and down as they dance among bemused audiences who might serenade him (Figure 3.4). That is, the Yangoron family plays a comic, rather than a threatening, role in the community.

Figure 3.4 Yangoron (right) with his parents who are escorting him to the boat

Photo: David Lipset, 1988

In the course of negotiations to buy the 'son' from his grade, I went to a meeting in the male cult house. The men of the Dimbwan masks were then being tasked with the installation of a taboo forbidding the harvesting of coconuts in the run-up to a female-cult initiation rite that was pending (see Barlow 1995). As men waited for a feast that the rite's sponsors were preparing, rather heated discussion arose.

> The Dimbwan grade, a man called Ker began to complain, had not fed the Bananain masks [of which he was a member]. He did not want the masks of his grade to gather stalks of sago palm and pound out fringe from them (*jaba'iin*), so the senior grade might then erect them as taboo markers. Wapo, a senior man in the Dimbwan masks, offered [to sponsor] a meal for the junior grade in the name of his cohort, so that the taboo could be properly installed.

The exchange, in which the junior masks should work for the senior masks in return for a feast and ritual support, is normative in Murik kinship. Youth expect that age will nurture them in return for which they will feel obliged to serve their elders. Ker was upset, in other words, that his grade was hungry. So why should they work?

Ker stood. He demanded to be initiated into the Dimbwan grade and complained that too many junior men had been promoted ahead of him. A firstborn son, he went on to admit, could replace his father in the senior man's grade, especially should he have grown old and his 'wood had rotted'. Sitting next to me, Sivik, who was a generation younger than Ker, whispered that he himself had taken his father's place in the Dimbwan grade just this way. Sivik pointed to Kaibong, younger than Ker, who had been promoted ahead of his cohort after giving his wife to his mother's brother, and had taken the opportunity to bring several junior men along with him, but not Ker.

Ker's reproach—that he had been ritually ignored by the senior masks— was based on an assumption, again coming from kinship norms, that needs to be made explicit. Not only are youth expected to be demanding, age fully acknowledges a desire to spoil them. But never vice versa. Age ought not ask anything of youth. To do so would degrade the self as 'young'. Cooperation from youth may be had only indirectly through strategic acts of care and nurture. Ker might have been grumbling, in other words, but as he belonged to the junior mask, his grievance was culturally normative. In Lacanian terms, if discourse arises from the loss of the other's desire, it signifies the empty phallus. From this standpoint, the generous presence that the youth would demand—expressed in age-differentiated norms of generalised reciprocity—recalls the other's absence and arouses desire for her desire all the more. Initiation into the senior mask, however much of a deprivation it might require, must signify both the mother and the castrating loss of her desire, thus binding the subject to the signifier, as Lacan's epigraph had it. The phallus—both symbolic and organic—is therefore never far to seek in the Gaingiin Society.

To wit: promotion in the Gaingiin Society is not fixed by chronological birth but is negotiable. Why is grade skipping warranted and how is it indemnified? It is justified in terms of the phallus. The substitution of the firstborn son, or other youth, for an ageing father was meant to preserve the phallus, not as metaphor, but now as organ, as a literal recipient of the desire of a junior masker's wife. It is also justified by the ambition of a junior man wanting to advance ahead of his cohort, which required sending his 'mother' to have intercourse with his 'father'. Grade skipping denoted the phallus, albeit in a characteristically Melanesian register. The subject enters a new level of 'the Symbolic' not by having to give up the desire of the other to the *Name-of-the-Father* but rather by trading upon that desire with 'him'.

Back at the male cult house, the co-sponsors of the women's initiation rite, Kaibong and his co-wife Tasi, were serving a meal. Its purpose was to obligate the senior maskers to taboo the gathering of coconuts so enough would be available to fulfil ritual needs. A leaf-covered set of plates filled with rice or sago pudding and garnished with fish was set out in the middle of the floor. Discussion continued about grade taking in the Gaingiin Society. Money, the men agreed, had replaced 'skirts'. Having previously sent his wife to his mother's brother, as I had been told, Kaibong had become the leader of the Dimbwan masks. In addition, to honour the retiring grade with a feast and *aragen*—the ceremonial porridge made of coconut milk and dried coconut meats—Kaibong now set the price for grade taking at K200.[6]

> Kaibong (standing before the meal): 'This little food [I now offer] is from my wife [and is meant to compensate Dimbwan] to set up the taboo markers (*jaba'iin*) in both Darapap and Karau [villages].'

> Mathew Tamoane (a Bananain member) stood: 'Our initiation [into the Dimbwan masks] should [take place] right away! It will take a bit of time to collect money from the members of the grade. We must take Dimbwan now and pay later!'

> Kaibong (in anger): 'You [Bananain masks] must pay us first!'

> Murakau (as a senior member of Dimbwan): 'Right!'

> Ker (as Bananain leader): 'Food is easy. We can give you food now. But money is a little harder. Can you give us a little time for it? The feast will be staged soon. If we want to get the money together, there will not be enough time to gather a lot of dry coconuts for the [ceremonial porridge].'

> Wapo (a senior member of Dimbwan): 'We won't allow debt. We want the food and the money at once. Otherwise, we will just put the Dimbwan [costumes] together and wear them ourselves!'

> Ker: 'I will go to [town] and come back and get the *jaba'iin* [sago fronds for the coconut taboo and the costumes] and beat them with my grade.'

> [The Dimbwan grade divided up plates of food among themselves and began to eat, acknowledging their obligation to set the taboo by doing so.]

The standing of the Gaingiin Society was relatively uncontested in 1988. Even Seventh-Day Adventist men, unlike the revivalists in Ilahita, were clearly not out to disband it. Ker, Wapo and Mathew Tamoane, who advocated holding the grade-taking rite as early as possible, were all leading Seventh-Day Adventists. Neither did anyone dismiss the Gaingiin Society as a waste of time that could be better spent on modern pursuits, such as the villagers' small-scale fishery.

---

6   In 1988, PNG K1 = US$0.85.

Instead, men assumed that the Gaingiin Society would and ought to go on. Their issue was how to reproduce it within the post-colonial context; in other words, how to convert the value of the phallus—for example, a 'mother's desire'—into money. How many PNG kina was a 'skirt' worth?

Grade Taking and the Metaphor of Money

The grade taking took place a few days later. Unfortunately, I had left Darapap by then to go back upriver to the Catholic Mission at Marienberg, where my Australian Museum colleagues and I were based. I did manage to collect one account of what took place when I subsequently spoke to Joshua Sivik, one of the retiring maskers, shortly thereafter.

> The Dimbwan grade decided that K200 was too dear. We cut the price in half. K30 was then paid us, leaving the rest as debt. Enoch, Ker and [another man] each paid K10 and became leaders of the grade. Kowre and Sauma [two senior men] accepted the money. The rest of us were not paid. Sauma gave his share of the money to Kiso, his wife, because she had intercourse with his mother's brother.

In the history of the Murik phallus, this substitution had already taken place in several other contexts. Now it was confirmed once again. The currency of the post-colonial state replaced—and was thus held to be functionally equivalent to—sexual intercourse. Money became a metaphor in the sense that its association with 'skirts' was that between two separate domains of meaning (Lakoff and Turner 1989:103). Ethically, what kind of metaphor had money become? It did not tip a Weberian shift from an otherworldly sexuality into an erotic sensuality (1946, 1978). Nor did it tip the arrival of a modern subject–object distinction. Inner life did not instantly become rationalised. From transactional and sociological viewpoints, the metaphor of money had not been exchanged between strangers. Although the Australian Museum did buy the Yangoron mask, the money for the Dimbwan grade taking was paid to mothers' brothers who were clearly not out to maximise profit. The senior grade offered a 'number two' price because they wanted to help the junior grade rather than exploit them. The money, to put it plainly, was *both* a gift that signified the Murik phallus and the universalist and rational phallus of modernity.

Let me finish discussing my informant's narrative of the grade taking. The senior Dimbwan maskers gave way to their junior counterparts whom he called the 'children's grade' (*naje'orub*). In the event, the ritual work of installing the coconut taboo was combined with the initiation of the Bananain maskers.

They gathered sago palm fronds in a motor-canoe. Both husbands and wives of the senior grade then beat the fronds [for the cloaks of the costumes]. The men assembled about twelve Dimbwan costumes inside the Male Cult Hall. Classificatory mothers' brothers made specific masks for their sisters' sons. I made the mask called Saboganap for Komsing and made Dagodago for Luke. The Bananain grade presented a feast to the Dimbwan grade for this work. The Dimbwan grade then beat the junior grade as they crawled through a tunnel of their legs.

Ker paraded through the village as Mwaraynor with the Mindamot lineage insignia (*sumon*) as a headdress. Coconuts were broken in his path to honor the insignia. The rest of the newly promoted Dimbwan masks followed him. They were trailed by two masks, called their 'mothers'.

The senior, retiring grade then made *aragen*, the ceremonial porridge, for the new Dimbwan grade to oblige them to begin the coconut taboo. Eight coconuts were harvested to prepare the porridge. Next day, six Dimbwan masks went to Karau village to install a taboo on groves there. The grade was well fed.

The relations of production between the grades, that is, had assumed anything but a 'fantastic form of a relation between things' (Marx 1990:165). Rather, the prevailing ethos was one of use value, domestic sociality and personification. The two grades were classed in patrifilial terms as 'fathers' and 'children'. Married couples worked together to prepare the fringe for the costumes as a cohort of masked spirits. The Dimbwan masks were individually named, and one mask, called Mwarenor, was decorated like a firstborn initiate privileged to display lineage heraldry (Lipset 1990). The initiation of the junior grade by the senior masks mimicked a rite of passage in to the Symbolic, on the one hand, but on the other it also invoked a kind of grotesque birthing imagery. The 'sons' succeeded the 'fathers' by crawling through a gauntlet of legs. The transfer of the masks seemed to recreate the phallus desired by the other.

The retiring Dimbwan maskers fed and were fed by their successors, who then installed the coconut taboo in two villages. When money replaced 'skirts', the relationship between people and masks remained relatively stable, in other words. The masks did not become governed by relations between people in a state of independence from each other. Nor had the ethical position of the subject suddenly become secularised. Outer life did not suddenly become de-spiritualised. Nor had inner life suddenly become spiritualised. The masks of the Gaingiin Society had rather moved the subject into a neither/nor—not quite one, not quite the other—world between the Murik and post-colonial

Symbolics. How did the masculinity of the Dimbwan mask fit the broader register of substitution and enchained signification in contemporary, post-colonial Murik culture?

Recall that Tuzin regarded the actions taken by revivalist Christians against the Itahita male cult in the mid-1980s as a symbolic act of 'murder' that 'killed' ritual masculinity, not as a metaphor, or chain of signification, by which the two institutions continued to reference each another. Culture in Ilahita was then divided up between rival nostalgic and depressed post-cultic men and the revivalists, who were desperately preparing for the Second Coming. As such, the millennial time then in play permitted little other than a perception of rupture and masculine anomie.

Facilitated by the cultural concept of replacement introduced earlier, at least two, interrelated chains of signification can be distinguished in Murik. The one dis-embeds and severs the cultic phallus from the Symbolic, by referencing nothing other than the commodity and the market, while the other makes a metaphor of the cultic phallus by associating modern ideas, objects and persons with it. These two chains of signification converge, I suggest, in a rather more complicated tone of masculine alienation than the tragic one Tuzin lamented so eloquently as having overtaken Ilahita.

Conclusion: The phallus in post-colonial Murik

Like Sahlins' Hawaiians (1985), as well as many Pacific peoples, the Murik began to call whites 'yabar goan', or children of the yabar spirits, at or soon after first contact, the yabar being a superior class of ancestor spirits who possessed great powers to transform the landscape and persons. In Durkheimian terms, the yabar were a collective representation of autochthonous mastery over space and society. In Lacanian terms, the yabar represented a lack, or a desire for the lost desire, of the other. The yabar spirits have long since disappeared from Murik animism, but the term yabar goan certainly remains in widespread use. Indeed, 'white man' is the most commonplace meaning of yabar, although not with a presumptively racialised valence (cf. Bashkow 2006). I have repeatedly heard it in reference to PNG nationals. The concept of yabar would thus seem to denote the technological space of urban capitalism where punctual subjects work for salaries, purchase goods and travel in yabar 'canoes'—cars, boats and airplanes—regardless of skin colour. The resources of the yabar—both as space and as social category—are viewed as morally problematic, challenging and difficult to deal with. Although they recognise and appreciate its vigour and wealth, both villagers and peri-urban Murik complain that they are made uncomfortable by it, not provisioned, protected or advanced by its meagre attentions. The moral agency of the *yabar* spirits might have exited Murik cosmology, but the contour of their enormous powers remains. *Yabar* has become a null signifier in their Symbolic. At the same time, *yabar* has come to refer to modernity. This semantic extension, I argue, exemplifies a chain of substitution that does not just signify rupture, but rather doubles the absent desire of the other, thus to build upon that archaic castration.

Let me cite several substitutions—large and small—of this emasculating kind. Today, men will prevail upon any makeshift kind of sealable container—for example, glass jars or little metal tins—to hold the lime powder they use when chewing betel-nuts. In the past, they had gourds engraved with geometrical designs, which only initiated men used, and which they named for the overseas lover who had given it to them (see Figure 3.5). As metaphors of a phallus contingent upon the lost desire of the Murik other, the jars and tins no longer refer to 'her' lack. Now, they refer to a second lack, which figures men as poor and unsophisticated 'grassroots', in the national slang (see Figure 3.6).

Figure 3.5 Man with lime gourd

Photo: David Lipset, 1988

Figure 3.6 Man with glass jar for lime powder

Photo: David Lipset, 1982

In pre-state society, rival moieties used to consecrate the male cult house (*taab*) by competing to ignite fire by friction, the victorious side then taking the honour of relighting the hearth fires in the community, all of which were extinguished prior to the event. This was part of an elaborate ritual dialogic between male and female, in which the male cult asserted a claim on maternal nurture (and the female cult answered by attempting to shake down the whole building by its pilings). Today, men still talk about this moiety competition in these very terms in connection with the consecration of new cult houses that are being built. But the relationship of the male cult to women's cooking and the illumination of the night, while still relying on firewood gathered from the Murik Lakes, have become mediated upon disposable butane lighters, kerosene, hurricane lamps and battery-powered flashlights. These commodities, as I propose, both do and do not refer to the male cult and 'his' absent other, the 'skirts' with which its moieties 'fought'.

In the contemporary technology of sleep, we might see a similar itinerary of the masculine signifier. Today, men and women sleep (with children) inside mosquito nets bought in town. Until the mid-1950s, the Murik slept in long, dark hand-woven bags (*arug*), together with the skulls of grandparents. In the morning, as they crawled out, they took the relics and 'fed' them cigarettes and betel-nuts. The interiors of mosquito nets do not demark spaces that have become completely disconnected from the lineage because people interact with ancestors in their dreams. But of course they are disconnected from the division of labour, the weaving of the bags having been women's work. Today, moreover, people sleep on foam pillows. Pre-state pillows—headrests—were made of wood propped up by little bamboo legs. They were engraved with imagery of ancestor-spirits and their zoomorphic totems—pigs in particular. Only men manufactured and used headrests, which is why they expressed male desire. Foam pillows do not signify their ornate predecessors. Foam pillows are gender neutral. *Qua* metaphor, they do not signify the Murik phallus. They rather index (the low level of) Murik integration in consumer capitalism. Pillows, however, together with mosquito nets, butane lighters, kerosene lamps and flashlights, remain links in a signifying chain of masculine negation, or, in Lacanian terms, of symbolic castration.

Like the substitution of money for sexual intercourse in the Gaingiin Society, the chains of signification that circulate in post-colonial ritual exchange index a complicated, multi-level kind of masculine alienation. There is, for example, a category of valuables called *mwaran* that includes several kinds of prestige goods, such as tobacco, betel-nuts and pigs, as well as shell ornaments, and a wide variety of ritual services, the most important of which was the exchange of 'skirts'. The Murik speak of hereditary feasting partners who donate ritual *mwaran* as belonging to the 'valuables route' (*mwara yakabor*). Today, *toea* coins appear together with shells woven onto the aprons of loincloths they give male-cult initiates. Instead of shell and teeth ornaments, appropriate *mwara* kin now place PNG bills on the chests of corpses soon after death for the deceased to use en route to the afterlife. In the past, the *mwara* kin used to give new loincloths, their apron panels painted with snake-phallus motifs (see Lipset 2009:57), to their partners as part of their provision of end-of-mourning services. Today, they give them new shirts, dresses and shorts. Disenchantment is certainly a reference of these clothes (Eisenstadt 1968), and use value is no doubt being dis-embedded by these commodities (Giddens 1990). They are, however, incorporated within, rather than displaced from, Murik social structure and its reciprocities, thus to evoke the symbolic castrations of the past in the present.

Perhaps most indicative of this chain of masculine alienation are the fibreglass boats in which the Murik travel along the coast from the lakes to the market town of Wewak. These little vehicles replaced the lineage outriggers whose prows were protected by male ancestor spirits and whose construction process and consecration rites also convened dialogue about the relationship of the cultic phallus to the desire of the other (see Barlow and Lipset 1997). Wooden planks, connoting an outrigger platform, are laid down to cover the floors of these dinghies (Figure 3.7), planks on which cargo is stored and people sit, continuing to divide themselves by gender as they used to do when riding on outriggers where men sat near the prow and women sat aft. Outboard motors have long since replaced coconut-bark sails. And their steering arms have long since replaced the big wooden steering paddles helmsmen used to hold (Figure 3.8), outboard motors whose power, of course, requires gasoline and clean sparkplugs rather than the desire of the other for the phallus (Lipset 2011:30–1).

Now, a bus named for a lineage outrigger carries fare-paying passengers through the streets of the provincial capital (Figures 3.9 and 3.10). As a metaphor of masculine alienation, the fibreglass boats, outboard motors and the bus all reference the pre-state castration for which they are substitutions. These objects not only rationalise the Murik phallus. They add a new lack onto the lack for which the phallus stood. They shift its dependency on the desire of the other, as in the Gaingiin Society, and move that lack into modernity, where money denotes both the old lack and the new lack. Tuzin's vision of 'the death' of masculinity in a millennial Ilahita finds a parallel in this chain of signification, to be sure. In this chapter, however, I have tried to show that the chain of masculine signification, the substitutions of local by modern values in Murik ritual exchange, material culture and semantic extensions might combine both continuity and discontinuity. The persistence of the phallus, as a paradoxical embodiment of deprivation in signification, suggests, rather than *anomie*, a rather equivocal picture of post-colonial masculinity, one that simultaneously fills out what is missing and represents its absence.

Figure 3.7 Man steering an outboard in a dinghy

Photo: David Lipset, 2008

Figure 3.8 Helmsman with steering paddle in outrigger canoe

Photo: Franz Kirschbaum, 1908

Figure 3.9 The outrigger canoe _Diskum_

Photo: David Lipset, 1982

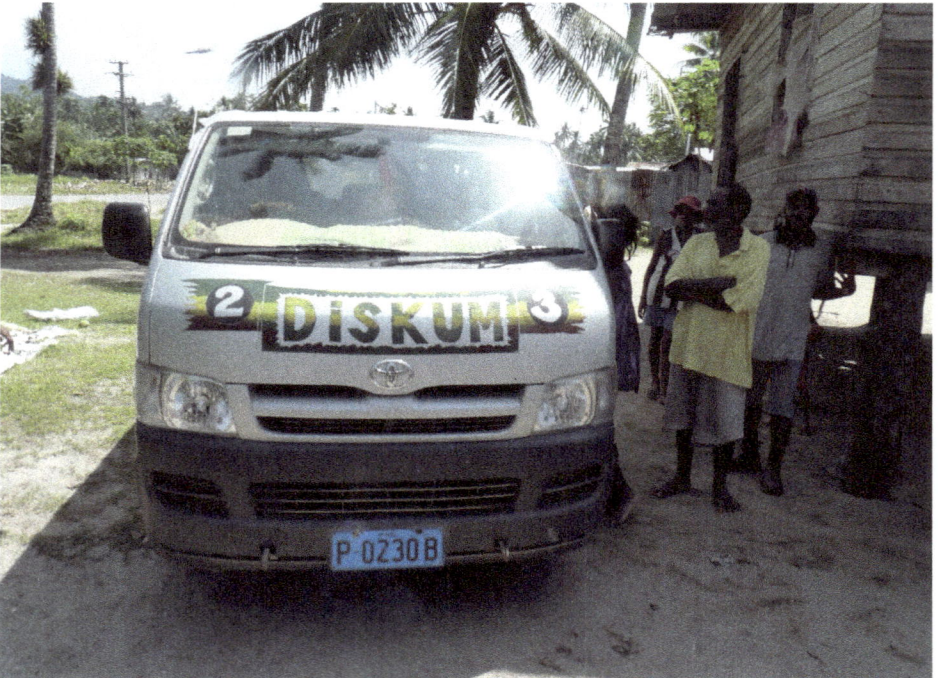

Figure 3.10 The bus _Diskum_

Photo: David Lipset, 2010

References

Barlow, Kathleen 1985. The Role of Women in Intertribal Trade Among the Murik of Papua New Guinea. *Research in Economic Anthropology* 7:95–122.

Barlow, Kathleen 1995. Achieving Womanhood and the Achievements of Women. In Nancy Lutkehaus and Paul B. Roscoe (eds) *Gender Rituals: Female Initiation in Melanesia*, pp. 85–112. London: Routledge.

Barlow, Kathleen 2010. Sharing Food, Sharing Values: Mothering and Empathy in Murik Society. *Ethos* 38(4):339–53.

Barlow, Kathleen and David Lipset 1997. Dialogics of Material Culture: Male and Female in Murik Outrigger Canoes. *American Ethnologist* 24:4–36.

Bashkow, Ira 2006. *The Meaning of Whitemen: Race and Modernity in the Orokaiva Cultural World*. Chicago: University of Chicago Press.

Bernardi, Bernardo 1985. *Age Class Systems: Social Institutions and Polities Based on Age*. Cambridge: Cambridge University Press.

Brison, Karen 1995. Changing the Constructions of Masculinity in a Sepik Society. *Ethnology* 34:155–76.

Dumont, Louis 1986. *Essays on Individualism: Modern Ideology in an Anthropological Perspective*. Chicago: University of Chicago Press.

Durkheim, E. 1984 [1933]. *The Division of Labor in Society*. Lewis A. Coser (trans.). New York: Free Press.

Eisenstadt, S. N. 1968. Introduction: Charisma and Institution Building, Max Weber and Modern Sociology. In *On Charisma and Institution Building, Selected Papers by Max Weber*, pp. Ix–lvi. Chicago: University of Chicago Press.

Fortune, Reo 1939. Arapesh Warfare. *American Anthropologist* 41:22–41.

Freud, Sigmund 1961. *The Interpretation of Dreams*. James Strachey (trans. and ed.). New York: Science Editions.

Giddens, Anthony 1990. *The Consequences of Modernity*. Stanford, Calif.: Stanford University Press.

Gregory, Christopher 1982. *Gifts and Commodities*. New York: Academic Press.

Hobbes, Thomas 1972 [1651]. *Leviathan*. Michael Oakeshott (ed.). Oxford: Basil Blackwell.

Jakobson, Roman 1971. The Dominant. In Latislav Matejka and K. Pomorska (eds) *Readings in Russian Poetics: Formalist and Structuralist Views*, pp. 23–30. Cambridge, Mass.: MIT Press.

Klein, Melanie 1932. *The Writings of Melanie Klein. Volume 2.* R. Money-Kyrle (ed.). New York: Free Press.

Knauft, Bruce 2002. *Exchanging the Past: A Rainforest World Before and After.* Chicago: University of Chicago Press.

Lacan, Jacques 1977a. Desire and the Interpretation of Desire in Hamlet. *Yale French Studies* 55–56:11–52.

Lacan, Jacques 1977b. *Ecrits: A Selection.* Alan Sheridan (trans.). London: Tavistock.

Lakoff, George and Mark Turner 1989. *More Than Cool Reason: A Field Guide to Poetic Metaphor.* Chicago: University of Chicago Press.

Leenhardt, M. 1979. *Do Kamo: Person and Myth in the Melanesian World.* Basia Miller Celati (trans.). Chicago: University of Chicago Press.

Lipset, David 1990. Boars' Tusks and Flying Foxes: Symbolism and Ritual of Office in the Murik Lakes. In Nancy Lutkehaus, Christian Kaufmann, William E. Mitchell, Douglas Newton, Lita Osmundsen and Meinhard Schuster (eds) *Sepik Heritage: Tradition and Change in Papua New Guinea*, pp. 286–98. Durham, NC: Carolina University Press.

Lipset, David 1997. *Mangrove Man: Dialogics of Culture in the Sepik Estuary.* Cambridge: Cambridge University Press.

Lipset, David 2005. Dead Canoes: The Fate of Agency in 20th Century Murik Art. *Social Analysis* 49:109–14.

Lipset, David 2009. A Melanesian Pygmalion: Masculine Creativity and Symbolic Castration in a Postcolonial Backwater. *Ethos* 37:50–77.

Lipset, David 2011. The Tides: Masculinity and Climate Change in Coastal Papua New Guinea. *Journal of the Royal Anthropology Institute* (NS)17:2–43.

Lipset, David and Kathleen Barlow 1987. The Value of Culture: Regional Exchange in the Lower Sepik. *Australian Natural History* 23:156–68.

Lipset, David and Eric K. Silverman 2005. The Moral and the Grotesque: Dialogics of the Body in Two Sepik River Societies (Eastern Iatmul and Murik). *Journal of Ritual Studies* 19(2):1–42.

Lipset, David and Jolene Stritecky 1994. The Problem of Mute Metaphor: Gender and Kinship in Seaboard Melanesia. *Ethnology* 33:1–20.

Marx, Karl 1990 [1867]. *Capital: A Critique of Political Economy. Volume 1*. Ben Fowkes (trans.). New York: Penguin.

Mauss, Marcel 1973. *The Gift: Forms and Functions of Exchange in Archaic Societies*. I. Cunnison (trans.). New York: Norton Library.

Mbembe, Achille 1992. The Banality of Power and the Aesthetics of Vulgarity in the Postcolony. *Public Culture* 4(2):1–30.

Moore, Henrietta 2007. *The Subject in Anthropology*. Cambridge: Polity Press.

Nobus, Dany 1999. Theorising the Comedy of Sexes: Lacan on Sexuality. In Bernard Burgoyne and Mary Sullivan (eds) *The Klein–Lacan Dialogues*, pp. 105–24. New York: Other Press.

Robbins, Joel 2002. *Becoming Sinners: Christianity and Moral Torment in a Papua New Guinea Society*. Berkeley: University of California Press.

Sahlins, Marshall 1972. *Stone Age Economics*. Chicago: Aldine-Atherton.

Sahlins, Marshall 1985. *Islands of History*. Chicago: University of Chicago Press.

Said, Edward 1978. *Orientalism*. New York: Random House.

Strathern, Marilyn 1988. *The Gender of the Gift: Problems with Women and Problems with Society in Melanesia*. Berkeley: University of California Press.

Thurnwald, Richard 1916. Banaro Societ: Social Organization and the Kinship System of a Tribe in the Interior of New Guinea. *American Anthropological Association Memoirs* 3:253–391.

Tuzin, Donald F. 1997. *The Cassowary's Revenge: The Life and Death of Masculinity in a New Guinea Society*. Chicago: University of Chicago Press.

Wardlow, Holly 2006. *Wayward Women: Sexuality and Agency in a New Guinea Society*. Berkeley: University of California Press.

Weber, Max 1946. *From Max Weber: Essays in Sociology*. H. H. Gerth and C. Wright Mills (trans and eds). New York: Oxford University Press.

Weber, Max 1978. *Economy and Society*. Guenther Roth and Claus Wittich (eds). Berkeley: University of California Press.

Weiner, Annette 1978. The Reproductive Model in Trobriand Society. In J. Spect and J. Peter White (eds) Trade and Exchange in Oceania and Australia. Special Issue. *Mankind* 11(3):175–86.

Weiner, Annette 1979. Trobriand Kinship from Another View: The Reproductive Power of Women and Men. *Man* (NS)14:328–48.

Weiner, Annette 1980. Reproduction: A Replacement for Reciprocity. *American Ethnologist* 7(1):71–85.

Wiener, James 1995. *The Lost Drum: The Myth of Sexuality in Papua New Guinea.* Madison: University of Wisconsin Press.

Young, Robert 2001. *Postcolonialism: An Historical Introduction.* Oxford: Blackwell.

Zimmer-Tamakoshi, Laura 1997. The Last Big Man: Development and Men's Discontents in the Papua New Guinea Highlands. *Oceania* 68:107–22.

Žižek, Slavoj 1989. *The Sublime Object of Ideology.* New York: Verso Press.

4. Men, Modernity and Melanesia

Bruce M. Knauft

During the period of Donald Tuzin's impressive fieldwork—from the late 1960s through the mid-1980s—themes of traditional male cults and masculine assertion in Melanesia (MMM1) had special purchase in the anthropology of Oceania and more widely. By the 2000s, another triplicate—of mobile men with money (MMM2)—has gained particular purchase (for example, Lepani 2008), along with various other dimensions of modern masculinity. In many of these more recent treatments (see Taylor 2008), Melanesian masculinity is often seen through the lenses of guns, drunkenness and pronounced, often brutal, male violence.

In 1997, an articulation between the first of these emphases and the nascent academic awareness of the second was attempted in a powerfully provocative book by Donald Tuzin: *The Cassowary's Revenge*. The present chapter takes stock of these trends on the basis of significant changes in masculinity that I have been able to document among the Gebusi of Papua New Guinea's Western Province (Knauft 1985, 2002a, 2010).

Donald Tuzin's imposing documentation of Ilahita Arapesh male cults and masculine practices (for example, Tuzin 1976, 1980, 1997) harboured several themes. Parallel with the then-prominent focus on male warrior-hood and sexual antagonism in Melanesia (for example, Allen 1967; Herdt 1982; Herdt and Poole 1982; Langness 1967, 1974; Meggitt 1964), Tuzin posited a functional dimension to elaborate male secret-cult activity among Ilahita Arapesh: male cults cultivated, organised and brought coherence to male organisation—and violence—in ways that were both instrumentally productive and ultimately constitutive of its culture, including its beliefs, values and ethics. Tuzin's first book (1976) documented how the elaborate dual organisation of Ilahita Arapesh society integrated diverse and, to some extent, refugee groups into itself in a Durkheimian manner—enabling a demographically large and militarily powerful extended community to repel the raids and incursions of neighbouring Abelam and other groups. In his second major book, Tuzin (1980) demonstrated the deep underpinning of the Ilahita social, organisational and masculine ethic of controlled violence—and misogyny—in the elaborate practices, rituals and myths of the multi-stage *Tambaran* male secret cult. In his third and most controversial volume (1997), he proceeded, based on ethnographic re-study, to document the demise of the *Tambaran* cult, the accompanying destruction of Ilahita Arapesh traditional culture and the death, as he termed it, of Ilahita masculinity itself (for example, 1997:181). Finally, Tuzin drew ominous links between the alienation of Ilahita culture and the alienation of masculinity in the absence of all-male institutions that could offer 'sanctuary' (1997:Ch. 8). As such, he created a broad if not sweeping connection between masculine insecurities in Melanesia and what was then just coming to be seen as the need for a coherent 'men's movement', organised by and for men, in California and other parts of the United States. As Losche (this volume) suggests, Tuzin's last major book on the Ilahita Arapesh differs significantly from the rest of his work in having a different tonality—more personally engaged, emotionally open and provocative—that expands upon his overall corpus.

In the earlier literature of the 1960s through to the early 1980s, speaking broadly, anthropologists suggested that Melanesian male insecurity was fuelled by warfare and other threats to male corporate integrity—and that the male response was collective bonding through ritual and social cult organisations exclusive to men and, commonly, institutionalised sexual antagonism that collectivised men over and against women. Though the functionalist assumptions of this line of reasoning were highly open to critique from feminist perspectives, more recent social changes have created a set of conditions that transformed and also maintained these tensions (however they arose to begin with). In particular, Melanesian masculinity has been threatened by increasing social emphasis on, but also great practical impediments to, obtaining money and Western commodities. Without these, men's status has been compromised, especially in relation to outsiders and the previous colonial presence (see discussion in Knauft 1997).

Consistent with the fact that commodity goods and money are often or typically considered individual in possession in Melanesia—notwithstanding their additional possible use in, or conversion for, collective exchange transactions—contemporary threats to masculinity in Melanesia have dovetailed with the de-collectivisation and individuation of masculine social life as widely reported in the literature on Melanesian social change, including male youth violence, criminal activity, opportunistic and/or extramarital sexuality and urban violence, including by so-called *raskols* (for example, Hart Nibbrig 1992; Strathern 1993; Wardlow 2007; cf. Haley 2008). Rather than fuelling traditionally collective and institutionalised sexual antagonism between men and women within communities, the modern inflection of gendered tension has arguably resulted in more focused individual and domestic, rather than collective, gendered antagonism (for example, Wardlow 2009). With the demise of collective cult activities, central longhouses or their equivalent, and the mythic and ritual moral authority of elders, younger men (as reported by Tuzin and many others) have been less restrained in individual aggressive or violent assertiveness towards women as well as with other men, including within the community, than they had often been before (for example, Sykes 1999). As a result:

> Male status remains culturally and morally dependent—in some ways more so than previously—on constraining female sexuality and limiting women's wider cultural and economic relationships. Male insecurity, opposition to women, and the desire for male collectivity have been reinstated in new guises at the same time that they have disengaged from customary institutions such as the male cult, the men's house, or the warrior society. At the same time, male social life involves an increasing proportion of transient and non-traditional affiliations, including work-groups and the relation of male comradeship through leisure activities such as drinking or gambling, which require money. (Knauft 1997:250)

These patterns are not disjoined or disarticulated from previous trends so much as they draw upon them in new contexts and guises amid individualised pressures. As Lipset (this volume) puts it, one now has at a minimum two alternative, local 'Symbolics' in Melanesian societies such as the Murik—the one made up of pre-state institutions and the other consisting of modernity—which together give rise to unpredictable, complicated chains of signification.

As pointed out by Holly Wardlow (Personal communication), an important link in reinforcing contemporary patterns of masculine insecurity and male violence is the threat posed not just by women in general but by the individualisation of women's agency under contemporary conditions—including the active or potentially active participation of women as agents in church, markets, in town and city businesses—and as sexual agents, including as 'wanton women' or *pasinja meri* (Wardlow 2006). Resentment and constraint against women by Melanesian men, often accompanied by a palpable sense of violent backlash against them, are prominent themes in an important suite of papers edited as a special issue of *The Australian Journal of Anthropology* by John Taylor (2008). In this and other works, the link between gendered change, masculinity and locally and regionally modern challenges to men seems substantively born out and amplified.

In significant respects, Donald Tuzin's later work (1997) illustrates this pattern from within a local village context; he considers a detailed case of male alienation and frustration in the wake of the demise of a key, if not all-encompassing, male cult system. Beyond Tuzin's premonition of deep anomie, however, he had little evidence or inkling of the extent and intensity of Melanesian male aggressiveness that were brewing in the modern Melanesian context, including in the nexus between alcohol, drugs and guns—nor of the great variations bequeathed from past traditions that were developing across Melanesia.

MacIntyre suggests for Melanesia that '[b]eer drinking and, to a lesser extent, marijuana use have become the quintessential ways that masculine sociality is expressed and they provide the means for expressing relations of conflict, aggression, and retribution' (2008:190). Furthermore,

> its most negative social effect is the way beer consumption and use of guns have become behaviours that differentiate men with wealth and power from those who have none…The image of a 'man with a gun,' primed for action, is pervasive in PNG and connotes not only the state's capacity to use force, but that of men to fight their own battles and to resist and subvert state control. (MacIntyre 2008:190)

Even among the Gebusi, who presently have a minimal rate of male violence, almost half of the schoolboys when asked to draw a picture of what they wanted to be when they grew up drew elaborate pictures of themselves as police officers or soldiers in the PNG Defence Force (Knauft 2002a:199-200).

Viewed in historical and cultural context, however, it remains important to consider current trends without positing them as a violent consequence of Melanesian modernities alone. For instance, as Bell (2006), Lipset (2006) and Halvaksz (Halvaksz 2006; Halvaksz and Lipset 2006) have illustrated, while the introduction and use of marijuana in Papua New Guinea connect with the perception of modern social ills, they also illustrate longstanding continuities of trade and exchange, substantialisation of personhood, and generational conflicts between senior and younger men.

In many areas of Melanesia, rates of violence and killing during the pre-colonial era, including in societies with active men's cult societies, were likely at least as high if not much higher than those presently evident (Knauft 1990). Though there is some truth to the suggestion that, prior to colonialism, ritualised male authority helped to channel and orchestrate male aggression from an intra to an inter-group focus, much of this functionalist reasoning is undercut by the fact that many forms of violence were more frequent and intense prior to colonial pacification. That ethnography grounded in structural-functionalist assumptions had its heyday during a period of relative late-colonial calm, during which social institutions from the past could be documented without experiencing the intensity of their prior violent actualisation, easily magnifies this sense of a 'palaeo-terrific', in which Melanesian masculinity was functionally ordered on its own except as disrupted by external forces and influences. At any rate, as MacIntyre notes:

> Studies of the violence of men in marginalized indigenous communities have in various ways attributed contemporary emphases on aggressive, self-assertive individualism to the emasculating effects of colonialism…

attributing contemporary violence to the breakdown of 'traditional' inter-generational authority structures…This historicist, exculpatory approach to the issue works at an abstract level but fails utterly as an explanation for any specific acts of violence. (MacIntyre 2008:187)

To concretise these issues in the present case—and to provide a complementary perspective—we can consider recent changes in masculinity and in violence among the Gebusi of Papua New Guinea. By 1998, Gebusi had experienced major changes that paralleled in some respects those documented by Tuzin (1997) for the Ilahita Arapesh. Longhouses had disappeared, initiations were no longer practised, indigenous costuming had been largely relegated to folkloric displays for government ceremonies, Christianity had supplanted traditional spirit rituals and seances, and communication with the unseen spirit-world forces was negligible. Among Gebusi as well as the Ilahita Arapesh, as Lipset puts it in his contribution to this volume, 'cultic men lost their position as the object of desire in society'. The rate of Gebusi violence—which included a very high homicide rate that made up 32.7 per cent of all adult deaths, mostly the execution of accused sorcery suspects—dropped to a fraction of this and then to zero after 1989 (Knauft 1985).

Along with these changes, and helping to account for them, was the post-colonial advent of Christianity, schooling for children, government development projects, a cash-based semi-weekly market, the mushrooming of small local stores, sports leagues and reliance on police to settle severe disputes and deal with the threat of significant physical violence (Knauft 2002a, 2002b). In terms of masculinity *per se*, I did not sense the anomie or alienation among Gebusi men that Tuzin reported for the Ilahita Arapesh but rather a decentralisation of male social life and an increasing modern 'bravado' of masculine speech styles, hortatory and urban-style dress and music, all of which contrasted with previous ritualised ways of asserting and maintaining masculine status, including through rituals of male initiation and traditional dancing (for example, Knauft 2010:Ch. 10).

Upon returning to the Gebusi 10 years later, in 2008, I was concerned to know whether the previous pattern of locally modern but non-lethal masculinity I had found a decade earlier would be continued—or overthrown as patterns of modern frustration, resentment and lack of economic development continued in this out-of-the-way corner of Papua New Guinea. My concern was magnified during my re-entry to the area, as the local airstrip had been closed due to poor maintenance, government inefficiency and neglect, and virtually all government workers at the local Nomad Sub-District Office had consequently left for Kiunga or other towns or cities in Papua New Guinea. As a result, local government services—including the elementary school, police force, development projects, sports leagues and folklore celebrations and sponsorships—were all defunct. The subdistrict health centre had no doctors or medicines, and the Nomad market had become desultory, affording few goods, fewer buyers and highly inflated prices for any outside commodities. Given that the region has no roads to other parts of the country and was highly dependent on the local airstrip, the closure of its airfield and the departure of the wage-paid government employees caused a collapse of the cash economy of the Nomad Subdistrict, including for the Gebusi communities within it.

How did Gebusi respond to these difficult circumstances? Against my expectations, the Gebusi living in the communities of my past association and study—the constituent hamlets of Gasumi Corners—had developed a striking resurgence of customs and practices that had been moribund and, I thought, virtually dead 10 years before, in 1998 (see Knauft 2010:Ch. 12). By 2007, a new central longhouse had been built. Male initiations were once again held, and traditional dancing, with costumes identical to those in 1980, was highly in evidence (cf. Lipset, this volume, concerning the persistence of male-cult activity among the Murik). Collective male etiquette that included the sharing of home-grown tobacco smoked from long bamboo pipes, the collective drinking of locally prepared kava, and heightened male sexual banter, camaraderie and horseplay were all pronounced. In significant ways, Gebusi male ethos was more similar in 2008 to what it had been in 1980 than to what I had observed and experienced during the Gebusi's locally modern phase in 1998.

Subsistence patterns had also become more traditional. In 1998, the dominant local crop was sweet potatoes—both for local consumption and to sell to cash-wielding family members of government officials at the Nomad market. Raising sweet potatoes required the Gebusi in Gasumi Corners to keep their pigs caged and fodder fed on the other side of the broad Kum River—that is, away from their root-crop gardens. Ten years later, in 2008, the domesticated pigs were back in the village. Root-crop gardens had been depleted and not replenished, and there was little incentive to cultivate produce for the Nomad market. In contrast, subsistence activity had returned more concertedly to the large expanse of the primary rainforest. In short, Gebusi resuscitated infrastructural as well as cultural patterns that were reminiscent of their pre-colonial past.

Some customs had not resurfaced or been rejuvenated. These included male spirit mediumship and men's collective seance communication with indigenous spirits for advice and divination. So, too, the rate of active sorcery divination, accusation and violent attack or execution of sorcery suspects had never resurfaced to its previous extraordinarily levels; it remained low to nonexistent. No homicides had occurred in my communities of association or were known from other neighbouring Gebusi communities during the preceding 10 years. As such, the homicide rate among the 150-odd persons whose descendants I had known well since 1980 had continued to be zero between 1989 and 2008, despite an extraordinarily high homicide rate among their predecessors from approximately 1940 to 1975. Though my stay was not long enough to effectively gauge changes in domestic violence or marital relations, the impressions I did have were that these were largely unchanged and were not more antagonistic than they had been either in 1998 or in 1980–82.

In some selective ways, to revisit earlier ethnographic contributions, Gebusi changes reaffirm possibilities that I think Don Tuzin would have liked, even if he did not envisage or imagine them for the Ilahita Arapesh or more generally. On the one hand, a palpable male collective social life based on camaraderie and longstanding collective ritual expression has again become alive and well among Gebusi. On the other hand, some of the more troubling traditional concomitants of this ritual, spiritual and cultural system—including extremely high rates of violent sorcery attribution and homicide—have been effectively reduced to very low levels, and this pattern has continued for more than two decades, from the late 1980s to at least 2008.

How and why Gebusi developed and are maintaining their present pattern of rejuvenated male social life but without significant violence—and after a period of intense locally modern adoptions during the 1990s (see Knauft 2002a)— are both important and challenging questions. It cannot be easily claimed that Gebusi patterns are widely evident across Melanesia. Gebusi themselves suggested in 2008 that neighbouring Bedamini peoples to the east had significant problems with marijuana use, the quest for guns, a sense of cultural alienation and elevated rates of male aggression.

In contrast with many peoples in Melanesia, Gebusi retain their distinct ability to return to the land and subsistence regimes that supported local populations for decades if not longer in the pre-colonial past. They have not been subject to significant wage labour, out-migration, cash cropping or the opportunities and challenges of connection by roads to other parts of the country. As such, they appear to have a particular potential as well as motivation under present conditions to rediscover or reinvent previous ways of being while also retaining introduced orientations, including Christianity, increasingly on their own terms.

After being first contacted by Australian patrols in 1962–63, Gebusi were effectively bypassed amid the colonial effort to pacify the more populous and militaristic Bedamini people to their east. On the other hand—also in contrast with many other groups in Melanesia—Gebusi had been on the verge of becoming a remnant population incorporated by aggressive neighbours. Perhaps consistent with this, they have not had a strong sense of their own cultural history or elevated cosmological past, even among the senior generation, against which current developments are seen as morally abased or degenerated. This historical and cultural context informs the Gebusi's 'presentist' emphasis, including their strikingly robust orientation to new, locally modern ways of life during the 1990s when these were most actively within their reach (Knauft 2002a).

As several contributions to this collection emphasise, including those by Lipset and Losche, large-scale arguments all too easily generalise or stereotype Melanesian gender relations and features of masculinity in particular. From nineteenth-century images of bloodthirsty Melanesian savages and mid–twentieth-century views of functionally controlled male ritual systems to early twenty-first-century views of male Hobbesianism—an almost *Lord of the Flies* perception of Melanesian male aggression—accounts have projected Western fears, or Western hopes, onto Melanesians (Knauft 1990; cf. Dinnen and Ley 2000). Against the grains of truth or significance that have informed and undergirded such generalisations in each case, individual Melanesian societies and circumstances evince their own distinctive development. On the one hand, for instance, the challenging and often troubling current trends of Melanesian masculinity as documented in Taylor (2008) appear to have significant purchase in various parts of Melanesia. As an overall emphasis, however, this orientation risks 'basket-casing' Melanesia and threatens to put the region back in the savage slot to which it has been relegated for much of anthropology's professional past (cf. Trouillot 1991).

Against this, it is important to reassert the importance in cultural anthropology of taking local cultural and historical features at their face value. Notwithstanding globalisation, and indeed because of locally derived appropriations of modernity (Knauft 2002b), Melanesia's diversity continues to belie generalities that derive primarily from a single group or a small cluster of societies, be it the Gebusi, the Ilahita Arapesh, the Enga, the Huli, the Lahiri people, the Murik, or others. Amid current economic retrenchment, the cutting back or collapse of rural government services and proliferating local ways of responding to new conditions across Papua New Guinea, Solomon Islands, Vanuatu and Fiji—not to mention West Papua and New Caledonia—it is hard to imagine that the cultural diversity of Melanesia, and of Melanesian masculinities, will wither rather than widen.

This suggests that a further emphasis in current perspectives is in order—an MMM3: a renewed awareness of our own continuing tendency, to misjudge Melanesian men. To historicise this misjudgment, we might recall the death of traditional Melanesian cultures that has been so sombrely predicted, inaccurately, since the mid-nineteenth century, including the widespread development of so-called 'salvage anthropology'. It is important not to downplay either the persistence of longstanding patterns of Melanesian belief or the orientation or periods and even epochs of great cultural reorientation, change and transformation. Both of these patterns continue as beliefs and practices from one period settle and morph upon those bequeathed from another. Some older patterns might never resurface while others lie dormant to be resuscitated in new guises of resurgence or rediscovery. In the mix, older patterns change if not transform even as they persist, while newer patterns establish continuities even as they break from the past.

Rosier and darker views of Melanesian masculinities might be considered in this light. For several centuries at least, much of Melanesia has seen patterns of violent male behaviour along with elaborate—and wonderful—cultural systems of belief and orientation that both reinforce and transcend or outstrip them. The remarkable diversity of these patterns is likely to continue. Amid this trend, it is easy to overlook exceptions to dominant current perceptions, including specific cultural environments, segments of social life, and masculinities that seem relatively peaceful or at least non-violent and pro-social. The Gebusi in current circumstances appear to fit this last characterisation.

In conclusion, I should register a limitation that the perspectives of Don Tuzin and I—our differences notwithstanding—have both in significant ways failed to transcend. This is the lack of an adequately articulated view of female-centred perceptions, actions and beliefs to parallel that of men's. Barlow and Lipset's (1997) discussion of the complementary and also dialogic aspects of Murik male and female perspectives is particularly important and illustrative in this regard. The truism that gender relations are neither male nor female is still rather inadequately confronted in much contemporary anthropology, including both an emphasis on men to the relative exclusion of women and the tacit complementary assumption that gendered anthropology is largely in fact an anthropology of women or of femininity. As the work of Holly Wardlow and others attests (see Hirsch et al. 2009), the task of documenting and articulating Melanesian male and female orientations often yields great ethnographic and analytic benefit even though—and in some ways for the very reason that—it can be difficult for a single primary researcher to initiate and methodologically maintain such complementary gendered perspectives during fieldwork.

In their introduction to this volume, Lipset and Roscoe describe Donald Tuzin as an 'anthropologist's anthropologist'. In my own experience, this is especially true of Don's ethnography. Tuzin's three big books on the Arapesh—*The Ilahita Arapesh*, *The Voice of the Tambaran* and *The Cassowary's Revenge*—are all marvels of intricate and nuanced ethnographic portraiture. By itself, detailed ethnography is not unusual; for a great number of world areas, one can find scores of rigorous scholarly monographs, however dry and tedious they might otherwise be. What sets Tuzin's work apart is his writerly ability not just to make the wonderful nuance of ethnography come alive but to construct a larger portrait, configure a broader purpose and, in the process, tell a bigger story. This makes Tuzin's ethnographic contributions endearing—and also provocative (see

Losche, this volume). Agree or disagree with his theoretical premise or analysis, the depth, richness and sheer power of his portrayals, mounting as they do towards crescendos of larger signification, force you to examine exactly how, when and for what reasons you might diverge from his view. Don Tuzin was both an ethnographer of cultural artistry and an ethnographic artist. Would that we could all be so lucky—or enjoy the process as much as Don himself always seemed to do.

References

Allen, Michael 1967. *Male Cults and Secret Initiations in Melanesia*. Melbourne: Melbourne University Press.

Barlow, Kathleen and David Lipset 1997. Dialogics of Material Culture: Male and Female in Murik Outrigger Canoes. *American Ethnologist* 224(1):4–36.

Bell, Joshua 2006. Marijuana, Guns, Crocodiles, and Submarines: Economies of Desire in the Purari Delta. *Oceania* 76:220–34.

Dinnen, Sinclair and A. Ley (eds) 2000. *Reflections on Violence in Melanesia*. Canberra: Asia Pacific Press.

Gregor, Thomas and Donald F. Tuzin (eds) 2001. *Gender in Amazonia and Melanesia*. Berkeley: University of California Press.

Haley, Nicole 2008. Sung Adornment: Changing Masculinities at Lake Kopiago, Papua New Guinea. *The Australian Journal of Anthropology* 19:213–29.

Halvaksz, Jamon 2006. Drug Bodies: Relations with Substance in the Wau Bulolo Valley. *Oceania* 76:235–44.

Halvaksz, Jamon and David Lipset 2006. Another Kind of Gold: An Introduction to Marijuana in Papua New Guinea. *Oceania* 76:209–19.

Hart Nibbrig, N. E. 1992. Rascals in Paradise: Urban Gangs in Papua New Guinea. *Pacific Studies* 15:115–34.

Herdt, Gilbert H. 1981. *Guardians of the Flutes: Idioms of Masculinity*. New York: McGraw-Hill.

Herdt, Gilbert H. (ed.) 1982. *Rituals of Manhood: Male Initiation in Papua New Guinea*. Berkeley: University of California Press.

Herdt, Gilbert H. and Fitz John P. Poole 1982. 'Sexual Antagonism': The History of a Concept in New Guinea Anthropology. *Social Analysis* 12:3–28.

Hirsch, Jennifer S., Holly Wardlow, Daniel Jordan Smith, Harriett H. Phinney, Shanti Parikh and Constance A. Nathanson (eds) 2009. *The Secret: Love, Marriage, HIV*. Nashville, Tenn.: Vanderbilt University Press.

Knauft, Bruce M. 1985. *Good Company and Violence: Sorcery and Social Action in a Lowland New Guinea Society*. Berkeley: University of California Press.

Knauft, Bruce M. 1990. Melanesian Warfare: A Theoretical History. *Oceania* 60:250–311.

Knauft, Bruce M. 1997. Gender Identity, Political Economy, and Modernity in Melanesia and Amazonia. *Journal of the Royal Anthropological Institute* 3:233–59.

Knauft, Bruce M. 2002a. *Exchanging the Past: A Rainforest World of Before and After*. Chicago: University of Chicago Press.

Knauft, Bruce M. 2002b. Trials of the Oxymodern: Public Practice at Nomad Station. In Bruce M. Knauft (ed.) *Critically Modern: Alternatives, Alterities, Anthropologists*, pp. 105–43. Bloomington: Indiana University Press.

Knauft, Bruce M. 2010. *The Gebusi: Lives Transformed in a Rainforest World*. Second edition. New York: McGraw-Hill.

Langness L. L. 1967. Sexual Antagonism in the New Guinea Highlands. *Oceania* 37:161–77.

Langness L. L. 1974. Ritual Power and Male Domination in the New Guinea Highlands. *Ethos* 2:189–212.

Lepani, Katherine 2008. Mobility, Violence, and the Gendering of HIV in Papua New Guinea. *The Australian Journal of Anthropology* 19:150–64.

Lipset, David 2006. Tobacco, Good and Bad: Prosaics of Marijuana in a Sepik Society. *Oceania* 76:245–57.

MacIntyre, Martha 2008. Police and Thieves, Gunmen and Drunks: Problems with Men and Problems with Society in Melanesia. *The Australian Journal of Anthropology* 19:179–93.

Meggitt, Mervyn J. 1964. Male–Female Relationships in the Highlands of Australian New Guinea. *American Anthropologist* [Special Publication] 66(4):204–24.

Read, Kenneth E. 1959. Leadership and Consensus in a New Guinea Society. *American Anthropologist* 61:425–36.

Strathern, Andrew 1993. Violence and Political Change in Papua New Guinea. *Pacific Studies* 16:41–60.

Sykes, Karen 1999. After the 'Raskol' Feast: Youth's Alienation in New Ireland, Papua New Guinea. *Critique of Anthropology* 19:157–74.

Taylor, John P. 2008. Changing Pacific Masculinities: The 'Problem' of Men. *The Australian Journal of Anthropology* 19:125–35.

Trouillot, Michel-Rolph 1991. Anthropology and the Savage Slot: The Poetics and Politics of Otherness. In Richard G. Fox (ed.) *Recapturing Anthropology: Working in the Present*, pp. 17–44. Santa Fe, NM: School of American Research Press.

Tuzin, Donald F. 1976. *The Ilahita Arapesh: Dimensions of Unity*. Berkeley: University of California Press.

Tuzin, Donald F. 1980. *The Voice of the Tambaran: Truth and Illusion in Ilahita Arapesh Religion*. Berkeley: University of California Press.

Tuzin, Donald F. 1997. *The Cassowary's Revenge: The Life and Death of Masculinity in a New Guinea Society*. Chicago: University of Chicago Press.

Wardlow, Holly 2006. *Wayward Women: Sexuality and Agency in a New Guinea Society*. Berkeley: University of California Press.

Wardlow, Holly 2007. Men's Extramarital Sexuality in Rural Papua New Guinea. *American Journal of Public Health* 97:1006–14.

Wardlow, Holly 2009. 'Whip Him in the Head With a Stick': Marriage, Male Infidelity, and Female Confrontation Among the Huli. In Jennifer S. Hirsch, Holly Wardlow, Daniel Jordan Smith, Harriett H. Phinney, Shanti Parikh and Constance A. Nathanson (eds) *The Secret: Love, Marriage, HIV*, pp. 136–57. Nashville, Tenn.: Vanderbilt University Press.

Section Two: Culture, the Agent and Tuzin's Methodological Individualism

5. Signs and Wonders: The uncanny *verum* and the anthropological illusion

Kevin Birth

As a Caribbeanist studying under Donald Tuzin, I was struck by the ways in which Don could make the implications of his ethnographic work relevant to my struggles with material from Trinidad. Often this involved delving into the ontological and epistemological relevance of ethnographic details, in order to create a context to relate Trinidad and New Guinea. This chapter is, in many respects, a continuation of some of those conversations.

An uncanny event is normally viewed as something unexpected and unexplainable. Even in anthropological thought, uncanniness is a phenomenological concept that serves as a catalyst for cultural meaning but eludes cultural control. Analytically inspiring, methodologically unplanned and ethnographically untamed, uncanny events gain significance for anthropologists and their subjects because of how they bind together a culturally constituted human quest to understand the vicissitudes of the world with anthropologists' quest to understand human thought and behaviour. Throughout his work, Tuzin explored the nexus between uncanny coincidence and cultural efforts to craft significance. Informed by works such as Charles Morris's *Foundations of the Theory of Signs* (1938), Susanne Langer's *Feeling and Form* (1953) and Isaiah Berlin's essay on Giambbattista Vico (1976), Tuzin confronted the uncanny in all its ontological obscurity and cultural salience. This chapter builds on this foundation to explore how the uncanny can be socially planned and culturally crafted rather than accidental.

An Uncanny Death in Trinidad

Soon before I returned to Trinidad in 1996, Constantine died. The circumstances of his death were disturbing. He had gone hunting with his dogs and several friends and, during the hunt, he became separated from his partners. When it was time to return home, he could not be found. The next day the hunters returned to look for him, and they found his body in a place where they thought they had looked the day before. Constantine's body was being guarded by one of his loyal dogs in a part of the jungle associated with *jumbies*—the spirits of the dead. Such places are here and there in the forest where one finds indications that somebody had once farmed—lone cocoa trees or fruit trees or stands of non-native species of tubers. Far from any current road or habitation, these places are disconcerting. They conjure up a spectral presence of human activity where none was expected. This is not merely a recent phenomenon: in his 1884 book, *Trinidad*, L. A. A. de Verteuil mentions a survey of the forest conducted in 1849, approximately 40 years before the first official titles were given to any land in this part of Trinidad. De Verteuil says the surveyors found evidence of previous occupation:

> These gentlemen observed, on their route, several cacao-trees: were they accidentally planted, or are they the natural growth of the country? They fell in also with brush-wood, and a few lime-trees; such being evidence that, during slavery, the *maroons* or fugitive slaves resorted to that spot as to a fastness. (1884:331)

Along with the occasional discovery of human bones in the forest, such places affirm that the jungle is a mysterious place with secrets. But the jungle is not a homogeneous space; only particular locations are spooky. Constantine died in one such place; his dog kept silent guard over his body in that place; and his body and dog eluded the efforts of his friends to find him for a day.

Significance was given not only to the place of Constantine's death but also to the timing. Constantine had died at a moment in his life when he was unusually embroiled in local conflicts. He had been a highly respected man. After he retired, he was still robust and full of energy. In addition to devoting himself to his land and to his hobbies, he became a leader in local politics. He was of unchallenged character, and his suggestion that there was local-level corruption garnered attention at the same time as it cultivated bitter animosities among his political foes. Only a short time before his death, political passions had reached fever pitch in a hotly contested parliamentary election that had resulted in a tie.

So Constantine had enemies. Death under such circumstances in a haunted place was a coincidence that evoked images of supernatural forces at work. As Khan (2004:109–18) has described for Trinidad, belief in such forces is part of the Trinidadian spiritual landscape, and these beliefs span the religious diversity of the island, which includes Christians, Hindus and Muslims. *Obeah* and 'science'—both means of manipulating supernatural forces and spiritual agents—are employed to address small and large problems and to redress major and minor offences. *Obeah* and science are also parts of the folklore of Trinidadian politics. Particularly powerful political leaders are associated with having supernatural powers—such as the ability of the union leader T. U. B. Butler to elude police capture during the labour riots of 1937. The leaders of Trinidad have never gone to the extent of Françoise Duvalier (Papa Doc), the Premier of Haiti from 1957 to 1971, in actually dressing to mimic the image of a spirit, as Duvalier adopted the dress and style of the *Vodun loa* Ghede—the guardian of the cemetery—but there have been moments when Trinidadian leaders have engaged in public performances with supernatural implications, such as Prime Minister A. N. R. Robinson's use of a *bois* while recuperating from injuries he suffered during the 1990 attempted coup d'état. A *bois* is ostensibly a walking stick, but it also has an association with *obeah* and the magic associated with stick-fighting. Robinson made no attempt to downplay this connotation that his new *bois* gave him magical strength, and in fact when convalescing posed for photographs with his new *bois*.

So the uncanniness of Constantine's death was built on a foundation of local shared knowledge about the forest and shared ideas about the supernatural. This was a death that needed to be explained in terms that transcended the religious and ethnic divisions found in Trinidad. The uncanniness of the event spurred an inter-subjective, inter-ethnic, interfaith acknowledgment of the truth of spiritual forces. At the wake, Hindus, Christians and Muslims all agreed on the strangeness of Constantine's death and displayed shared feelings, in response, that there is more to existence than the familiar.

In fact, the discussions at the wake for Constantine were quite unusual. I have attended many Trinidadian wakes, and usually discussions about the cause of death are expressed in terms of either biomedicine or humoural medicine. Even unexpected deaths are explained in these terms, such as when a seventeen-year-old died a few years before Constantine. In this case, the youth's autopsy indicated that he suffered from an aneurysm, and the discussions at the wake focused on his engaging in 'hot' activities followed by taking a cold shower in the middle of the night that caused a blood vessel in his brain to 'bust'. The uncanniness of Constantine's death was not merely that it was unexpected, and not merely that he died in a part of the forest associated with *jumbies*, and not merely that his body was not found for a day despite his companions' attempts to find him, but the combination of all these factors with the conflicts in which Constantine had been embroiled. The constellation of elements associated with his death pointed to forces beyond body humours and medical conditions, and, for that matter, beyond the religious differences between Hindus, Christians and Muslims.

The Uncanny and Cartesian Epistemology

In some respects, the feeling of the uncanny evoked by Constantine's death is discussed in Freud's essay 'Das Unheimliche'. Cixous describes this essay as 'a commentary on uncertainty' (1976:525), but its equivocations and elisions display signs of Freud's own uncertainty, as well. In the essay, Freud occasionally admits and recounts some of his own uncanny experiences and, in so doing, he generates a problem for himself. While he intellectually dismisses uncanny experiences as a problem of reality testing and repetition compulsion, his claim that superior rationality and reality testing allowed him to dismiss the uncanny becomes compromised by his admission of a certain reality to the uncanny:

> We—or our primitive forefathers—once believed that these possibilities were realities, and were convinced that they actually happened. Nowadays we no longer believe in them, we have *surmounted* these modes of thought; but we do not feel quite sure of our new beliefs, and the old ones still exist within us ready to seize upon any conformation. As soon as something *actually happens* in our lives which seems to confirm the old, discarded beliefs we get a feeling of the uncanny…Conversely, anyone who has completely and finally rid himself of animistic beliefs will be insensible to this type of the uncanny…The whole thing is purely an affair of 'reality-testing,' a question of the material reality of the phenomena. (Freud 1976:639; emphasis in original)

For Freud, the uncanny creates uncertainty, and he seems unwilling to accept or believe that it has ontological implications. He assumes, *a priori*, that it creates an illusion grounded in the repetition of some unconscious anxiety. Yet, the phrase 'actually happens' haunts Freud enough for him emphasise it, and this phrase will continue to haunt the discussion here of the uncanny. Freud is caught in a dilemma: his idea of reality testing forces him to dismiss beliefs used to understand something that 'actually happens' and which, therefore, involve 'the material reality of the phenomena'.

Freud's dilemma emerges from his Cartesian epistemology. The uncanny often refers to events in the world that 'actually happen', but Freud can only address and eventually dismiss the interpretation of the events, not the 'material reality' of the events themselves. In the case of Constantine's death, the place and time were not psycho-dynamically determined. One could argue that there was still no need to explain his death beyond natural causes, yet what disconcerts contemporary Trinidadians about the part of the forest that gave Constantine's death its uncanny character also disconcerted de Verteuil in 1884 and surveyors in 1849. The uncanny is uncanny because, in Freud's words, some aspect of the 'material reality of the phenomena' in the world 'actually happens', and this material reality demands an explanation.

In his separation of the mental from the material world, Descartes suggests that there are different methods of study for each. Descartes claims that we know our minds better than our bodies and that the knowledge of mind is due to 'natural enlightenment' (1983:6). The material world consists of 'objective reality' outside human thought (Descartes 1980:70–1). But in Descartes' discussion of his idea of objective reality one again finds the seeds of conundrum posed by the uncanny:

> [I]f we posit that something is found in the idea that was not in its cause, then the idea would get it from nothing; but as imperfect a mode of being as this is, by which a thing exists in the intellect objectively through an idea, it nevertheless is surely not nothing; hence it cannot get its existence from nothing. (Descartes 1980:72)

The Cartesian dilemma seems to be that the uncanny is either a part of objective reality or it comes from nothing. Freud's solution is to attribute it to repetition compulsion; uncanniness derives from a previous objective reality being added to present perception. The problem of the anxiety about Constantine's death was not due simply to memories and cultural ideas of *jumbies* but to coincidence: the 'objective reality' of his death in a place with traces of long-disappeared human cultivation in purportedly virgin rainforest.

Descartes' division of knowledge led to an emphasis on observable and measurable facts in the social and physical sciences. Empirical research had to be contextualised as investigating a world of facts. As Poovey (1998) has shown, the ontological status of these facts is not as secure as many might hope. The definition of fact, she argues, has its roots in rhetoric—namely, in how information is represented as objective. She notes that the modern fact only emerged in an episteme that distinguished between observed particulars and theory so that these observed particulars could become evidence capable of supporting or disproving theories (Poovey 1998:92). Built upon Descartes' division of knowledge, matters of spirituality lie outside of the realm of observed particulars.

This creates a dilemma for the scientific study of religion as separate from theology, for it excludes the phenomenology of the spiritual from analysis on grounds that it is not observable evidence. Based on Descartes' famous statement 'I think, therefore I am' (1983:5), it also separates the study of matter from the issue of ontology; the 'I am' is a consequence of 'I think', and thought has an ontological status superior to that of the material world that would exist even if the body did not (Descartes 1980:18). In fact, the existence of the material world is simply taken for granted: 'that there really is a world, that men have bodies, and other such things, concerning which no one of sound mind has ever seriously doubted' (Descartes 1980:54).

In this dualism, the uncanny is disruptive. The coincidences on which the sense of the uncanny are founded are observable particulars, but these coincidences serve as an indicator of mystical connections beyond observation. In this way, it is similar to Otto's exploration of *mysterium*—one component of his discussion of the idea of the holy. Mysterium involves a sense of something 'hidden and esoteric, that which is beyond conception or understanding, extraordinary and unfamiliar' (Otto 1950:13). But the ease with which the experience of mysterium can lead to the idea of the holy suggests a bridge across the Cartesian divide, and, as a post-Cartesian troll, Freud does not want that bridge crossed. Part of the Cartesian dilemma posed by the uncanny, then, is that it involves something that 'actually happens', which evokes mysterium.

The Cartesian dualism thus places Freud in an uncomfortable if not untenable position. In response to the uncanny, Freud suppresses it in favour of a non-spiritual, observable reality as determined by his preconceived notion that reality testing only includes observable particulars and therefore must exclude the spiritual.

Donald Tuzin had no such problem. Tuzin invoked Vico's critique of Descartes' dualism as a means to avoid being impaled on the horns of the Cartesian dilemma of choosing between the spiritual and the material. He was particularly enamoured of Isaiah Berlin's discussion of Vico in *Vico and Herder*. Berlin (1976:25) represents Vico's view on Cartesian dualism as: 'Descartes is the great deceiver, whose emphasis on knowledge of the external world as the paradigm of all knowledge has set philosophy on a false path.' In contrast, Vico developed a distinction between *verum* and *certum*—truth and certainty. His idea of truth was that it was created by the human mind; according to Berlin (1976:13–14), only 'where we make or design something out of literally nothing, can we be said fully to understand what we have made; for in that situation to create, and to know what and why we are creating, is a single act. This is how God creates.' *Certum*, on the other hand, refers to the human mind's relationship to the physical world. In this relationship, the world is perceived, not directly constructed. This gives natural scientific knowledge of the world an epistemological status different from that of truth. In contrast, the study of human efforts at creation—the study of history for Vico and the study of culture for Tuzin—allows a window into *verum*. As Berlin put it: 'In history we are the actors; in the natural sciences mere spectators' (1976:67).

The concept of *verum*—the creation of truth—is an important dimension of Tuzin's study of the *Tambaran* cult of the Ilahita Arapesh. Tuzin was not a simple Vichean, however. He coupled truth with illusion: truth 'cannot even be known to exist—except through the medium of illusion' (1995:298). Tuzin's idea of illusion in religion is better thought of as the magician's creation of experience to generate wonder rather than as Freud's (1961) cynical emphasis on delusion in his *The Future of An Illusion*. Tuzin emphasises the aesthetic of the magician's creation of illusion, including the awareness of the Arapesh men that they are the ones engaged in the creation of the illusion and that secrecy is necessary to pull it off.

Tuzin coupled Vichean dualism with Suzanne Langer's (1953) approach to aesthetics and Charles Morris's (1938) pragmatism. One of his favourite quotes was from Langer's *Feeling and Form*: 'But the status of the unfelt feelings that inhere in art objects is ontologically obscure' (Langer 1953:22). Langer's emphasis on the ontological obscurity of the unfelt feelings in art fits well with Morris's pragmatic dimension of meaning. As Tuzin put it, the symbol 'is apperceived to have intrinsic import' (1977:197). The apperception is at once both an individual process and a collective endeavour. The object of religious art, such as the *Tambaran* spirit house, is an object in the world, but the powerful feelings attached to the object are less ontologically clear; are they in the object or in the mind? Tuzin adopts a Vichean response to this question; the focus on apperception rather than perception indicates an active process in the creation of meaning rather than a passive process in the perception of meaning.

The active process in the creation of meaning involves not simply reaction to objects but also the creation of objects—one of Langer's crucial insights. In a statement of Langer's contribution to his thought, Tuzin wrote that works of art 'are not expressive of actual, untransformed emotion, but rather they express the *idea* of emotion' (1977:198). For Tuzin, the idea of emotion in the art spurs a cultural response through social processes; for Tuzin, who was trained in the British social anthropological tradition, this was a Durkheimian rather than cultural-constructivist perspective. For instance, the paintings associated with Nggwal, the spirits of the highest initiation level in the *Tambaran* cult, are an important meeting place of collective religious sentiment and individual expression. The Nggwal involves 43 named spirits in which 'each individual's relationship with his nggwal is personified in a painting' (1980:175). These paintings are then displayed in the outer sanctum of the spirit house on the wall that divides the inner and outer sanctums. Tuzin says of this display:

> By its design the gallery wall elevates the symbolic office of these paintings to a higher level. Here, in graphic rendition of the conceptual realm, the individual spirit is socially ennobled by virtue of its placement in a mosaic which orders while pictorializing the collective spirituality of the village. In the logic of the Tambaran, therefore, the men are quite correct when they proudly proclaim that Nggwal—the image par excellence of the village collectivity—dwells in his house. Had the scheme been designed by Durkheim himself, it could not have expressed better the mirror which religious ideology holds up to the social order. (1980:180)

Tuzin's Durkheimian twist on the combination of Langer's and Morris's approaches to symbols removes the interpretation of symbols from the strictly Freudian realm of the connection of the symbol to the individual unconscious and instead places the interpretation of symbols into the nexus of individual and collective experience and emotion.

This raises a contrast between Freud's post-Enlightenment intellectualism and Tuzin's approach to Arapesh religion; in the former, the uncanny is disruptive and in the latter, it is catalytic. Yet, Freud's suppression is not the only form of post-Enlightenment response to the uncanny. The colonial encounter created another form of suppression: the uncanny could be dismissed as the naive superstition associated with the colonised or uneducated masses. In the Caribbean, the uncanny is a prevalent component of representations of the West Indies, whether it be *zombis* associated with Haitian Vodun, *obeah* or spirit possession. Palmié (2002:216) traces how *brujeria*, Cuban witchcraft, came to be seen by Ortiz, a student of Malinowski, as 'an affliction, not of concrete people but of the republican mind; a hybrid formation, not just in the literal sense, but also in terms of the way in which it seemed to disfigure the identity of the *clases responsables* of the neocolonial republic'. The uncanny in the Caribbean is not denied, then, as Freud does, but is seemingly dismissed as attached to a deviant, counterproductive state of mind. Within a Cartesian dualism, this dismissal is made possible by transforming the uncanny into merely a state of mind. But Constantine's death still haunts this transformation, not because of a state of mind but because of the coincidence of when, where and how he disappeared and died. The feral, non-native yams and fruit trees in the forest are not a state of mind in the Cartesian framework but a component of the material world—observed particulars out of which scientific knowledge should be able to be constructed. That is what makes Constantine's death unsettling—namely, the empirically observed particulars that unsettle the analytic ability to dismiss cultural efforts at interpretation. Even within the colonial logic, as with Freud, labelling the interpretations as irrational or deviant only dismisses them, not what 'actually happens'.

Even before Tuzin explicitly invoked Vico in his work, he expressed concern about Cartesian dualism and anthropological concepts. His first book, *The Ilahita Arapesh: Dimensions of Unity*, concluded by revealing ontological uncertainty in Lévi-Strauss's theory of binary oppositions. Tuzin wrote: 'as it is usually presented the theory presupposes a Cartesian metaphysic of Mind—the absolute autonomy of "reality" as distinct from "experience"—and once this logical Rubicon is crossed, there is no further inquiry which is not either teleological or formally meaningless' (1976:329). Later, he wrote: 'we must resist an unwitting participation in the cosmology we are studying which presumes that both it and our own scientific ontology are merely different manifestations of a common

Cartesian principle' (1976:334). The surprising conclusion of *Dimensions of Unity* implies that Cartesian epistemologies possibly pose a challenge to empirically grounded ethnographic research. The implication is that theoretical constructs that assume distinctions of mental and observable phenomena are ontologically dubious. It is difficult to tell whether they emerge out of observed particulars or whether they are preconceived categories imposed on observed particulars. What, after all, is the ontological status of social structure, or culture? Or, if the readers of a volume otherwise dominated by Melanesian studies will indulge me, what is the ontological status of the concepts of creolisation and hybridity that dominate current discussions of the post-colonial Caribbean?

As descriptive labels, creolisation or hybridity seem to lend themselves to an analysis of the discourses of local politics and *jumbies* evoked by Constantine's death. In the hands of Caribbeanists, these ideas are constantly deployed to discuss the nexus of political action and significance with spiritual dimensions that seem to have an African or South Asian origin. In Trinidad, the connection between *jumbies* and political strife can be explained by reference to Trinidadian's long experience of colonially created ethnic divisions and post-colonially cultivated rancorous politics. There is a rhythm to these tensions such that they are heightened during and immediately following parliamentary elections, which must occur no later than every five years. Constantine was embroiled enough in political debates and died close enough to parliamentary elections that the coincidence was an important component of conversations to make sense of his death. *Jumbies* are viewed as specteres whose powers can be harnessed through the practice of *obeah*. Hence, it makes sense that being in a place associated with *jumbies* when one has enemies would be potentially dangerous. Creoliszation and hybridity focus on dynamic processes that produce this mix, but the mix, like the uncanny, often bridges the Cartesian divide.

There is a problem, however, with perspectives such as creolisation and hybridity. One might label an explanation of Constantine's death as a form of hybridity or as a consequence of creolisation, but this, in fact, bypasses the problem that nags Freud. Hybridity and creolisation are concepts that refer to the consequences of contact between different peoples, but the place and time of Constantine's death are not determined by such contact. His death might evoke a creolised response, but it was not creolisation in the conventional sense of the term that brought about Constantine's death in a stand of feral cultigens. There are events that 'actually happen' that seem outside the purview of these concepts from post-colonial studies, and this limit on these concepts is not confined to singular events such as Constantine's death. In response to these events that actually happen, creolisation and hybridity merely serve as labels after the fact, not really as a means of explaining what has happened.

Within anthropology, the challenge of addressing what 'actually happens' is an important part of the longstanding tradition within the field of disrupting Western epistemological complacency, such as Evans-Pritchard's representation of his discussion with Azande about the collapse of an old granary. 'That it should collapse is easily intelligible, but why should it have collapsed at the particular moment when these particular people were sitting beneath it?' (Evans-Pritchard 1937:69). Evans-Pritchard admits: 'We have no explanation of why the two chains of causation intersected at a certain time and in a certain place, for there is no interdependence between them. Zande philosophy can supply the missing link' (p. 70).

The Planned Uncanny

While the uncanny might refer to anomalies, it does not include only the accidental and unexpected. This is implied by Freud's use of a work of fiction, Hoffman's *The Sand-Man*. If, as Nietzsche argues in *The Birth of Tragedy and the Genealogy of Morals* (1956), the plot of tragedy is known, and this knowledge gives its affective import to the audience, the use of a work of fiction to demonstrate and explore the uncanny suggests the possibility that the uncanny is expected. Freud equivocates on this when he writes: '*in the first place a great deal that is not uncanny in fiction would be so if it happened in real life; and in the second place…there are many more means of creating uncanny effects in fiction than there are in real life*' (1976:640, emphasis in original). This equivocation is itself based on Freud's Cartesian distinction between 'reality' and 'fiction', but, from Tuzin's point of view, this boundary is not as clear as Freud wishes. Tuzin argues that the uncanny can be created through ritual practice. The sound created by the bullroarer is one such case. In his article 'Miraculous Voices', he argues that

> a certain type of naturally occurring sound has a perceptual effect on some, possibly many, animal species that is *intrinsically* mysterious and thus anxiety arousing; that this sensation is humanly interpreted and its accompanying anxiety cognitively resolved by referring it to the mystery that is allegedly inherent in the supernatural realm; and that certain kinds of ritual sounds capitalize on this iconic resemblance by simultaneously mimicking, as it were, factual and artifactual mystery, thereby summoning the senses to bear witness to the noetic truth of the sound's religious meaning. (Tuzin 1984:579)

In his discussion of the association of the bullroarer with *Lefin*, the *Tambaran* cult's second age grade and the name of a *Tambaran* spirit, Tuzin emphasises that 'the *active* aspect of Tambaran power, to the extent it can be known, is conceived by men to reside in its voice' (1980:57, emphasis in original). This voice is manifested by the bullroarer. When played, this instrument creates the sound of *Lefin*, a 'big-mouthed, red-haired dwarf' (Tuzin 1980:60), crying 'I am a great, great man; I am a great, great man' (Tuzin 1984:582).

Tuzin states that the sounds produced by the bullroarers '*are* the cult spirits represented in their voices' (1984:582). He argues that the volume and tone of the bullroarer not only are heard but are felt; they create infrasonic waves. Consequently, the experience of the sound of *Lefin* is perceived not only through normal auditory perceptual paths but is felt through non-auditory paths as well (Tuzin 1984:586), thereby fostering a sonic experience and consequent mental state that evoke 'sensations of the uncanny, the dreadedly obscure' (p. 587). In effect, the sense of mysterium Otto described and which is crucial to the uncanny can be created and reproduced. It can be deployed to give significance to moments of time.

In this sense, the creation or reproduction of a sense of mysterium can be related to Benjamin's (1969) idea of messianic time—the uncanny disrupts homogeneous empty time through the demand that the uncanny be given meaning. As Robbins (this volume) states, messianic time connects 'potential emancipation' with events in the present. But I want to maintain a distinction between messianic time and uncanny disruptions to homogeneous empty time. Uncanny coincidences provoke the creation of meaning that makes a moment unique and significant, but they need not convey any messianic hope.

What messianic and uncanny forms of temporal disruption share is the co-presence of a sense of existence beyond the lived moment with the mundane sequences of life. Such co-presence is at the heart of Augustine's discussion of memory and time in his *Confessions*, where he argues that the tension between time and change and God's unchanging eternity is what gives time meaning (1997:266–72; see also Ricoeur 1984:5–30). One can also view these uncanny times as moments when, as Hauser-Schäublin (this volume) discusses, there is a co-presence of the transcendental with the lived moment. Put into a rubric of time that echoes Augustine's discussion of time and eternity, such co-presence can be a moment when a sense of eternal or transcendent time intersects with the sequences of lived existence.

In Hauser-Schäublin's chapter in this volume, one gets a sense of how a logic of concealing and revealing in the rituals of initiation into grades of the *Tambaran* cultivates such a co-presence. As Tuzin's *The Voice of the Tambaran* showed, staging these rituals is not an easy or trivial matter, but involves immense preparation; the sense of mystery evoked in these rituals through the play of revealing and concealing is therefore anticipated and planned. The uncanny disruption of homogeneous empty time can be a staged and planned event.

In Trinidad, the seasonal timing of ritual observances of different religious traditions is a source of the uncanny because of the coincidences created by the intersections of Christian and Hindu calendars. The cycles of holidays in calendars from different religious traditions intersect to create moments of significance. As in Constantine's death, the coincidences are what foster the sense of the uncanny—of a beyond that is not fully known yet actually there. Every year, the Hindu celebration of Divali nearly coincides with the Roman Catholic celebrations of All Saints' Night and All Souls' Night. Divali involves lighting *deyas*—small clay lamps with a cotton wick; All Saints' Night involves lighting candles outside the home; and All Souls' Night involves lighting candles on the graves of loved ones. During my first All Souls' Night in Trinidad, standing in the cemetery among a crowd of Muslims, Hindus and Catholics seeking the graves of their deceased loved ones in order to light candles, many of my neighbours impressed upon me the parallels between Divali and All Saints'; to them, both represented the victory of light over darkness. Divali, in fact, is thought to occur on the darkest night of the year—a new moon after the autumnal equinox. How might the coincidence of such different religious traditions be explained? The Trinidadian cultural response is to engage in a form of creolised ecumenical theology—that the similarities between religious events reveal a deeper truth than any of the religions individually.

This local-level, theological explanation emerges from the contact between different groups exploring the similarity in timing of some of their religious practices—their effort to create a collective truth. The local explanation is an example of hybridity and creolisation, but the materiality of the uncanny—the component that 'actually happens'—indicates something beyond a coincidence of religious practice. The way in which these calendars interact is a catalyst for creolised interpretations but is not caused by creolisation; colonialism brought into contact pre-existing calendars from different parts of the world but did not create the calendars. In fact, it is the perception of an independent origin of these two calendars that makes their coincidence seem uncanny.

At least in Hinduism, if one moves from religious practice to the justification of the practice, one is confronted with an ethno-astronomical explanation. Divali is associated with an event in the night-time sky. Hinduism is fixed on the skies in ways that contemporary Christianity is no longer. Hinduism, in particular, emphasises the coincidence of celestial bodies as crucial to understanding one's fate and making wise decisions. The Hindu claim that Divali falls on the darkest night of the year is not merely a cultural claim but an ethno-astronomical one based on the decrease in sunlight after the autumnal equinox and a new (or dark) moon after what, in the West, is known as the Harvest Moon—the full moon nearest to the autumnal equinox that is reputed to be brighter than other full moons.

It is possible to step out of the context of creolisation in Trinidad and enter into a broad play of the uncanny coincidence of the recognition of autumnal celestial darkness, since the American celebration of Halloween also coincides with this darkest time of the year, as does the Mexican Day of the Dead (which coincides with All Saints' Day and All Souls' Day).

Such ethno-astronomical awareness was once part of Christianity, gave significance to some holidays and determined the dates of other commemorations. For instance, in an essay attributed to Anatolius of Laodicea in the third century, the timing of Easter was described in terms of ethno-astronomical significance:

> [A]s long as equality between light and darkness endures, and is not diminished by the light, it is shown that the Paschal festival is not to be celebrated. Accordingly, it is enjoined that that festival be kept after the equinox, because the moon of the fourteenth, if before the equinox or at the equinox, does not fill the whole night. (Anatolius 1926:149)

In 1733, Isaac Newton also suggested a tie between astronomy and religious commemoration in Christianity:

> They who began first to celebrate [Christian holidays], placed them in the cardinal periods of the year; as the annunciation of the Virgin Mary, on the 25th of March, which when Julius Caesar corrected the Calendar was the vernal Equinox; the feast of John Baptist on the 24th of June, which was the summer Solstice; the feast of St. Michael on September 29, which was the autumnal Equinox; and the birth of Christ on the winter Solstice, Decemb. 25. (Newton 1998:143)

But ethno-astronomy goes only so far as a form of explanation. Easter is tied to Passover, and Passover is determined by astronomical events. Why is it that these events coincidentally occurred around the spring equinox when light is ascending? Again, the full moon coinciding with the vernal equinox is a coincidence observable in the material world.

The juxtaposition of discussions of the resonances between Hinduism and Catholicism in Trinidad and with de-contextualised examples about the sacred dimensions of celestial events from Anatolius and Newton is meant to stir a sense of uncanny similarity between societies that are not directly connected. This, too, was something that Tuzin explored, in his work with Gregor comparing Amazonia and Melanesia (Gregor and Tuzin 2001). The uncanny resemblances seem to point to elements of psychic unity and, in the case of the impressive sound of bullroarers and the coincidence of autumnal holidays, disparate cultures that note repeatable, widespread phenomena that 'actually happen' but which generate a sense of mysterium. Tuzin's willingness to broach these issues in a spirit of scepticism and openness in fact revives the possibilities of broad-based comparisons of cultures. In Tuzin's approach, this is not to place them in broad classifications but to understand components of the human cultural creative process. The origins of the bullroarer are shrouded by time, and whether its presence in Melanesia and Amazonia is the result of diffusion or independent invention was of little interest to Tuzin. What was of interest was how the bullroarer created similar experiences in Melanesians, Amazonians and ethnographers, and the fact that the similarity of experience prompted cultural interpretation. There is also the recognition that societies differ in whether they cultivate planned experiences of the uncanny, and the question of how societies accomplish this. In fact, even though it is obvious, it bears to be stated: a coincidence between the practices of two societies does not mean that there must be a coincidence between the practices of all societies for a sense of the uncanny to emerge. After all, Islam does not have a commemoration that regularly corresponds with Divali or All Saints'/All Souls' because the Islamic calendar is strictly lunar. It therefore has a year that is 11 days shorter than the solar Gregorian calendar and never readjusts the lunar to the solar year through an embolismic month, as does the Hindu calendar. Yet, even though Islam is not part of the uncanny coincidence of Catholicism and Hinduism in Trinidad—at least in my field site—Muslims appear at the cemetery on All Souls' Night to light candles and join in the discussion of how all religions celebrate the victory of light over darkness.

Still, the existence of coincidences between cultural practices and the practice in many societies of cultivating uncanny experiences allowed Tuzin to plumb the depths of common ways to stir the human spirit while leaving open how such stirring is culturally employed and interpreted.

Ritual, then, can involve not only the creation of truth in response to the uncanny, but also the creation of the uncanny by reference to features of the environment that 'actually happen'. The sonic qualities of Arapesh ritual are not accidental, and the coincidence of sound and ritual action is planned and practised rather than unexpected or unpredictable. Likewise, the coincidence of Divali and All Saints' is part of the annual cycle of holidays. The uncanniness derives from the coincidence of two holidays from two different religions representing very different cultural traditions within Trinidad. Examples of an expected uncanny experience do not diminish its effect; the uncanny qualities of the sound still create a numinous experience in Arapesh ritual, and the uncanny coincidence of holidays still spurs theological musings.

The Uncanny and Anomie

Just as the uncanny can be created in order to stir the spirit and create truth, Tuzin provides an account of the uncanny being denied. *The Cassowary's Revenge* explores an idea that is complementary to Vico's wisdom: the criterion of the false is to have unmade the true. The dismantling of the *Tambaran* made it false, but in *The Cassowary's Revenge* there remains scepticism about the falsehood of the *Tambaran*. In this ethnographic description, scepticism ceases to be opposed to religion but is opposed to any system of truth/falsehood; and the persuasiveness of truth and falsehood is against the ground of scepticism but, under the new circumstances, the uncanny does not lead to collective conscience but to anomie—a move from Durkheim's *The Elementary Forms of the Religious Life* (1995) to *Suicide* (1979) as a source for insight. In fact, Tuzin laments this in the last chapter of the book, where he discusses the possible functions of men's cults. Maybe there are here clues to understanding the disruptiveness of the uncanny for modernity. In an ontological system that dismantles collective responses to ontological uncertainty in favour of individualised ontological doubt, the uncanny has little power to mobilise.

In the case of post-*Tambaran* Ilahita, this disruption had not led to the re-establishment of a collective consciousness, although it seems that millenarianism has had this outcome in other parts of Melanesia (see Robbins, this volume). In this regard, the inability to fully resuscitate ontological obscurity in the face of socially sanctioned doubt created anomie. Augmenting Durkheim, Tuzin's approach to anomie merges the problem of social isolation with a phenomenological experience of anxiety about reality. In one way, this parallels Heidegger's (1962) treatment of the uncanny as a primordial experience of the world and the individualised disruptiveness of the uncanny, but Tuzin does not agree with Heidegger's claim that the uncanny is always an individualised experience. Instead, he seems to imply that the individualisation of the uncanny is a consequence of social disintegration. The public face of the uncanny had no concealed dimension of socially sanctioned secrecy. When it is assumed that everything known is revealed then the uncanny is unsettling. The possibility of a reservoir of ontological obscurity allows for the creation and cultivation of secrets that can be deployed socially. The disclosure of the *Tambaran* cult's secrets did not dispose of ontological obscurity, only this reservoir of secrecy with which the obscurity could be handled.

Tuzin's *The Cassowary's Revenge* suggests that, in the wake of the revelation of the *Tambaran* cult's secrets, the uncanny is not denied, but there is no cultural structure remaining that can adequately address it. As Palmié (2002) suggests for the Caribbean, the uncanny is more often disavowed than denied. It is much more like the situation that Ewing (1997:163) describes in Pakistan, where '[m]any highly educated Pakistanis who regard themselves as modern, rational, and professional are…caught between ideologies, inconsistent in their self-representations, uncertain about how to articulate their relationships to Islam and to modernity. Many are drawn to Sufism and yet avoid identifying themselves as Sufis.' The congruence of Melanesia, South Asia and the Caribbean suggests a condition of the post-colonial world. In effect, in the post-colonial context, the uncanny reveals the incompleteness of European Enlightenment hegemony about being and knowing. Concepts such as culture, social structure, hybridity and creolisation serve to deflect attention from the uncanny that 'actually happens'. The emphasis is shifted from the uncanny event to the interpretation of the event. In effect, uncanniness is split into the materiality of what actually happens and interpretation of what actually happens, with the materiality ultimately being neglected or dismissed.

The ontological obscurity of the spirits in art, ritual and uncanny events makes Tuzin's work an unusual intervention in understandings of the role of the uncanny in anthropology with implications for understanding fissures in post-colonialism and modernity. The tacit adoption of Descartes' epistemological dualism has led anthropology either to dismiss the uncanny or to assume the uncanny and its accompanying ontological anxieties are a disruptive force, but Tuzin's ethnographic discussions lead him to view it as a socially creative force. Rather than dismiss or disavow the uncanny, his synthesis of Vico and Langer allows him to embrace the ontological uncertainty it creates and the culturally creative consequences of this uncertainty based on events that 'actually happen', which stir the spirit. Cartesian dualism has led to a social scientific fear of having the spirit stirred in response to what actually happens. Tuzin had no such fear.

By adopting a Vichean dualism, Tuzin allowed his spirit to be stirred without necessarily going down the road to religious faith. He emphasised and celebrated scepticism, but his Vichean approach to the uncanny allowed his scepticism free rein to include both religion and claims of rationality. Repeatedly, Tuzin describes how scepticism about the existence of spirits and sorcery lays the foundation for the extraordinary collective experience of spirits and sorcery in ritual or in response to unexpected events or strange coincidences; the stirred spirit is all the more remarkable when it emerges out of scepticism. For instance, he describes one informant who intimated that 'just as the fiction of a *physical* Nggwal enables men to dominate women, so the fiction of an *invisible* Nggwal enables the senior initiates to dominate their junior colleagues. The lie is itself a lie' (Tuzin 1980:212). Tuzin remarked on the resemblance of this statement to certain forms of atheism and existentialism; 'belief in self replaces belief in Nggwal; the human actor assumes the godlike functions of Nggwal' (1980:213). But then, a few days later, this informant had a dream in which he was chased by animated Nggwal statues, and this dream changed his imagination of Nggwal: 'No longer the free-wheeling agnostic, he had reverted to an anxious literalism that verged on the abject credulity which, in happier moments, he scornfully ascribed to women' (1980:214).

Tuzin's attention to sensory perception—the sights of the spirit house, the terror evoked by the din of bullroarers, the exquisite pain of ritualised penile bloodletting—adds a phenomenological dimension to his link between the ontology of spirits and the imagination of community. Rather than being disruptive of society, the counterpoint of uncanny events, sensory experience and scepticism becomes the foundation for Durkheimian social connections.

In Tuzin's work, then, the uncanny is consistently portrayed as a productive, creative force. It is creative in how it prompts the collective imagination and creation of truth, and this catalyst of the imagination plays an important role in religious experience and, in an interesting, parallel fashion, in anthropological methodology. In both cases, the uncanny is something that requires attention—signifying a moment of potential insight through its unsettling of ontological complacency.

Returning to the Caribbean vignettes I have offered, Constantine's death and the congruence of Divali and All Saints' are uncanny events that, according to Tuzin's logic, must either produce a social response at creating an illusion of truth or create individualised anomie. This allows some insight into the Vichean problems of post-colonial studies. The social divisions created by colonialism and its enlightenment heritage seem to highlight the opposed Durkheimian paths to collective conscience or to anomie. For instance, M. G. Smith's (1965) model of cultural pluralism seems to suggest social disintegration except for the power of the state. This was a model that Tuzin learned quite well at the hands of his undergraduate anthropology professor, Leo Despres, a specialist in the study of Guyana who was an advocate of Smith's cultural pluralism theory. Tuzin's familiarity with this model seemed to breed contempt for it; he was utterly unconvinced by the anomic representation of such societies. He was more sympathetic towards creolisation, but still regarded it as a grand term that probably obfuscated a diversity of practices and ignored points of tension and fissure in Caribbean societies. I do not think he would have been much more satisfied with hybridity—a label that is often confused with being an explanation. From a Cartesian perspective, all of these are models attempting to label observed particulars. From Tuzin's Vichean perspective, they are acts of anthropological creation. Cultural pluralism, creolisation and hybridity are all models that explain what they themselves create, and in the Caribbean this is highlighted by the prevalence of scholars who are also policy makers and advisors. Such scholar-politicians use social scientific theory in their policies and strategies. In Trinidad, they approach policy making as if cultural pluralism were truth, and in creating institutional structures that treat the social world in terms of cultural pluralism, they make cultural pluralism true. Behind the imposing pluralist, creolised or hybridised masks are mere humans.

Conclusion

The social creation of truth to understand the uncanny is, from Tuzin's Durkheimian perspective, a cultural and social process; through the human spirits stirred to create a shared vision about the world, there is a creation of social connection. In the process, Tuzin's insights make the ontological status of all our theoretical constructs uncertain. They, too, are creations of human action rather than objects in the world to be studied, and what is of greatest importance ethnographically is to study the process of creation not the reification of categories for purposes of objective and objectifying analysis.

This leads to a significant ontological and epistemological implication of Tuzin's work. From his Vichean perspective, human action is the act of creation, and the act of creation establishes truth. The ethnographic enterprise, then, must attend to the act of creation, and the ability to create is a common human bond between ethnographers and their subjects. If attention is given to the act of creation then ethnographers can gain special insight into cultural and social processes that approach *verum* and maybe gain insight into acts of creating new social systems. But if attention is given to the study of ossified categories that anthropology creates to filter and shape the world the ethnographer studies then, at best, one can achieve only a form of *certum* that is a pale imitation of that in the natural sciences and, by privileging the pre-ethnographic conceptual creations over what actually happens, develop a Cartesian blindness to the uncanny. In mentoring me to study the Caribbean, Don Tuzin encouraged me to observe and even participate in creation; that seemed to stir his spirit in our discussions to allow us to transcend the distance between Ilahita and Trinidad.

Acknowledgments

I would like to thank Alex Bolyanatz, John Collins, Ted Sammons, and two anonymous reviewers for their comments on earlier versions of this chapter.

References

Anatolius 1926. The Paschal Canon. In A. Cleveland Coxe (ed.) *Ante-Nicene Fathers. Volume 6*, pp. 146–51. Grand Rapids, Mich.: Christian Literature Publishing Company.

Augustine 1997. *The Confessions*. New York: Vintage.

Benjamin, Walter 1968. Theses on the Philosophy of History. In Hannah Arendt (ed.) *Illuminations*, pp. 253–64. New York: Schocken.

Berlin, Isaiah 1976. *Vico and Herder*. New York: Viking.

Cixous, Hélène 1976. Fiction and its Phantoms. *New Literary History* 7:525–48.

Descartes, René 1980. *Discourse on Method and Meditations on First Philosophy*. Indianapolis, Ind.: Hackett.

Descartes, René 1983. *Principles of Philosophy*. Dordrecht: Kluwer.

de Verteuil, Louis A. A. 1884. *Trinidad: Its Geography, Natural Resources, Administration, Present Condition, and Prospects*. London: Cassell.

Durkheim, Emile 1979. *Suicide: A Study in Sociology*. New York: Free Press.

Durkheim, Emile 1995. *The Elementary Forms of the Religious Life*. New York: Oxford University Press.

Evans-Pritchard, E. E. 1937. *Witchcraft, Oracles and Magic Among the Azande*. Oxford: Clarendon.

Ewing, Katherine 1997. *Arguing Sainthood*. Durham, NC: Duke University Press.

Freud, Sigmund 1961. *The Future of An Illusion*. New York: Norton.

Freud, Sigmund 1976. The 'Uncanny'. *New Literary History* 7:619–45.

Gregor, Thomas A. and Donald Tuzin 2001. *Gender in Amazonia and Melanesia*. Berkeley: University of California Press.

Heidegger, Martin 1962. *Being and Time*. New York: Harper.

Khan, Aisha 2004. *Callaloo Nation: Metaphors of Race and Religious Identity Among South Asians in Trinidad*. Durham, NC: Duke University Press.

Langer, Susanne 1953. *Feeling and Form: A Theory of Art*. New York: Scribner.

Morris, Charles 1938. *Foundations of the Theory of Signs*. Chicago: University of Chicago Press.

Newton, Isaac 1998 [1773]. *The Prophecies of Daniel and the Apocalypse*. Hyderabad, India: Printland Publishers.

Nietzche, Friedrich 1956. *The Birth of Tragedy and the Genealogy of Morals*. New York: Doubleday.

Otto, Rudolf 1950. *The Idea of the Holy: An Inquiry into the Non-Rational Factor in the Idea of the Divine and its Relation to the Rational*. Oxford: Oxford University Press.

Palmié, Stephan 2002. *Wizards and Scientists: Explorations in Afro-Cuban Modernity and Tradition*. Durham, NC: Duke University Press.

Poovey, Mary 1998. *A History of the Modern Fact*. Chicago: University of Chicago Press.

Ricoeur, Paul 1984. *Time and Narrative. Volume 1*. Chicago: University of Chicago Press.

Smith, M. G. 1965. *The Plural Society in the West Indies*. Berkeley: University of California Press.

Tuzin, Donald F. 1976. *The Ilahita Arapesh: Dimensions of Unity*. Berkeley: University of California Press.

Tuzin, Donald F. 1977. Reflections of Being in Arapesh Water Symbolism. *Ethos* 5:195–223.

Tuzin, Donald F. 1980. *The Voice of the Tambaran: Truth and Illusion in Ilahita Arapesh Religion*. Berkeley: University of California Press.

Tuzin, Donald F. 1984. Miraculous Voices: The Auditory Experience of Numinous Objects. *Current Anthropology* 25:579–89, 593–6.

Tuzin, Donald F. 1995. Art and the Procreative Illusion in the Sepik: Comparing the Abelam and the Arapesh. *Oceania* 65:289–303.

Tuzin, Donald F. 1997. *The Cassowary's Revenge: The Life and Death of Masculinity in a New Guinea Society*. Chicago: University of Chicago Press.

6. Comparison, Individualism and 'Interactionalism' in the Work of Donald F. Tuzin

Don Gardner

Introduction

Don Tuzin left a magnificent corpus of work on the Ilahita Arapesh, one that presents a compelling analysis of two remarkable transitions in the history of a people. His work is also striking because of the sheer range of issues on which he focused his fine analytical eye; his work might focus on the emotions, dispositions and moral conflicts of particular persons or categories thereof (specific elders, initiands, or Christians, men, women) as readily as on the structural or historically contingent circumstances within which agents must act, and which tend to produce grand historical transformations. There are also significant essays that complement both these analytical poles with a consideration of apparently general human susceptibilities to certain sorts of sensory experience and their relevance to religious life.[1] Finally, Tuzin was given to posing questions about the relevance of this sort of ethnographic analysis, of this sort of society, to broader comparative and theoretical matters in the social sciences. He usually did so in the course of an analysis of some aspect of Ilahita's social life, but sometimes he considered such questions specifically and explicitly; when he did so, he was liable to proclaim his allegiance to 'methodological individualism'. Such statements of position have struck even some of his closest admirers as dated or doctrinaire relative to the discipline's orthodox orientation and given the actual breadth of his analytical vision.

---

1   Thus, the religious imaginings of Ilahita's prophet, Samuel (a 'rather extraordinary individual' [Tuzin 1989:187]), and the political significance of the contingencies of birth order in a given family (Tuzin 1991) are no less a part of the village's history than its extraordinarily involuted dual organisation; and the tenderness that marked intra-familial relations as well as the moral equivocation—in the context of the burden that the *Tambaran*'s productive demands placed upon women—these induced in senior men (Tuzin 1982) were as integral to Ilahita's political dynamics (Tuzin 1974) as was the competition between exchange partners (Tuzin 1976). On a different but wholly complementary tack, Tuzin also considered the work of pre-cultural experiences of certain sounds (1984), sights (2002) and smells (2006) in the construction of specifically Ilahitan cultural forms, which were thereby identified as cognate with specific forms found elsewhere. Similarly, certain Ilahita experiences, and the institutions that they thematise, bespeak the psycho-social qualities of human relationships as such, and, therefore, the comparability of culturally prepotent institutions from widely dispersed settings (Tuzin 2001).

I will here consider his methodological commitments in the light, first, of his analysis of Ilahita culture and history (which I will suggest changed slightly over time) and, second, in relation to what we should make of this doctrine today and its bearing on our assessment of the work Don left.

I shall take it as uncontroversial that Tuzin saw his four books and numerous articles as dealing with interlinked dimensions of his project to portray the history of Ilahita and the lives of Ilahitans. I shall also take it for granted that Tuzin saw his analytical practice and his theoretical or meta-theoretical orientations as, at the very least, mutually consistent. Accordingly, I will probe Tuzin's methodological commitment—avowed in his first and his last books—to the principles of Popperian methodological individualism (hereinafter MI), in relation to the consistency of his analytical vision. I believe it was his sense of the complexity of the total human person in a definite historical setting, rather than any *methodological* primacy of 'the individual' as such, that drove and rationalises his analytical work. I will try to suggest that his strongest convictions concerned the depth of the connections at work in what he termed the culture–society–individual nexus and, therefore, the interest and legitimacy of a very broad range of questions that anthropology might pose of human life, in general or in particular. Yet it was important to him that his views be both morally and theoretically defensible, which is what drew him to Popperian MI, with its twin emphasis on science and liberal values.

Any discussion of MI today has to take account of more recent refinements in the discussion of the *knot of issues* that it involves. The Popperian terms in which Don made his methodological claims implicate some daunting conceptual and metaphysical issues; they also rather too easily evoke moral-political sensibilities associated with terms such as 'choice', 'reduction' and 'determinism'. The sort of ecumenical project that Tuzin's corpus represents can now be conceived in ways that he himself did not consider, and which have the virtue of avoiding certain conceptual difficulties while—in principle, anyway—not provoking anyone to mount the theoretical barricades. In short, recent considerations of the ontology of social states and processes suggest that some clarity on the vexed issues that Don felt the need to address can be achieved. I will introduce one effort to make a place for both traditional holist and traditional individualist intuitions: Philip Pettit's is one example of an attempt to differentiate questions of methodology and ontology in a way that can connect with the empirical practices of social scientists while isolating those moral-political convictions to their proper domain. With the waning of the hegemony of deductive models of explanation, and a more nuanced consideration of the ontology of social life (the sorts of dependencies it involves), old accusations of 'reductionism' lose their sting; once we make the right sort of conceptual space for psychological and the sociological questions, the narrowness of the opposition between 'the individual' and 'society'—which has exercised more influence than any other intellectual construct since Durkheim—becomes apparent.

A Complex Science

The historical and social sciences have always been concerned with the entire range of features relevant to human life: with persons, nations, and states, with personal situations and cultural specificities, and with the idiosyncratic and the utterly general characteristics of human sociality across time and space. Tuzin's work as a whole evinces a commitment to the idea that a similarly wide range of factors, of different degrees of generality, is relevant to the comprehensive, single-case study he undertook. This is for the most part implicit in his different books and articles on Ilahita, but it is sometimes stated plainly, as when in 'Miraculous Voices' he indicates his debt to a vision:

> [One] advocated in various contexts by, among others, Freeman (1983), La Barre (1980), and Spiro (1978). Skeptical of the deterministic cant of much social-science discourse these scholars hold that human behavior is constitutive of a cultural, psychological, and biological wholeness; that human experience, in its immediacy, is profoundly oblivious of the internal partitions that gerrymandering theorists impose on it; and that the idea of the 'psychic unity' of our species should be treated neither as an empty slogan nor as a brief for the judicious neglect of biological factors in the study of culture, but as a challenge to engage the unsolved problems of the human condition in its most universal expressions. Both humane and humanistic, theirs is an anthropology of great moral and scientific importance. (Tuzin 1984:580)

An anthropology 'both humane and humanistic...of great moral and scientific importance' seems to summarise aptly the deep ambition thematising Tuzin's vision. He later explains that such an anthropology—one principled enough to follow an empirical problem wherever it might lead—would have to involve an 'interactionalist' paradigm, in which information from disciplines concerned with different aspects of 'the human condition' are brought together (Tuzin 1984:589). Here, and elsewhere, it is clear that Tuzin differs from those who see the human condition as defined by some key feature; his outlook on the human condition is sensitive to many local and universal factors, which is why its study must depend upon the synthesis produced by research perspectives in interaction. It might seem, though, that this rather pointedly raises doubts about Tuzin's uncompromising insistence on Popperian MI.

I will begin what I intend to be a sympathetic reading of Tuzin's position by setting out some social-science commonplaces concerning persons and the societies that encompass them. Doing so will help my case, which suggests that we now (perhaps, with the waning of logical positivism, and its hostility to metaphysical notions) have better resources for characterising the complexities that prompted the old divisions than formerly.

If we consider in a Searlean manner (Searle 1995, 2010) the enormously heterogeneous range of states that a human being might be in (being pregnant or undernourished, for example, contrasts in important ways with being the local bank manager, under indictment for a crime or in debt to your maternal kin), we can see how they depend upon rather different sorts of worldly conditions. Similarly, if one contemplates the range of events or processes a person might be engaged in (eating a grape versus blessing clan sacra or studying for a driving test) or undergoing (fighting a fever versus undergoing initiation or defending a thesis) then coordinate differences become obvious. Again, if one thinks about the state, event and process terms that could be predicated of the last person left on Earth, it seems clear that some would and some would not have a use (being injured or afraid or near the beach versus under arrest or close to becoming the vice-chancellor or a ranking elder). And under that terrible condition, the suite of values, reasons and ambitions (to name just one species of motivation) that a person might have and act upon would be dramatically transformed (in logic, if not—given the historicity of human being—in psychological fact). What these considerations seem to show is not just that many of our most definitive characteristics are relational (which is true of many of the non-social predicates applying to individuals), but that the relations involve persons and their relations with other persons and institutions. (It is worth mentioning that this is also true of the social properties of physical objects; what makes a suit a police uniform, for example, has nothing to do with the intrinsic properties of the material from which it is made. This is even more clearly the case with money.)

Less dramatically, but no less clearly, while any one of us was born at the same moment as legions of other mammals (think of all those rodents), and in the same part of the world as some of them, we acquired immediately a set of identities (for they are usually packaged together) that has no counterpart to the events and conditions we might use to individuate members of those other species; we are identified relationally (by our parents and their families, our clan, our initiation class or nation-state, our legal status, and so on), even while we cannot identify *with* those identities. And the significance—constitutive and causal— of those identities, not only to what I am at that point in time, but also to the sort of being I can become, is obvious once one takes thought. The facticity of these features of ourselves is shown, among other things, by the impossibility of discounting their relevance to us, whether or not we identify with particular identities (*pace* claims about the 'performative' nature of social identities). Repudiating those identities, which in any case is possible only later in life, if at all, is no less testimony to their facticity than embracing them with pride. And if one thinks about the institutionalised settings of much of contemporary life (in which one may need to be concerned with—among many other things—whether one is or is not a citizen of the state, a registered resident of a town, an enrolled student or voter, a discharged bankrupt, a licensed driver or dog-owner, a member of the union or the gym, the legal owner of what one is consuming or using, the bearer of legal tender or counterfeit notes, or even an authorised passenger on the train), then it can seem that a great many of the things we care about involve states, events and processes that have no counterpart in the sad life of the last person on Earth. Finally, if we scrutinise the minutiae of our interactions with others, we see other significant factors—Goffmannian, we might call them—that have complex dependencies upon conventions, rules and practices that also enjoy a facticity with respect to ourselves, yet inflect our own actual and potential experiences, by defining the interpersonal setting in which we each find ourselves, and, hence, the sense of self we can sustain. Particular individuals are rarely in the position to control the definition of a social setting or the exact quality of its interactions and their outcomes.

If we change our focus now and consider somewhat broader states of affairs and processes, it seems we can make connected distinctions: indexes of economic inequality are higher now in the West than a few years ago, as are levels of carbon dioxide in the atmosphere; the world is, apparently, currently undergoing a change in climate, but it is also undergoing an economic crisis; the universe is expanding, but so are average household debt and unemployment. Corporations, classes and clans are subject to the vicissitudes of worldly happenings no less than moons, mountains and molehills. Nation-states and Melpa clans go into debt, declare war and join organisations of one sort or another. Connected with these and other events and processes, values, beliefs and desires undergo epidemiological processes that leave individuals and collectivities changed, sometimes decisively.

Questions—essentially *ethnographic* questions—about what is going on, and why, can arise about any of the features of social life indicated above; accordingly, an alternative way of making the point here would be to follow Geertz's (1973:7–9) discussion of his frequently cited 'note in a bottle', which he took to indicate the range and heterogeneity of the information relevant to the 'thickening' of the ethnographic story of the Moroccan trader's misadventures (including Cohen's history and personal characteristics, North African Jewish customs, Berber social organisation, *mezrag* pacts between Sheiks and traders, and French colonial history). We should also keep our eyes open to what might be thought of as the complement to Geertz's point, which is that we could invoke Cohen's particular circumstances to explain why, when the French were in charge and safely ensconced in their forts, the *mezrag* pact was still relevant to social events. If, generalising from these particularities, we think through how the different questions requiring ethnographic answers interconnect, then we can see (along with thinkers as different as Durkheim, Weber and Wittgenstein) how ethnography's significance outruns its role in providing purely local understandings. We account, for example, for a woman's self-sacrifice by reference to her determination to save her group's reputation, which she could not achieve in any other way, and to the value of the honour of one's natal group to someone *produced* by that way of life, which is sometimes sufficient to trump the value of life itself. And if someone contemplating the woman's actions cannot see how such values *can* play so central a role in anyone's life, then more exposure to the thick descriptions that good ethnography provides is all we can recommend. Similarly, someone who cannot see how anyone *could* labour fiendishly to amass valuables to give to a rival, rather than enjoy them himself, is suffering a very particular blindness. As Geertz always stressed, the questions ethnography addresses in small settings are not thereby small questions, and—as he also stressed—such an interlocutor's failure to comprehend is most importantly in *self*-understanding.

What has been said so far underlines the complex dependencies that enmesh particular lives and their cultural contexts (and while I have invoked Geertz to help make the point, I could just as easily have cited Sahlins' work on historical change and continuity in Oceania). Ethnographically, descriptions need to be thick and omnidirectional if they are to play a role in answering questions about events on different scales. Social-science theorists' ambitions tend, however, to outrun intuitions concerning interconnections between the various orders of facts that ethnography and historiography describe. Theorists of social life working under very different conceptions of what adequacy amounts to have agreed that some verdict must be reached about the fundamental direction in which genuinely *explanatory* dependencies run.

Tuzin also felt the need to enter the lists on these matters, and he did so with some passion. I will argue that more recent reflection on them indicates that different aspects of Tuzin's project need to be evaluated separately—in particular, his interests in an interactionalist approach to social life and his concern with comparison are not particularly well defended by his MI; indeed, they are more defensible once his Popper-inspired methodological dicta are set aside.

The Account of Ilahita and Methodological Individualism

The Earlier Works

Tuzin gives his only reasonably extended account of what it means to adopt MI in the course of the introductory chapter of his first book, *The Ilahita Arapesh*, where he also defends what might seem to be 'the arrant parochiality' of asking what made the village become so extraordinarily large and what enabled it to maintain its unity (1976:xxi).

In this first volume, the focus is the complex dual organisation of Ilahita village, which Tuzin sees as a structural accommodation to the difficulties—in particular, the population pressures—caused by refugees displaced by the Abelam expansion (see Roscoe, this volume). The book argues that the elaborate organisation that resulted is traceable to, and is maintained by, the cumulative effects of individual actions of interconnected, culturally similar agents responding to the circumstances they face. The complex, crosscutting structures of dual classes are detailed and their effects in binding together the various segments of this large population demonstrated by the rich ethnographic material Tuzin commanded and used expertly. He left for his second volume almost all ritual aspects of these structures, but their importance was a constant background theme in the first.

Tuzin presents a historical picture in which a local system, made up of a social order—with its own 'inherent dynamic' that 'tends to homeostasis'—is integrated into a more or less constant environmental setting to produce something approximating equilibrium. Wider historical forces necessitated adjustments in the narrower social process since they presented problems that the prior homeostatic system was not required to face (Tuzin 1976:xxii–xxiv). The most pressing of these problems relates to Ilahita's adaptive increase in size, which nullified the possibility of 'remedial changes of residence' that the previously more fluid settlement patterns permitted; 'the various problems chronically infecting relations of proximity, kinship and political rivalry' (which his own ethnographic data document) were not only harder to resolve in the new Ilahita, they increased (Tuzin 1976:xxiv). Accordingly, the need to 'manage' the difficulties and resolve the tensions was great; the response was 'the elaboration of regulatory, integrative mechanisms'. Of particular significance was the evolution of the intricate web of complementary identities that constituted Ilahita's highly complex dual organisation, which was '[r]eplete with cohesive functions' (Tuzin 1976:xxiv–v).

It is at this point—where, so to speak, management needs, responses and functions have been rather equivocally invoked—that Tuzin sees 'yet another processual mode' as being implied, one wherein the components of the dual organisation are created and re-created 'from the lower levels' of quotidian existence in the expanded community. The dual organisation's many components depend upon this input from 'mundane behavioral spheres', in their initial development and for their reproduction; and, it is important to stress, his account 'predicates the rarefied dual structures on the motivations of individuals operating within a changing socio-cultural setting' (Tuzin 1976:xxv). So the 'management' he speaks of is not, or not only, to be interpreted as a metaphor for the feedback connections within the system, but as something the need for which confronts particular people through the problems some of their interpersonal relations now represent. As a result of the expansionary pressures of southern groups, Arapesh people faced difficulties in their lives—the arrival of refugees, the threat of raids, difficulties with subsistence, and so on—to which they had to respond. Their responses, grounded in their pre-existing values and beliefs, were what, over time, crystallised into the complex structures that had mystified regional specialists such as Anthony Forge, who advised Tuzin to conduct research in Ilahita.

Notice that Tuzin has used both psychological motivations and social functions in explaining Ilahita's adaptive responses; the ancestors of contemporary Ilahitans responded to novel demands on their existing relationships with one another by using cultural items to hand (conspicuous among which was the regionally characteristic practice of defining social categories in terms of a dual organisation [Tuzin 1976:xxv]) to deal with the new social setting. In so doing, new conceptions of relatedness and shared identity emerged that proved adequate to the new social setting. It is at this point—early in setting out his thesis about Ilahita's growth—that Tuzin refers to Lévi-Strauss for the first time. He does so only to stress that he will later argue against the structuralist accounts of dual organisation, foreshadowing that his views and those of Lévi-Strauss 'embody fundamentally distinct philosophical orientations, intellectual stances whose relevance extends far beyond theories of dualism per se to demarcate alternative perspectives on culture, society and the individual' (Tuzin 1976:xxv). And it is here, having referred to the three elements whose relationships constitute the 'central problem of anthropology' (Tuzin 1976:338), that he tells us that his analysis of Ilahita dual organisation 'will be guided in large measure by the principle of methodological individualism' (p. xxv)—a notion he then discusses in rather definite terms.

The most important point—'the heart of the principle' (Tuzin 1976:xxvii)—is that social structure arises out of what Tuzin, quoting Popper, characterises as the '"indirect, the unintended and often unwanted by-products" of decisions and actions', which agents take 'according to the logic of their situation'; actions taken by individuals are represented in MI as the source of both social stasis and social change (p. xxvi). The rationale, he seems to suggest, is importantly given by its negation, methodological collectivism or holism, which, 'in its pure form', portrays individuals as 'a reifying fiction, a walking bundle of social rules, statuses, values and similar abstractions' (Tuzin 1976:xxvi). The individuals invoked by MI are not particular historical persons, but anonymous agents, each of whom is also 'presumed to be a competent member of a society, steeped in [its] norms and values', not the mythical pre-social individual postulated by reductionist nineteenth-century theorists (Tuzin 1976:xxvii). Nevertheless, the norms and values possessed by those competent members of society themselves 'originate in, and are actualized through, the interactions of individuals, and, therefore, cannot logically precede these interactions' (Tuzin 1976:xxvii). Tuzin later makes the point that the individuals invoked by MI might indeed possess 'holistic concepts', but these are to be treated as *data* by the analyst (1976:335)—as part of what is to be explained, rather than what provides explanatory resources. Although MI holds that the social structural effects of actions are unintended and unforeseen by individuals, even when they are consciously planning to affect social structure, it does not exclude 'rationality or premeditation' (Tuzin 1976:xxvii). On the contrary, our actions are indeed 'governed by relatively immediate considerations…we apply to any given situation a calculus, not only of social prescriptions and values, but also of personal strategies, psychological proclivities and other factors which are, in principle, determinable' (Tuzin 1976:xxviii). Once these individual-level processes have been analytically identified, it is possible to link them to societal consequences. Here Tuzin makes a reference to Adam Smith and his principle of individual expediency as the basis for economic institutions (although he does not explicitly invoke the 'invisible hand').

The strength of MI, Tuzin continues, is that it sets on centrestage the individual—an 'empirically isolable unit of observation'—that is also a 'conceptual link' between the psychological and the sociological sciences and 'our guide through many of man's domains' (Tuzin 1976:xxiv). Accordingly, MI expects (indeed, it 'celebrates') variation between individuals and sees 'change as an *inherent property* of human groups' (Tuzin 1976:xxix, emphasis in original). In the context of his account of Ilahita and its increase in size and structural complexity, this methodological orientation entails the study of the factors impacting upon the population of individuals and their interactions, given both what they share culturally—the concepts, norms and values— and how they differ (with respect to their situations and inclinations). It also involves tracking how, under historically new, challenging conditions, what he calls the 'actional field' becomes constituted by this configuration of responses. More generally, Tuzin continues, 'by *deducing* the "unintended" repercussions of this actional field' (emphasis added), we come to understand what Watkins called the 'organic-like' feature of social systems, wherein a collection of people whose actions affect one another 'mutually adjust themselves to the situations created by the others in a way which, without direction from above, conduces to the equilibrium or preservation or development of the system' (1976:xxix–xxx, quoting Watkins 1957:114). Tuzin then takes Watkins' final formulation for his own purposes: 'In the present study, the system whose equilibrium, preservation and development we are seeking to explain is the social entity of Ilahita village' (1976:xxx).

If Tuzin is emphatic about MI's virtues, so too is his case for viewing Lévi-Straussian commitments as empirically inadequate to a comprehensive anthropology: structuralism indulges itself with 'other concerns, such as the imponderables of metaphysics and unreconstructable history…the elusive objects of pleasurable speculation' (Tuzin 1976:338–9). Yet the book is overwhelmingly concerned with a complex and convincing empirical analysis of Ilahita's social organisation; rereading it and the second volume (Tuzin 1980), and reading back over some of his earlier papers, makes it clear how *theoretically* wide ranging Tuzin was; and, despite occasional polemical flourishes and firm statements, he rarely seems doctrinaire. I believe that even at this early stage, the real attraction of MI for Tuzin was that it provided the sort of meta-theoretical orientation that could rationalise the distaste he felt for 'gerrymandering' theory. It also provided a context for a perspective on cultural order as 'processual' in nature and in complex two-way dependencies with the actions taken by individuals and, hence, with their psycho-dynamic characteristics; all this he took to be demanded by the unusual empirical situation Ilahita presented. His works repeatedly return to the 'fit' between processes of cultural reproduction and the behaviours generated by the existential conditions of individuals' lives. Strikingly, he insists that the scepticism, deception and playfulness that life can induce, as well as the moral tensions generated by routine interaction, are as necessary to particular institutional processes as are the cultural norms and values that channel them. All of these particular factors and their interactions are discussed in terms that are highly sensitive to the general historical conditions of cultural contexts and persons. Such a concern with the mutual conditioning of factors usually thought of as at different levels, and the sensitivity of historical outcomes to the subtlety of that conditioning, evokes something like a Weberian perspective on 'the relationship between culture, society and the individual', as I shall underline later. Be that as it may, Tuzin insisted from his earliest works that the conspicuous elaboration of ritual and social form in Ilahita is to be grasped as a *process*, initiated and then sustained by historical circumstances, not simply a *product* of the passage of time or an abstract endogenous force: 'the elaboration *and* maintenance of [the dual] organization is traceable to the cumulative effects of individual actions conditioned by the press of broadly shared circumstances amid the constraints of equally shared cultural understandings' (Tuzin 1980:335, emphasis added). I submit that the historical contingency of social processes became analytically more central over the period between his first and his last books.

Social Complexity in the Making

With his later work, *Social Complexity in the Making* (2001), Tuzin sought to reposition his ethnographic findings from Ilahita in relation 'both to general issues of social evolution and, more specifically, to the major transitions undergone by Ilahita that have also occurred in many other times and places in world history' (p. xii). He begins, though, with another critique of the discipline's usual orientations. The overreaction of anthropology to nineteenth-century evolutionism led to the exclusion of history, and *a fortiori* evolutionary history, from the analysis of social forms, in favour of synchronic descriptions and a fundamentally typological approach to comparison (Tuzin 2001:2–3). Accordingly, anthropology overlooked 'one of society's most prominent features: incessant change in adaptive response to internal and external contingencies' (Tuzin 2001:4). He adds that it is only when we see this, and take it into analytical account, that we can understand 'social dynamics in the here and now' as well as how 'historical circumstances selectively affect social systems' (Tuzin 2001).

On Tuzin's account, the search for ways to understand social transformations was (luckily) carried on by archaeology, but its models tended to be unconvincingly materialistic and/or typological. One might have expected ethnographers to offer suggestions that would overcome these problems, but, because of anthropology's own history, few practitioners are ready to think about the functional relationship between how population size and societal complexity articulate with 'questions of causality, cognition, agency, and intentionality' (Tuzin 2001:6) to produce historical change significant on a societal scale: evolutionary change. Tuzin argues that material and typological models will remain inadequate as long as they are uninformed by more subtle understandings of the processes through which ideological and social factors are integrated with the material, in mechanisms driving changes in social morphology. Such changes, whether they occur in a 'forward, backward or sideways' direction, always occur in a concrete 'adaptational matrix bounded by space, time and population' (Tuzin 2001:9). He draws a parallel here with organic evolutionary theory, which became convincing only once Darwin provided a framework ('descent with modification by natural selection') that directed attention to the dynamic mechanisms of change (Tuzin 2001:7). Real social evolutionary inquiry seeks to understand 'processes of change and the emergence of novelty within sociocultural systems' (Tuzin 2001:8).

Tuzin's analysis of 'the evolving society of Ilahita village and the external events and internal mechanisms implicated in its increasing size and complexity' (2001:10) aims to underscore the poverty of typological approaches that lack models of the dynamic mechanisms involved. It sought to show: a) the adaptive nature of organisational complexity based on ritual institutions structured by dualistic principles; while also elucidating b) 'the rather severe limits to settlement growth and organizational complexity facing societies of Ilahita's type' (Tuzin 2001:10). If he speaks of 'types' here—the very term he has worried about earlier—it is because he believes his study will indicate general patterns in 'the movement of simpler, small-scale societies to more complex, large-scale societies' (Tuzin 2001:124). To that extent, analysis of societal dynamics generates its own, *causally* relevant types (Tuzin 2001:9), while making room for 'unique communal biograph[ies]' (p. 124).

The book once more tells (with some significant differences in emphasis) how nineteenth-century population changes connected with warfare and migration posed an urgent question to the traditional socio-cultural forms in one part of the Sepik region shared by Arapesh, Kwanga and Abelam populations. Ilahita's Arapesh population suddenly faced an influx of refugees from these other groups. The answer to the question could not come from Ilahita's 'subsistence base or technology' (Tuzin 2001:17), but was found in the elaboration of a new form of the regional 'cult of war and human sacrifice', produced by the iteration of dualistic ritual categories and resulting in 'the most complex system of its type ever documented', with eight crosscutting dual categories (and, therefore, 256 distinct ritual-categorical identities). He stresses, though, that '[f]rom top to bottom, the dual organisation is cast in ritual terms'; furthermore, because it also embraces kin relations, economic activities (production for exchange and for consumption) and political competition and conflict (between descent and residential groupings), even the most 'practical' actions are seen by Ilahitans to be mandated by the *Tambaran* cult and 'suffused with spiritual meaning' (Tuzin 2001:83).

Tuzin emphatically concluded (in rather Weberian tones) that the *Tambaran* cult in Ilahita amounted to 'the emergence of *a rationalised religious ethic*—a body of doctrine against which behaviour could be compared, evaluated, and, if necessary, punished...[and], moreover, which summarized and transcended the level of individual clan spirits' (2001:103, emphasis in original). It featured a unique, 'transcendent' spiritual patron for the village as a whole, one that 'allied itself with the elders of the cult' (Tuzin 2001:103). These elders—men spread across the village's components—were (also uniquely, in the cults of the region) united by a special grade and charged with making the most of the politically significant interventions, which they made in their own and the village's interests and with the full moral weight of the *Tambaran*, whose power was at their disposal. But the cult and its divisions also provided an arena for the competition and conflict generated by the rather pervasive intra-village strife, so that even social discord acted to enfold the binding, dualistic structure into the quotidian emotions of residents. In turn, the dual structures and the ritual prescriptions they embodied were reinforced by the interpersonal and inter-group antagonism that life in this large village engendered (Tuzin 2001:119–20).

Let us now consider some of the new orientations in *Social Complexity in the Making*. In Tuzin's earlier work, the spirit if not the letter of structural-functionalist conceptions of 'system' were patent; his bifurcated view of the process leading up to Ilahita's increase in size and complexity (described earlier)—with a social system having an internal dynamic that tends to homeostasis moving through an historical ambience that can usually (but not always) be counted upon to remain stable—evokes much of late structural-functionalist thought, which had still not entirely relinquished its attachment to the organismic analogy. Tuzin stressed both 'the equilibrium, preservation and development' of the 'organic-like' social systems and their susceptibility to being sustained or transformed by individuals' actions, even while these are themselves 'conditioned' by cultural understandings (which tend to be shared, of course). In the later works, though, the conditioning and the effects of individual actions implicate circumstances broader than those specific to the social system, which nevertheless tends to remain the unintended—and perhaps rather fragile—outcome of decisions and actions taken by individuals. The actors focus on the *Tambaran* and 'miss' the systemic connections that its power in their lives presupposed; 'the [actors] look after the details and the system looks after itself' (Tuzin 2001:83), but the process is 'non-teleological'. The 'logic of the situation' of the actors, given the circumstances and other factors 'accidental to the structure of the overall system', suffices to bring about the evolutionary transformation of Ilahita; but it was 'an emergent property of experience: the actions, perceptions, and ideas of individuals in a collective, temporal setting' (Tuzin 2001:84).

By 2001, then, society's tendency to 'incessant change' is stressed (Tuzin 2001:4), although Tuzin still cites Radcliffe-Brown on the evolution of systems as though the process were endogenously driven, and still sometimes evokes 1960s theoretical divisions.[2] Yet, he also writes of the need to appreciate the role of 'the mechanisms at work in *the adaptational matrix bounded by space, time and population*; for it is only through those mechanisms that societies move' (Tuzin 2001:9, emphasis added). And while, in the next paragraph, he will

---

2   Thus, for example, 'while the dual organization gives the Tambaran structural coherence and social effectiveness, the Tambaran infuses the dual organization with cultural meaning' (Tuzin 2001:14), which, for me, very strongly calls to mind the function/meaning duality that thematised the notion of a cultural system for Geertz during the 1960s.

again use terms that suggest a dichotomy between internal social mechanisms and external processes, the particularities of historical processes themselves, which are as responsible for the reproduction of social systems as for their transformation, and which are 'always already' open (and can be closed only as an analytical strategy), are more securely established as the focus of his concern with how cultural systems change. Tuzin, it seems to me, is by 2001 fairly clearly thinking about social life and change in terms of contingent, open systems, the elements of which are in interaction with one another; local cultural traditions, human psychological capacities and the broader environment of the concrete population (broadly construed, to include the socio-political as well as the physical ecology) are all aspects of the systematicity, or otherwise, of social life.[3]

I do not want to be dogmatic about the depth or extent of the transformation in Tuzin's views, but I do think he defined more precisely what an anthropology grounded in the 'cultural, psychological and biological wholeness' of human behaviour would involve. And this happened, I think, as he discussed with himself and his colleagues (and, at UCSD, he was well located for such discussions; see Lipset and Roscoe, this volume) the articulation of cultural, sociological and psychological perspectives in accounting for specific ways of life. He also came to appreciate how the works of such psychologists as Nicholas Humphrey and Elisabeth Spelke, and those of such adventurous, synthesising anthropologists as Dan Sperber and Pascal Boyer, related to his own (Tuzin 2002).

In 1984, Tuzin had already had to defend himself against some rather crude charges that his argument about the role of the experience of certain auditory properties in religious practices was 'reductionist', and he had accepted and elaborated upon Michael Young's suggestion, in the latter's commentary on that essay, that it sought to argue from 'culture to nature to brain/mind and back again' (Young 1984:594). By 2002, Tuzin was happy to risk 'anti-reductionist rage' (2002:10) in considering the cognitive basis of intuitive expectations relevant to the experience of art in ritually prepotent contexts. I have nothing but his texts to go on, but I think that when, through the late 1980s and 1990s, his pursuit of his interactionalist paradigm led him into the burgeoning literatures in developmental psychology and cognitive science, he came to reconceptualise not just how the cultural, psychological and biological were interrelated but how each realm was itself constituted. It seems that he came to share the sense of incredulity at mainstream anthropology's lack of interest in widely dispersed or universal psychological characteristics that, for example, Sperber had expressed in many forms, and which Boyer addressed at length in relation to religion in his 1994 work (published, perhaps significantly, by University of California Press).

---

3   Although I will not deal with his account of the demise of the *Tambaran* cult (Tuzin 1997) and the fracturing of Ilahita's unity, I think these events, which were contingent on the effects of colonial forces within Ilahita's social fields, acted to confirm Tuzin in his perspective.

Perhaps he was also persuaded to consider these theorists' epidemiological, processual perspectives on culture, which tend to undermine the very notion of social life as a systems-theoretic phenomenon. While, I admit, this line is somewhat speculative, *Social Complexity in the Making* presents formulations of Ilahita's past that contrast with his earlier accounts, and it does so in ways that suggest that Tuzin had been influenced by models of social process that involve selection on populations of variants over time. While this is not fundamentally at odds with his earlier perspectives, the analytical space that he had previously assigned to social systems at equilibrium, and to structural explanation, would seem to have diminished. Nevertheless, the continuities over the 25-year span are very striking. He still, for example, conspicuously invokes Popper and his non-Hobbesian individualism, so I now broaden the discussion in an effort to show that Tuzin's analytical commitments are not best supported by such invocations.

Individuals, Individualism and Processes

In this section, I will try to detach Tuzin's interactionalist practice from his avowed attachment to Popperian MI. I will briefly discuss Popper's views and those of his most influential followers, such as Watkins and Agassi, mostly to suggest that these never amounted to a coherent position. I will then suggest, even more briefly, that Tuzin's analytical ambitions could fruitfully be compared with those of Max Weber, as could, perhaps, the spirit of his defence of MI and Weber's views on the matter. Finally, I will say something about more recent attempts to set the relations between ontological and methodological considerations on a more precise footing, which, for many scholars, have resulted in a more reasonable picture of the import of the distinction between holists and individualists.

Popper's Agenda and Tuzin's Analysis

Recall that for Tuzin the relationship between culture, society and the individual constitutes the central problem for anthropology; on the face of it, this statement implies the existence of all three sorts of entity whose relationship is at issue. What in facing the matter of their integration led Tuzin to align himself with the views of Popper, Watkins and Agassi? First, unlike other approaches that proclaim their methodological individualism, Popper's MI usually insisted on the autonomy and facticity of the social (institutions, norms, and so on) no less than the agency of subjects. Popper applauded Marx for having shown, against John Stuart Mill, that the social sciences must be autonomous of the psychological sciences, since the actions of individuals could not be explained without reference to institutions (Popper 2003:100), which 'set limits or create obstacles to our movements and actions almost as if they were physical bodies or obstacles'; indeed, they 'are experienced by us as almost literally forming part of the furniture of our habitat' (Popper 1994:167). Tuzin emphasises Popper's rejection of atomistic individualism of the sort associated with Hobbes and repeatedly endorses the connected Popperian view about the crucial role of the unintended consequences of actions in human social history. Popper came to stress more and more the role of institutions and the responsiveness of individuals to the 'logic' of their situation, to the point where he gave up the term 'methodological individualism' (Udehn 2001:206). In their attempts to defend the position, Watkins, Agassi and Jarvie responded in contrasting ways, bringing out some of the ambiguities of Popper's original formulations (Udehn 2001:211–24).

It is hard, I think, not to have some sympathy for those who felt bewildered by the divisions that Popper's intervention in social-science methodology precipitated. What the debates (and their cross-purposes) indicate is the instability of the positions the protagonists adopted. Ruben states bluntly that 'methodological individualism has never been stated with enough clarity and precision to permit its proper evaluation' (1985:132). In its Popperian version, MI presented reasonable arguments against those who postulated a *telos* to local or universal history; and while insisting that human agency (purposes, decisions, theories, intentions, and so on) was an irreducible element of social life and its trajectories, and therefore of the history of the physical world as well, it affirmed the facticity of institutions. This mixture of the repudiation of (pre)deterministic doctrines, an insistence on human freedom and the openness of historical outcomes (with their unavoidable but causally relevant unintended consequences) proved unstable. Popperian MI was historically significant just because it addressed major questions in the philosophy of science while simultaneously opposing anti-humanist conceptions of society and history. With hindsight, it is apparent that the deductive models of explanation (in either covering law or falsificationist form) prevalent at the time restricted ideas about causal relations and their role in social life. In addition, the association of such models with inter-theoretical reduction in science made it rather obvious that the unwillingness of Popper and his followers to contemplate reduction of human cognitive powers to non-cognitive processes—given their insistence that social events (for all the facticity of their outcomes) be reduced to the actions of their human participants—was motivated by humanist politics rather than methodological considerations. Of course, the instabilities of MI were no less apparent in the holist positions that opposed and complemented it (many of which were also inspired by humanist political sensibilities), which is perhaps why today there are prominent MI defenders of Marx and thriving anti-individualist currents in mainstream economics.

In concluding this cursory examination of Popperian MI and its tribulations, it is worth stressing that Tuzin's interest in this orientation stemmed from its empirical focus and its presumed capacity to *explain* both the reproduction of and the change in cultural forms, by providing an account of the social dynamics at any given time. Under all circumstances, social trajectories are inflected—but not set—by the decisions and actions taken by individuals in the face of the circumstances they confront.

Tuzin and Weber on Culture and History

This perspective was probably inspired by Tuzin's reading of Popper and Watkins, but it also seems close to the following: 'in sociological work... collectivities must be treated as solely the resultants and modes of organization of the particular acts of individual persons' (Weber 1978:13). Weber, though, will go on to warn that it is 'a tremendous misunderstanding' to think that a methodological focus on individuals has anything to do with individualistic political values, just as it is to think that a methodological interest in agents' reasons for acting indicates a 'belief in the predominance of rational motives, or even a positive valuation of rationalism' (1978:18). Weber's and Tuzin's views imply a demand for transparency in social explanation, and we have this only when we can relate social phenomena to how they are understood by the agents partaking of social phenomena. To take an utterly mundane example, what explains the shopkeeper's willingness to accept the pieces of paper I give her for a basket of good food is only elliptically explained when we refer to the laws or traditions of the place. What really explains what she does is her *observance* of the rules or traditions, or her *concern* about the law; the demand, then, is for the social facts *and* the 'subjective meanings' of individuals, for only then is the explanation complete (even though it is only rarely necessary to mention the obvious like this). Again, even if a decision or action is intimately tied to the individual's position—as a king, say—and motivated by the incumbent's knowledge of the cultural expectations attaching to it, it remains the individual's action, no less than when the king effects some historical coup only through a bold move that strategically violates those expectations.

The rationale for Weber's methodological focus on the individual is emphatically not, then, the political or ethical status of the human being, but the fact that it is the individual who takes action, and who is, therefore, the locus of an element that constitutes a central explanatory factor in many (but not all) of the circumstances of interest to the social scientist or historian. Weber's (1978:4) definition of sociology is predicated on this view. Action (that is, behaviour that is 'subjectively meaningful' to the agent), including, of course, *inter*action, is what makes for differences in the flow of social life, in cases when change is the historical outcome and when it is not. If we want *causal* understanding of the course of social life, and thereby the capacity to explain particular and general aspects of it, looking to people's actions is indispensable, Weber argues, no matter how routine the cultural context is for the agents. To the extent that it is action that is causally important, then it is somewhat misleading to think of Weber's methodology as stressing the individual *rather than* the collectivity, as Heath (2008) also points out (see also Ringer 1997:Ch. 4, 2002).

Two further points should be made here (even if they cannot be fully defended): first, the interpretation of subjective states relevant to action does not amount to a special kind of understanding, although it is a special kind of causal understanding; for Weber, we might say, there is no gap between identifying *why* somebody acted as she did, the subjective meaning the action had, and *what* action she performed. Second, the central role that Popper (and other methodological individualists, in economics as well as other social sciences) assigns to institutions ('rules of the road, police regulations, traffic signals… language, markets, prices, contracts and courts of justice' [Popper 1994:166–7]) is also a crucial dimension of this Weberian scheme, where they feature as an aspect of the action itself (defined relative to its subjective meaning, as when I obey the traffic rules in stopping at the red light—or break them in an act of defiance) or an aspect of the outcomes the action causes (the anger of other motorists or the fine that results when I do not obey the lights) or, more usually, both. Together, these two points suffice to indicate something I shall return to below—that the Weberian picture set out so far does not amount to a *psychological* individualism of the sort Mill held (and Homans endorsed [1982:287]), which asserts that the

> laws of the phenomena of society are, and can be, nothing but the laws
> of the actions and passions of human beings united together in the social
> state. Men, however, in a state of society, are still men; their actions and
> passions are obedient to the laws of individual human nature. Men are
> not, when brought together, converted into another kind of substance,
> with different properties; as hydrogen and oxygen are different from
> water. (Mill 1882:608)

For Weber, in contrast, it is clear that the historical and cultural context of an action is central to its very identity and therefore to its causal significance (as well as to the sorts of 'human nature' one will encounter in agents). If one were inclined, one could here invoke Geertz's (1973) account (by his own testimony, Weberian) of how our minds' properties (our 'moods and motivations' as well as our conceptions of the 'general order of existence') radically depend upon the historical state of the 'web of cultural meanings' we inherit, but it will be safer, given Geertz's mercurial shifts in perspective, to stick to Weber's original accounts. The point is merely to stress that there is nothing in Weber that suggests that what we need in understanding the subjective states relevant to *socially* significant actions should be looked for in the theories and findings of (sub-personal) psychology.

The reason for this (and for the complexity of Weber's analytical schemes, even taking account of his use of ideal types) is that action is constituted by the subjective meanings of the agent and these are highly conditioned by particular circumstances, so that social outcomes typically depend upon the minutiae of the setting. Sub-personal psychological and even biochemical factors are sometimes causally relevant to the development of the subjective meaning that constitutes an action, but the action itself has to be interpreted—indeed, defined—in relation to that meaning. On the other hand, there is nothing at all in Weber to encourage those who wish to see the return to centre stage of the inscrutable 'voluntarist' individual, the uncaused cause of micro and macro-social trajectories (the 'intolerably spoilt child' that the social sciences worked so hard to displace [Lévi-Strauss 1981:687]). The meanings in terms of which the subject acts, and therefore the actions taken that inflect to a greater or lesser extent the course of social(-historical) events, are themselves contingent on the social biographical circumstances (which, of course, implicate the institutions and social currents of the milieu).

Many of Tuzin's explicit statements about MI could be read as echoing portions of Weber's methodological writings, but a more telling convergence of perspective, as I have already claimed, is revealed by the profile of ethnographic studies Tuzin produced—in particular, the *variety* of factors he held to be relevant to the explanation of the growth of Ilahita, the maintenance of its social form and then its demise. Of particular significance is his insistence that we should focus on individuals, their particularities and their actions because of their *causal* significance for socio-historical processes as factors involved in the interaction between the historical traditions of Ilahita culture, the population and its environment (construed in the broadest terms). It seems, then, that for Tuzin (especially in his later work), as for Weber, societies are best conceived as processes. Less speculatively, for Tuzin, as for Weber, while society and its cultural forms are unintentionally produced and reproduced by acting individuals, their actions are irreducibly dependent upon the culture into which they are born. Cultural context, the individual meanings to which these are causally relevant (and which are partly constitutive of action) and the unintended consequences of agents' activities are equally indispensable to the social and historical disciplines.

Holist Individualism

If, as I have suggested, Weber could have provided Tuzin with better support for his interactionalist perspective than the brand of MI he drew upon, it remains to answer someone who might be preoccupied with the idea that, nevertheless, Popper provided the sort of philosophical or meta-theoretical perspective that Tuzin sought in opposing prevailing structuralist paradigms. Well, I think this worry can be addressed.

The debates about *methodological* individualism that took place through the 1950s and 1960s were deeply affected by the program of inter-theoretic reduction intimately associated with the deductive model of explanation, a paradigm of which was the reductive deduction of the gas laws from the kinetic theory. The difficulties of that program (which stemmed not only from the failure of attempts to generalise the paradigm just mentioned, but also from, for example, the complex and clearly non-deductive relations between domains within biology [Bechtel and Hamilton 2007]) also played an important part in changing the focus of debates about MI and, connectedly, in the development of a novel construal of the ontology of social life and its methodological implications. For, while awareness of the difficulties of the deductive picture of inter-theoretic reduction spread (along with broader concerns about empiricist and positivist models), it was nevertheless hard to abandon the conviction that there was indeed a fundamental relationship between mean kinetic energy of molecules and temperature, between the molecular gene and the gene of population genetics or, most notably (given the advent of cognitive science), the mind and the brain. These and other factors ensured that the search for micro-foundations for biological and cognitive phenomena remained important (Bechtel and Hamilton 2007; Bickle 2008; Oddie 2001). Accordingly, other, more subtle notions of the dependency between domains were explored and developed.

Discussions of such 'supervenience' relations and cognate notions pertaining to the metaphysics of identity have galvanised the philosophy of mind and the cognitive sciences since the 1970s (although it has also been important in ethics, aesthetics and the philosophy of science). The term 'supervenience' applies to the relations between properties in two domains, S and B, and is usually expressed by a slogan along the lines of 'changes in S-properties only if there are changes in B-properties'. So, properties relevant to one domain (the mental, say) supervene upon those of another (the neurophysiological, say) when the former can undergo no change that is not a change in the latter ('base' or 'subvening') domain. Thus, there can be no change of mental properties without a change of neurophysiological properties; it is important to note, however, that changes in base properties do not entail changes in the supervening ones.[4]

The impact of this notion stemmed from its introduction in the philosophy of mind, where it seemed to offer the possibility of a non-reductive account of the relations between the mental and the physical, while also defining an ecumenical space wherein the various particular disciplines ('the special sciences') could retain their autonomy. Moreover, each could do so without having to commit to any process or principle that might bring it into conflict with the fundamentals of the picture painted by physics. Accordingly, it was not long before scholars began thinking about the relations between the realms of the individual (or some more precise notion) and the socio-cultural in terms of supervenience, for it seemed to hold out 'the promise of prizing apart the methodological and ontological issues, enabling, for example, both the metaphysical strictures of the [ontological] individualist and the methodological dispositions of the holist to be accommodated' (Oddie 2001:12858). This was undoubtedly a liberating departure, for it facilitates a realisation that seeing individuals and social entities on a model of parts and wholes is metaphysically inadequate. Supervenience is, however, a modal notion; it says what is *necessary* and, therefore, what is *possible* (for the two terms are inter-definable); this means that it is susceptible to treatment within the technical apparatus of contemporary modal logic. Complexity is also guaranteed by the fact that different kinds of necessity/possibility can be at stake: 'necessity abounds', Fine observes (2005:235), in logic, mathematics, metaphysics and nature, and it is no easy matter to sort and classify 'this abundance'. A recent authoritative overview, for example, lists six categories of supervenience, each divided into two or four subcategories (McLaughlin and Bennett 2008). Rather than even think about introducing further discussion of supervenience, I will quickly describe one influential attempt to deploy the basic idea in thinking through the issues that preoccupied the Popperians, as well as Don Tuzin: Philip Pettit's *The Common Mind* (1993).

In this ambitious synthetic work, Pettit links political orders to social orders and the latter to human psychological characteristics, at the core of which are our powers as intentional, thinking subjects.[5] In place of the usual dichotomy between holism and individualism, Pettit considers the relations between

---

4 Equivalently, identity between two entities (objects, events, states) in their subvening properties entails their identity in supervening properties, but not vice versa.

5 On Pettit's view, developed in the first of the book's three sections, thinking subjects are a subset of intentional beings; an intentional being is one who has states (pre-eminently, wants or aims and 'beliefs'— cognitive, truth-evaluable states) appropriately connected to its environment and whose characteristics explain its behaviours, while thinking beings also have the capacity to make their first-order intentional states the subject of desires and complex sets of beliefs. Briefly, if you and your pet dog believe the snake that just reared up before you is dangerous, you, as a thinking subject, will, in contrast with your dog, believe that it is true that the snake is dangerous (you will argue the toss with those inclined to doubt it), hold that there is

the social and the psychological orders in terms of two distinctions: between individualism and collectivism and between atomism and holism. He argues that the conflation of these two distinctions has been encouraged by the mistaken idea that individual agents stand to the societies of which they are members as parts to wholes. He characterises the difference between the distinctions in terms of a spatial metaphor: individualists and collectivists differ on the significance of the *vertical* relations between regularities that obtain in domains of social life, while atomists and holists differ on the question of the *horizontal* relations between the essential features of agents and those of society:

> Individualists deny and collectivists maintain that the status ascribed to individual agents in our intentional psychology is compromised by aggregate social regularities. Atomists deny and holists maintain that individual agents non-causally depend on their social relations with one another for some of their distinctive features. (Pettit 1993:118)

Pettit spends a chapter on each distinction, arguing against the collectivist in one and against the atomist in the other; not only is our intentional psychology not compromised by aggregate social regularities, it is also necessary for them, while our intentional psychology—our status as thinking subjects—'is superveniently dependent' (1993:228) upon our being members of a linguistic community of socially interacting subjects. In sum, Pettit argues for holistic individualism, which preserves the insights of romantic and historicist philosophers, as well as major social-scientific theorists, while avoiding the postulation of ontologies that are hard to reconcile with those of other sciences. The separation of ontological and methodological issues central to the discussion of supervenience and associated notions offers metaphysical austerity and the plurality of autonomous sciences: biological, psychological and social phenomena are scaffolded by, but irreducible to, physically fundamental processes. As Pettit's work shows, this powerful vision is naturally extended to areas of social and political theory. And while important, connected questions about causal relations and the nature of explanation remain for the friends of supervenience (as they do for friends of other approaches), the program of non-reductive physicalism has certainly shown the confusions that attend the failure to distinguish between the *supervenience* of A properties on B properties, the *reduction* of A properties to B, and the *elimination* of A properties in favour of B properties. It is reasonable to expect that if these distinctions became more widely available in the social sciences, some of the anxieties (and sloganeering) about determinism and reductionism might become things of the past.

---

evidence to that effect in the circumstances (which you are prepared to point out to your doubting friend), wish, perhaps, that it were false that the snake was dangerous, and so on. His argument that being a thinking subject involves non-causal dependencies on social relations is crucial to the remainder of the book.

The sort of non-reductive individualism that Pettit sets out amounts to the replacement of the dualism between the social and the individual with a continuum between the macro-social through the meso-social to the micro-social, where we encounter particular persons. The most important implication is that persons are socio-historical beings, in fact and by metaphysical necessity. (To that extent, the continued use of an undifferentiated notion of the individual is to be avoided, for it too easily evokes those Hobbesian atoms that are projected as only contingently social beings.) So, on the arguments of Pettit and others (such as Currie 1984, 1988, 2001), persons are 'always already' social entities, for they are necessarily defined relationally. Pettit (1993:229) goes on to elaborate a view that he (and Frank Jackson) calls explanatory ecumenism, according to which 'intentional, structural, historicist and rational choice styles of explanation are complementary enterprises' (see also Jackson and Pettit 1992a, 1992b; Pettit 1998). Calling them 'styles of explanation' does not really do justice to Pettit's conception of the relationships involved in these different areas of endeavour. What matters is being precise about the question we wish to pose: are we asking about the decisions of this clan leader in that context, or about the context, or about the broad institutional setting that defined the context in that way, or about the history of that configuration of institutions?

What makes the sort of ecumenical, 'interactionalist' approach Tuzin favoured, and Pettit explicitly defends, so important is that it subverts the simple individual–society couple that has inflected debate since Durkheim. Pettit's analysis, however, and the considerations upon which he grounds it, also undermines Tuzin's stated MI grounds for his approach. It would be possible— and for many purposes, desirable—to pursue further the approach Pettit takes and the many questions and difficulties it raises. But given limitations of space, it seems more worthwhile to conclude by returning to my introductory rehearsal of social-science commonplaces.

Concluding Remarks

Those commonplaces indicate that a great many of the states any given person is in are defined socially and relationally; so description of a person already entails the sort of relations that MI is sometimes aimed at accounting for. Social properties are contingently acquired by an individual through the process of socialisation (which amounts to ontogenesis), but having a particular social property—such as being a citizen, taxpayer, or an enrolled school student, or in a particular Arapesh initiation class—is non-contingently dependent upon enjoying the right sort of relations with aspects of society (just as what it is for something to be legal tender is a matter of its relational history [Searle 2010]). Admittedly, a general account of the relations relevant to overall personhood is a difficult ontological question. But there are physical entities and states that are defined by their having the right sort of causal historical relations with prior events: footprints, skid marks, sunburn, shaving cuts and whiplash injuries are obvious examples; but being a tiger or an oak is a matter of causal history, while being a thermostat is less a matter of physical constitution than causal powers. While these examples are helpfully suggestive, the relations involved in someone's being a divine king, cult elder, citizen, mayor or judge, or for something to be a signature or a football field, are more complex still. In fact, the relations that matter seem to be between agents and appropriate states of mind (Currie 1988)—prior states of one's own mind (as my currently being under contract entails prior actions, and therefore intentions, of mine) and, more importantly, states of other minds, recursively linked together, as they are in linguistic communication. So not only are social states and processes relational, they apparently involve irreducibly mental states—states it is notoriously difficult to identify with any non-mental substrate (not least because they too are relational).

Interestingly, once we abandon hope of accounting for aspects of the social life of humans in terms that abstract from our status as intentional, social beings (which is akin to trying to account for the natural history of sharks in terms that abstract from the properties they have as predatory fish), it becomes difficult to specify a sense of individual that is not parasitic on the one we use pre-theoretically. So social relations depend (supervene) on mental states, which, in turn, have dependencies on the conventions and practices of social life (in the sense that my worrying whether my dole cheque is on its way is a state of mind that entails the existence of certain socio-historical conditions).

All this is not to deny that there is—and necessarily so—some substrate that is the possessor of a social property; and it is hard to see how this could be anything other than a being with a sufficiently rich psychology (rich enough to permit language learning, for example), or something (such as the football field) defined as such by beings of that sort. While, though, there are obvious candidates for bearers of social properties (human beings), specifying them in ways that do justice to typical cases (mature cultural beings) without presupposing the socio-cultural is a forlorn hope, as the difficulties of MI indicate. This, in turn, means that it makes little sense to think of concrete individuals as basic parts of social wholes (Currie 1984, 1988; Pettit 1993, 1998; Ruben 1985). And if one thinks carefully about the relations among armies, soldiers and the people who signed up, or between the team, the club it represents and the players, or between the clan, its subclans and the current members, one can appreciate that we are dealing with something other than simple aggregates—like those who are waiting right now at the local bus stop. If I am one of the group waiting at a particular bus stop, and that group is one of the many making up the larger group of people waiting for buses on the high street, I am a member of the larger group, whereas (as Ruben shows), if you are an Australian citizen, and Australia is a member of the United Nations, it does not follow that you are a member of the United Nations. And whereas the group of people sitting in the café or residing in an Ilahita ward changes as persons come or go, neither the library committee nor the Afinga clan is transformed when one member is replaced with another (even if this has effects on other interpersonal relations, the tenor of meetings or the chances of internal disputes, and so on).

Coping with the complexities of the relations between social entities is, then, a metaphysically challenging task, and that makes formulating explanations capturing causal relations among them less than straightforward. This state of affairs *need* not worry us, however; we might still think (as Weber did, and historians usually do) that there is still much analytical satisfaction to be had from showing how, for example, economic depressions, wars or the rise of new social classes causally relate to the actions and decisions of individuals and identifiable social collectivities, picked out in the usual intuitive terms; or from appreciating how certain religious doctrines, which might demand a great deal of interpretation on our part, grew and spread through one stratum of society, but not others. It was only in this (folk psychological) sense that Weber was an individualist; he seems to have crafted his sociology to be ontologically and methodologically continuous with history and with our folk psychology. And these resources might be all that we need to understand how Ilahita, under pressure from expanding populations around them, made accommodations that involved, among other things, the elaboration of existing practices and their deployment in the novel historical circumstances, and that what eventuated was something unprecedented in the area. Of course, we will have lots of questions about those practices, their histories, their connections with one another, and with human psychology; and when it comes to some very particular aspects of events (why the turn to Christianity at *that* juncture [Tuzin 1997]), we might want to know about the personal characteristics of individuals (such as Samuel). Usually, however, the characteristics of typical individuals with locally specific, shared understandings set in the broader contexts of their human condition will suffice.

Finally, where does this perspective leave Don Tuzin's interactionalist paradigm and his hopes for an anthropology 'both humane and humanistic...of great moral and scientific importance'? I think it leaves it in as good a shape as he might have wished for when he began his stunning exposition of Ilahita's fortunes in the 1970s. Indeed, I would argue that it leaves his version of interactionalism in a somewhat stronger position than that of prominent others who share Don's interactionalist ambitions, such as Sperber and Boyer. Don could help himself to what we might call 'the anti anti-reductionist' case that these scholars have made so strongly over the years (see, for example, Sperber 1996) and to the openness to integration with evolutionary history that this naturally provides. Yet, the sensitivity of Don's approach to those particular historical features that Sperber's model of culture packages together as 'ecological factors' makes it more apt than Sperber's for the single-case historical-ethnographic study. And just such studies are the ones prized by those who want anthropologists to continue to produce cultural accounts thick enough to warrant Rorty's description of us as 'agents of love' (1986), or who think the discipline should remain dedicated to addressing what Geertz insisted on calling our 'moral imagination' (1983). What makes Tuzin's work so outstanding is that it can appeal no less convincingly to both perspectives, even while they see themselves as opposed.[6]

References

Bechtel, William and Andre Hamilton 2007. Reduction, Integration, and the Unity of Science: Natural, Behavioral, and Social Sciences and the Humanities. In Theo A. F. Kuipers (ed.) *Philosophy of Science: Focal Issues*, pp. 377–430. New York: Elsevier.

Bickle, John 2008. Multiple Realizability. In Edward N. Zalta (ed.) *The Stanford Encyclopedia of Philosophy*, Stanford, Calif.: Stanford University, <http://plato.stanford.edu/archives/fall2008/entries/multiple-realizability/>

Boyer, Pascal 1994. *The Naturalness of Religious Ideas*. Berkeley and Los Angeles: University of California Press.

Currie, Gregory 1984. Individualism and Global Supervenience. *British Journal for the Philosophy of Science* 35:345–58.

Currie, Gregory 1988. Realism in the Social Sciences: Social Kinds and Social Laws. In Robert Nola (ed.) *Relativism and Realism in Science*, pp. 205–27. Amsterdam: Kluwer Academic.

Currie, Gregory 2001. Methodological Individualism. In Neil J. Smelser and Paul B. Bates (eds) *International Encyclopedia of the Social and Behavioral Sciences*, pp. 9755–60. Amsterdam: Elsevier Science.

Durkheim, Emile 1973. The Dualism of Human Nature and its Social Conditions. In Robert N. Bellah (ed.) *Emile Durkheim on Morality and Society*, pp. 149–64. Chicago: University of Chicago Press.

---

6 These closing—admittedly rhetorical—remarks are a little unfair to Sperber's views, which need to be seen as but a small part of a broader and extremely interesting vision that cannot even be sketched here.

Fine, Kit 2005. *Modality and Tense: Philosophical Papers*. Oxford: Oxford University Press.

Freeman, Derek 1966. Social Anthropology and the Scientific Study of Human Behaviour. *Man* (NS)1:330–42.

Freeman, Derek 1983. *Margaret Mead and Samoa: The Making and Unmaking of An Anthropological Myth*. Cambridge, Mass.: Harvard University Press.

Geertz, Clifford 1957. Ritual and Social Change: A Javanese Example. *American Anthropologist* 59:32–54.

Geertz, Clifford 1973. *The Interpretation of Cultures*. New York: Basic Books.

Geertz, Clifford 1983 [1977]. Found in Translation: On the Social History of the Moral Imagination. In *Local Knowledge: Further Essays in Interpretive Anthropology*, pp. 36–54. New York: Basic Books.

Heath, J. 2008. Methodological Individualism. In Edward N. Zalta (ed.) *The Stanford Encyclopedia of Philosophy*, Stanford, Calif.: Stanford University, <http://plato.stanford.edu/archives/fall2008/entries/methodological-individualism/>

Hedström, Peter, Richard Swedberg and Lars Udehn 1998. Popper's Situational Analysis and Contemporary Sociology. *Philosophy of the Social Sciences* 28:339–64.

Homans, George C. 1982. The Present State of Sociological Theory. *Sociological Quarterly* 23:285–99.

Infantino, Lorenzo 1998. *Individualism in Modern Thought: From Adam Smith to Hayek*. New York: Routledge.

Jackson, Frank and Philip Pettit 1992a. Structural Explanation in Social Theory. In David Charles and Kathleen Lennon (eds) *Reduction, Explanation, and Realism*, pp. 97–131. Oxford: Clarendon Press.

Jackson, Frank and Philip Pettit 1992b. In Defence of Explanatory Ecumenism. *Economics and Philosophy* 8:1–21.

Kottak, Conrad P. 2008. *Mirror for Humanity: A Concise Introduction to Cultural Anthropology*. New York: McGraw-Hill.

La Barre, Weston 1980. *Culture in Context: Selected Writings of Weston Labarre*. Durham, NC: Duke University Press.

Lévi-Strauss, C. 1981. *The Naked Man*. J. & D. Weightman (trans). Introduction to a Science of Mythology. Volume 4. New York: Harper & Row.

McLaughlin, Brian and Karen Bennett 2008. Supervenience. In Edward N. Zalta (ed.) *The Stanford Encyclopedia of Philosophy*, Stanford, Calif.: Stanford University, <http://plato.stanford.edu/archives/fall2008/entries/supervenience/>

Marx, Karl 1963 [1869]. *The Eighteenth Brumaire of Louis Bonaparte*. New York: International Publishers.

Mill, John Stuart 1882. *A System of Logic, Ratiocinative and Inductive*. [Eighth edition.] New York: Harper & Brothers.

Moore, Wilbert E. 1979. Functionalism. In T. B. Bottomore and Robert A. Nisbet (eds) *A History of Sociological Analysis*, pp. 321–61. London: Heinemann Educational.

Oakley, Allen 2002. Popper's Ontology of Situated Human Action. *Philosophy of the Social Sciences* 32:455–86.

Oddie, Graham 2001. Reduction: Varieties of. In Neil J. Smelser and Paul B. Bates (eds) *International Encyclopedia of the Social and Behavioral Sciences*, pp. 12 857–63. Amsterdam: Elsevier Science.

Pettit, Philip 1993. *The Common Mind: An Essay on Psychology, Society, and Politics*. Oxford: Oxford University Press.

Pettit, Philip 1998. Defining and Defending Social Holism. *Philosophical Explorations* 1:169–84.

Popper, Karl R. 1994. *The Myth of the Framework: In Defence of Science and Rationality*. M. A. Notturno (ed.). London: Routledge.

Popper, Karl R. 2003 [1945]. *The Open Society and Its Enemies: Hegel and Marx. Volume 2*. Oxford and New York: Routledge.

Ringer, Fritz K. 1997. *Max Weber's Methodology: The Unification of the Cultural and the Social Sciences*. Cambridge, Mass.: Harvard University Press.

Ringer, Fritz K. 2002. Max Weber on Causal Analysis, Interpretation, and Comparison. *History and Theory* 41:163–78.

Rorty, Richard 1986. On Ethnocentrism: A Reply to Clifford Geertz. *Michigan Quarterly Review* 25:525–34.

Ruben, David-Hillel 1985. *The Metaphysics of the Social World*. London: Routledge and Kegan Paul.

Searle, John R. 1995. *The Construction of Social Reality*. New York: The Free Press.

Searle, John R. 2010. *Making the Social World: The Structure of Human Civilization*. Oxford and New York: Oxford University Press.

Schütz, Alfred 1973. *The Phenomenology of the Social World*. George Walsh and Frederick Lehnert (trans). Evanston, Ill.: Northwestern University Press.

Sperber, Dan 1996. *Explaining Culture: A Naturalistic Approach*. Oxford: Blackwell.

Spiro, Melford 1978. Culture and Human Nature. In George D. Spindler (ed.) *The Making of Psychological Anthropology*, pp. 331–60. Berkeley: University of California Press.

Turner, Stephen P. and Regis A. Factor 1994. *Max Weber: The Lawyer as Social Thinker*. London: Routledge.

Tuzin, Donald F. 1974. Social Control and the Tambaran in the Sepik. In A. L. Epstein (ed.) *Contention and Dispute: Aspects of Law and Social Control in Melanesia*, pp. 317–44. Canberra: Australian National University Press.

Tuzin, Donald F. 1976. *The Ilahita Arapesh: Dimensions of Unity*. Berkeley: University of California Press.

Tuzin, Donald F. 1980. *The Voice of the Tambaran: Truth and Illusion in Ilahita Arapesh Religion*. Berkeley: University of California Press.

Tuzin, Donald F. 1982. Ritual Violence Among the Ilahita Arapesh: The Dynamics of Moral and Religious Uncertainty. In Gilbert H. Herdt (ed.) *Rituals of Manhood: Male Initiation in Papua New Guinea*, pp. 321–55. Berkeley: University of California Press.

Tuzin, Donald F. 1984. Miraculous Voices: The Auditory Experience of Numinous Objects. *Current Anthropology* 25:579–96.

Tuzin, Donald F. 1989. Visions, Prophecies, and the Rise of Christian Consciousness. In Gilbert Herdt and Michelle Stephen (eds) *The Religious Imagination in New Guinea*, pp. 187–210. New Brunswick, NJ: Rutgers University Press.

Tuzin, Donald F. 1991. The Cryptic Brotherhood of Big Men and Great Men in Ilahita. In Maurice Godelier and Marilyn Strathern (eds) *Big Men and Great Men: Personifications of Power in Melanesia*, pp. 115–29. Cambridge: Cambridge University Press.

Tuzin, Donald F. 1997. *The Cassowary's Revenge: The Life and Death of Masculinity in a New Guinea Society*. Chicago: University of Chicago Press.

Tuzin, Donald F. 2001. *Social Complexity in the Making: A Case Study Among the Arapesh of New Guinea*. London: Routledge.

Tuzin, Donald F. 2002. Art, Ritual, and the Crafting of Illusion. *Asia Pacific Journal of Anthropology* 3:1–23.

Tuzin, Donald F. 2006. Base Notes: Odor, Breath and Moral Contagion in Ilahita. In Jim Drobnik (ed.) *The Smell Culture Reader*, pp. 59–67. New York: Berg.

Udehn, Lars 2001. *Methodological Individualism: Background, History and Meaning*. London: Routledge.

Udehn, Lars 2002. The Changing Face of Methodological Individualism. *Annual Review of Sociology* 28:479–507.

Watkins, J. W. N. 1955. Methodological Individualism: A Reply. *Philosophy of Science* 22:58–62.

Watkins, J. W. N. 1957. Historical Explanation in the Social Sciences. *The British Journal for the Philosophy of Science* 8(30):104–17.

Weber, Max 1952. *Ancient Judaism*. Hans H. Gerth and Don Martindale (eds and trans). London: Allen & Unwin.

Weber, Max 1978. *Economy and Society: An Outline of Interpretive Sociology*. Guenther Roth and Claus Wittich (eds). Berkeley: University of California Press.

Young, Michael W. 1984. Response to Miraculous Voices: The Auditory Experience of Numinous Objects. *Current Anthropology* 25:593.

7. Stories from Childhood: Windows on experience or cultural meta-narratives? Evidence from Papua New Guinea

Stephen C. Leavitt

Introduction

Childhood stories in personal narratives of Western subjects often convey pivotal moments of experience aimed at communicating personal identity. Such strategies rely on cultural models that see identity as the product of past life events, with childhood experience especially important. But what do personal childhood stories reveal in societies with very different cultural models of early life's role in shaping identity? Among the Bumbita Arapesh of Papua New Guinea—a group bordering the Ilahita Arapesh—childhood is the time of life when a new growing being takes in essential life substance from parental nurturing, supplemented by ritual transformation in initiation and maturation ceremonies. In their view, childhood experiences do little to shape personality; instead, they work to define one's essential being, in substance and position, through nurturing and transactions of food. Individuals' stories of their childhood, then, convey themes of personal identity as refracted through local Bumbita understandings of what a person is.

This chapter draws its inspiration from Donald Tuzin's ethnographic vision, focused as it is on understanding cultural themes as they are expressed in individuals' minds, with all of the contingencies of a life as lived. In his work, Tuzin emphasised that one's cultural views depend as much on the emotional conditions of one's individual experience as they do on the learned cultural systems. His paper 'Of the Resemblance of Fathers to Their Children: The Roots of Primitivism in Middle-Childhood Enculturation' (1990) presents a clear example of his point of view. In that work on the psychological impact of beliefs in spirits, he looked to the context in which those beliefs were first learned in middle childhood. His point is that the experiential context of a child is very different from that of adults, and that experience is what shapes the emotional valences of adults' beliefs. He writes: 'Children creatively interpret received cultural elements in such a way as to give substance to their emergent sense of identity, thus establishing an indivisible union between the person, on the one hand, and the culture that provides its ideational constituents, on the other' (Tuzin 1990:72).

To understand the emotional framework of beliefs in adults, one needs to understand the story told by those beliefs to children, for it was as children that those beliefs were first learned and understood. Children learn features of their culture from other children (Tuzin 1990:82), and the versions they learn are 'inevitably partial and distorted because they are based on limited life experiences' (p. 84). The process produces 'childish residues' in adult culture, and in that context some of the more ghoulish elements of adult culture make more sense (Tuzin 1990:99). So, in this context, the beliefs of fathers—formed originally in the context of child-to-child interactions—resemble the primitivisms found in children's beliefs.

By placing beliefs in a specific ethnographic and experiential context, Tuzin's approach is one example of several recent efforts to view cultural beliefs through the lens of individual experience. Recent research in anthropology and psychology, for example, has shifted its focus to the activity of narrative production, arguing that people everywhere build stories that make a point; as the linguist Labov (1981) put it some time ago, the stories must answer the question 'So what?' Individuals use personal narrative to make sense of their lives, to negotiate among different versions of self, and to fashion responses to dominant cultural discourse. In their review of approaches to the study of personal narrative, Ochs and Capps emphasise that by using all these strategies, 'interlocutors tell personal narratives about the past primarily to understand and cope with their current concerns' (1996:25). Narratives are thus driven by motives with particular, immediate aims. Researchers across a range of analytic traditions have put forward new approaches that accommodate narrators' active attempts to use stories to place life events in a desired context. Thus, cognitive anthropologists have worked to build models of mental process that can address specific circumstances. Strauss and Quinn, for example, draw on a connectionist model for mental schemas that can be 'highly context sensitive' (1997:53). By looking at schemas as embedded in a host of associations networked together, researchers can consider specifics, so that 'the particular features of any given event can lead to different outcomes from one situation to the next' (Strauss and Quinn 1997:53). The model allows for greater attention to the 'directive force' of cultural schemas to better appreciate narrators' commitments to specific ideas at specific times (D'Andrade and Strauss 1992). At the same time, psychoanalytically informed anthropologists have looked at the often inconsistent and conflicting identities mobilised by narrators to apply to specific situations in giving life accounts (see especially, Ewing 1990, 1997). Researchers in cognitive psychology have cultivated an interest in 'taking narrative seriously' (Chase 1995) as a tool for better understanding mental processes. And theorists of autobiographical memory emphasise how memories of the past are mobilised through a narrative process with specific aims, so that remembered stories 'communicate what is significant in [people's] lives' in such a way as to 'seek to convince others to see some part of reality in a particular way' (Garro and Mattingly 2000:11).

When stories deal with the very personal topic of one's own childhood, it is likely that the rhetorical strategies for self-presentation will play a prominent role in the shape of the story told. The stories almost by definition seek to convey something about self-understanding. But stories of childhood also, to an exceptional degree, rely on often unarticulated ethno-psychological premises about just what a person is, so that they might serve as a particularly effective venue for exploring how local cultural forms bear on universal processes in narrative production. The challenge for the researcher is to articulate these universal features while at the same time avoiding inferences about motives that might depend on a Western model of how childhood shapes adult selfhood. So, for example, in dealing with Bumbita personal narrative, it might be appropriate to infer that a narrator is making an argument about how to understand his or her experience, but it would be inappropriate to infer that the narrator aims to build a narrative that explains personality traits or emotional preoccupations. While the stories from childhood might seek to convey something about 'who I am today', the cultural forms that underlie that self-assessment might be dramatically different across societies.

I shall use the case of a personal narrative of a Bumbita young man to pursue two separate aims. The first seeks to illustrate in a detailed way how basic Bumbita assumptions about the nature of personhood define the terms through which the narrator presents his stories from childhood. Bumbita conceptualise a person as the product of the nurturing activity of parents and others in the community, and that nurturing is conceptualised in terms of a literal transfer of substance through the activity of cultivating and providing food. Thus, the Bumbita say that people age only because their vital strength is continuously being sapped by dependents who are consuming food produced by the caretakers. They understand the process as a literal transfer of substance between generations. One implication is that a person becomes who he or she is only through a process of literally ingesting the vitality of parents and other caretakers. The Bumbita frame the moral obligations of children to their parents in these terms. You must look after your parents in old age, they say, because your own strength has caused their weakness. In the Bumbita view, it is not the case that one's personality is shaped by, say, the child-rearing priorities of one's parents; in fact, they see childhood experience as irrelevant in shaping one's character. Instead, they see one's personal vitality and integration within the community as the products of caretakers' vigilance in providing adequate transfers of food to dependents. I shall show how these themes underlie the narrative structure of the young man I have chosen to present.

At the same time, this young man's narratives also reveal rhetorical strategies that I believe are characteristic of personal stories everywhere. In spite of the dramatically different cultural frame for his stories of childhood, he still makes an active effort to present himself in a particular way. In this context, the local Bumbita understandings of the meaning of childhood become a backdrop for a more active, individual rhetorical move to prove a point about what the childhood experience means. My second aim in this chapter, therefore, is to draw attention to a relatively underdeveloped dimension of the universal process of rhetorical argument in narrative production. Specifically, I argue that the inevitable rhetorical dimension to telling stories requires us to look at the story as making an argument about the experience. Once we look at the arguments that underlie a given story, we have to consider also what it is that the arguments are mobilised against. In asserting a certain point about how to understand a story, the narrator seeks to suppress alternative versions. Those 'suppressed meanings' (Leavitt 1995, 2007) should be integral to our analytical approach. The actual meaning of the narrative emerges only by juxtaposing the asserted argument against these suppressed meanings. The young Bumbita man who talked to me about his childhood transactions of food was at the same time constructing an argument about his place in the community. And he was building that argument to combat suppressed fears about what he suspected was actually a precarious position in that community.

Transactions of Food in Bumbita Childhood Stories

During my first weeks in Bumbita, I was struck by how easy it was to ingratiate myself with people by simply feeding them. In those early days, I had several tasks (including the large one of building my house) that had to be paid for, and while the adolescents who helped me were willing to take money for their work, I found that they seemed to feel better compensated if I simply offered them a meal at the end of the day instead. The deep significance of transactions of this kind is a well-known feature of Melanesian social relations. On one level, it is not surprising that in exchange-based societies people would see gifts as potent declarations of goodwill. In talking about the Kaluli of the Papuan Plateau, for example, Schieffelin (1976:150) notes: 'As human relationships are actualized and mediated through gifts of food and material wealth, so these things come to stand for what is deeply felt in human relationships.' Gifts convey concern.

To appreciate what gift relations actually mean for Melanesians, it is necessary, however, to look as well at how such relations come to participate in people's most intimate sense of being. Marilyn Strathern has described how Melanesians see transactions as ways of transporting parts of one's being in a literal sense. She distinguishes 'mediated' exchange of valuables where objects 'circulate as parts of persons' (1988:192) from 'unmediated' exchange where the products of work contribute directly to the creation of others (such as in the case of parents feeding children) (pp. 177–8, *passim*). In both types of exchange, the essence of being is conveyed from person to person through transaction. In the first case, the objects themselves determine a temporary state of relations between people (as 'donors' or 'recipients'). Over time, as gifts pass back and forth, the relations are reciprocal. But in the second case, the unmediated transfer of substance means the donor has a direct influence on the minds and bodies of the recipients, so their status as recipients is more enduring. As a result, 'the capacity to have an unmediated effect creates a distinguishing asymmetry between the parties' (Strathern 1988:178). This asymmetrical relationship, which finds its prototype in relations between parents and children, provides the conceptual frame for Bumbita thoughts about their childhood experiences.

It is not simply that children, in accepting food from their parents and others, learn about unmediated exchange of substance; they also come to associate those ideas with themes and conflicts that arise from the pragmatics of growing up. In the case I present here, the young Bumbita man related to me a series of vignettes from his childhood focusing on the theme of his integration into a community of peers through transactions with food. His stories draw upon Bumbita cultural themes emphasising how transactions of food provided, through a literal transfer of substance, a vehicle for integrating oneself into the community. He emphasises how, through guile and manipulation, he was able to compel older boys to accept him into their social group. His stories argue implicitly that he was successful.

The episode was related by Aminguh, a young man in his early twenties. He was the youngest son of a powerful village leader who served several years as village councillor. The father died when Aminguh was in his early teens. Of the informants with whom I conducted detailed personal interviews, Aminguh was among the most enthusiastic. Occasionally, he would wake me up to talk in the middle of the night, and often he said he had thought a lot between sessions about what he wanted to tell me in the next interview. By the time of my departure, we were close friends. After one of my early formal interviews with him, I told him that the next time I would like him to tell me some stories that he remembered from his childhood. I told him just to tell me anything that he remembered. He returned the next week and began relating to me a whole series of childhood incidents. All together, they took up the better part of three interviews. He seemed to want to entertain me with the humour of a child's plight. He told of cutting himself in his fumbling attempts to learn to use a bush knife, of eating food that made him sick to his stomach, of burning himself in cooking fires. In taking this perspective, he also sought to capture the feelings and thoughts of a young child as opposed to those of an adult. His stories of relations with others therefore conveyed his experience with an immediacy often lacking in similar stories from other informants.

He began his rendition of his childhood by relating to me a series of incidents involving his attempts to follow along with his classificatory brothers in their forays into the bush to find food. Most of his stories shared themes about wanting to be included. Because of Bumbita cultural assumptions about defining group membership through sharing of substance accomplished through transactions of food, Aminguh used the theme of transactions of food to articulate his points about being included in the group. By manipulating his brothers into sharing food with him, he became a part of their group. What is striking about his account from a Western perspective is how irrelevant motives are. Westerners would consider acceptance through manipulation as a decidedly unsatisfying way of becoming a part of a group. From our perspective, the important thing would be whether the brothers *wanted* to include Aminguh in their group—the extent to which Aminguh could, through personality traits or commendable personal action, convince his brothers that he should be a part of their group. But such issues matter little in Aminguh's story. The first incident goes as follows:

> We went to cut the bush. At this time I didn't wear any trousers [he was about ten years old at the time]. When we cut gardens, we would work at night, with the moon full. Sirimbom, Rengur and some others, we would work at night, cutting the bush. I was just a kid so I just sat and looked at them [as they worked]. One morning [my 'brothers'] went off to find eggs from wild fowl. I wanted to go with them, but they pushed me away, pushed me away, so I just sat down [to wait for them]. Then they came back to cook, in the afternoon, to cook the eggs and wild fowl they had caught. I got up and walked very quietly and sat at the back of Ohitum ['eB']. I sat there and they talked among themselves, saying, 'Hey, you all eat in a hurry, the kid's going to come back soon!' They started to eat and I sat at the base of a tree and then hit a piece of sugar cane against the tree. They turned to see me and then they got up to hit me now! Mangen ['eB'] and the others chased me up the hill, but I didn't go away. I just waited for them to go back so I could come up and they would ['have to] give me a piece of meat. I came up and Sirimbom ['yB', but older than A.] gave me some and then told me to leave, and I said, 'I am going to tell my father, say that they are eating wild fowl'—you see

they had forbidden them from eating it because they had already done [their initiations]. I said that I'd go tell them and they started cajoling ['*grisim*'] me, telling me not to. They sat there and gave me a piece of meat—Sirimbom had given me some before—but now [the two others] gave me some and they said, 'You can't go and tell them, just keep quiet about it.' We ate together, finished, and we came on up.

There are two avenues that I wish to pursue here in explicating this incident. The first is to assess Aminguh's characterisation of the people's motives and interactions as an indication of his general view of human behaviour as framed by Bumbita understandings about the significance of transactions of food. The second is to identify the social predicament his story works to fortify him against and to address what suppressed meanings might motivate him to frame his stories in the way he does.

Aminguh's immediate goal here, as he presents it, is to finagle some food out of his 'brothers'. But the details he selects indicate that for him there is an association between getting the food and being a part of the group—that is, if he gets the food, that means he is one of them. He begins by saying, 'We would work at night', implying that he remembers being one of this group of classificatory brothers. But then he immediately establishes a narrative tension by throwing his affiliation with the group into doubt, stating that when they went off on that cherished social activity of boys, finding food, 'They pushed me away'. When the brothers return, he hides from them in order to overhear them conspiring to keep from him the food they have caught. He includes this sequence in the story to verify that their hiding the food from him is an active exclusion, not simply an oversight. For him, that situation is intolerable. He reacts by getting them to share the food with him. It is only then that he can feel included.

In telling how he managed to get them to share, Aminguh reveals his understanding of human behaviour in such situations. First, his brothers do not have any prior inclination to share with him despite his being their kin. They try to eat in a hurry in order to avoid having to give him some. He characterises them as being self-interested, excluding him so as not to have to share. Second, they respond to his efforts to reveal them. He first distracts them so that they will know that he has heard them trying to eat behind his back, and then, after they chase him, he continues to come back because he knows that if he comes back, 'They would have to give me a piece of meat'—even though they were capable of sending him off completely, using their fists. His message here is that people will not share unless they are forced into doing so. And even then that is not sufficient since they only give him 'some'—that is, not an equal portion. Getting the equal portion requires further manipulation. Here he uses the threat that little boys often use, the same threat that keeps them from being included in the group to begin with: he says that he will tell their parents that they are eating forbidden food. This last manipulation produces the desired results. Suddenly, the older boys take him in and give him his proper share of the food, and they all go off together back to their camp. Aminguh sketches here a pattern of interaction that shows individuals acting in their own interests at the expense of others but at the same time responding well to manipulation and to the threat of being exposed. Through this manipulation, Aminguh gets his food and at the same time is included in the group.

Aminguh's act of manipulation raises another theme to his story, one that is implicit but important to identify given his position as the son of a deceased village counsellor and leader. He gets his way through artful manipulation, and successful manipulation is in the Melanesian context a measure of personal power. For example, Bumbita yam growers manipulate ancestral spirits through their yam magic, coercing them to help the yams grow. Similarly, successful leaders manipulate others into doing their bidding. In Melanesia, 'status in the local community is achieved through processes of political manipulation. Through these manipulations a man becomes a big man. Successful big men become village councilors' (Barnett 1979:770). Missing are the negative connotations associated with political manipulation in the Western context. Aminguh's stories here are clearly success stories. He manages to manipulate his 'brothers' into sharing with him, and in so doing he shows himself to have some of the ingenuity recognised as characteristics of village leaders.

It is important to note here that once he does get them to share with him, he sees the conflict as resolved and the previous rejection as nullified. It is this characteristic of the story that makes it seem so peculiar when looked at through Western assumptions about what it means to belong to a group. To a Western audience, such a story would convey at best a tenuous resolution to the predicament of social belonging. Aminguh's having to resort to guile and manipulation would be seen as a sign that he had failed in a fundamental way to resolve the issue. It would be tempting to view his story as an appeal to sympathy due to an unfortunate, even tragic, instance of social rejection. But Aminguh attaches no such meanings to his story. For him, the story is a success story about exercising leadership in becoming a part of his group of brothers. What matters is the actual transaction of food; how the food was obtained is not an issue for him. In fact, the dynamic that Aminguh presents from his childhood recapitulates Bumbita understandings of prototypical negotiations between children and parents over food. According to Bumbita understandings of child-rearing patterns, when children are young, they learn that conflicts with their parents can be resolved by demanding food, that eventually their parents will 'feel sorry' for them and give in to the demands. Parents regularly describe their own behaviour as eventual acquiescence to persistent pestering.

Westerners regard such patterns as evidence of some kind of failing on the part of parents. Manipulation of parents by children is part of the Western model of what might go into 'spoiling' a child. But in the Bumbita view, guile and manipulation to obtain the transaction of desired food are a fundamental part of the process of transaction. Young children do it with their parents, and once they reach older childhood they extend this model of interaction to relations with peers, describing more subtle methods of manipulation. This manipulation becomes a basis for exercising leadership among men.

An appreciation of local Bumbita understandings of transactions over food is therefore pivotal in understanding the significance of Aminguh's story. Only by looking through the local cultural lens can one see the story's heroic features. It is a story that begins with a rift in social relations causing feelings of rejection, a manipulation of others through guile and persistence, and a successful resolution of the conflict through the proper sharing of food even when done grudgingly.

Suppressed Meanings

Anthropologists might at one time have used a story such as Aminguh's to illustrate prevailing features of local cultural models or schemas. But in recent years attention has shifted to identifying some of the contingencies of personal narrative that might shape how it appears at any given point in time. Personal narratives present an understanding of the self, but they do so through a rhetorical process that seeks to foreground certain themes and suppress others. Psychologists following the pioneering work of Jerome Bruner have sought to articulate some of the activities involved in presenting a particular version of the self. Bruner writes, in fact, that '[r]hetoric is as pervasive a feature of Self construction as narrative itself, and though we tend to dismiss it on moral grounds as mere "self-justification", such dismissals fail to recognize to what degree the concept of Self (and autobiography itself) is a form of apologia' (Bruner 1994:49). Researchers, he argues, have to recognise that such self-justification is a fundamental characteristic of how people everywhere think about themselves. Behind the activity of self-justification lie alternative scenarios, what I have called 'suppressed meanings', which contribute to the shape of the story. As Susan Chase (1995) puts it, any asserted story of self contains a 'submerged' story that might point to a 'feeling of inadequacy'. She argues that 'as interviewers we need to attend to submerged stories and invite their telling' (Chase 1995:17).

So what possible submerged story or suppressed meanings might we infer from Aminguh's stories of his childhood? Without a detailed account of his entire life, I can only hint at suggestions, but there are clues even in the accounts that he presents here. First, it is important to point out that the themes articulated in the story above appear over and over in his stories about his childhood. Establishing a sense of belonging to the peer group was a preoccupation. His other stories of childhood show what he experienced there as part of a more general pattern. So, for example, after relating the incident above, he went on to talk about the time his friends and 'brothers' caught some fish and another bird. Aminguh again tried to tag along, saying that they sent him off, 'They always got rid of me'. When they spied him following behind them, they rubbed stinging nettles on him and threw him into the water. When they caught a bird, he says, 'They left me behind, they didn't think of me, just thinking of their bird. I walked along [he imitates sniffling] as if I were about to cry.' Afterwards, they prepared to cook the bird but did not show it to him, lying to him and keeping an eye on him so that he could not see what they were cooking. But by astutely looking at the materials they used for cooking, he surmised that they must have caught something substantial. When they offered him some fish and told him to leave, he said, 'No, I want to see what it is that you are planning to bake', and he told them again that he would tell their parents if he did not get some. So they included him, saying, 'Sit down, sit down, sit down', and they all ate together.

In a third incident under similar circumstances, his 'brother' sneaked a pigeon to Aminguh before the others returned and told him to hurry and eat because otherwise '[w]hen they come they'll see that you've already eaten and they'll say that you've already had enough'. He cooked and ate the bird in a hurry and then received a small share of the catch of the others when they returned. After receiving his share, he said, 'Hey, give me another one!' and they said, 'That's enough for you!' He then went on to describe how in the morning they discovered the feathers from the first bird he had eaten and thus saw that he had manipulated them into sharing when he had already eaten a large portion on his own. He portrays himself here as being as selfish as the others by trying to get more than his share. After he had related all of these incidents, I ventured the question, 'Why were they always trying to get rid of you?' He responded:

> Because they said I was just a kid. It wouldn't be good if I were to tell on them, tell the women and the other kids, saying, 'These guys here are guys who hide and eat meat', to shame them, so that the women would say, 'Hey, we don't like these guys who eat meat', it's like that.

Here the question of who trusts whom runs the other way around. Before, Aminguh could not trust them to share the food because of their greed. Now, he says that they could not trust him to keep their eating a secret. The implication is that one should not expect to be able to trust other people; he portrays himself as unreliable as well. In Aminguh's view, it is the inability to trust others that lies behind the difficulties people have in accepting others. And, of course, Aminguh's subsequent manipulation only reinforces that view among his peers.

These stories carry some persistent patterns, and Aminguh consistently presented them to me through constructing a version of himself as a child, a version he wanted me to see and accept. He invited me to share in his childhood frustrations at being shunned by his brothers and peers and then presented for me a 'childhood Aminguh' who, through his skill at guile and manipulation, was able (temporarily at least) to overcome the exclusion he felt. These vignettes cannot accurately reflect Aminguh's overall childhood experience, but they can reflect his interpretation of important features of that experience and identify enduring issues of conflict. Taken together, they suggest that, for him at least, being outside the group, excluded by others, was a problem that he felt he needed to address. The tension in each incident derives from his setting himself in opposition to the group. In each case it is Aminguh versus 'them', with the 'them' being a solidified group of peers. Their exclusion of him makes him feel hurt so that he 'sniffles' or murmurs stoically to himself, 'It's all right, it's nothing'. And each time he eventually responds by revealing that he knows they are hiding food from him and by eventually manipulating them into letting him join them.

Taken together, the series of vignettes does not imply a deeply psychological defence structure against unacceptable meanings. But they do have a coherent set of points—likely cultivated in his own private reflections on his past experience—that insist on a particular interpretation of the events described. The central argument is that he, through his own individual initiative, was able to coerce his brothers into accepting him into the group. In the Bumbita cultural context, transfers of substance, through the sharing of food, imply a fundamental sharing of being that Aminguh accomplishes through his own initiative. Once his argument is understood in that context, it is possible to infer the alternative scenarios that might be suppressed. The critical issue is what he can actually accomplish through individual initiative. Lurking behind the stories is the possibility that personal initiative is not in fact sufficient for becoming a part of the group. In fact, the Bumbita cultural model of substance transfer implies that individual initiative is not sufficient. All Bumbita are fundamentally dependent upon the nurturing activities of others.

It turns out that, in Aminguh's case, the premature death of his father left him with a profound sense of dislocation that he was wrestling with throughout our interviews together. As he understood it, maturing without a father entailed the risk that he would not be able to acquire the substance and knowledge that would make him a complete adult. While the vehicles for the transfer of vitality are primarily those of food and energy spent on the cultivation of food, the Bumbita tend to see other transfers, such as ritual knowledge, magic and wisdom, as a form of nurturing essential to the proper relationship between father and son. In the case of ritual knowledge and magic, the scrupulous secrecy and the competitive uses of such things require that one learn about them from just a very few sources, and the most important is one's father. Certain techniques of yam magic, for example, are highly individual and are passed from fathers to their sons. Such magic is regarded as essential to harvesting abundant crops. The importance of acquiring knowledge from one's own father is also reflected in the magical potency of heirlooms such as axes, nets for hunting pigs, and curing packets. These objects are imbued with the essence of clan ancestors so that they are not effective if used by anyone besides an appropriate heir. Young men also rely on more informal practical wisdom about how to live with women and how to succeed politically. The Bumbita feel that anyone else besides their own fathers will be unwilling to impart such knowledge. Aminguh, in his interviews with me, communicated a profound anxiety over being able to take his father's place in the community without his father's guidance and continued transfer of substance. Here is an example of how he talked about his position when lamenting the death of his father:

> I am here and…there is no other 'father' to come and teach me things. I know, each father must teach his own children about everything. If he goes wrong like this, his father will say, 'You must do it this way.' That's how it is, so I think of this all the time. I think, 'Why did he die like that, he didn't want to wait until I was big, like I am now, so that he could teach me first and then later go ahead and die?'

He starts by saying that his clan fathers (all of whom have died) might have taught him had they lived, but then reflects that really it is only his own father who would have been likely to do so consistently. Clan 'fathers' have their own sons. Aminguh's feeling of loss is accentuated by the ideology that parents create adults out of their children through a transfer of substance, vitality and energy. Here he speaks only of ritual knowledge and wisdom, but his understanding of relationships between generations leads him to see the loss of his father's teachings as leaving him incomplete in some fundamental way. When I asked him if he thought that he would be like his father, he said, 'I want to become like him, I think that way. I think, will I become like him or not? If I had gotten some stories from him, then I could be like him. But I have missed out, so I can't know.'

What is striking about these comments is the explicit fear that he will not, through his own initiative, be able to take his proper place in the community. What he is unsure about is whether he has already acquired enough of what it takes to be an effective adult man. In his mind, the jury is still out; he says, 'I can't know'. Masculine vitality is for Bumbita men a fundamental feature of self-assessment. Men learn to gauge their own effectiveness as males by observing the products of their own individual initiative. If a yam crop yields abundance, a man can infer that he has the requisite vitality to cause that result. The proof lies in the results of individual initiative.

It is in this context that his stories of guile and manipulation take on a new meaning. In being successful at getting the young men to include him, he is in essence re-enacting an activity appropriate for village leaders, for people like his own father. His stories are of a heroic nature, with the young Aminguh successfully getting his way. In framing his stories in this way, he is suppressing the doubts that we otherwise know concern him, that the loss of his father has meant he has lost the training necessary to become a village leader himself. The stories are a way for him to indirectly play out the role of a successful leader, who, through manipulation, gets others to give him what he wants and becomes a part of the community in the process.

Aminguh's stories of his childhood, when understood now in the context of a preoccupation with masculine vitality, become narratives through which he seeks to prove to himself that he already has enough personal effectiveness to integrate himself into the group without the continued guidance from his father. He understands that he now depends on the same community of classificatory brothers that he successfully manipulated in his stories about their childhood interactions. His stories of success fortify him against fears that his own personal initiative will be insufficient to make him a successful adult.

Thus, by understanding Aminguh's childhood stories as active attempts to define reality in a particular way, we can better appreciate the fundamental issues that define his experience.

Conclusion

I have used Aminguh's case material to illustrate the value of attending to the active rhetorical dimension of narrative construction. I have deliberately chosen stories that do not call attention to their argumentative dimension. It was not the case that Aminguh insisted to me that I must understand these stories in a particular way. He was not aware of building any strong argument. Nevertheless, the stories do reveal a consistent set of themes pointing to a particular interpretation of childhood events. I have tried to show that an appreciation of Bumbita cultural understandings of the process of development in childhood is essential to the interpretation of themes from childhood stories. Without a sense of those understandings, Aminguh's stories, as stated, make little sense. But at the same time the stories illustrate universal features of the narrative process that I argue should be applied to narrative constructions across cultures. Appreciation of Aminguh's experience requires attending to psychologically based motives that contribute to the structure of his stories. He presents a particular version of events in an effort to convince himself of his own personal effectiveness in manipulating and ultimately relating to his close relatives. The version he presents is a fortified one, built to defend against an alternative suppressed version that would leave his personal effectiveness in doubt. Those suppressed meanings emerge in other contexts, such as when he invites my commiseration over his predicament of having to grow up without a father. Aminguh's childhood stories, then, do rely on cultural meta-narratives, but they also—when viewed with their rhetorical intent as a part of the analytical calculus—provide a window on experience.

References

Barnett, Tony 1979. Politics and Planning Rhetoric in Papua New Guinea. *Economic Development and Cultural Change* 27(4):769–84.

Bruner, Jerome 1994. The 'Remembered' Self. In Ulric Neisser and Robyn Fivush (eds) *The Remembering Self: Construction and Accuracy in the Self-Narrative*, pp. 41–54. Cambridge: Cambridge University Press.

Chase, Susan E. 1995. Taking Narratives Seriously: Consequences for Method and Theory in Interview Studies. In Ruthellen Josselson and Amia Leiblich (eds) *Interpreting Experience: The Narrative Study of Lives*, pp. 1–26. Thousand Oaks, Calif.: Sage.

D'Andrade, Roy and Claudia Strauss (eds) 1992. *Human Motives and Cultural Models*. Cambridge: Cambridge University Press.

Ewing, Katherine P. 1990. The Illusion of Wholeness: Culture, Self, and the Experience of Inconsistency. *Ethos* 18:251–78.

Ewing, Katherine P. 1997. *Arguing Sainthood: Psychoanalysis, Modernity, and Islam*. Durham, NC: Duke University Press.

Garro, Linda C. and Cheryl Mattingly (eds) 2000. *Narrative and the Cultural Construction of Illness and Healing*. Berkeley: University of California Press.

Labov, William 1981. Speech Actions and Reactions in Personal Narrative. In Deborah Tannen (ed.) *Analyzing Discourse: Text and Talk*, pp. 219–47. Washington, DC: Georgetown University Press.

Leavitt, Stephen C. 1995. Suppressed Meanings in Narratives About Suffering: A Case from Papua New Guinea. *Anthropology and Humanism* 20(2):1–20.

Leavitt, Stephen C. 2007. Positioned Meanings in Personal Narratives. In Jurg Wassmann and Katharina Stockhaus (eds) *Experiencing New Worlds*, pp. 78–94. New York: Berghahn Books.

Ochs, Elinor and Lisa Capps 1996. Narrating the Self. *Annual Reviews of Anthropology* 25:19–43.

Schieffelin, Edward L. 1976. *The Sorrow of the Lonely and the Burning of the Dancers*. New York: St Martin's Press.

Strathern, Marilyn 1988. *The Gender of the Gift*. Berkeley: University of California Press.

Strauss, Claudia and Naomi Quinn 1997. *A Cognitive Theory of Cultural Meaning*. Cambridge: Cambridge University Press.

Tuzin, Donald 1990. Of the Resemblance of Fathers to Their Children: The Roots of Primitivism in Middle-Childhood Enculturation. In L. Bryce Boyer and Simon Grolnick (eds) *The Psychoanalytic Study of Society. Volume 15: Essays in Honor of Paul Parin*, pp. 69–103. Hillsdale, NJ: Analytic Press.

8. On Messianic Promise

Joel Robbins

Introduction

I have learned many things from Don Tuzin's books. One of the formative texts of my education, as a graduate student interested in religious secrecy, was *The Voice of the Tambaran* (1980), and I poured over *The Ilahita Arapesh: Dimensions of Unity* (1976) just as carefully. Later, *The Cassowary's Revenge* (1997) became a guiding light for me during the process of writing my thesis on Christianity and cultural change among the Urapmin of Papua New Guinea. As it has for many of my generation, this book has been a condition of possibility for my own work—a book from the pen of a major figure of what we might call traditional Melanesian ethnography that provided proof that anthropologists could take Christian revival movements and the cultural changes they wrought seriously as objects of study and could, in doing so, produce ethnographies every bit as rich and satisfying as those of the past. A work of exceptional subtlety and rigorous, inventive argument, *The Cassowary's Revenge* was, to many who read it, a classic from the moment it appeared. I mention all this by way of saying that Don Tuzin, the writer, has been with me almost from the beginning of my engagement with Melanesian studies, and his work has been a major presence at every stage of my intellectual development.

And in 1998, Don Tuzin became my colleague and mentor. In those capacities, he taught me much more than I can begin to recount here. But I want to dwell on one lesson I learned from him that has been important to me and that bears on the argument of this chapter. That lesson is that people can be close and supportive colleagues even in the face of important intellectual differences as long as they are willing to argue those differences out whenever they come up. Don taught me this lesson because although he and I agreed about a great many things— not least the importance of Melanesian ethnography—deep down we favoured very different kinds of anthropological theory. As he laid out clearly in the opening pages of *The Ilahita Arapesh*, Don was a methodological individualist and, correlated with this, a nominalist (Tuzin 1976:xxv–xxx). Put very roughly, for him the world was created anew at every instant by individuals acting in the situations in which they found themselves. I, on the other hand, am much more comfortable in the other camp—a camp that is harder to name (Tuzin 1976:xxvi– xxvii), but that tends to be labelled holism or realism. Trained as a structuralist, I focus in my own work on standing cultural complexes, which I take to be real in some meaningful sense, and on their power to shape the way social life unfolds. Broad theoretical distinctions such as those between nominalists and realists are always too blunt, and I can point you to realist-looking parts of Don's work (and in fact he was a great ethnographer of what I would call cultural structures) and to nominalist-looking parts of my own. But it was still the case that in the midst of my and Don's many long intellectual conversations—a genre of interaction of which Don was a master—often the areas of disagreement would run along these nominalist/realist lines, with him wanting to privilege individuals in one way or another and me wanting to privilege cultural structures. Don taught me how valuable it was to keep revisiting such recalcitrant issues as friends and as colleagues, even when perfect agreement is not on the horizon. This was one of the many important lessons in how to be an intellectual and a colleague that I learned from Don, a man who excelled in both roles.

I bring up this particular lesson here because the split between nominalism and realism bears on the topic I want to address in the rest of this chapter—that of messianism. Ever since I read *The Cassowary's Revenge* very soon after it came out (see Robbins 1998), I sensed that this was the book of Don's that fitted my own theoretical predilections most closely. For a long time, I thought this might just be because Don's methodological individualism had mellowed a bit with age, but now I am inclined to think that the drawing closer of our two outlooks that I see in this book also has to do with its focus on messianism as a kind of cultural change. For if we take messianism to aim for (even if it never fully achieves) change that is deliberate, rapid and radical then the kinds of cultural spaces messianism opens up are ones in which even realists will have to attend to how concrete individuals bring about momentous change—how they, as Don puts it, take 'history into their own hands' (Tuzin 1997:36). At the same time, inasmuch as messianic periods are ones in which all manner of cultural resources are in play—periods in which 'culture, history and psyche unite to create a "mythic" moment in which the barriers separating metaphysical domains are lifted' (Tuzin 1997:67)—even nominalists will have to attend to the kinds of cultural structures messianics shatter into the fragments they then redeploy to make a new life. Don made just this kind of cultural turn in *The Cassowary's Revenge*. This is evident both in his consideration of how the Nambweapa'w myth shaped historical action in Ilahita and in his complex argument about the way in which a central contradiction of Ilahita culture 'pressed for its own resolution' in the messianic Ilahitan destruction of their men's cult (Tuzin 1997:65).

Because my own theoretical interests and those that preoccupied Don come together so nicely around issues of messianism, I want to devote this chapter to some thoughts on what we might call the messianic promise: the possibility that messianism always holds out that life might be lived otherwise. Some of the theorists of messianism I discuss in what follows were not ones who interested Don much, but I am convinced that the spirit of this inquiry is in line with some of the main issues that animated his own work.

On Hearing the Messianic Promise

What does it mean to hear the promise of the messianic? If I were to answer that question on the basis of self-evidence, I would have to refer to several experiences: taken in order of occurrence, these would be encountering anthropology as a young student in the late 1970s and early 1980s; reading the literature on millenarianism in Papua New Guinea and later doing fieldwork with a group of people in that region who were adept at listening for the messianic promise; and, finally, reading and rereading Walter Benjamin's (1969) 'Theses on the Philosophy of History'. In this chapter, I want to try to make these experiences speak to each other in a way that might be productive for anthropological practice, or at least for my own anthropological practice. In order to work towards that goal, let me proceed in reverse personal experiential order, starting with Benjamin (and addressing Derrida along the way), moving on to Papua New Guinea and finally to anthropology.

One might say that Benjamin's theses need no introduction among contemporary academics, but of course they always do. They are cast in a writerly style that demands that they be received as an event in the lives of their readers, and to say anything interesting with or about them you have to put your reading on the table. Mine has always focused most on time but has in the past few years also taken up Benjamin's related critique of progress. I start with time here and come back to progress in my conclusion. The crucial point about time on my reading of the theses is that messianic time arrests another kind of time. Homogeneous empty time is Benjamin's historically grounded name for the kind of time the messianic interrupts, but perhaps we can include workaday linear causal time here as well so as not to exclude from consideration the messianism of those who have never lived in the homogeneous empty time of modernity. Benjamin's images of how the messianic arrest of linear time occurs are justly famous: the messianic makes the continuum of history explode; it pulls the emergency brake on the locomotive of history. But what does this arrest of time establish? Here Benjamin refers to historical memory, suggesting that messianic arrests happen when the past flashes 'up at a moment of danger'. This is to say that critical to the construction of messianic now-time is the effort to read history as a repository of some moments of potential emancipation that shine through the gloomy muck of its record of oppression, suffering and disappointment.

When such moments resonate with what is happening in the present the two can form a fusion that happens to time, not just in it, and opens up radically new possibilities for action.

How do we listen for the promise of the kind of messianism Benjamin has in mind? On this topic, Benjamin is not so strong. Certainly, he tells us to approach history differently, attending more to its unrealised potentials than to its linear unfolding. And we can argue that he himself has modelled this kind of listening for us in his own raising up of an old tradition of Jewish messianism in these theses written in the aftermath of the Molotov–Ribbentrop pact. But still, there is something Benjamin is not telling us about how to live what he calls in the notes to the theses a critical 'organized pessimism' that does not foreclose hearing the messianic call (Benjamin 2003:404). And this, I think, is where Derrida comes in.

In *Specters of Marx*, Derrida (1994:180–1) first introduces the concept of 'the messianic without messianism' in a footnote on Benjamin. He will in a later essay distance his idea of the messianic without messianism from Benjamin, but this initial conjunction—no matter how hedged and cautious—ought not be ignored. For I think Derrida has taken just the kind of step towards specifying what it would mean to listen for the messianic promise that one needs to take if one is to answer the questions about living messianically that Benjamin leaves largely unaddressed in the theses.

'Messianicity', Derrida tells us, is a 'universal structure of experience' (2008:248). It is a stance of 'waiting for an event, for someone or something that, in order to happen or "arrive", must exceed and surprise every determinant anticipation' (Derrida 2008:251). It is an openness towards, or even an expectation of, an unexpected future. This, on Derrida's account, is the messianic. The 'messianism' Derrida would have us do without is a tethering of the messianic to any kind of traditional content of expectation that would see the future as determinate (1994:59). Most often this content comes from a religious tradition and is represented by the figure of a known messiah, but of course Marxism and other post-Enlightenment political ideologies can supply it as well. Those who adhere to a messianism with determinate content too easily try to make progress towards realising it by shutting down other options. In the face of this danger, Derrida enjoins us to keep the structure of experience he calls messianicity in its pristine openness and to be vigilant in guarding against the messianism that would rob it of its ability to allow the event of a messianic cessation of time.

As an aside, I would note that though Derrida worries that Benjamin has fallen into the trap of tying his messianicity to a particular messianism—in his case a Jewish one—I am not sure this really is a trap or, if it is one, that Derrida has himself avoided it. As Jacoby (2005) has recently reminded us in quite eloquent terms, the tradition of Jewish messianism has always under-specified the future in just the way Derrida demands. Starting from the prohibition on making images of the absolute, it has proffered what Jacoby calls iconoclastic utopias (or in our case, eschatons), rather than ones based on blueprints for what is to come. Derrida's epoché of messianic content would thus not place him as securely outside Benjamin's tradition as he might imagine.

But more than perhaps entangling him in a Jewish tradition of messianism without the messianic that predates his coinage, Derrida's insistence on openness—on the disavowal of messianic content—also leaves him vulnerable to the question of whether or not anyone can really live this way. Can one listen for the messianic promise without listening for something specific? Would this reduce, as Eagleton (2008:87) remarks in a hostile response to Derrida, to something as unfortunate as harbouring 'a perpetual excited openness to the Messiah who had better not let us down by doing anything as determinate as coming'? My argument in the next part of this chapter is that we can learn from Melanesian millenarians that messianicity without messianism need not lead to this kind of absurd, unliveable stance.

On Messianic Living in Melanesia

We arguably have more detailed ethnographic accounts of lived millenarianism from Melanesia than from anywhere else in the world. A huge literature on cargo cults and a more recent one of Christian millennialism in the region combine to give us an unusually rich archive of materials bearing on this topic. We can and have quibbled about whether we have the categories right—whether the notion of cargo cult in particular shelters too many disparate kinds of social phenomena under its capacious canopy to be a useful concept. But there is little doubt that messianicity and messianism are both well documented in the region in contemporary as well as in earlier works (Jebens 2004a; Robbins 2004b).

The main focus of the Melanesianist writing on millenarianism is well known. It is trained on recognisable social movements, generally organised around an intensified ritual life and aimed at achieving fairly well-articulated goals such as acquiring manufactured goods, ridding one's territory of foreigners or achieving Christian salvation. In the terms we have borrowed from Derrida, these movements represent messianism—an attempt to bring about a determinate future. But the Melanesianist literature is also marked by a more subterranean theme. Most groups that engage in full-scale millenarian movements do not do so constantly, or even for particularly long stretches of time. Instead, periods wholly devoted to ritual performance focused on achieving clear goals alternate with quieter periods in which people live in workaday linear causal time. But anthropologists have found—and this is the key point here—that even when they live outside full-scale millenarian movements, many Melanesians live with a kind of millenarian openness that maps well on to what Derrida is calling messianicity. In these quieter times—times of what I have called elsewhere everyday millenarianism—people go about their normal business but remain ready for unexpected change, anxious to hear a messianic promise should it be made (Robbins 2001).

Even as anthropologists have not accorded everyday millenarianism the kind of attention they have given to full-scale millenarian movements, they have sometimes tried to describe it. In their accounts, we see both Derrida's openness to the event and Benjamin's hope that the unappreciated aspects of the past might sometimes knock the present off the tracks that its more appreciated aspects have laid down. Hence, for example, Burridge (1995) has talked about the myth-dream that proceeds and then underlies cargo cults as the rolling development of what Lindstrom (1993:49) nicely calls an 'unarticulated aspiration' for a future different from the present. Jebens (2004b:64), pointing to something similar, talks about the openness of much cargo language, a language in which it is quite possible to repeat phrases of the kind 'something will happen' without being heard to talk nonsense (see also Robbins 2004a:165–8). And while everyday millenarianism remains open to the future in just the ways Derrida would ask for, it also scans the past incessantly for elements that might find a place in a coming now-time, just as Benjamin would hope. As Don shows in his powerful analysis of the way a traditional myth came to legitimate a radical Christian revival movement that aimed to sweep all other aspects of tradition aside among the Ilahita Arapesh, during this millennial period, 'distinctions of past, present, and future dissolved' in a way that allowed a wholly new cultural configuration to arise (Tuzin 1997:128).

I hope to have at least indicated in somewhat abstract terms that there are riches to be gleaned in the Melanesian literature by those looking to learn what living a messianicity without messianism might look like. Before concluding, I want to give one more extended, concrete example of this kind of living. This is a very humble example from my own fieldwork among the Urapmin of Papua New Guinea.

The Urapmin are a group of 390 people living in West Sepik Province. They converted en masse to a charismatic form of Christianity in the late 1970s and since that time have been waiting intently for Jesus's return. Sometimes they feel sure that His coming is imminent, and they drop everyday life altogether for a week or more at a time and in classic millenarian-movement fashion devote all their time, day and night, to performing Christian rituals. More often, however, they accommodate their millenarian attentiveness within the bounds of their daily routines, constantly looking for and talking about the possibility of dramatic change but doing so while they garden and hunt. During these times, their millenarian hopes encompass, among other things, not only Jesus's return but also the possibility that mineral prospecting on their land might lead to the development of a major mine like the one that was built during the 1980s in Tabubil, a town on the land of their neighbours five days' walk to the south.

One day during one of these quieter periods, a young man arrived at my door rather breathless to ask if I had bought gardening gloves recently. This was a reasonable question, since after picking up a scorpion-like spider while clearing a garden about a month before I had told my companions I needed to get some of these gloves the next time someone went to Tabubil, where I knew they were sold in the supermarket. But no one I knew well had gone to the mining town since then, so I had not bought any gloves yet. I told my visitor this, and he expressed some agitation. He told me that a pair of gloves had turned up in the bushes by the main path people follow to make the six-hour walk home from the nearest airstrip where one can fly to and from Tabubil. People thought the gloves were mine. But if they were not, what could their appearance in Urapmin mean? Not sure what to answer, I followed my visitor to the area in which the gloves had been found. A small crowd had formed, and when I told them the gloves did not belong to me, they collectively began to ponder the significance of their appearance. Gloves were white-people things, they noted. Could this mean a mine would be built and Urapmin would become a white town like Tabubil? Could it mean that Jesus—Himself white—was finally returning to gather the faithful? Open-ended speculation along these lines developed apace, and, as people's excitement rose, they sent an emissary to consult a powerful Spirit man—a housebound man capable of consulting the Holy Spirit to learn about things that might happen in the future. For some time, all of us waited to hear what he would say.

Let me interrupt this narrative momentarily to point out that it would not have been that difficult for people to provide a simple, locally sensible explanation for the appearance of the gloves. First of all, they were in a recognisable yellow bag emblazoned with the Tabubil Supermarket logo, so there was no mystery as to where they originated (it seems that, even when one operates the only electrified full-scale supermarket within several days' walk of any real competition, branding is still important). They were also stashed along the main path one would use when coming home after flying to Tabubil. And finally, people often stash things they are tired of carrying in the bush by the side of the road, to come back for them later. It is true that no Urapmin had bought gardening gloves before, or at least not that anyone could remember, but people were always picking up new bits of modern life they could afford and bringing them home to try out, so it was not out of the question that someone would take a chance on gardening gloves in this respect and leave them by the side of the road to pick up later. At least for me, this line of reasoning rendered the gloves comprehensible.

But my main point here is that no Urapmin chose to take this line of reasoning. Instead, they took the appearance of the gloves as a chance to stop and listen in case they might be making a messianic promise—a promise about a future in which the gathered Urapmin people were not sure what to expect except that it would be different from the present. As it happened, about an hour into waiting for news back from the Spirit man, Deni showed up. Deni is a man in his mid-thirties who is very ambitious and who likes to accumulate as many fancy modern accoutrements as he can; he is one of the few Urapmin, for example, who often wears sunglasses. He had heard about all the commotion and had come to tell us all the gloves were his. His young daughter had got tired of carrying them home from the airstrip and had set them in the bushes to come back and get later. His announcement ended all speculation. In light of it, I guess I had been right. This time around, the gloves were making no messianic promise. But then again, had they been making such a promise, I would have missed it, and the Urapmin would not have. In this minor passing incident, as in many others, they showed they were ready quite quickly to let time stop and to organise around such a promise should it be made. The differences between myself and the Urapmin in this regard bring me to anthropology by way of conclusion.

On Messianism and Anthropology

In many ways, this chapter is inspired by two recent articles: one by Guyer (2007) and the other by Bialecki (2009). In both of these articles, the authors deploy ethnographic work on evangelical Christian messianism (in the Derridian sense of an anticipation of a determinate future) as a mirror for anthropological relations to time and event. For both, those who hold to schemes of Christian messianism lose their ability to plan for and act towards the near future in politically potent ways. Guyer's argument lays this out clearly, and Bialecki builds on it to demonstrate that in addition to eliding the time frame of meaningful strategic planning, left-leaning North American charismatics also foreclose political action by assuming that any meaningful transformation will come as a miraculous rupture and that, if they themselves work to bring about a change, the very fact of their effort will ensure that whatever it produces cannot be the millennial transformation for which they hope. For both Guyer and Bialecki, there are lessons in their ethnography for anthropologists, who are equally vulnerable to losing sight of the near future and to focusing on notions such as hope that attenuate their focus on the ways human beings actually bring about change.

These pieces have inspired me to ask here if there is not a kind of millenarianism worth living for anthropologists—a kind that might allow for the efficacy Guyer and Bialecki are seeking in anthropological practice and that, we should not forget, the anthropologists, sociologists and historians who first made millenarianism a major topic of contemporary study in the 1960s hoped to find in their subject matter. I have sought to find that kind of liveable messianism in this chapter in Benjamin's notion of moments in which homogeneous empty time stops and the present ceases to govern one's sense of possibility, and in Derrida's specification of messianicity as a structure of experience that stands open to the possibility of an other-than-present beyond current expectations. I presented material from New Guinea by way of suggesting that it is possible to live in the ways Benjamin and Derrida promote.

As a student in the 1970s and 1980s, I encountered an anthropology that I found saturated with what I, at least, thought was just this kind of messianic impulse. It was an anthropology committed to ethnography as at least possibly an encounter with an otherness it did not predefine, and in figures such as Mead and Benedict it had a history of making reports of such otherness effective at home in ways that on occasion interrupted homogeneous empty time by appearing as an event. After a long period of productive and necessary self-critique, anthropology has almost wholly lost this messianic openness to otherness. I cannot recount that history here, and we all know it in any case. But we should also recognise that without that openness to otherness, we now often adopt the linear time line of progress Benjamin so adamantly attacked; we are now much more about seeking means of amelioration in a world of stably defined goods such as human rights, health, political participation and economic wellbeing than we are about listening for messianic promises that might explode the progressive time line along which these goods are arrayed. In saying this, I want to write carefully. I recognise that anthropologists are led by their current preoccupations and temporal sensibilities to do good and necessary work. But—to use a phraseology that belongs wholly to models of time oriented to progress—I worry that this work keeps us so busy that, unlike the Urapmin, and, I would argue, unlike earlier anthropologists, we would have trouble stopping to listen when, in the field or at home, a messianic promise might be being made.

Coda

As a methodological individualist (see Gardner, this volume), Don Tuzin was always interested in the ways people made their own worlds. They might not always realise the kinds of worlds they are making, he was quick to note, but unless social life goes very wrong they are always free agents making their lives by choosing how to respond to the situations that confront them. A holist or realist, I am always in contrast more apt to stress the weight culture brings to bear on the acting person even if he/she construes his/her life largely in terms of individual choice. But when it comes to examining moments of messianic fervour, I have tried to suggest here, we need to attend to acting individuals— those who choose to hear the messianic promise—at least as much as we attend to the cultural structures from which they hope they are about to become disembedded. In the study of the messianic, I have suggested, the theoretical opposition that Don and I so often explored in our conversations tends, like so many other oppositions, to at least attenuate itself, if not collapse.

Don often made verbally a point I cannot recall ever seeing him put in print. Melanesianist anthropology, he liked to argue, had probably produced proportionally more major anthropological theories and theorists than any other region of the world. It punched above its weight in this way, he liked to suggest, because Melanesianists knew that they would never be able to claim the discipline's interest on the basis of the geopolitical importance of the countries they study or on the sheer numbers of people who lived in them. Instead, to be listened to at all, Melanesianists have always known they had to strive to address issues of very general interest in theoretically novel ways. I would not claim to have accomplished such a lofty goal here, but in Don's memory I did want to try to move in that direction, and that is why this chapter has addressed a topic of general interest at the moment (millenarianism), has tackled it in broad theoretical terms, and has tried to ground its argument in at least some discussion of Melanesian ethnography. Don excelled at this kind of complex, multi-voiced writing, and he enriched Melanesian studies immeasurably by his work. I hope to have been able to evidence a little bit of what both Don and his work have meant to me in my own effort here to follow his lead.

References

Benjamin, Walter 1969. *Illuminations*. H. Zohn (trans.). New York: Schocken.

Benjamin, Walter 2003. *Selected Writings. Volume 4*. H. Eiland and M. Jennings (eds). E. Jephcott et al. (trans.). Cambridge, Mass.: Harvard University Press.

Bialecki, Jon 2009. Disjuncture, Continental Philosophy's New 'Political Paul', and the Question of Progressive Christianity in a Southern Californian Third Wave Church. *American Ethnologist* 36(1):110–23.

Burridge, Kenelm 1995 [1960]. *Mambu: A Melanesian Millennium*. Princeton, NJ: Princeton University Press.

Derrida, Jacques 1994. *Specters of Marx: The State of the Debt, the Work of Mourning, and the New International*. P. Kamuf (trans.). New York: Routledge.

Derrida, Jacques 2008. Marx & Sons. In M. Sprinker (ed.) *Ghostly Demarcations: A Symposium on Jacques Derrida's Specters of Marx*, pp. 213–69. London: Verso.

Eagleton, Terry 2008. Marxism Without Marxism. In M. Sprinker (ed.) *Ghostly Demarcations: A Symposium on Jacques Derrida's Specters of Marx*, pp. 83–7. London: Verso.

Guyer, Jane 2007. Prophecy and the Near Future: Thoughts on Macroeconomic, Evangelical, and Punctuated Time. *American Ethnologist* 34(3):409–21.

Jacoby, Russell 2005. *Picture Imperfect: Utopian Thought for an Anti-Utopian Age*. New York: Columbia University Press.

Jebens, Holger 2004a. Introduction: Cargo, Cult, and Culture Critique. In H. Jebens (ed.) *Cargo, Cult, and Culture Critique*, pp. 1–13. Honolulu: University of Hawai'i Press.

Jebens, Holger 2004b. Talking About Cargo Cults in Koimumu (West New Britain Province, Papua New Guinea). In H. Jebens (ed.) *Cargo, Cult, and Culture Critique*, pp. 157–69. Honolulu: University of Hawai'i Press.

Lindstrom, Lamont 1993. *Cargo Cult: Strange Stories of Desire from Melanesia and Beyond*. Honolulu: University of Hawai'i Press.

Robbins, Joel 1998. Review of D. Tuzin's 'The Cassowary's Revenge: The Life and Death of Masculinity in a New Guinea Society'. *American Anthropologist* 100:516–17.

Robbins, Joel 2001. Secrecy and the Sense of an Ending: Narrative, Time and Everyday Millenarianism in Papua New Guinea and in Christian Fundamentalism. *Comparative Studies in Society and History* 43:525–51.

Robbins, Joel 2004a. *Becoming Sinners: Christianity and Moral Torment in a Papua New Guinea Society*. Berkeley: University of California Press.

Robbins, Joel 2004b. On the Critique in Cargo and the Cargo in Critique: Towards a Comparative Anthropology of Critical Practice. In H. Jebens (ed.) *Cargo, Cult, and Culture Critique*, pp. 243–59. Honolulu: University of Hawai'i Press.

Tuzin, Donald 1976. *The Ilahita Arapesh: Dimensions of Unity*. Berkeley: University of California Press.

Tuzin, Donald 1980. *The Voice of the Tambaran: Truth and Illusion in Ilahita Arapesh Religion*. Berkeley: University of California Press.

Tuzin, Donald 1997. *The Cassowary's Revenge: The Life and Death of Masculinity in a New Guinea Society*. Chicago: University of Chicago Press.

Section Three: Comparativism, Psychoanalysis and the Subject

9. Klein in Bali and Ilahita: A reflection on cultural fantasy and the deep unconscious

Michele Stephen

Although many anthropologists would not even accept the existence of a deep unconscious such as outlined by psychoanalytic theory of various persuasions, the ethnographic data often provide examples of cultural constructs that seem such vivid realisations of themes described in psychoanalytic practice that one can only stand amazed. If there is no 'unconscious', from whence do these extraordinary visions emerge and how is it they have such constancy across cultures? In this chapter, I employ Melanie Klein's work on gender, fantasy and psychosocial development as a framework for comparing Balinese and Ilahita imaginings of the feminine and the maternal.

If Freud's insights concerning the region of the unconscious were unpalatable to many—dethroning as they did reason and consciousness as the sources of human motivation—Melanie Klein's theories might be considered truly repellent. At least Freud's theories put the father figure and patriarchal authority at the centre of unconscious conflict. Klein, however, was bold enough to declare that the real lynchpin of all emotional development was the relationship with the mother. Prior to the unconscious guilt attached to a fantasised patricide went envy and paranoid fears aroused by a fantasised matricide. Masculinity and femininity were shaped against a mother image of such terrible power that both genders felt themselves to be damaged as a result of the struggle. In Klein's view, human life began in pain and suffering; it was not an optimistic view of the human condition. Yet she believed that it was only in relationships that emotional life developed and she emphasised that guilt, envy and fear were balanced by an equally strong positive urge to make reparation.

Contemporary feminist theorist Julia Kristeva (2001:15) observes: 'Melanie Klein ranks amongst those who have done the most to further our understanding of our being as an endemic state of ill-being in all its diverse manifestations: schizophrenia, psychosis, depression, mania, autism, delays and inhibitions, catastrophic anxiety, fragmentation of the ego, and so forth.'

Although Klein took psychoanalysis in new directions, she did so within the framework of Freudian thought. Kristeva (2001:11) notes: 'Klein successfully introduced a new approach to the theory and practice of the unconscious without ever abandoning the fundamental principles of Freudianism (which distinguishes her from Jung and from the other "dissidents").' Her significance for anthropology is perhaps only beginning to emerge, especially as anthropology's comparatively recent interest in gender directs new attention to the maternal in cultural fantasy (Gregor and Tuzin 2001). I do not expect that my readers will find Klein's ideas more intuitively persuasive than Freud's; quite the contrary. Yet I contend that she has much to offer anyone who seeks to explore the extraordinary images of the maternal found in Bali and Melanesia.

The inspiration for this chapter goes back several years to when I first began to take an interest in Kleinian theory. Don Tuzin commented to me at the time that his mentor at The Australian National University, Derek Freeman, always said that the Hindu goddess Durga was a Kleinian fantasy *par excellence*. Later, when I came to work in Bali, Indonesia, I began to understand why, and I promised myself that one day I would attempt a Kleinian interpretation of Durga. It thus seems especially fitting that I should offer this essay as a tribute to Don's wide-ranging psychoanalytic and comparative interests. In the process of writing, I began to realise that Klein's ideas not only threw new light on my Balinese material but also strongly resonated with Don's own work on masculinity and femininity among the Ilahita. I had previously published a piece on male cults in the New Guinea Highlands from a Kleinian perspective (Stephen 2003); I began to wonder how the same approach might work with respect to Sepik male cults. Engaging with Don's analysis of the Ilahita cult enables me to identify significant points of similarity and difference with Balinese imagery of the 'Terrible Mother', pointing to the ways in which cultures deploy to different ends, and with different consequences, imagery drawn from the deep unconscious. My Kleinian framework also brings me to challenge some aspects of Don's analysis of the male cult, as will be explained later. In doing so, I seek to honour the fertile and stimulating qualities and the breadth of Don's theoretical reach.

This chapter is not offered as ethnography but as an interpretation that draws upon extensive bodies of ethnographic work, sketching in with bold brush strokes links and parallels leading to reflections upon the nature of masculinity and femininity as shaped by culture and the unconscious. My arguments and conclusions do not pretend to be conclusive but aim to draw new attention to the mystery of the maternal, especially its negative aspects, in cultural imaginings. I begin with the horrific imagery of the Balinese Durga[1] and then turn to a consideration of the role of similarly Terrible Mothers among the Ilahita of New Guinea.

---

1   I have elsewhere described the Balinese goddess Durga (Stephen 1999, 2001, 2005, 2006), but have not previously attempted a psychoanalytic interpretation of her iconography, except to the extent that it is connected to the witch figure.

Klein and Durga in Bali

The Divine Mother has many refractions in Hinduism, and Durga is one of the most prominent. In Indian iconography, Durga is a warrior goddess, her 10 arms each carrying a weapon, riding on a lion into battle. Yet, though she is bloodthirsty, and offerings to her consist of meat and blood, she is usually depicted as young and beautiful in form. She is addressed as 'Ma Durga'— Mother Durga—and praised as defender and saviour by her followers. She seems to stand midway between gentle and benign forms of the goddess such as Sri and Sarasvati, and horrific forms such as Camundi and Kali (Kinsley 1988).

Durga is defined thus in the *Rider Encyclopaedia of Eastern Philosophy and Religion*:

> '[T]he unfathomable one'; one of the oldest and most widely used names for the Divine Mother, the consort of Shiva.

> Her ten-armed figure, standing on the back of a lion, symbolizes the great power that the Vedic texts describe her as wielding, either to punish or to confer grace on human beings. She destroys the demon of ignorance, nourishes the poor, and confers blessings of love and knowledge upon all those who strive for God-realization. (Schumacher and Woerner 1999:96)

The Balinese Durga[2] differs from her Indian counterpart, although both figures might be said to be recognisable as variations on similar themes. Indian traditions seem to emphasise Durga as a warrior goddess.[3] She is revered as the slayer of terrible demons—in particular, the buffalo demon, Mahisha. In this form of demon slayer, and thus as the saviour of gods and humans, she is usually depicted as a young and beautiful woman. Durga, the slayer of the demon Mahisha, is known in Bali, and her image is found in old Javanese sculpture. A famous statue of Durga at Pura Kedarman in Bali depicts the goddess in human form,[4] but the Balinese Durga is more usually depicted very differently. Her iconography more closely resembles the Indian goddess Kali, a horrific manifestation of Durga.

---

2   The relationship between Balinese Hinduism and Hinduism (in its many varieties) as found in India has been the topic of much scholarly debate over many years, with some scholars arguing that at best Hinduism in Bali is but skin deep, and others that it is much more deeply rooted (see Stephen 2005). I do not intend to re-enter that debate here but to describe the imagery of the Terrible Mother as encountered in its specifically Balinese cultural forms. My aim is not to compare the Balinese and Indian variants of the goddess—a project well worth undertaking but one that could not be contained within the limits of a single essay. Emigh (1996:89) suggests that the iconography of the Balinese Durga/Rangda might be derived from several different Indian goddesses. Overall, his exploration of the Balinese Rangda clearly demonstrates the ways in which she encapsulates many aspects of the Shakti traditions of India.

3   Variations in the role of goddess over time and in different regions of India are, however, noted by Kinsley (1988:96, 114–15).

4   See Bernet Kempers (1991:32) for an illustration; compare with Mookerjee (1988:48).

As the Divine Mother, Kali is usually represented as dancing or in sexual union with Shiva. Whereas Shiva represents the transcendental aspect, Kali symbolizes the dynamic aspect, primal energy…Kali wears a belt made of dismembered arms and a necklace of skulls; of her four arms, the lower left hand holds the bloody head of a demon, the upper left wields a sword. With her upper right hand she makes a gesture of fearlessness, while the lower right hand confers benefits. She destroys ignorance, maintains the world order, and blesses and frees those who strive for the knowledge of God. Kali is the symbol of dissolution and destruction. (Schumacher and Woerner 1999:170)

Kali is usually shown with staring eyes, a red, lolling tongue, sharp fangs and fierce expression; her skin is black and her hair long, matted and wild (see Mookerjee 1988 for illustrations). When she appears with Shiva, her spouse, she usually stands or sits astride his recumbent body.

The Balinese Durga is depicted in temple sculpture and paintings as a kind of female monster or ogress, the body large and heavy, with emphasis on pendulous breasts and belly, the head like that of a wild beast. She is gigantic in size, as is the mother in respect to the infant. With great bulging eyes, a pig-like snout, huge curved fangs and a great gaping maw opened to release a flaming red tongue, her face is that of a terrifying animal. A mass of matted, tangled hair cloaks her back and sides, reaching to the ankles. Her feet and hands have the huge claws of a beast of prey. Entrails, bones and dismembered human body parts constitute her necklaces, earrings and various ornaments. How does such a hideous figure come in Bali to represent the Divine Mother?

Balinese mythic representations reveal that Durga is the terrible form taken by the gentle and beautiful goddess Uma,[5] wife of Siwa (Shiva). As Siwa's *sakti*, Uma is the active creative principle that gives rise to the physical world and all its contents. She is the Divine Mother as creatrix; however, myths recount that having created the world and human beings, Uma suddenly turned upon her creations in anger and, taking the terrible shape of Durga, began to destroy them. The *Purvaka Bhumi*, a Balinese text explaining the origin of the universe, describes the goddess's horrific transformation thus:

The Goddess then looked upon Her Self
And full of wrath She then became.
Her urge was then to eat mankind;
She screamed, and like a lion roared.
Her teeth were long and sharp, like tusks,
Her mouth an abyss in between,

---

5 'Uma' is more common than 'Parvati' as the name of Shiva's divine consort in Bali, while 'Shiva' is usually pronounced and spelt 'Siwa' or 'Ciwa'.

Her eyes shone, they were like twin suns,
Her nostrils, deep and cavernous.
Her ears stood like two thighs, straight up,
Matted and twisted was her hair;
Her body was misshapen, huge,
There was nothing that broke its height.
It pierced The Egg of the Universe,
Reached to the centre of the Sky.
Such then, was the Goddess Durga,
That was the name that She then bore. (Hooykaas 1974:64–5)

The myth continues with the god Siwa (Shiva) also taking the form of the terrible god Kala. Together, Durga and Kala create all manner of hideous creatures, and, residing in the graveyard, they begin to feast on humankind:

Could then the Goddess have been seen,
She was arising from the Deep,
And with her was the God Kala,
What was the aspect She had then?
With blood, as ashes, She was smeared,
And garlanded with human skulls,
Intestines were draped over Her,
She wore a scarf of red and black.
Her minions were escorting Her,
The creatures of the God Kala,
With all their brood attending them.
Then in the graveyard She did dwell.
In the graveyard of the infants,
Uncanny trees, branches drooping,
Where the God Kala's creatures dwelt,
The frenzied Dremba ate mankind. (Hooykas 1974:71)

Various myths recount how Siwa provoked Uma's anger, causing her to descend to the Earth as Durga and wreak destruction upon its inhabitants (Stephen 2002, 2005:64–71). Other myths attribute to her the origin of disease and of witchcraft (Stephen 2006). Human beings who aspire to obtain destructive occult powers (*pengiwa*) must pray to Durga in the cemetery in order to obtain them, and all human witches are said to be her followers and servants. She resides in the Pura Dalam (one of the three temples found in every Balinese village), where the souls of the dead awaiting cremation also stay. Clearly, she is associated with death, disease, witchcraft and destruction.

Durga is the inspiration for various sacred dances/dramas in which two formidable monsters, Barong and Rangda, confront each other, apparently in battle, but one in which no side is ever victorious. Rangda is danced by a single performer wearing a long wig of matted hair, a fearsome mask and striped bodysuit representing a grotesque female form. Her opponent, Barong, is danced by two performers, one carrying the front and the mask, the other the rear end with its long, arched tail. The body of the Barong is covered with long black, and sometimes white, hair and gives the impression of a great hulking beast, yet he has about him an air of both the ludicrous and the playful. I have elsewhere interpreted these two figures in detail to reveal their mystic significance as the goddess Durga and her spouse, the god Siwa, in his terrible form as Siwa Kala (Stephen 2001, 2005). Their ritual encounter in dance depicts the occasion quoted earlier in which Durga and Kala meet on Earth to create all terrible and destructive entities. As the *PurvakaBhumi* explains, in their divine forms, the goddess Uma and the god Siwa create the world, human beings and all good and useful creatures, then in their terrible forms as Durga and Kala they create fearsome and destructive entities. The aim of human ritual, while recognising the negative aspect of creation, is to ensure that Durga and Kala never again devour mankind but instead are persuaded to assume their benign forms as Uma and Siwa and to return to Heaven. The *PurvakaBhumi* tells that human beings were taught how to make the offerings necessary to satisfy the terrible hunger of Durga and Kala and their minions:

> And then a covenant they made:
> That mankind in the Middle Sphere,
> At full of moon and when at new,
> Should not by Kala be accurst,
> Should not by Durga be accurst.
> God Kala shall not eat of him,
> The Goddess Durga eat him not;
> …
> Gone is the form that They then had,
> To their first form They have returned;
> God Kala, Guru has become,
> And Durga, Uma has become. (Hooykaas 1974:75)

The aim of Balinese ritual is to ensure that the capacity for divine forces to turn destructive is balanced by the return to a positive state. Through ritual action, all negative, coarse and dangerous forces and entities can be transformed back into the positive entities from which they originated (Stephen 2002, 2005).

The dangerous and disruptive entities created by Durga and Siwa Kala—the *bhutakala*—can be transformed from enemies into protectors and guardians. Furthermore, since Durga and Kala gave rise to these entities, they control them and thus in terrible form can provide protection from them. The masks of Rangda and Barong used in the sacred dance dramas are kept in the village temples, along with other sacred symbols. Collectively, these items are referred to as the '*sesuhunan*'.[6] The Rangda and Barong masks are brought out and displayed on various occasions, and are revered as the protectors and guardians of the village, although not all people are aware of their mystical significance as emanations of Uma and Siwa. One hears much more of Durga in Bali than of Uma, her benign, gentle form, and her ferocious images are much more evident.

Kleinian Perspectives on the Terrible Mother

Durga/Kali, as found in India or Bali, is such a repellent image that one can only imagine how colonialists from Britain and Europe must have shuddered at such strange expressions of religious fervour (Urban 2003). What could be more disgusting, more alien—an ultimate manifestation of 'otherness'—for nineteenth-century European minds? No wonder even today the very name Durga tends in the popular imagination to conjure images of blood-soaked temples and thuggery. There is little or nothing here to overtly suggest commonality across cultures, so repellent is Durga/Kali that she surely must be the creation of a specific cultural logic, or fantasy. Ostensibly, she provides a case in point for the anthropological perspective that only an elucidation of the cultural webs of significance in which such a figure is enmeshed could provide any understanding of it. Intuitively, we can see no common ground with such a figure. Why should the Great Mother, the cosmic principle of creativity, be described in such extraordinarily ambivalent terms? Why in Bali is the tender, nurturing beautiful Mother equally a hideous monster who devours her own young and wreaks disease, havoc and destruction on all? What in these cultures might give rise to such horrific images of the feminine and place such emphasis on the hideous and grotesque in the maternal figure?

Freudian approaches lead to the assumption or argument that Indian child-rearing practices give rise to the splitting of the mother figure, and more specifically to the horrific image of Kali.[7] Are we to assume that the same arguments might explain the Balinese images? Some very famous anthropologists have certainly thought so, and have attempted to explain the figure of Rangda as a product of Balinese child rearing (Bateson and Mead 1942). But can child-rearing practices alone account for the sheer horror and force of such imaginings?

If we turn to the pages of psychoanalyst Melanie Klein (a younger contemporary of Freud), we can find descriptions of the fantasies of Western individuals

---

6   The *sesuhunan* are sacred objects representing divine powers, including masks and other items, belonging to the village temples.

7   Freudian interpretations of Kali have been extensively explored by Jeffrey Kripal (2003:196–222).

concerning the mother figure that closely parallel, in all their grotesque detail, the Balinese iconography of Durga. A Kleinian perspective thus might lead us to give more weight to unconscious sources of such cultural imagery.

Klein's psychoanalytic theories of emotional development came to focus on the persecutory anxieties and fears experienced by the human infant from its earliest moments from birth onwards. She argued that the first six months of the child's life were dominated by what she came to refer to as the 'paranoid/ schizoid position', which then gradually moved into a phase she referred to as the 'depressive position' (Klein 1993a:2–4). These two crucial developmental phases were what in Klein's view determined all later and adult emotional adjustment. Furthermore, failure to move through each phase satisfactorily became the basis for neurosis and even psychosis in later life.

In the paranoid-schizoid phase, the infant is exposed to an external world of experiences totally beyond its capacity to control or understand. In its relation to its primary care giver—usually the actual mother—the infant is totally dependent on her to satisfy all its basic needs. This first 'other' is initially experienced by the infant as a series of pleasurable, satisfying and comforting sensations—as when fed or held at the breast, and touched and handled in a comforting manner—and a series of painful, frightening and frustrating sensations, when the infant is hungry, wet, cold or in pain. Thus, in Klein's view, a sense of a good, satisfying external object is built up on the one hand, and on the other, a bad, frustrating and persecutory object. At first, due to its emerging cognitive capacities, the infant does not understand that the 'good object' and the 'bad object' are parts of the one person, the mother. Klein refers to this process as 'splitting' and to the 'good breast' and the 'bad breast' as the two objects or images that form in the infant's mind. Only later, as the child reaches the depressive position, does it begin to realise that the two are aspects of the one person.

'Splitting' along with projection and introjection become important defence mechanisms against anxiety during this early phase and later. Through projection, the nascent ego is able to rid itself of badness and danger, and, through introjection, it is able to incorporate the good object within itself (Klein 1993a:6–7). By splitting, the ego is able to keep the good object, the 'good breast', totally separate from the bad, frustrating breast, thus not only are the two kept widely apart but the very existence of the bad can be denied (at least for a time). In other words, the initial ambivalence in which experience of the mother is grounded also serves to protect the infant ego from realising that good and bad sensations emanate from the same external source. The infant 'phantasises'[8] the

---

8 In Kleinian theory, the term 'phantasy' is employed to indicate unconscious imaginative processes taking place outside conscious awareness, as distinct from 'fantasy', which takes place in consciousness. See

destruction of the bad breast while still being able to keep intact in its mind the good object. Thus, the complex process of introjection of good, and projection of the bad, can take place. Klein points out, however, that projecting the bad has its costs as it also involves denial and annihilation of a part of the ego—that part from which the bad feeling towards the object emanates (Klein 1993a:7).

Overwhelmed by its fears of the persecutory object—the 'bad breast'—the infant comes to hate it and wishes to destroy it by whatever means possible. Accordingly, it begins to picture, in the imagery thought that is all that is available prior to the development of language, retaliatory attacks upon the 'bad breast'. These attacks take the form of biting, chewing and burrowing into the 'bad breast', tearing into it with nails and teeth and sucking out all its contents. Klein (1993b:63) explains:

> If we consider the picture which exists in the infant's mind—as we can see it retrospectively in the analyses of children and adults—we find that the hated breast has acquired the oral-destructive qualities of the infant's own impulses when he is in states of frustration and hatred. In his destructive phantasies he bites and tears up the breast, devours it, annihilates it; and he feels that the breast will attack him in the same way. As urethral- and anal-sadistic impulses gain in strength, the infant in his mind attacks the breast with poisonous urine and explosive faeces, and therefore expects it to be poisonous and explosive towards him. The details of his sadistic phantasies determine the content of his fear of internal and external persecutors, primarily of the retaliating (bad) breast. (Klein 1993b:63)

Klein recognises that this picture of a terrified infant trying to defend itself against a hated persecutor who is none other than an internal representation of its mother seems scarcely credible given our assumptions about the angelic innocence of babies. Nevertheless, she argues that the evidence is undeniable for those familiar with the clinical data:

> The idea of an infant of from six to twelve months trying to destroy its mother by every method at the disposal of its sadistic trends—with its teeth, nails and excreta and with the whole of its body transformed in phantasy into all kinds of dangerous weapons—presents a horrifying, not to say an unbelievable picture to our minds. And it is difficult, as I know from my own experience, to bring oneself to recognize that such an abhorrent idea answers to the truth. But the abundance, force and multiplicity of the cruel phantasies which accompany these cravings are displayed before our eyes in early analyses so clearly and forcefully that

Hinshelwood (1991:32–46). In my discussion of Klein, I shall follow this usage throughout this chapter.

they leave no room for doubt. We are already familiar with those sadistic phantasies of the child which find their culmination in cannibalism, and this makes it easier for us to accept the further fact that as its methods of sadistic attack become enlarged so do its sadistic phantasies gain in fullness and vigour. (Klein 1994:130)

These escalating sadistic trends in turn give rise to more and more horrific images of the persecutor and what might be expected in retaliation. Thus, as the child begins by desiring to attack the 'bad breast' by sucking and scooping it out, then later by tearing into it with teeth and nails, and finally with explosive excreta and burning urine, so it expects to be annihilated by the 'bad breast' in exactly the same manner. Eventually, these desires move to the mother's body as a whole, which the infant desires to pierce open, burrow into and rob of all its desired contents—that is, those things the child assumes she is withholding for her own pleasure: milk, excrement, babies, and, by this stage, the father's penis. So the child comes to imagine a Terrible Mother figure that desires to rip open, suck dry and devour him. Klein (1993b:62) stresses the dominance of oral greed and aggression in this situation.

As the child develops, however, it begins to fear that, in its imagined attacks upon the bad breast/mother, it might have injured or destroyed the 'good breast' on which it depends for every comfort and need. This fear ushers in the next phase of development: the 'depressive position', where remorse and guilt over damaging or killing the 'good mother' prevail over paranoid fears of attack by the 'bad mother'. In order to deal with the feelings of loss that now emerge, the child must engage in reparative phantasies in which the damaged, wounded or dead mother is put back together and returned to life. The depressive position comes into play somewhere towards the beginning of the second half of the first year of life.

The first year of life begins with phantasies concerning sadistic attacks upon the bad mother and, in turn upon the self; then, as the child begins to realise that the good and bad breast are aspects of the one person (the mother), it is dominated by fears of loss, guilt and remorse. The splitting of the experience of the mother is determined at first by the infant's limited mental capacity, as it seeks to attach sensations—pleasurable and painful—to imagery. But as the child develops, the splitting begins to serve as a defence mechanism, shielding the child from recognising that the two are actually one.

From a Kleinian perspective, we see that the child's emotional life is dominated by the mother imago—that is, the internal image generated in the child's mind. All pleasurable and negative experiences are linked to aspects of this figure, and dealing with the love, hate, fear, remorse and guilt that it evokes not only constitutes the earliest challenges the child faces but also the foundation for later emotional life continuing into adulthood. In Klein's view, failure to negotiate satisfactorily the first two phases—the paranoid/schizoid and the depressive position—sows the seeds of adult neurosis and psychosis. The key to emotional life—the mother imago—is inherently ambivalent and furthermore is the subject of horrific sadistic and paranoid phantasies.

A Kleinian approach thus suggests that the unconscious basis of the Durga/Kali image lies in the early experience of every human infant. The radical splitting of the Great Goddess into totally benign, nurturant figures such as Uma/Parvati and demonic figures such as Kali/Rangda closely correlates with the primal experiences described by Klein. This ambivalence, we have seen, is inherent in the very nature of the infant's early experience of the mother. Furthermore, the terrible Devouring Goddess, who turns upon her own creations and devours them, is equally prefigured there. The iconography of the Balinese Durga—the emphasis on fangs, lolling tongue, sharp talons, and the frequently depicted casual gnawing on an infant—emphasises the central theme of oral greed. The ornaments—earrings, necklaces and garlands of dismembered body parts: heads, skulls, chopped off hands and arms, strings of entrails—evoke the phantasy attacks on the mother's body and its contents, and the retaliation expected in kind. The infant does not simply want to kill the mother; it wants to rip her apart with teeth and nails, and suck and scoop out all her body contents. The huge body of the goddess, with its heavy breasts and belly, depicts the mother's body full of milk, excrement, babies and all that the child desires to grab for itself, but now this treasure house of riches becomes a looming monster about to obliterate the child.

We do not need to look to cultural factors to interpret these images; they are the unconscious phantasies described by Klein writ large. Yet they are also clearly cultural forms. The basis for such forms lies dormant in all human beings, we might assume, but the question for the cultural analyst remains: why have such horrific images been worked into culturally elaborated symbols?

The Goddess and the Witch

I have argued elsewhere that the universality of the image of the witch owes its origin to the phantasies of the Terrible Mother described by Klein. The Balinese Durga's link to witches and witchcraft has already been noted. Yet while many cultures have beliefs in witches, how often do we encounter Devouring Mothers as goddesses? The witch, I have argued (Stephen 1999), is in essence a projection of guilt and anxiety—a projection of the 'bad breast'—and is a figure provoked in times of loss and bereavement.

A Terrible Devouring Goddess, who is not merely some kind of minor symbolic figure but explicitly an important aspect of the Great Goddess, creatrix of the whole physical universe, is clearly significantly different from a witch figure. She brings into consciousness something most of us, and probably most cultures, would prefer to deny: the deep ambivalence in our most primal experience of love and nurturing. Encountering this terrible aspect of the goddess is to face the very roots of our emotional being. It expresses a fundamental truth about human nature and the very nature of embodied existence. In terms of its spiritual significance, it brings the seeker after truth to recognise the inherently conflicting nature of human love: its origins in fear, anxiety and guilt. This, however, is not a cause to reject human love but to seek that which transcends it and thus to move beyond the dualities of love and hate, good and bad, positive and negative, creative and destructive that limit the operations of the mind, as we find in the philosophical teachings of Tantrism (Avalon 1974; Feuerstein 1998).

At a more mundane psychological level, we can see that whereas the witch is a product of unconscious 'splitting', the goddess is rather an attempt to bring the unconscious identification of the mother as the bad breast/object into awareness. The image of Durga involves recognition of the deep ambivalence that human beings have towards their first love object: the mother. As such, this cultural image surely serves to bring into awareness both sides of the ambivalence, thus resolving it for those who engage deeply with the symbol. By openly stressing and exploring both positive and negative aspects of the unconscious mother imago, these cultural forms enable the undoing of the unconscious splitting of the feminine and thus avoid the need to project the 'bad mother' onto actual women.

Of course, it might also be that the image of the Terrible Mother can be employed in a defensive manner, enabling the worshipper to identify (projective identification) with the Terrible Mother, as in Balinese witchcraft and sorcery (Stephen 2006), so that the victim becomes the persecutor. On the whole, however, at least in Bali, the cultural imagery that vividly depicts both sides of the ambivalence attached to the mother imago helps to foster cultural attitudes towards women that recognise both their gentle, nurturing and loving capacities and the awesome power they hold. Woman indeed is an embodiment of Sakti, the power of the material world, and deeply revered as such. In relation to woman, the male represents spirit rather than matter, but just as Shiva is powerless to bring the physical world into being without Sakti—his creative energy—so the human male is powerless without his consort.

Although I would not want to make such the proof of my arguments, the position of women in Balinese culture—both in the past and today—tends to support my position. Balinese women are respected and valued, and value themselves, as females in a way that is quite different from Western cultures, where the women who are respected are those who have succeeded in a man's world. In a book first published in 1937 and still in print, Miguel Covarrubias (1973:44–5) noted the high status of Balinese women, their role as sellers and moneychangers, their dominance of local markets and their economic independence in general:

> A woman has definite rights; the income she derives from the sale of her pigs, her weaving, or the garden produce she sells in the market is her own, and she may dispose of her belongings without the knowledge of her husband. Most women are not only economically independent, but contribute to the expenses of the household. A woman's debts are her own and her husband is not liable for them. The women keep the finances of the family and control the markets. (Covarrubias 1973:83)

He also observed in family life 'a strong feeling of equality, of politeness, and friendly frankness in the relationship between husband and wife' (Covarrubias 1973:155). Although Balinese have definite ideas about the type of work appropriate to the different sexes, Covarrubias explains that this by no means meant that women were confined to the home and domestic duties only. Indeed, they routinely undertook such labour as 'transporting building materials, carrying coconuts…delivering charcoal, or obtaining broken coral from the beach to make lime', and even house painting and masonry work (1973:82). These remarks are as apposite today as they were more than 70 years ago. As any visitor to the island can observe for themselves, Balinese women still work as labourers on the roads and building sites, and in the rice fields; they are still active as traders and sellers, and many are taking advantage of new opportunities available in business, tourism and government service.[9]

Well-known Balinese author, public commentator and psychiatrist Luh Ketut Suryani (2003:42–9) observes that Balinese Hindu women are not taught to think of themselves as weak or as of less strength and ability than men, as are females in many other—including Western—cultures. On the contrary, she points out, Balinese Hindu women are deeply respected and honoured as mothers, as the source of creativity and nurturing, indeed as emanations of the great Mother herself, while their propensity for materialism, greed, destructive anger and jealousy is equally recognised. The beautiful, gentle human mother quickly takes on monstrous form if not given her due. In Bali, the power of the Mother is the basis of all life, activity and success—and of all destructive and negative forces as well. In a study of contemporary Balinese artist Ketut Budiana, I have described his most compelling inspiration as 'the power of the Mother':

---

9   Nineteenth-century travellers and explorers made similar observations concerning the high status of Balinese women. See Geertz (1980:93) and Vickers (1989).

> Budiana's works reveal that the Goddess, in her many refractions, can take forms both beautiful and terrifying. She is the tender loving mother who gives birth to and nurtures all beings; she is the hideous ogress who devours and destroys all in her path. This dual aspect of the Goddess/Mother is central to knowing and understanding the nature of her power. Indeed in Budiana's works, as in Balinese religious art in general, monstrous figures of the divine mother predominate over the gentle and benign. The Mother is not only the origin of life; she is also the origin of death, and womb and tomb are often equated. In the womb, material elements are brought together to form a body that is the vehicle for a new life…Life and death are part of a continuous cycle of transformations of physical substances into different forms. (Stephen 2005:48)

The unconscious imagery is there for all to draw upon, but how that imagery is employed by different cultures links, I believe, to cultural ideas concerning gender identity—and to misogyny and violence towards actual women in real situations.

Women also fear the mother imago; indeed, they have especially strong guilt related to phantasised attacks upon the mother's body. Female psychosexual development, in Klein's view, involves a deep-seated fear that they have been wounded or maimed by the mother, in return for their attacks upon her. I have argued in more detail elsewhere that this unconscious belief leads to a sense of inherent badness or weakness, which results in women feeling themselves to be inferior (Stephen 2003). They thus become vulnerable to, and easily convinced by, cultural images that portray them as inferior beings to men. Where men introject the good aspect of the mother imago and project the destructive and inferior aspects onto women—as we can see vividly depicted in many male initiation cults—women come to accept this projection as it meshes with their own unconscious phantasies of being damaged by the mother.

Carl Jung (1980:37), who believed that the Mother Figure constituted an archetype in the human unconscious, also drew attention to the deep ambivalence attached to this figure and to the many symbolic representations of the Terrible Mother, including Kali. He argued that in patriarchal religions, such as Christianity, the removal of all feminine figures results in an impoverishment, and a failure to engage with the fullness of those symbols of the sacred that arise naturally in the human mind.

Klein and Vengeful Mothers in Ilahita

In their important comparative study *Gender in Amazonia and Melanesia*, Gregor and Tuzin (2001:338) observe that gender distinctions play a key role as organising principles in Hindu Tantrism, as well as in the male initiation cults on which they focus. My argument in this chapter has been that the Tantric figure of Durga in Bali, although it is based on 'splitting', serves as a cultural symbol to undo the split and its defensive consequences. I have argued elsewhere (Stephen 2003) that male initiation cults in the New Guinea Highlands can be understood as classic Kleinian defences against the guilt and terror provoked by the splitting of the mother imago. Gregor and Tuzin's comparative work enables me to apply my arguments more widely to include the cultures they examine, and thus to elaborate on the differences with Balinese Tantrism.

Male cults, as Gregor and Tuzin point out, are prevalent not only in Amazonia and Melanesia but also in Aboriginal Australia, and echoes of them remain even in Western culture in exclusively male clubs and organisations. Their psychoanalytic interpretation clearly identifies the defensive nature of the cults and the insecure masculine identity that they serve to defend. A Kleinian perspective, which Tuzin (1997:122) acknowledges as especially pertinent to his data, can help, I think, to elucidate yet further the nature of the unconscious desires and phantasies involved in the cult rituals. I will focus my discussion on six important features Gregor and Tuzin identify as central to the cults found in 'Melazonia'.

1. The Matriarchal Myth

The 'myths of matriarchy' that characterise the cults are summarised by Gregor and Tuzin thus:

> The myths tell of a time when the women discovered, invented, or possessed the cult objects, bullroarers, flutes, or trumpets that are the central symbols of the men's cults. These objects permitted the women to dominate the men or at least to live apart from them…Banding together, the men forced or tricked the women into giving up the sacred objects, resulting in their possession of the generative powers of the flutes, the reordering of society, and, in some case[s], the establishment of patriarchy. (2001:310)

The primal unconscious phantasy that the Mother is possessed of all good and desirable things, and the infant's desire to rob her of them, is clearly reflected in this mythic structure, which, like a dream, provides the fulfilment of the wish. The desire to rob the Mother is now realised, but with this satisfaction come guilt and fear of the Mother's terrible retaliation. These 'myths of matriarchy' reflect in barely disguised form the central phantasies that constitute what Klein refers to as the 'paranoid/schizoid position' described earlier in this chapter.

2. The Importance of Body Imagery

There is much acceptance in anthropology that the body provides a natural symbol for society and many other things as well (Gregor and Tuzin 2001:339), although why certain substances and structures should be privileged over others is not so clear. Few anthropologists, however, consider the unconscious significance of the body. From a Kleinian perspective, the body that provides the template for unconscious phantasy is the Mother's body. The maternal body is believed to contain every good thing the child desires: milk, food, babies, excrement and the father's penis, all of which the Mother is thought to be withholding for her own enjoyment. Klein observes:

> I have found that aggressive impulses and phantasies arising in the earliest relation to the mother's breast, such as sucking the breast dry and scooping it out, soon lead to further phantasies of entering the mother and robbing her of the contents of her body. Concurrently, the infant experiences impulses and phantasies of attacking the mother by putting excrements into her. In such phantasies, products of the body and parts of the self are felt to have been split off, projected into the mother, and to be continuing their existence within her. (1993c:142)

Such nightmarish combinations of body parts, male and female genitals, and body substances are just what form the symbolic material elaborated in male cults. Gregor and Tuzin observe: 'The detachability of genitals from their owners anticipates their mutability as male and female organs. Penises, clitorises, vaginas, anuses, breasts, mouths, noses and tongues are symbolic permutations of one another. They condense, merge, and differentiate' (2001:313).

The Mother's body containing the Father's penis is a key Kleinian phantasy, and the core of the figure of the combined parental imago (Klein 1993b:79). The Father's penis is also equated with babies (and faeces) contained in the Mother's body (Klein 1993b:78), providing an exact parallel with the apparently bizarre idea of the Gimi people of Highlands New Guinea that 'fetuses are conceived of as phalluses, with the newborn's fontanel as the urethral aperture' (Gregor and Tuzin 2001:313).

3. Reproduction and Procreativity

Male cults, as Gregor and Tuzin (2001:314) observe, typically focus on concerns with reproduction and creativity in general, asserting that both are the exclusive province of men. This is clearly a defence against male fears of precisely the opposite, and correlates with the primal envy inspired by the Mother's body. According to Klein, the phantasy image of the 'good breast' is the prototype of all creativity:

> I would not assume that the breast is to him [the infant] merely a physical object. The whole of his instinctual desires and his unconscious phantasies imbue the breast with qualities going far beyond the actual nourishment it affords.

> We find in our analysis of our patients that the breast in its good aspect is the prototype of maternal goodness, inexhaustible patience and generosity, as well as creativeness. It is these phantasies and instinctual needs that so enrich the primal object that it remains the foundation for hope, trust, and belief in goodness. (Klein 1993d:180)

Thus, in unconscious phantasy, the Mother is the source and prototype of not only sexual and reproductive power, but of all cultural creativity as well, and thus the focus of intense envy.

4. Women and Projective Identification

In an article entitled 'Male Mothers and Cannibal Women', I have argued at length that male initiation rites in Highlands New Guinea are cultural fantasy systems involving a splitting of the mother imago into exclusively good and bad parts, the former being appropriated symbolically by men, the latter being projected on to actual women (Stephen 2003). Thus, men ritually assert that they give birth to and nurture if not all human beings, then certainly the most important: men. Women on the other hand are seen as dangerous, polluting and weakening to males, and capable of producing only unimportant females—or indeed, if we look to the beliefs of the Gimi people, as inclined to devour all offspring unless subject to the controlling influence of men!

Similar if not identical phantasy processes of splitting, appropriation (projective identification) and projection of the mother imago are evident in the broad spectrum of cultures that Gregor and Tuzin consider. Male cults 'project a view of women as dangerous and powerful', while men take on the procreative powers of mothers for themselves (Gregor and Tuzin 2001:321).

5. Secrecy, Vigilance, Terror and Violence

Having, in unconscious phantasy or myth dream, successfully stolen all the desired things the maternal body is felt to contain, the culprit is then consumed by paranoid fears of the Mother's retaliation. In order to ward off the Mother's revenge, secrecy must be preserved at all costs, but the fears are by no means abated; indeed, the more intense the activities of the cult, the greater are the fears of revenge by the Mother. It is not simply men's insecurity in relation to their masculinity, though there is that of course, but their guilt concerning the theft of the Mother's power, and their intense fear of her revenge, that charges their emotional investment in the cult with such force. Guilt and terror, not merely insecurity, provide compelling motivation. 'Secrecy', 'vigilance', 'terror and violence' (Gregor and Tuzin 2001:316, 318, 319) are the hallmarks not only of these male cults but also of the paranoid/schizoid position described by Klein.

6. Phallic Aggression

The desire to attack, destroy and control from within the maternal body is central to the Kleinian paranoid-schizoid position:

> From the beginning the destructive impulse is turned against the object and is first expressed in phantasied oral-sadistic attacks on the mother's breast, which soon develop into onslaughts on her body by all sadistic means. The persecutory fears arising from the infant's oral-sadistic impulses to rob the mother's body of its good contents and from the anal-sadistic impulses to put his excrements into her (including the desire to enter her body in order to control her from within) is of great importance for the development of paranoia and schizophrenia. (Klein 1993a:2)

The cultists' phallic aggression against women—be this rape or murder (Gregor and Tuzin 2001:320)—might thus be understood as an acting out of unconscious phantasies of destroying the Mother.

The Demise of a Cult: Opportunity for reparation?

From the Kleinian perspective argued here, the 'anguish of gender' identified by Gregor and Tuzin (2001) is generated by men ritually embracing the paranoid-schizoid phase of emotional development, splitting the Mother and appropriating for themselves the characteristics of the 'good breast' while projecting on to actual women the 'bad breast'. No wonder the cults have myths of an original theft from the Mother; this is precisely the nature of the phantasies Klein describes. The fears of the men that women will find out are fuelled by the paranoid fears of retaliatory attacks from the Mother. The cults serve to provide a defence against envy and fear of the Mother, but they come at the price of continuous paranoia. By dismantling the cults and admitting their sins, as occurred in the case of the Ilahita *Tambaran* cult (Gregor and Tuzin 2001:326–8; Tuzin 1997), the men, it seems, might now be able to enter the reparative stage, which begins in mourning and loss but at least provides the opportunity to attempt to repair the damage done in phantasy to the Mother.

The paranoid/schizoid position moves into the depressive position as the child begins to fear that, in his attempts to destroy the bad Mother, he has injured, damaged or even killed the good Mother. A growing sense of loss and depression can be overcome only by the repairing of the dead or dying Mother imago so that she is restored in phantasy as a good inner object. This process of reconstruction Klein terms 'reparation', and in her view it is crucial to normal emotional development. The child unable to make reparation remains locked in the paranoid/schizoid position and this provides the basis for psychosis in adult life.

Tuzin (1997) describes the cultural disintegration and sense of mourning and loss that followed the deliberate unmasking of the Ilahita *Tambaran* cult. For him, the disintegration of the cult, with all its admitted abuses and even horrors, led to cultural chaos and a worsening of actual relationships between men and women in Ilahita society. He concludes from this experience that the *Tambaran* cult had served in a positive manner to provide men with 'sanctuary'—a ritual space wherein a painfully acquired sense of masculinity might find shelter. He argues that male gender identity is more difficult to achieve than female, which is based, it would appear, on women's natural physiological attributes and the comparative psychological ease with which girls might identify with mothers (Tuzin 1997:191–2, 228). At this point, however, a Kleinian perspective would challenge his argument.

Masculinity, Femininity, and the Mother

As Tuzin himself points out, in examining male cults, we are not simply dealing with gender relations as such; rather, we are dealing with the unconscious relationship to the first object, the Mother.

> What men did not realize was that while the Tambaran may have engendered fears at one level, it dissipated fears on another. Those fears, older and more primitive than the Tambaran, were not really fears about women at all, but about Mother—though, of course, it was and is women who suffer because of them. (Tuzin 1997:177)

In turn, this primal relationship determines how gender identities are formed and what is considered to be the proper relationship between genders.

But is masculine identity more difficult to achieve, as Tuzin suggests, than female identity? I have argued elsewhere (Stephen 2003) that women are more prone to see themselves as damaged and inferior, especially if subjected to male ideology along these lines. Freud's notion that women in unconscious phantasy picture themselves as castrated men has, understandably, not been popular with feminists. Yet I think there is a truth in Freud's insight that women feel themselves to be wounded—a truth that is developed and clarified by Klein, who shows that female gender identity is much more complex than usually assumed. The girl has her own pressing fears and guilt concerning her phantasy attacks on the Mother. The unconscious belief that the inside of her own body has been damaged in retaliatory attacks is, according to Klein (1994:225–7), confirmed by the onset of menstruation—a fear that is not overcome until she bears a healthy child of her own, and sometimes not even then. According to Klein, the girl's progress through the oedipal phase is in fact more difficult than the boy's, since the male child eventually returns to his original love object, his mother, while the girl has in the end to reject the mother, her first love object also, and turn to the father and other males:

> There are great differences in the Oedipus complex of the girl and boy, which I shall characterize only by saying that whereas the boy in his genital development returns to his original object, the mother, and therefore seeks female objects…the girl to some extent has to turn away from the mother and find the object of her desires in the father and later on in other men. (Klein 1993e:252)

We can see from this perspective that female identity and relationship to the mother are much more problematic than is recognised by some feminist theorists such as Chodorow, as quoted by Tuzin (1997:228). I think any argument that male identity is more problematic than female needs qualifying. Rather, both genders founder on the reef of the Terrible Mother, but in different ways: male envy and fear of retaliation, female envy and the fear girls have that they have already been attacked and wounded. Thus, unconscious female fears that the insides of their bodies have been damaged easily mesh with male insistence on female 'badness' and inferiority. Such fear reinforces the practical circumstances of child-bearing and nurturing that tie women to these tasks. Men are indeed fortunate to be able to convince women that all they are fit for are the menial tasks of caring for children, when really it is men's control of cosmic or cultural forces that constitutes real creativity—be this making money or ritually ensuring fertility and procreation. As technology comes to free women from the slavery of child-bearing and nurturing, or at least gives them the choice, the question of who will produce children becomes critical—much as Tuzin's Ilahita Arapesh men feared. Who will willingly choose the drudgery of women's labour?

If men continue to attempt to appropriate the Good Mother for themselves, while trivialising and demeaning women by projecting onto them the Bad Mother, gender relations will continue to be dominated by unconscious fears of, and actual violence towards, women. Evidently, this is a situation that prevails far more widely than the male cults of Melazonia, including contemporary Western societies. Klein's insights suggest that both men and women need to become more aware of the unconscious power of the Mother imago. Where women are culturally encouraged to identify with both negative and positive aspects of the mother figure, as in Bali, I think they will seek to realise their identity as mothers. Nor is it enough to assure women that they are only really fulfilled as mothers; how can they accept that when everything associated with women and children is in actuality trivialised? All they are good for then is second best. Is it possible, as some believe (McDermott 2003), that Western women can successfully identify with the goddess? This clearly will depend on how Western men can respond to such identification.

Defences Against Primal Envy

Gregor and Tuzin point to male envy of women as a theme of central importance in the ritualisation of male gender identity. Yet why should men envy women? As Tuzin (1997:120) notes for the Ilahita Arapesh, the mythic cassowary maiden, Nambweapa'w, was tricked into an 'artful bondage' in which she relinquished her freedom for 'the captivities of childbirth, motherhood, sexual slavery, food getting drudgery, and all the rest'—in short, the traditional female role.[10] It is obvious that at a conscious level there is very little in women's roles in these cultures to envy, but as Tuzin (1997:177) notes, Ilahita Arapesh fears (and envy) of women are not really to do with women at all but concern the Mother.

Primal envy of the Mother and all she is believed to possess and be keeping for her own pleasure is, according to Klein, a key factor in early emotional development. She identifies several defences used to deal with that envy: splitting, projection, introjection, denial, and idealisation. All, I believe, can be identified with specific cultural attitudes to women: splitting, projection and introjection in Melanesia and Amazonia, denial in modern Western culture, idealisation perhaps in medieval ideals of courtly love and the cult of the Virgin Mary. In contrast, in Hindu Bali, as we have seen, there is a conscious recognition

---

10   Strathern's (1990) work on women's labour and domesticity might also be considered here.

in religious symbolism of the ambivalence held by the mother figure, and a deliberate honouring of the double-sided power held by women in their role as mothers.

Might not the Balinese Durga still be the product of child-rearing practices? Do teasing, frustrating or aggressive mothers give rise to images of Durga/Kali, as argued by Bateson and Mead (1942)? Although the figure of Durga in Bali can be understood as a product of 'splitting' the mother imago into good and bad aspects, the fact that she is honoured and worshipped in terrible guise—with the aim of returning her to her benign aspect—reveals that cultural rituals actually serve to undo the splitting. The equal emphasis on both benign and terrible aspects underlines the point that both are aspects of the same figure: the mother. In this way, I believe, unconscious processes are brought into consciousness and the deep ambivalence to the mother figure is made the subject of conscious reflection and indeed spiritual insight. This contrasts dramatically with Melanesian and other cultures where male cults serve to perpetuate the split, appropriating the good aspect of the mother imago for men and projecting the bad on to women. The Balinese Durga, I suggest, provides both men and women with a means of dealing with their ambivalence towards the Mother imago, the results being that men respect women as the embodiment of the Great Mother, in both her aspects, and women are able to identify with both powerful and nurturing aspects of the Mother. Certainly, men are still able to assert superiority in this scheme of things, since female equates with material substance and physical power, whereas masculine equates with spirit, consciousness and transcendence. Yet the two are utterly interdependent and the necessary basis of all existence. It might of course be that such clearly demarked categories could be used as the basis to enforce even more rigid cultural notions of gender inequality, yet this is not the case in Bali.

In my view, Tantrism reflects the opposite of the Melanesian gender situation; in Melanesia men deal with their envy and fear by attempting to ritually appropriate the good aspects of the mother figure (not just female in general, but as Mother). In Tantrism, envy and fear are overcome by bringing into cultural consciousness the negative and acknowledging and honouring both aspects of the powers held by women. The Tantric hero, the *vira*, is a hero as he is able to confront his own ambivalence.[11] But this, of course, does not apply to all men—only to the Tantric adept. The esoteric symbols are there available for those who wish to engage with them but, for the majority, defensive responses to the Mother imago, and her carriers, will probably still prevail.

I would expect that certain kinds of child-rearing practices do in fact tend to elicit or favour cultural emphasis on images of the Terrible Mother but that the

---

11 My view of the *vira* contrasts with Kripal's (2003) Freudian interpretation.

psychic images themselves are an inherent part of the human condition. All cultures must deal with them in some way—even if it is to simply repress and deny them, as we find in modern Western cultures—but they then find outlets other than religion; for instance, in the popularity of violence and monster figures in film and entertainment, but that is another argument.

The question remains why do particular cultures elaborate on particular defensive fantasies? Why do cultures in Melanesia, Amazonia and Aboriginal Australia possess such strikingly similar male cults, while Hindu cultures worship Terrible Mothers? I can do no more than raise the question here and make a few final comments. In small-scale, technologically simple societies, unconscious phantasy themes seem to emerge in more direct, less disguised forms, and to be closer to their unconscious roots. This emerged as a major finding from a survey study of the Oedipus complex cross-culturally (Johnson and Price-Williams 1996:7). This finding also applies to the male cults, where the direct parallels with Kleinian phantasies are no less than astonishing. Although the terrible goddesses of Hinduism also seem very direct representations, and no less confronting, a difference emerges in the way the phantasies are culturally employed.

Along similar lines, Obeyesekere (1990:60–1) has pointed out that in cultures such as the Sambia of Melanesia, symbolic systems seem to remain tied to unconscious themes and conflicts, while in Hinduism (and Buddhism) the symbolic systems follow a different trajectory, moving away from primal concerns to link to more refined concepts and understandings. His insights seem relevant to my arguments here about terrible goddesses providing the symbolic means to transcend the unconscious splitting of the mother figure, whereas the male cults provide a defensive reaction against the splitting. As we see in Tuzin's (1997) account of the demise of the Ilahita *Tambaran* cult, circumstances can change, however, and the defensive mechanisms of the past might no longer suffice, bringing about internal as well as external revolutions. In these circumstances, new cultural systems will eventually need to be developed that can provide the opportunity for reparation to the damaged Mother. It is perhaps too early yet to know how the Ilahitans might achieve that transition, but Tuzin's unique study has captured precisely for us the moment of change.

Conclusion

Psychoanalytic perspectives of whatever persuasion inevitably direct our attention to what is common to the human condition. As Donald Tuzin has extensively argued in his own work, comparative perspectives in anthropology are essential unless the discipline is simply to wither into relativist trivia;

a truly human science must engage with what it means to be human cross-culturally. The Kleinian approach I have taken in this chapter can, I believe, add to Freudian insights concerning the nature of unconscious phantasy processes. Freudian concepts of ambivalence, anxiety and repression—used to powerful effect by some cultural analysts—can be sharpened and given more explanatory force in view of Klein's understandings concerning the primal forces shaping emotional life. The phantasies she describes, in all their bizarre detail, are to be found in our ethnographies, and the richer these are, the clearer are the parallels with Klein, as I have found with the Ilahita cult and the Balinese Durga.

Critics of psychoanalysis have often maintained that it is demeaning to claim that the religious beliefs of other cultures reflect the fantasies of children and the insane in Western culture. Such arguments, I believe, involve a false reading of psychoanalytic theory, which suggests not that cultural products such as religious beliefs are no different from infantile fantasy or the delusions of the insane but rather that the unconscious mind provides a common stream of fantasy thought on which different cultures draw and then elaborate, and which also emerges in raw, unworked form in the fantasies of Western individuals. The Balinese Durga is a culturally mediated construct, the subject of complex philosophical reflections, mythological elaborations and rich artistic formulations in dance, drama, sculpture and painting. She is quite specific to Balinese culture and yet she encapsulates and crystallises in a very specific cultural form what are also universal themes of the deep unconscious. The same observations equally apply to Ilahita male cults.

The match between the ethnographic data discussed here and the phantasies identified by Klein seem just too specific and too striking to ignore in my view, yet anthropologists in the main rarely bother themselves with psychoanalytic theory, let alone the Kleinian variety.[12] Perhaps the confronting 'otherness' of such images, stemming as they do from primal experience not usually available to adult consciousness, prevents us from recognising the recurring patterns cross-culturally. Donald Tuzin was an intrepid explorer of these twin dangerous seas of psychoanalytic theory and the comparative method. We who follow in his wake will sorely miss his brave and fair-minded leadership.

---

12 Witness the complete overlooking of Klein's work by Kripal (1998, 2003) in his groundbreaking psychoanalytic studies of Kali. The recent edited study *Encountering Kali: In the Margins, at the Center, in the West* (McDermott and Kripal 2003) does not so much as list Klein in its index or bibliography. Fossey (2008:4) explicitly rejects Freudian approaches to Rangda, and does not even refer to Klein.

Acknowledgments

I would like to thank two anonymous reviewers of this chapter for pointing out several problems with an earlier draft and the editors of this volume for their support and encouragement.

References

Avalon, Arthur (Sir John Woodroffe) 1974. *The Serpent Power: The Secrets of Tantric and Shaktic Yoga*. New York: Dover Publications.

Bateson, Gregory and Margaret Mead 1942. *Balinese Character: A Photographic Analysis*. New York: The New York Academy of Sciences.

Bernet Kempers, A. J. 1991. *Monumental Bali: Introduction to Balinese Archaeology & Guide to the Monuments*. Berkeley, Singapore: Periplus.

Covarrubias, Miguel 1973 [1937]. *Island of Bali*. London and New York: Kegan Paul International.

Emigh, John 1996. *Masked Performance: The Play of Self and Other in Ritual and Theatre*. Philadelphia: University of Pennsylvania Press.

Feuerstein, Georg 1998. *Tantra: The Path of Ecstasy*. Boston: Shambhala.

Fossey, Claire 2008. *Rangda, Bali's Queen of Witches*. Bangkok: White Lotus Press.

Geertz, Clifford 1980. *Negara: The Theatre State in Nineteenth-Century Bali*. Princeton, NJ: Princeton University Press.

Gregor, Thomas A. and Donald Tuzin 2001. The Anguish of Gender: Men's Cults and Moral Contradiction in Amazonia and Melanesia. In Thomas A. Gregor and Donald Tuzin (eds) *Gender in Amazonia and Melanesia: An Exploration of the Comparative Method*, pp. 309–36. Berkeley and Los Angeles: University of California Press.

Hinshelwood, R. D. 1991. *A Dictionary of Kleinian Thought*. Northvale, NJ: Jason Aronson.

Hooykaas, C. 1974. *Cosmogony and Creation in Balinese Tradition*. The Hague: Martinus Nijhoff.

Johnson, Allen and Douglass Price-Williams 1996. *Oedipus Ubiquitous: The Family Complex in World Folk Literature*. Stanford, Calif.: Stanford University Press.

Jung, C. G. 1980. *Four Archetypes: Mother, Rebirth, Spirit, Trickster*. London and Henley: Routledge and Kegan Paul.

Kinsley, David R. 1988. *Hindu Goddess: Visions of the Divine Feminine in Hindu Religious Tradition*. Berkeley: University of California Press.

Klein, Melanie 1993a [1946]. Notes on Some Schizoid Mechanism. In *Envy and Gratitude and Other Works 1946–1963*, pp. 1–24. London: Virago Press.

Klein, Melanie 1993b [1952]. Some Theoretical Conclusions Regarding the Emotional Life of the Infant. In *Envy and Gratitude and Other Works 1946–1963*, pp. 61–93. London: Virago Press.

Klein, Melanie 1993c [1955]. On Identification. In *Envy and Gratitude and Other Works 1946–1963*, pp. 141–75. London: Virago Press.

Klein, Melanie 1993d [1957]. Envy and Gratitude. In *Envy and Gratitude and Other Works 1946–1963*, pp. 176–235. London: Virago Press.

Klein, Melanie 1993e [1959]. Our Adult World and its Roots in Infancy. In *Envy and Gratitude and Other Works 1946–1963*, pp. 247–63. London: Virago Press.

Klein, Melanie 1994. *The Psycho-Analysis of Children*. London: Virago Press.

Kripal, Jeffery J. 1998. *Kali's Child: The Mystical and the Erotic in the Life and Teachings of Ramakrishna*. Chicago: University of Chicago Press.

Kripal, Jeffery J. 2003. Why the Tantrika is a Hero: Kali in the Psychoanalytic Tradition. In Rachel Fell McDermott and Jeffery J. Kripal (eds) *Encountering Kali: In the Margins, at the Center, in the West*, pp. 196–222. Berkeley and Los Angeles: University of California Press.

Kristeva, Julia 2001. *Melanie Klein*. Ross Guberman (trans.). New York: Columbia University Press.

McDermott, Rachel Fell 2003. Kali's New Frontiers: A Hindu Goddess on the Internet. In Rachel Fell McDermott and Jeffery J. Kripal (eds) *Encountering Kali: In the Margins, at the Center, in the West*, pp. 273–95. Berkeley and Los Angeles: University of California Press.

McDermott, Rachel Fell and Jeffery J. Kripal (eds) 2003. *Encountering Kali: In the Margins, at the Center, in the West*. Berkeley and Los Angeles: University of California Press.

Mookerjee, Ajit 1988. *Kali: The Feminine Force*. Rochester, Vt: Destiny Books.

Schumacher, Stephen and Gert Woerner (eds) 1999. *The Rider Encyclopaedia of Eastern Philosophy and Religion*. London and Melbourne: Rider.

Obeyesekere, Gananath 1990. *The Work of Culture: Symbolic Transformation in Psychoanalysis and Anthropology*. Chicago and London: University of Chicago Press.

Stephen, Michele 1999. Witchcraft, Grief, and the Ambivalence of Emotions. *American Ethnologist* 26:711–37.

Stephen, Michele 2001. Barong and Rangda in the Context of Balinese Religion. *Review of Indonesian and Malaysian Affairs* 35:137–93.

Stephen, Michele 2002. Returning to Original Form: A Central Dynamic in Balinese Ritual. *Bijdragen tot de Taal-, Land- en Volkenkunde* 158:61–94.

Stephen, Michele 2003. Male Mothers and Cannibal Women: A Kleinian Interpretation of Male Initiation in the New Guinea Highlands. *The Psychoanalytic Review* 90:615–53.

Stephen, Michele 2005. *Desire, Divine and Demonic: Balinese Mysticism in the Paintings of I Ketut Budiana and I Gusti Nyoman Mirdiana*. Honolulu: University of Hawai'i Press.

Stephen, Michele 2006. Imaginary Violence and the Terrible Mother: The Imagery of Balinese Witchcraft. In Andrew Strathern, Pamela J. Stewart and Neil L. Whitehead (eds) *Terror and Violence: Imagination and the Unimaginable*, pp. 192–230. London and Ann Arbor, Mich.: Pluto Press.

Strathern, Marilyn 1990. *The Gender of the Gift*. Berkeley and Los Angeles: University of California Press.

Suryani, Luh Ketut 2003. *Perempuan Bali Kini*. Surabaya: Paramita.

Tuzin, Donald 1997. *The Cassowary's Revenge: The Life and Death of Masculinity in a New Guinea Society*. Chicago and London: University of Chicago Press.

Urban, Hugh B. 2003. 'India's Darkest Heart': Kali in the Colonial Imagination. In Rachel Fell McDermott and Jeffery J. Kripal (eds) *Encountering Kali: In the Margins, at the Center, in the West*, pp. 169–95. Berkeley and Los Angeles: University of California Press.

Vickers, Adrian 1990. *Bali: A Paradise Created*. Hong Kong: Periplus.

10. Hierarchy and Equality in Fijian Kindergartens

Karen J. Brison

Introduction

In 1983, when I was a graduate student, Donald Tuzin changed the course of my career by writing a National Science Foundation grant, part of which funded my dissertation research among the Kwanga of the East Sepik Province of Papua New Guinea. Tuzin proposed an ambitious comparative study of four neighbouring Sepik cultures. He argued that an important part of socialisation came through experience with other children. Among the Ilahita Arapesh, boys tell each other fearsome stories about cult spirits, and even though they later learn that these stories are just lies designed to frighten women and children, they continue as adults to have frightening dreams of cult spirits (Tuzin 1987). The same belief system, Tuzin argued, might have quite different personal meaning for individuals depending on how children were positioned in society and on the nature of their early experiences with these cultural beliefs. Even though the Ilahita Arapesh and three neighbouring groups had very similar male initiation cults, he continued, the personal meanings of these beliefs for individuals could be different in the four groups if children's early exposure to the belief systems differed.

My PNG research did not end up focusing on children's peer groups, but I was intrigued by Tuzin's ideas and realised, when I later put together courses on the anthropology of childhood, religion and other topics, that he was ahead of his time in suggesting that children internalised many of their assumptions about self and culture through interacting with other children. Kulick (1997), for instance, argues that children of Gapun village in the East Sepik lead the shift away from bilingualism to monolingualism in Tok Pisin—one of the two PNG lingua franca. Adults want their children to be bilingual but child caretakers generally use Tok Pisin with younger children in an effort to enhance their own authority by drawing on the associations of Tok Pisin with reason and wisdom. More generally, Corsaro (1997, 2003), Harris (1999), Tannen (1990) and many others all suggest that children are not directly socialised by adults. Instead, children understand from an early age that they are children, and they form their ideas about appropriate behaviour and values by internalising routines and assumptions in a world of peers. One peer culture gives way to other peer cultures as children grow up, but our understandings of self and society are acquired through this succession of peer cultures rather than through adult instruction.

In 1997, when I began new fieldwork in Fiji, my research agenda was shaped by Tuzin's ideas about peer socialisation. I argued that Fijian children—relegated to the bottom of the status hierarchy in a culture that ranks everyone by age, gender, lineage membership and other criteria—internalise many of their assumptions about self and society through playing with other children, because they are excluded from many adult activities and spend much of their time in the company of other children while higher-status adults pursue important communal activities. In this chapter, I compare the ways urban and rural Fijian children enact and interpret hierarchy and equality in their play in order to revisit another of Tuzin's insights: that the same cultural system can have very different meanings depending on the ways that children experience those beliefs.

In Fiji, as in neighbouring Samoa (Ochs 1988) and Tonga (Morton 1996), low-ranking people must obey and accommodate those further up who are thought to be wiser and to have a greater capacity to understand and act for the good of society. This principle structures interactions from the way adults talk to infants (Ochs 1988) and the fostering of children to meet the needs of adults, to interactions among siblings where the older siblings are expected to take care of younger siblings, who owe deference and obedience in return. In rural villages, a large part of children's experience of hierarchy comes from spending their lives in mixed-age peer groups where they both obey older children and discipline younger children. I shall argue that children's experience of the cultural principle of hierarchy is quite different in urban areas where they spend much less time in mixed-age groups and a great deal more time in the same-age cohorts favoured by educational systems all over the world (Anderson-Levitt 2003). As a result, they interact with a large group of unfamiliar equals—their classmates—and experience hierarchy as a binary opposition between those with authority, the teachers, and those without, the children. In contrast, rural children are part of a world of kin where no-one is equal and differences in rank are gradual and continuous, starting with the child one month one's senior and extending through to the oldest grandfather.

I suggest that the new experiential world of children is changing the way they internalise understandings of self and society and that these differences are reflected and reinforced in play. Rural children experiment simultaneously with being higher and lower in rank in their mixed-age play groups. Urban children, on the other hand, develop strategies for negotiating their way through a world of equals by strategically defining in-groups and out-groups. They experience themselves as being powerless in the face of powerful adults and play a variety of games, such as pretending to be monsters, superheroes and other powerful figures, which allow them both to defy authority and to play at being powerful. Such play is similar to that of children in American and European schools, who are faced with a similar situation of being powerless in a world where they will some day be required to be autonomous adults (Corsaro 2003; Jones 2003; Paley 1986). These games reflect concerns and assumptions of self and society fundamentally different from those in the games of rural children, who always see themselves as 'dividuals' embedded in a community, neither powerless now nor destined to be powerful in adulthood, but always high with respect to some and low with respect to others. Moreover, the experience of rural children in shifting their behaviour from context to context—depending on the age of the other children present—causes them always to think of themselves as playing roles in a larger communal structure rather than as individuals whose unique characteristics determine their relationships.

Hierarchy in the World of Rural Children

Cultural assumptions about hierarchy and the correct relationship between adults and children were largely similar in rural and urban areas, but the experience of children was fundamentally different. Morton (1996) and Ochs (1988) note strong cultural assumptions in Tonga and Samoa that children are born foolish, wilful and selfish and only gradually develop the capacities to reason, to think of others and of communal good, and to curb their impulses. On the one hand, these assumptions lead to authoritarian parenting strategies; since children have a limited capacity to reason and are naturally naughty, adults must be firm, in control and often need to use a bit of corporal punishment to impress upon children the right way to behave. On the other hand, since adults are of high status, they should not spend their lives accommodating children's needs; instead, adults are often distant, assigning much of the work of caretaking to older children. Children should not be underfoot, distracting adults from important communal work, and they must accommodate the needs of adults by, for instance, doing manual labour. These cultural assumptions shaped the behaviour of rural Fijian parents (Brison 1999) and also urban kindergarten teachers (see below), but the experiential worlds of urban and rural children were rather different because urban children spent more time in schools and less time in neighbourhood and extended kin groups.

In the rural area of Rakiraki, four and five-year-olds lived almost exclusively in a world of kin. I kept track of 13 children between three and five years old over a period of several days in 1997, noting what they were doing and who they were with at random intervals. They were almost always found with members of their own families, most often in the company of their own siblings or closely related children. Rakiraki children in general were discouraged from wandering far from their own homes and from entering the compounds of other lineages, unless visiting relatives from those lineages. In 2003, a small kindergarten opened in the compound of the lineage with which I lived. Visits to the kindergarten, however, revealed that it was frequented primarily by children who were closely related to each other and knew each other already, since there was another kindergarten at the other end of the village serving children there. Children in the kindergarten also ranged in age from three to six since parents liked to send siblings to school together.

One consequence of these patterns was that children were almost always part of a kin hierarchy since they were seldom away from siblings and cousins. At home, there were generally few enough children in any one lineage that all the children—from two-year-olds to teenagers—often ended up playing together. In such a world, children experimented with being both a higher status and a lower status person (Brison 1999; see also Morton 1996), and the lived experience of hierarchy was one of a continual gradation of closely connected individuals. Children's focus on relative rank was apparent, for example, in one interaction I observed involving two four-year-olds, Mere and Tukana, who lived near each other and often played together; Minroti, a six-year-old boy; and two three-year-olds, Merioni and my son, Jeffrey (Brison 1999). Mere and Tukana were pretending to be soldiers until they saw Merioni and Jeffrey climb on to the foundation of a new addition to a house. The two older children showed their internalisation of age hierarchy when they immediately headed over to get the two younger children off the foundation, saying, 'Jeffrey, forbidden, you are a baby', and then chasing Merioni off, counting as they had heard adults doing: 'Quickly, four, five you have to be missing from here!' The children were then joined by the slightly older Minroti who now assumed the authoritative role, telling Tukana not to hit smaller children when Tukana tried to frighten Merioni off the foundation. On other occasions, I saw Minroti, who was the youngest in his sibling set, being ordered around by his older siblings. On these and other occasions, rural children experienced hierarchy as a continuous gradation. Children continually moved from being high to being low as the composition of groups changed; they lived in a world where no-one was equal but where there was no clear dichotomy between power and powerlessness either. They also took seriously their responsibilities to supervise younger children and to defer to older children.

I suggest here that one consequence of this situation was a relative absence of 'monster' play or other kinds of play that involved working through relationships with remote, powerful others. Corsaro (2003) observed monster play in both American and Italian preschools. One child would assume the role of monster, and the others would first sneak up on the monster and then run away shrieking in mock terror. Jones (2003), Lanclos (2003), Paley (1986) and others have argued that such play helps children who are sociologically small and weak but know they will grow up to be independent adults experiment with power. They work through fears of a dangerous outer world in safe ways by 'killing monsters' and, conversely, they assume powerful monster or superhero roles to gain the experience of being powerful and venting aggression in safe ways.

Fantasies of power were not common in rural Rakiraki children's play. Rakiraki boys of ten or older did sometimes imitate superheroes. I once watched two boys both pretending to be Jean-Claude Van Damme (Brison 2007). But there was no clear villain nor was power over others much emphasised; instead, the boys imitated a scene from a movie that had recently been shown in the community hall in which Van Damme struggled to prevent a jeep from pulling away. Each boy took the role of the jeep driver making engine noises so the hero–villain opposition from the original was lost. Relative power was also not emphasised in a game of house I witnessed played by four small children (Brison 2007). 'Mum' and 'Dad' were significantly absent from this game with each child taking the role of an adult visiting with friends.

In short, I suggest that for Rakiraki children there is no clear dichotomy between adult power and childhood powerlessness in a world where children are sometimes high and other times low in peer groups. Like the perfect 'socio-centric' self described by Becker (1995) and Mead (2001), rural children always think of themselves as playing a role vis-a-vis others, in a ranked community, alternately taking responsibility for lower-ranking people and deferring to higher-ranking people. Children are constantly reminded when the composition of groups changes that expectations of them are linked less to their unique personalities than to the position they occupy in the group of the moment.

Hierarchy in Fijian Kindergartens

Suva kindergartens were shaped by the same assumptions about rank that moulded rural parenting. But the experience of urban kindergarten children was much different because classrooms contained a large cohort of unrelated children of the same age who were all relatively powerless in contrast with teachers.

Suva kindergarten teachers clearly had beliefs about the need for wise adults to have firm authority over foolish children. Corporal punishment was not allowed in Fijian schools, but most teachers felt that using corporal punishment would have been helpful since children lacked the capacity to reason so time-outs had limited impact. Assumptions about rank also moulded teaching strategies. Teachers insisted that learning was a matter of listening to adults;

if you did not understand it was because you had not listened. One teacher, for instance, routinely contrasted 'clever' children who listened obediently with 'naughty' children who failed to pay attention on the implicit assumption that learning was a process of allowing your foolish mind to be guided by the higher wisdom of an adult. One outcome of these ideas was what one teacher called 'parrot teaching'—a popular strategy where the teacher would tell the children a piece of information and then have them repeat it. For instance, when one teacher read her class the story of a sheep, Wooly, she read each line and then repeated it back omitting some key word: 'On this farm there was a sheep named Wooly. On this farm there was a sheep named_____?', waiting for the children to obediently repeat back the information after every sentence. When teachers asked more open-ended questions, they often had a single correct answer in mind. One teacher, for example, told me that her goal was to make her kindergarten children independent. This meant, she continued, that they should learn in kindergarten what they were expected to do so that they could just do that without being told. She assumed there was a correct way to think about things and that being independent involved grasping that correct way so one could do what the teacher wanted without being told. For example, teachers often reminded children that near the end of the school year, or even midway through, they should not need to be told to sit quietly, sweep floors, or wipe tables; they should already know that these things needed to be done and do them on their own initiative. Similarly, when another teacher told me that her main goal was to make children confident, she elaborated by explaining that confidence involved knowing the right thing to do in each situation so that one could feel sure one was behaving correctly.

Equally evident was the influence of cultural assumptions about the importance of children accommodating adults. For example, many kindergartens comprised large groups of 30 to 50 children rather loosely supervised by two or three adults. Teachers often left children to sort out their own problems, only occasionally intervening, and to play as they chose while teachers talked with each other or to visiting parents and so on.

While cultural assumptions moulding interaction between adults and children were similar in rural and urban areas, children's experience of hierarchy was, in practice, different. Rural children experienced hierarchy as a continuous gradation where one was sometimes high and other times low and often not around adults at all. But urban kindergarten children were unambiguously low in a school hierarchy that involved a clear binary division between teachers and children. The home world of many urban children also had this character since urban children were much more likely to be kept within their own house's compound than allowed to play with mixed-age neighbourhood groups of children. For example, the two children in the household I lived with in Suva were generally in their own house, watching TV or playing together. There was always an adult present, and the older child was never encouraged to supervise the younger child. Under these conditions, children experienced their social world as consisting of a large cohort of relatively powerless equals who stood in opposition to powerful adults. These conditions encouraged two kinds of play that I seldom saw in Rakiraki—that is, routines for controlling peers by defining in-groups and out-groups, and fantasies involving either exercising arbitrary and often negative power over others or acting out against oppressive authority figures.

Corsaro (2003), Jones (2003), Lanclos (2003), Paley (1986) and others observed a great deal of 'power' play among American and European children. One child assumed an exaggerated authority role, and the others would resist or act out. Children experimented both with getting out their aggression against authority figures and with being powerful in a world where they were generally powerless. Jones (2003) argues that such play helps children vent frustrations in safe ways and also alleviates anxieties about powerlessness by assuming powerful fantasy roles. In short, this kind of play is typical of children who feel powerless in society and will be expected at some time to become autonomous.

Playing with power was frequent in Suva's urban kindergartens. An obvious example of this kind of play was the game of pretending to be a teacher, which I observed in two or three preschools. In one small preschool, for instance, the teacher often threatened misbehaving children with a yellow plastic belt, which she referred to as 'my yellow friend'. One day when she was in another room, preparing for lunch, one boy, Christopher, who was frequently threatened with the 'yellow friend', grabbed the belt and started pretending to be the teacher, wielding his authority over the anthropologist (KB), and his classmates Ryan, Richard, Ethan and Aaron. From my notes:

> Christopher is holding the yellow belt, and says 'Enough you two! This yellow flend!' hitting at KB. Ryan grabs at the yellow belt. Richard looks at KB and says, '*Lasu Lasu*' (liar liar) for no apparent reason, and two others take up the chorus. They all run to Aaron who is giving away lollypops, usually doled out by the teacher as rewards…Ethan now grabs possession of the belt and hits Richard while Christopher yells at Ethan (a chubby child), 'Fatty booma!' Ethan then hits the floor with the belt, and Christopher gets up on the table and walks right over the colouring books of a group of girls. The teacher now comes back in and orders them all into the other room. Aaron comes running in with a blue ruler the teacher sometimes uses to threaten children, and the teacher says 'Oh my blue friend! Who wants my blue friend?'

On this occasion, the children, in a rare moment of freedom from adult supervision, 'cut loose', doing all sorts of forbidden things such as calling the ethnographer a liar, walking on tables and on colouring books, insulting others for being fat and so on. They also assume autocratic adult roles, threatening each other gleefully with the teacher's 'yellow friend' and 'blue friend', and doling out forbidden treats. These behaviours all reflect a world with a clear dichotomous hierarchy. Rural children are often unsupervised; they are often in situations where they must guide and direct younger children; they do not act out against authority but instead take on responsible adult roles in the presence of younger children. Urban kindergarten children, in contrast, are used to being controlled by adults and are seldom put in charge of other children. They experience themselves as powerless in the face of teachers; when given the chance they play gleefully at being autocratic authority figures and at acting out against such figures in the safe context of play with peers who will not punish them.

Similar themes were evident in another urban kindergarten, when a group of boys started playing teacher and students after the teacher had left the room to go talk on the telephone. That morning, during story time, the teacher had threatened to swat a couple of the boys over the head with her book for talking and moving around while she was reading. When she left the room, one of the boys in the class sat in her chair and started imitating her while his friends lined up on the floor in front of him, assuming the role of children in the class. From my notes:

> Epeli sits on the teacher's chair holding a book while a group of five boys sit on the mat facing him, where the class would usually sit. One of the boys in the 'class', says 'Teacher, teacher somebody play here.' Another boy in the 'class' keeps pointing to the books saying, 'Monkey, monkey there!' Epeli waves his arms and says, 'Move back! Move back!' as the teacher often does with her class. Epeli slaps one of the boys on the head with the book, and they all move back grinning. The boys grin and move forward toward the teacher and he grabs the teacher's ruler and threatens them…Epeli says, 'Listen to Teacher! Hear that story.' The boys in the class take turns getting up and standing in front of Teacher Epeli and saying, 'Teacher', and being pushed back down. Epeli now starts pushing his chair backward, and the boys follow him sliding forward on their bottoms. Epeli swats one of them on the head and then starts sliding his chair forward, and they all grin and start crawling quickly away from him. Epeli gets up and walks away, and three of the boys race for his chair and then turn giggling and run away when he comes back. One of the boys gets up and hands the book to Epeli and says, 'Teacher, a book', and then starts dancing around in front of Epeli

daring him to hit him. Epeli grabs the teacher's ruler and starts chasing the boy, and then picks up the books and starts chasing his 'class' with it. The boys run away giggling.

Again, the boys here are having fun assuming the role of arbitrary and abusive power and then acting out against an authority figure, reflecting the concerns of children who feel powerless, and experimenting both with defying authority and with assuming power.

Experimenting with power was also evident in another sequence in the same preschool where Melea, Sera and Amy were playing house. Rakiraki girls playing house had imitated friends going to visit each other. There were no parents and no apparent power differences in their game. In the urban kindergarten, in contrast, Melea became 'Mum', ordering the other children around and wielding a ruler against misbehaving boys, who baited her. From my notes:

> Sera says to Melea, 'Mom, Mom the baby is crying.' Melea and Amy ignore her. Two boys come into the house corner, and Melea swats them with the teacher's ruler. Melea points her ruler and says to Sera, 'Make the baby a drink.' Sera feeds the 'babies' (three teddy bears) who are 'sleeping' on the lower of two tables stacked one on top of the other. Sera then brings Melea a cup, and she pretends to drink tea and eat a biscuit. Melea notices three boys have gone under the table, disturbing the babies, and swats one of them with her ruler telling them to get out. The boy looks surprised and then calls her name 'Melea, Melea' and purposefully reaches in to disturb the sleeping babies. He runs away as she starts hitting him with the ruler. He laughs, and she yells at him to stay out of the house. The three boys sneak toward the house chanting, 'Melea, Melea', and she chases them with a ruler until she corners one of them and hits him until he starts crying.

Here, house play became a game of power. The friends visiting each others' houses in the rural game are replaced with an authoritarian mother who orders her children to feed the babies and to make tea and then punishes children for misbehaving. The children experiment both with being an aggressive, powerful, adult authority figure (the Mum) and with acting out against such an authority in the (relatively) safe context of play with other children.

Children's superhero play also had a different character than that of the rural children. The rural boys each emulated Van Damme with no clear opposition between hero and villain. Urban kindergarten boys, on the other hand, clearly focused on wielding power over others. From my notes:

> Christopher is sitting on the first floor of the playhouse with Peter. They have toy airplanes. Richard says, 'Me got the DVD [title inaudible].'

> Ethan says, 'I got the video game,' and Christopher says, 'And I got big video; it's X Man and Batman, Superman, X Man.' Peter: 'Me got da Superman DVD.' Richard says, 'You know, that be my Nemo DVD.' Christopher says, 'And I got Nemo DVD.' Richard: 'You know, shark, shark him got bite.' Christopher: 'Me a Power Ranger.' Richard picks up one of the airplane parts and Christopher takes it away saying, 'No, no, no.'…Christopher gets up and says, 'And Superman can punch the building.' Richard: 'And Batman can beat the balloon.' Christopher: 'No he can't; he only can punch the car and punch the robot and punch people and punch Peter and punch Ethan, but he can't punch me because I'm stronger!' Ethan: 'And I'm X Man'…Ethan to Christopher: 'I can punch your face.' Christopher: 'No I can punch my brother, cut my brother to pieces, and I can cut you to pieces.' Richard, 'And me can.' Peter: 'Me can do,' he makes a judo stance; 'Teacher I can punch my brother.' Richard, 'And I can punch my Daddy.' Christopher, 'No!' Richard, 'Me can punch my Daddy! Look, look, look me can punch mine Daddy! Yes me can, me can punch my Daddy!' Christopher, 'I'm going to be Batman. I'm going to change into Batman. I have to be the Daddy. I am Batman and I can spray light!'

Here the boys were clearly concerned with relative power. As in the interactions described above, these boys saw power as extreme, aggressive and somewhat arbitrary. Again, I suggest that this comes from the typical experience of children in urban society of being relatively powerless in a world dominated by adults—a condition not experienced to the same extent by rural children who inhabited a world of mixed-age peers. The boys' conversation also reflects the desire of urban kindergarten children to establish their place in a world of equal and unrelated peers. Each wants to establish his power relative to the others. This concern was much less pressing for rural children who were generally in the company of relatives and for whom relative status was ascribed by age. I turn below to urban children's attempts to define their relationship with classmates and the influence of this kind of play on their views of self and society.

Friendship in Urban Kindergartens

Urban kindergarten children moved from home situations where they were closely monitored by adults to large classes where they had to negotiate their way through a group of unfamiliar peers of equal status. In many kindergartens, children were only loosely supervised by adults and therefore needed to develop strategies to protect themselves from aggressive children, to develop predictable routines and relationships, and to protect these from incursions from other children (see also Corsaro 1997). The absence of any clear hierarchy among the children created a situation where children had to come up with strategies to try to control their peers and establish some kind of predictable social order.

Corsaro (2003) demonstrates that Italian and American preschool children establish social order among their peers through friendship routines, and I observed a similar preoccupation with friendship among urban Fijian kindergarten children, who used friendship to define who was in and who was out in particular situations to transform chaos into predictable routines. In more controlled kindergartens, children used friendship to develop some kind of autonomous identity and social structure in situations largely dictated by teachers.

All over Suva, I encountered the ritual of the 'friendship thumb'. One child would extend his or her thumb towards another in friendship, who would respond by pressing it with his or her own thumb to confirm the friendship. Children also tried to establish in-groups through carefully sharing only with select others, even though teachers resisted this, encouraging children to share with everyone. Bonds were also forged through establishing points of similarity. For example, I observed one boy who had joined a kindergarten late in the term frequently pointing out similarities between his lunch, his clothing and so on and those of other children by calling out, 'Eh look, same-same!'

The use of friendship to try to establish social networks was evident during lunch period at one kindergarten. From my notes:

> Christopher opens his lunch box revealing pieces of birthday cake neatly wrapped in tin foil. Aaron immediately holds out his hand asking for some. Christopher, takes a piece, breaks it in half, and offers some to Aaron and some to Richard. Ethan and then Aaron reach across the table and offer their thumbs to Richard who presses each in return. Aaron then tells one of the girls, Seini, to offer her thumb to Bessie, another girl sitting across the table, and the two girls press thumbs together. Richard holds up a roti (flatbread) in front of his face like a steering wheel, making car noises and then bites a hole through the middle and looks at the other boys near him giggling. Christopher points to Anil, a two-year-old sitting next to Richard, and says, 'He doesn't like it. He's scared.' But then Christopher picks up his own chicken bone and holds it in front of his eye like a telescope looking first at Anil and then at Richard. Ethan has been watching and offers a friendship thumb to Richard, who accepts, and then to Aaron, who pushes Ethan away and gets up. Ethan grabs Aaron's arm trying to get his thumb, but Aaron pulls away.

Here, the children manoeuvred quietly at lunch to define who was in and who was out by sharing food, pressing thumbs and engaging in each other's games, while the teacher exhorted them to eat their lunch and not to talk and otherwise socialise. 'This is eating time! NO talking!' Christopher carefully doled out his birthday cake to most of the boys but to only one of the girls, the daughter of a national rugby star and the single girl the boys routinely played with. When the teacher suggested that Christopher give some cake to me and to a girl who had forgotten to bring her lunch that day, he ignored the suggestion, using his cake to define his circle of friends. He also quietly suggested that boys were friends with boys and girls with girls when he suggested that Bessie and Seini press thumbs but did not offer his own thumb to either of them. These friendship routines reduced the chaos potentially present in a large group of children by defining who interacted with whom and what they played—as when Richard and Christopher joined together in using their food as devices to look at other children. These routines are also used to resist the teacher's authority since most teachers insisted that all of the children should be friends, that they should focus on the teacher not on other children, and that mealtime in particular was supposed to be a quiet activity. The children also used offers and rejections of friendship to control their peers, as when Aaron refused Ethan's proffered friendship thumb to express displeasure at some unknown cause.

In more highly structured schools, children's use of friendship to resist too much control by teachers over their lives was particularly apparent. In one such preschool, one of the few occasions when children had any control over their companions was when they chose tables for eating their snacks. In this preschool, the children carefully manipulated table choice to establish friendships. On one occasion, a girl called Emma told another, Lani, not to sit next to her because that chair was for her 'friend'. But when Emma's friend came in and sat somewhere else, Emma called first one boy and then another girl to sit next to her, trying to keep the seat for a friend. Lani, in the meantime, came and told me that her friend was Kenny and went and sat next to him. In this way, children established alliances and a sense of independent identity in a world where the teacher controlled much of what they did.

Children also used friendship to try to control each other. At one preschool, for instance, one of the boys was from Bangladesh and had a British mother. This child, who was clearly not used to local school conventions, routinely interrupted the teachers to tell long stories about Bangladesh and got up and wandered around the room while the other children sat quietly. He also often insisted on being chosen when the teachers were picking out children to do some favoured activity. The children reacted to this behaviour by implicitly refusing to be his friend. One day, when he walked in after retrieving his lunch bag and sat down, all the other children got up and moved to another table. As more children filed into the room, they avoided the boy alone at his table and filled up other tables until the teacher came in and told two boys to sit with the Bangladeshi boy.

Corsaro (2003) argues that children use friendship to try to establish control in unfamiliar environments with no clear social structure, and this seemed to be the case in Fijian kindergartens. Friendship among equals, however, is a rather different kind of social principle than the age hierarchies of rural children, all of whom know each other well and whose relationships to each other are clearly defined. When urban children form friendships, they look for those who are similar in some way, often focusing on some principle not particularly important in the adult world. For instance, in one kindergarten, the children routinely compared lunches, hitting upon chance similarities in the colour of juice bottles and so on to form friendships. From my notes, as the children come in with their lunchboxes and chose table companions for lunch:

> Tevita sits next to Martin: 'Hey, us two!' Martin: 'Us two! Hey, same-same bag!' (pointing to their lunchboxes). Tevita: 'Us two! Us two Martin!'

> Martin, to a third boy, Simon, who enters with his lunch bag: 'Us two, all of us!'

> Simon to Martin and Tevita: 'Us two!' At another table, Ana and Sera sit down together and compare their juice bottles: Ana: 'Eh, same-same!'

> Sera: 'Eh, same-same!'

In these examples, children establish and cement relationships by finding common ground. Rural children interact mostly as occupants of fixed roles in larger kinship structures. In contrast, urban children interact as autonomous individuals each trying to control his or her own environment. In the process, not surprisingly, they often define their identities in terms of consumption, commenting on clothes, lunchboxes, toys, or, as in the superhero conversation among Christopher and his friends, possession of DVDs and computer games. This suggests a clear shift in children's sense of self, consistent with the preoccupation with autonomy and power evident in much of their play. These children internalise distinctively Fijian assumptions about hierarchy in an experiential world that prompts them to think of themselves as autonomous individuals who must control their world.

Conclusion

Tuzin was ahead of his time in suggesting that the same cultural beliefs can take on different meanings for people depending on the ways that these beliefs impinge upon their experiential world in childhood. Male cult secrets were carefully guarded from women and children among the Ilahita Arapesh, and children were tricked with stories of dangerous and aggressive cult spirits. When children tried to understand their world and contemplate its dangers they told each other fearsome ghost stories that continued to shape their emotional reactions to religious beliefs even after they learned that these stories were lies told to trick women and children. To understand people's conceptions of self, society and culture, one must examine not only the belief system itself but also the ways that it is experienced by children, who are in general distinctively positioned in society and exposed to cultural beliefs and social principles in different ways than are adults.

Tuzin's ideas—similar to models since developed by Corsaro, Tannen, Harris and many others—give us new kinds of insight into contemporary Fiji. Indigenous beliefs about rank and human nature continue to shape the ways that adults treat children at home and at school. But the distinctive social experiences of urban children, particularly in kindergartens, transform the ways that these assumptions are internalised by children so that, I suggest, Fiji's urban children will grow up to think of themselves as autonomous individuals in a larger social hierarchy that is not necessarily god-given but could, in fact, be contested.

Acknowledgments

I observed children's play in Rakiraki, a village in the north-east of Fiji's main island, Viti Levu, in 1997, 2000 and in 2003 (Brison 1999, 2007). I then observed children in nine Suva kindergartens for periods of two to six weeks each in 2006 and 2007. I chose kindergartens associated with a range of ethnic and religious groups and social classes, some affiliated with schools and others private. Research was funded by two National Science Foundation summer grants and by Union College. I thank Sara Melton and Carly Aimi for helping me with the Suva kindergarten research.

References

Anderson-Levitt, Kathryn M. (ed.) 2003. *Local Meanings, Global Schooling: Anthropology and World Culture Theory*. Palgrave Macmillan: New York.

Becker, Anne E. 1995. *Body, Self, and Society: The View from Fiji*. Philadelphia: University of Pennsylvania Press.

Brison, Karen J. 1999. Hierarchy in the World of Fijian Children. *Ethnology* 38:97–119.

Brison, Karen J. 2007. *Our Wealth is Loving Each Other: Self and Society in Fiji.* Lantham, Md: Lexington Books.

Corsaro, William A. 1997. *The Sociology of Childhood.* London: Pine Forge Press.

Corsaro, William A. 2003. *We're Friends, Right?: Inside Kids' Culture.* Washington, DC: Joseph Henry Press.

Harris, Judith Rich 1999. *The Nurture Assumption: Why Children Turn Out the Way They Do.* New York: Touchstone.

Hirschfeld, Lawrence A. 1988. On Acquiring Social Categories: Cognitive Development and Anthropological Wisdom. *Man* 23:611–38.

Hirschfeld, Lawrence A. 1990. Acquiring Social Categories. *Man* 25:146.

Holland, Dorothy, Debra Skinner, William Lachicotte jr and Carole Cain (eds) 1998. *Identity and Agency in Cultural Worlds.* Cambridge, Mass.: Harvard University Press.

Jones, Gerard 2003. *Killing Monsters: Why Children Need Fantasies, Super Heroes and Make-Believe Violence.* New York: Basic Books.

Kulick, Don 1997. *Language Shift and Cultural Reproduction: Socialization, Self, and Syncretism in a Papua New Guinean Village.* Cambridge: Cambridge University Press.

Lanclos, Donna M. 2003. *At Play in Belfast: Children's Folklore and Identities in Northern Ireland.* Piscataway, NJ: Rutgers University Press.

Mageo, Jeannette Marie 1998. *Theorizing Self in Samoa: Emotions, Genders, and Sexualities.* Ann Arbor, Mich.: University of Michigan Press.

Martini, Mary 1994. Peer Interactions in Polynesia: A View from the Marquesas. In Jaipaul L. Roopnarine, James Ewald Johnson and Frank H. Hooper (eds) *Children's Play in Diverse Cultures*, pp. 73–103. Albany, NY: State University of New York.

Mead, Margaret 2001. *Coming of Age in Samoa: A Psychological Study of Primitive Youth for Western Civilisation.* New York: Harper Perennial Modern Classics.

Morton, Helen 1996. *Becoming Tongan: An Ethnography of Childhood.* Honolulu: University of Hawai'i Press.

Ochs, Elinor 1988. *Culture and Language Development*. Cambridge: Cambridge University Press.

Paley, Vivian Gussin 1986. *Boys and Girls: Superheroes in the Doll Corner*. Chicago: University of Chicago Press.

Schwartzman, Helen B. 1978. *Transformations: The Anthropology of Children's Play*. New York: Plenum.

Tannen, Deborah 1990. *You Just Don't Understand: Men and Women in Conversation*. New York: Morrow.

Toren, Christina 1990. *Making Sense of Hierarchy: Cognition as Social Process in Fiji*. London: Athlone.

Tuzin, Donald F. 1987. On the Resemblance of Fathers to Their Children: The Roots of Primitivism in Middle-Childhood Enculturation. In L. Bryce Boyer and Simon A. Grolnick (eds) *The Psychoanalytic Study of Society. Volume 15: Essays in Honor of Melford E. Spiro*, pp. 69–104. Hillsdale, NJ: Analytic Press.

11. The Torments of Initiation and the Question of Resistance[1]

Thomas A. Gregor

We are told that in certain happy regions of the earth, where nature provides in abundance everything that man desires, there are races whose life is passed in tranquillity and who know neither compulsion nor aggressiveness. I can scarcely believe it, and should be happy to meet these fortunate beings.

— Sigmund Freud, Letter to Albert Einstein, 'Why War?'

The Problem

In 1982 Donald Tuzin published a short but trenchant article titled, 'Ritual Violence Among the Arapesh: The Dynamics of Moral and Religious Uncertainty'. The work probes a question of broad human significance. The Ilahita Arapesh, in the course of their long initiatory cycles, terrorised their children and subjected them to excruciating ordeals. Tuzin self-consciously ascribes the word 'brutal' to these acts, partly because many of the Ilahita themselves so saw them, but also because we, if we are honest with ourselves, do so as well. Ilahita ritual (which no longer takes place) was particularly disturbing in that it was at the sacred core of the society.

Rituals of initiation, which encompass many discomforting practices, are the centrepiece of religious life among many Melanesian societies. It is in the course of initiation that young men learn the deepest secrets of the men's cults, that they come to possess its most sacred symbols, and that they learn the most profound values of the society. When we consider that initiation can last many years (in the case of Ilahita, it is a 50-year cycle), we only hyperbolise slightly when we say that ritual, in many Melanesian societies, is initiation. What does it mean when such ritual encompasses the cruelties that Tuzin and others have documented? How, Tuzin asks, can such 'good people do bad things to one another?' (1982:323). Consider, as an example, the Ilahita custom of *laf*, or ritual killing. During one of the stages of initiation, wearers of certain ritual masks who are possessed by the spirit of the men's cult, may kill people with impunity:

1   This material was based partly upon work supported by the National Science Foundation under Grant No. 0650859. The article has also benefited from the comments of Warren Shapiro.

'nothing can vacate a hamlet so quickly as one of these spooks materializing out of the gloom of the surrounding jungle.' The 'heaviness' of the mask transforms its wearer into a compulsive killer: 'his own child or brother would not be spared if he came upon them' (Tuzin 1980:50).

Are we dealing with social pathology, and, if so, how can a relativistic discipline such as ours, especially one that, as Tuzin put it, 'make[s] no provision for affect' (1982:320), even begin to describe it?

Ritual violence is not wholly strange to us in that *religious* violence is familiar territory. It is responsible for the deaths of millions, and it confronts us in each day's news. But religious violence is invariably, in terms of its ideology, defensive in nature. Hence those who die in its service are martyrs to the cause, destined to a place in heaven, as in the case of jihad in radical Islam or the crusaders during the eleventh century. Seen from the point of view of the perpetrator, such violence defends the religion against its external enemies.

Religious violence might also turn inward, as in the persecution of heretics. There are abundant historical examples in Western Christianity, culminating in the Inquisition. But here, too, looked at from the perspective of the inquisitors, we find the religion defending itself, albeit by turning upon the enemy within.

Ritual violence, unlike religious violence, neither guards the periphery of religion nor assures the purity of its core. Our only experience with it, as Tuzin points out, is in highly sublimated versions such as those associated with the Eucharist. Violence directed against the self—as in self-mortification described in Catholic liturgy—comes closer, but it too, while discomforting, is largely alien territory.

Tuzin suggests that, as anthropologists, we practice our own sublimations, in that ritual violence becomes an unexamined part of the background of ethnographic accounts. To be sure, the ethnography is plain enough, but the moral and emotional implications of the violence are often rendered nearly invisible by theoretical frameworks that anaesthetise us from feeling (Tuzin 1982:322). 'One problem entailed in studying the literature of an ethnographic area such as New Guinea', he writes,

> is that the reader risks being desensitized—losing his cultural distance and with it his 'fresh eye'. Penile incision is reported often in the New Guinea ethnography. The resulting contempt-bred-of-familiarity takes the form of coming to view this practice as 'just another' customary observance equivalent in most analytic respects to members of the culture brushing their teeth with coconut husks or marrying their cross-cousins. (Tuzin 1980:67)

There are exceptions among ethnographers—notably Tuzin himself, but also Read (1954, 1965) and especially Gilbert Herdt, who writes of his own 'shock, fear, anger and sorrow in the rituals' (Herdt 1981a:7). More normally, such reactions stay well separate from the accounts. Although Tuzin does not state it, this is useful in that it permits description free from extraneous judgment. But it comes at a cost in that it numbs us to the reactions of those we study. Are they so different from us that they do not perceive the violence they perpetrate as cruel? And if so, why do the tormented eventually turn upon their children and pass the suffering to the next generation?

My intention is to examine these questions from the perspective of research in Melanesia, which offers many relevant examples. The reader is warned that my focus is primarily on a few societies where the data are rich, and the level of ritual pain is extreme. The question I will address is that of *resistance*. Is there evidence that those who perpetuate the torments of initiation question what they are doing? Do they feel remorse for what they have done or shame for its effects? The puzzle of ritual violence and the possibility of resistance reflect on our capacity to love and empathise, on broad issues of ethical relativism and on the universality of human values.

The Background of Ritual Violence: Male initiation in Melanesia

Male initiation is about making men out of boys. Ritual violence, therefore, occurs in a larger sexualised context. Roger Keesing (1982:6–13) and Gregor and Tuzin (2001) summarise the characteristics of male initiation rituals, many of which can be reasonably extended to cultures beyond Melanesia. The most salient fact is that in ritually violent cultures males and females are different kinds of beings in their physiology, their bodily fluids and their essences (Keesing 1982:7). These contrasts radiate outwards so that the mythology, folk medicine and expressive culture are themselves, in Shirley Lindenbaum's (1987:222) useful phrase, 'gender inflected', so that 'the polarities of male and female articulate cosmic forces thought to be located in the human body'. Outside Melanesia, the pattern is less marked but still vivid. The most cosmic example of which I am aware is in Amazonia, where the Tukuna regard the phallic sun god as being in permanent copulation with the womb-like under layer of the cosmos, which is constantly being fertilised by his semen in the form of the sun's rays.

The primary symbolic currency of the initiatory symbolism is formed by sexual body parts and fluids. They appear not as rooted in different sexual natures but as permutations, one of the other. Penises, clitorises, vaginas, anuses, breasts, mouths, noses and tongues condense, merge and differentiate. Among the

Sambia, semen is equated with breast milk: 'the milk of women is the same as milk of men' (Herdt 1981a:186–7). The penis, as the source of milk, is referred to as the 'glans-breast'.

The initiatory systems we will examine are 'pseudo-procreative' (Hiatt 1971) in that men coopt women's capacity to gestate and give birth to new life. Growth and manhood are achieved through giving birth to initiates, through injecting them with life substance, especially through the oral ingestion of semen. The concept of pseudo-procreativity is literalised most vividly in the practice of subincision among the Australian Arunta (Arrernte), wherein the initiators drip 'postpartum' blood from their newly opened subincision scars, which are called vaginas, and the blood is identified as postpartum blood (Hiatt 1971). Among the Iatmul, 'male initiators are identified as "mothers" of the novices' and the doorway to the initiatory structure is literally the 'clitoris gate' (Bateson 1958:282). A similar pattern is repeated among the Wogeo in the form of male 'menstruation' and in many other Melanesian and Amazonian contexts, albeit in slightly less intense and elaborate forms (see, for example, Gregor 1985). A logical corollary is the disturbing possibility of male pregnancy, which is a fear expressed by Sambia (Herdt 1981b:237) and the Awa (Newman and Boyd 1982). There seem to be few limits to the ingeniousness of initiators in claiming the generative capacity of women (see Bettelheim's [1954] more general treatment).

These ideas are images of dreams, the stuff of primary process thought. As relativising anthropologists, we rarely say it, but they are factually wrong, they are based on 'error' (Keesing 1982), and they are, in fact, objectively 'preposterous' (Hays 1988). Nonetheless they have real consequences for initiates, for women and for the moral systems they infuse. Thus, the men who utilise feminine symbolism in the creation of initiates are not grateful. Women are dangerous. They and their menstrual blood are contaminating. The overwhelming burden of the ideology of the initiating cults is that women are inimical to masculinity and, in Tuzin's words, 'the bane of a peaceful society' (1980:106). The process of initiation strips away all that is feminine from boys who have been too long in association with their mothers, through rituals that purge female influence from their skin, blood, intestinal tracts, words and thoughts.

In a few cultures, the opposition and uneasy relationship of men and women spill over from initiation to appear in other areas of social life, with women often being the victim of male aggression. Among the Nama, as described by Read (1954:22–3), 'women suspected of adultery have sticks thrust into their vaginas…fights are staged at marriages, when, characteristically enough, a man is required to shoot an arrow into the thigh of his future wife'. Sexual violence itself is encompassed in an atmosphere where aggression is a norm. Again following Read (1954:33), 'punishment for wrongdoing characteristically includes public beatings and vicious humiliations…self-injury and mutilation are customary ways of expressing sorrow and loss...dominance and submission, rivalry and coercion are constantly recurring themes, manifest alike in day-to-day contexts and in ceremon[y].'

The Torments of Initiation

The ideology of masculinity and sexual opposition sets the stage for ritual violence within the cycle of initiation. Boys are not simply roughly treated. Rather they are systematically terrorised. Let us look at the process from the perspective of the novices.

Lack of Preparation or Explanation

Initiates are often unprepared for what will happen to them. Cruel treatment, once explained, becomes bearable, and initiation has a high purpose of making men from boys. But, as I read the literature, the explanation often comes after the torment. Hence among the Awa, 'the sequence of male initiation begins when these boys are forcefully taken to the men's house...The boys are surprised by this abduction' (Newman and Boyd 1982:247). Adult men, recalling the experience, describe themselves as unprepared: 'they cried and shook when taken away to the men's ground' (Newman and Boyd 1982). Further along in the process of initiation, the boys have learned to expect abuse, so much so that anticipation itself becomes anguish. Recalling such a moment, one of the men says: 'There was something else besides washing. We heard that, and we all started to shake' (Newman and Boyd 1982:253). Similarly, Tuzin (1980:94) describes the novices as 'wondering what will happen' just prior to being forced to run a gauntlet in which they are rubbed with nettles and clubbed, some knocked unconscious.

On the occasion when children are prepared for the ritual, the story might be even more terrifying than the reality. Sambia boys are told 'the spirit wants to get you, she wants to kill and eat you!' (Herdt 1981a:110). Among the Ilahita, prior to having their penises lacerated, the boys are told that the *Tambaran* spirit will force them to 'slide down the spiked trunk of a falanga sago palm, and thus rip open their bellies' (Tuzin 1982:338). From a child's perspective, these stories are genuinely terrifying. The events associated with them must seem unpredictable, catastrophic and lethal.

Separation from Mothers

We must keep in mind that the initiates are boys as young as six or seven, who will be separated from their mothers in seclusion camps or villages for periods of months or years. The tears of mothers as their sons are led away to initiation are thoroughly justified. Among the Sambia, after the boys learn (for the first time) that they must have oral sex with the bachelors to consume semen, they are marched in front of their mothers as novice warriors. This is the last time they will see their mothers and sisters for more than 10 years. Herdt explains that a boy loses his mother totally. Physical contact, commensality and even direct gaze are forbidden. Having learned the secrets of the cult, he is forbidden this warmth 'for fear he might reveal these secrets' (Herdt 1981a:112). In other cultural settings as well, the long process of initiation and the barriers between men and women seem sufficient for sons to 'forget' their mothers. When their mothers might see them again, they will have been forever changed.

The Novices Are Guilty

The first explanation the novices might receive for their torment is that it is their own fault: initiation is punishment for real and imagined misdeeds. Among the Sambia, Herdt notes that this is a formal part of the justification for the ritual: 'first-stage nose bleeding is a punishment for insolence', and the more defiant the child is to the initiators, the more he is tormented. The sense of retaliation is explicit, in that, in the words of a Sambia initiator, 'for those acts we now pay you back' (Herdt 1982:225). Among the Awa, the men harangue the boys for their purported misconduct and blame them for the deaths of warriors who were killed when they were too young to have participated in their defence. The men's anger at the boys is genuine: 'So great is [the patriclansmen's] hostility towards the boys that they are not allowed to be directly involved in the purging ritual lest they handle a nose bleeder, vomiting cane or bamboo blade in such a manner as to cause serious injury on their relatives' (Newman and Boyd 1982:283). Ilahita Arapesh initiators are equally furious at their charges, explaining to them that they are guilty and will be punished.

Terrorisation: Staging

Beyond separation is psychological terror, which is deliberately inflicted on the initiates. Among the most violent of the initiators, the Marind Anim ordeals included 'submitting them to an ostensible headhunt attack so realistic that most of them fainted' (Knauft 1993:150). Terror is enhanced by deliberate staging designed to produce fear, including frightening masks, strange sounds and seclusion enclosures with moveable walls. Herdt writes that among the Sambia the boys are tied on the backs of their sponsors so that escape is impossible. They then 'confront a massive vibrating wall of thick green foliage'. There is a bedlam of 'eerie sputtering sounds', shaking walls, and what seems to be blood dripping from the vegetation (Herdt 1981a:141). The boys are terrified and cry out for their mothers. Tuzin writes of the Arapesh:

> What cannot be conveyed in a short space is the full emotional force of this violence: it is one thing to be thumped in the head or have your penis lacerated, but when these attacks are staged in a dramatic atmosphere of weird customary, unearthly sounds, and frenzied stomping, screaming and singing by scores of armed warriors, each of whom seems madly intent on your destruction, the experience is transformed into nightmarish horror. (Tuzin 1982:337)

What comes across in the literature is that the terror is not a by-product of necessary procedures, which are, regretfully, frightening. Often terror itself is the objective.

Pain

It is easy to inflict excruciating, unbearable pain. Pressure, heat and blows are sufficient. A device as simple as a water board can make it unbearable. But there is something quite different about ritual pain. It seems designed, often ingeniously, to violate self-boundaries, to humiliate and to induce terror and fear of death. Hence the torments focus on bodily orifices and boundaries—usually the neurally most sensitive and intimate tissues, including the nostrils and nasal cavity, the mouth, throat and oesophagus, the genitals and, with somewhat less frequency, the eyes and the anus. The overwhelming theme is that of penetration and laceration, using sharpened canes, bamboo rods, tiny stone arrows and similar devices. A full catalogue of techniques is the stuff of nightmares. Alan Morinis, who has examined pain in initiatory rites, lists 'being beaten, starved, incised, scarified, pierced, tattooed, terrified, mutilated, circumcised, infibulated, cicatrized, bound, and subject to removal of parts of… bodies, especially teeth and fingers' (1985:151).

In Melanesia, it appears that initiators are more than commonly imaginative, in that they add such techniques as cane swallowing, nose bleeding and being rubbed with and forced to swallow nettles, and, at least among the Sambia, being forced, in the dark, without preparation, to have oral sex with strange adult men.

Of these ordeals, cane swallowing deserves special note. A photograph of Awa cane swallowing subtitled 'a man forces the vomiting cane down an initiate's throat' can be found in Newman and Boyd's (1982) article 'The Making of Men'.

The canes penetrate more than a foot inside the throat and oesophagus, and they are intended to produce defecation and vomiting. Herdt (1981b:224) quotes an informant: 'This is for removing food belonging to the mother', which is the sweet potato, hence the term for 'cane swallowing' translates as 'sweet potato/ food; elimination'. Cane swallowing also is designed to induce defecation, which eliminates not only maternal food but also maternal symbols: 'Out with the feces pass the depreciating "words" of the mother' from which the boy must be separated (Herdt 1981b).

Closely associated with cane swallowing among the Sambia is nose bleeding (the term translates as 'cleansing and expulsion'), which is regarded as the most painful act. It is performed upon the boys 'without warning' in an assault so violent that it constitutes physical and psychical trauma (Herdt 1982). The boys' first experience with nose bleeding is horrific, and they cry out for their mothers. Adults recalling the experience are 'virtually unanimous in expressing the feeling that they believed they were to be killed on the spot' (Herdt 1982:225).

In all of the groups I have reviewed, the physical attacks on the boys inevitably turn to an assault on the genitals. One example is sufficient. Among the Ilahita Arapesh, the men make a surgical instrument 'by sharpening a piece of bamboo to a razor's edge' (Tuzin: 1980:69), which, when decorated, is the incisor of a ritual pig. The 'pig'—one of the initiators—is a 'balefully weird creature', his skin painted black. A mask covers the face. He lies in wait beneath the floor of the initiation chamber until called by the boys' sponsors. In the midst of shouting and singing designed to terrify the initiates and drown out their screams for their mothers, the pig suddenly appears 'to bite them'. The pig delivers 'deep cutting strokes on their glans penis' (Tuzin 1980:71). Younger boys, who watch in horror, are also attacked. They are 'held down while their penes and scrota are vigorously rubbed with singing nettles' (Tuzin 1982:338). Then all of the boys are thrown in a pool previously filled with stinging nettles (Tuzin 1982).

Beatings, cane swallowing, nose bleeding and assaults are often combined with each other and with still more excruciating patterns of abuse. Hence Van Baal reports that among the Marind Anim, initiates were the targets of anal rape and that they 'had their mouths, noses and eyes smeared with excrement that had been mixed with semen…they were forced to lie in seclusion until maggots appeared on their befouled faces' (Knauft 1993:150).

Death

Several ethnographers note that initiation is extremely dangerous for the boys, and some in fact die. Cane swallowing is known to be particularly risky in that it can cause internal haemorrhaging. We do not know how frequently boys actually die in the course of initiation, but it is not infrequent. Campbell (1983:144) reprints a historical photo from Arnhem Land showing the corpses of seven young initiates who died as a consequence of being 'exposed to a broiling sun and to a torment of stinging insects'.

Explanations of the Torments of Initiation

Ethnographers' explanations often focus on the role of initiation rituals in creating solidarity among the boys who have together survived the ordeal and their subordination to the power of the senior males. Initiation entails secrecy and gradual revelation of cult knowledge—a period of many months, years or even a lifetime, as in the case of the Ilahita. Those who breach the secrets may be put to death. The unity of men—held together by secrets and the common bonds of shared torment—is crucial in communities at war, which is traditionally a chronic state of affairs. Perhaps the logical extreme in this process is reached among the Sambia, who force the boys to have sex with the bachelors and thereby create homoerotic bonds among them. Pacification, as Herdt (1981a:210) predicted, brought the initiatory cycles to an end, and along with it aggression towards women.

More psychologically oriented approaches emphasise the peculiar role of pain in establishing solidary relationships (Morinis 1985), the repetitive compulsion in which trauma is mastered by inflicting it on others, and, specifically in the Melanesian context, 'flash-bulb memory', by which pain intensifies and engages the initiate with ritual experience (Whitehouse 1996).

Resistance

Resistance

The term 'resistance' has been overworked in the postmodern literature, and it rolls too easily off the tongue. Michael Brown (1996), in a perceptive essay, 'On Resisting "Resistance"', points out that a primary function of the concept has been to establish the user's moral bona fides as an objector to oppression. Brown notes that in the world of cultural studies, 'cross dressing, tattooing, women's fashions, dirty jokes and rock videos are routinely held up as examples of cultural resistance'. In the context of this essay, my use of the term is more literal. 'Resistance' to ritual violence consists of efforts to escape; scepticism and disavowal; discontinuance of custom; and remorse and shame. We shall find all represented in the literature, though less than might be expected, and less than we, while wearing our humanitarian hats, might wish.

The Clash of Values and the Origins of Resistance

Standing against the opposition of men and women and the extremes of ritual violence are domestic relationships. In the case of the Ilahita Arapesh, domestic relationships are positive. Tuzin describes the 'extraordinary warmth and affection' between a man and his sister and between husband and wife. In marriage, there is a sense of spiritual harmony that begins with a new couple's 'pledge of eternal love and fidelity' (Tuzin 1982:329–30). The contradictions of domestic values and those of the men's cult are likely to be especially serious in this setting, and we shall see that it is just those values that seem to explain the scepticism and alienation that Ilahita men have from their own initiatory system.

Among the Sambia, however, marital relationships are strained to the point of disintegration. Women come from enemy villages; they may be 'stolen' or traded. 'Sex', Herdt writes, 'is fraught with anxiety. Physical fights are common... Sambia wife beating occurs and it is an ugly stain on the tenor of village life' (1981a:174).

But even among the Sambia, marriage confers a lifelong bond and has at least a measure of happiness. One of Herdt's informants notes: 'When a couple walk together from the forest, and everyone sees you returning from the gardens, your family and friends are happy for you' (Herdt 1981b:189). Following Herdt, 'joy is undeniably there for a moment' (1981b). At minimum, even in the most polarised of the Melanesian societies, men are bound to women for their own identity: 'only a wife and children bring full manhood' (Herdt 1981a:34).

Primary relationships stand in stark contrast with the ritual violence associated with the cults. The affection of husbands and wives and parents and children is incompatible with the extremes of initiation. Conflict within the family expresses the disjunction, in that the world of men is partly rejected by both boys and their mothers. Hence, among the Sambia, boys almost always side with their mothers in marital conflicts: 'Boys express anger and fear towards their fathers over this abuse of their mothers. I have seen boys try to hit their fathers in defense of their mothers' (Herdt 1981a:174).

The love of mothers for their sons spills over into the sacred territory of initiation rituals. Sometimes their resistance is symbolic in that they might put up a pretence of shielding their sons from masked initiators. But at other times it is a serious battle. Herdt describes an altercation of more than an hour as mothers 'attempt to extract their sons from the crowded dance ground...there are scuffles and arguments. Several times men angrily curse the women, who move back only to approach again...the atmosphere is tense enough for a brawl.'

The men respond by attacking the women; 'more startling is the treatment of the mothers who are hit even harder by the men...some are hit hard enough so that they fall on the ground' (Herdt 1981a:137).

Efforts to Escape

The most unmistakable signs of resistance are the efforts of the initiates to flee. They scream, shout and cry and try to run away. The most dramatic examples I have found are Herdt's sensitive observations of the Sambia:

> A boy refuses to be hoisted on his sponsor's back...it takes three men to do the job. His mother approaches...he grabs hold of her bamboo necklace...tears wash down his face as he repeatedly cries 'No, no,' and 'Mother, mother.' The poor woman...is nearly in tears herself...the men severely swat the boy with blow after blow. (Herdt 1981a:137)

One of the boys 'struggles fiercely, so four men lift him off the ground, he is forcibly nose-bled...the smell of blood and fear sours the air' (Herdt 1981a:143).

Herdt further documents that boys sometimes actually do escape, albeit briefly. When they do, search parties are sent out, and when the boys return they are beaten and treated more severely as a consequence. The central point that Herdt makes is ultimately obvious to the boys: *there is no escape*. All boys must be initiated. The fact that they resist at all, however, forms essential data. Despite the obvious rewards of maturity, they do not enter manhood gladly.

Shame

Men's cults—with their clash of domestic and cult values—are inherently unsteady edifices. One of the markers of instability is shame in perpetuating them. Among the Sambia, the men are deeply ashamed of their homosexual relations with one another and of forcing their sons to fellate the bachelors. The matter was a deep secret, revealed at pain of death.

Tuzin also describes the shame of the men in deceiving both the women and the initiates:

> Aware that much of what passes for religious 'truth' is nothing but artifice, cult members are placed in the embarrassing position of having to confess to initiates that they—the initiates—have been systematically deceived...[They] openly admit that they feel deeply shamed at having their true role revealed to their sons. (Tuzin 1982:349)

For fathers, the gulf between the cult and reality is so wide that they seek to put off the inevitable day when their sons learn that by their father's own standards, the voice of the *Tambaran* cult spirit is a fraud.

Rationalisations

A 'rationalisation' differs from 'an explanation' in that it is an intellectualised defence from guilt or remorse. The data are not always sufficiently fine-grained to make this claim. Thus, indigenous explanations of initiation emphasise the separation of boys from women and the magical techniques needed to make men of them. Following Herdt, '[m]en are doing boys a favor in initiating them'. The torments 'are directed at the boys' contaminated innards, which, alas, must be violently penetrated to cleanse them' (Herdt 1982:225–6). Is this a rationalisation or an explanation? I believe it is the former, in that the torments inflicted on the initiates are extreme, and the men's anger towards the boys is visceral. I have already described how the men tell the boys that they are being punished (which does not fit the prevailing ethos of making men out of boys), and they must at times be restrained from doing permanent physical harm. Tuzin captures the implicit sadism of the rituals when he notes that even if the torments are intended positively, they are also acts 'of raw aggression and dominance assertion' (1980:74). Moreover, 'the ordeal is carefully and successfully designed to inspire maximum horror on its victims' (Tuzin 1980). In the case of the Sambia, we learn that when 'the boys are carried through a gauntlet of men with whips…the men take delight in it. Most of the initiates cry' (Herdt 1981a:137).

Among the Avatip (a middle Sepik society), men scarify the boys to purge them of female blood. But they claim that the boys have been 'gored by spirits, whom they portray as anthropomorphic beings with tusks' (Harrison 1985:418). Harrison (1985) directly interprets this as a 'concession to the values prevailing outside the ritual sphere'. It is certainly that, but that such concessions are needed at all suggests the fragility of the enterprise and the real possibility of shame and guilt, which are but one step away from active resistance.

Scepticism and Disbelief

Donald Tuzin's work is unique in that he closely explored the scepticism and moral uncertainty that marked the Ilahita cult. The cult persisted in its island of secrecy but was everywhere else challenged by positive domestic relationships. These erode certainty about the contaminating nature of women and ultimately subvert masculine ideology. Tuzin writes that more than once it was intimated to me that just as the fiction of the physical [spirit] Nggwal enables men to dominate women, so the invisible Nggwal enables the senior initiates to dominate the junior colleagues. The lie is itself a life. Astonished upon hearing this I asked my informant, 'What, then, is the truth about the Nggwal?' to which he replied 'Nggwal is what men do'. (Tuzin 1982:348)

How did the cult persist in the face of such scepticism? Tuzin argues that the men's cult is 'a cultural addiction, in which the pain of continuing these ritual customs is exceeded only by the pain of relinquishing them' (1982:350).

Disbelief is surely an example of 'resistance'. Herdt, however, objects. He suggests that Tuzin's perspective is culture bound and not that of the Arapesh. He argues that the apparent guilt really reflects a post-colonial world, in which the heart of the cult has been eaten out by the pressures of evangelism and social change (Herdt 2003:205–7). The statement that the *Tambaran* is 'what men do' suggests that faith in Nggwal is at the end of a process of cultural change and 'the dissolution of collective ritual into alienation' (Herdt 2003:207). Had the Ilahita men's cult been in full flower, presumably Tuzin would not have observed this scepticism, which, like the underlying guilt, would seem to be a sentiment 'reminiscent of Western middle class emotional constraints' (Herdt 2003:195).

Tuzin might respond that primary relationships and men's cults are in chronic disequilibrium. The imbalance among the Ilahita Arapesh leads to a degree of reflection and eventually to disenchantment and alienation. It is inherent to the system; 'there is no reason to suppose that these reservations are not as ancient as the beliefs themselves' (Tuzin 1980:315).

Herdt's argument is more complex and sophisticated than we can do justice to here. But I would argue that scepticism is normal in human affairs, that doubters and local atheists are recurrent features of all social landscapes. Melanesian men's cults, however, would appear to be fertile ground for scepticism in that the values of the cult are in such radical conflict with primary relationships. Secrecy, as Herdt (2003) convincingly documents, makes it possible to sustain both in their separate compartments, but it surely saps faith and credibility. To an extent, even the Sambia recognise this. Hence, by the logic of equating semen with breast milk, fathers should inseminate sons to make men of them, just as mothers nursed boys. But of course this does not occur, despite its theoretical plausibility. And in no case of which I am aware do fathers inflict the most painful initiatory torments on their sons. There is, therefore, a separation between domestic life and the cult, and from this space might grow resistance to the formal system.

Scepticism and ambivalence might therefore be more than the bitter fruits of culture contact, force-fed by judgmental officials, police patrols and missionaries. Societies are not homogeneous and individuals are reflective even if their voices are drowned out or actively suppressed by the chorus of believers and enforcers. There are simply too many losers in the Ilahita, Sambia and other initiatory systems for them to go without dissent. Surely, throughout initiatory societies, there are mothers and fathers who would prefer that their sons opt out, and I am quite sure the same thought has regularly occurred to the initiates themselves. Senior men might be beneficiaries, but not women, not children, not initiates manqué, not 'rubbish men' and not others who were marginalised by the system.

Finally, we note the rapid collapse of such systems, as occurred among the Sambia with the suppression of war. Herdt (Email, 14 December 2010) informs me that not only has initiation ceased, but also the entire men's cult is a thing of the past. Tuzin's (1997) own account of the spontaneous self-destruction of the Ilahita men's cult makes the same point just as dramatically. Men's cults are fragile, if dark, institutions, narrowly adapted to overwhelming need for masculine solidarity. But they are fraught with contradiction, which we can observe even while the system is in place.

Conclusions

Why does the suffering of the initiates disturb us, and why are we motivated to seek resistance to it? I began this chapter by suggesting that we have no true analogue to ritual violence. The closest approximation we have is that of torture—a deeply evaluative word that anthropologists avoid in describing the ordeals. We can, however, find many superficial resemblances between torture and the ordeals in their exquisiteness, their technology and their intuitive understanding of how to violate the human self. As Tuzin says of Ilahita, the cult 'engenders acts that are physically, emotionally, or, indeed, fantastically terrorist' (1982:347). But if we grant some resemblance, it shifts the direction of the question: why is torture repugnant? The answer would seem to lie in the intentionality of the act, the physical closeness of the torturer and the victim and the relationship of the two. What torture violates is the fundamental human capacity for empathy, upon which all morality is ultimately based. Ariel Dorfman, a Chilean essayist, wrote: 'Torture…requires, it craves the abrogation of our capacity to imagine others' suffering, dehumanizing them so much that their pain is not our pain.' In other words: 'Torture obliges us to be deaf and blind and mute' (Dorfman 2007).

The fact of resistance shows that initiators are hardly indifferent. But at times the raw sadism of many of the acts, in which the higher purposes of the ordeals might not even be explained to the victims, point in another direction. What overwhelming rage can nourish such an institution so that it was not only invented and enacted, but also perpetuated by those who suffered at its hands? This question takes us in a different direction. We might invoke the reasons offered by Whitehouse and Morinis in their discussion of pain, and the need to create a firmly bonded group of men. The psychological mechanisms that facilitate this process such as identification with the aggressor and its association with traumatic stress disorder might also be part of it. But does this suggest that the pattern is pathological, and that the society itself, is, by extension, emotionally disturbed? Many anthropologists are uncomfortable with such judgments because we lack a clear standard for diagnosing a society's mental status as opposed to that of an individual. In the present instance, the sum total of behaviour associated with men's cults has the *look* of pathology but does it have its substance? Freud, who did not hesitate to read culture and behaviour as if they constituted a single personality, was himself aware of the danger of conflating the two. Hence, he noted that the striking resemblance of taboos and the obsessive-compulsive neurosis 'may be no more than a matter of externals, just as the branching structure of trees and crystals are essentially unrelated' (Freud 2004:31).

Are men's cults therefore simply unusual cultural scripts, or, in Tuzin's terms, 'cultural addictions', but not reflective of individual personality? I am inclined to believe otherwise. The ego-dystonic nature of the cults, with their concomitant rationalisations and sense of shame, is all too suggestive. The fact that the cults might collapse from the internal weight of moral ambivalence (as in the case of the Ilahita), or with a relatively gentle external nudge (as in the instance of the Sambia), is further evidence. Finally, the inventive nature of the sadism, and the extraordinary brutality towards initiates, is surely deeply rooted in primary process thought.

For the moment, however, it is enough to say that the participants in the cults are not themselves of one mind. Ideology and conduct are sufficiently disjoined so that some do object. They distance themselves from the initiations, they disbelieve, they resist. This does occur—less frequently than we might wish, but often enough to at least partly dispel Freud's bleak view of the human condition with which I began this chapter.

References

Bateson, Gregory 1958. *Naven*. Stanford, Calif.: Stanford University Press.

Bettelheim, Bruno 1954. *Symbolic Wounds*. Glencoe, Ill.: The Free Press.

Brown, Michael F. 1996. On Resisting 'Resistance'. *American Anthropologist* 98:729–35.

Campbell, Joseph 1983. *Historical Atlas of World Mythology*. San Francisco: Harper & Row.

Dorfman, Ariel 2007. Are There Times When We Have to Accept Torture? Are We Really So Fearful? *South Central Review* 24:95–100.

Freud, Sigmund 2004. Taboo and Emotional Ambivalence. In *Totem and Taboo*. London: Routledge.

Gregor, Thomas 1985. *Anxious Pleasures: The Sexual Lives of an Amazonian People*. Chicago: University of Chicago Press.

Gregor, Thomas A. and Donald F. Tuzin 2001. The Anguish of Gender: Myths of Matriarchy and Men's Cults in Amazonia and Melanesia. In Thomas A. Gregor and Donald F. Tuzin (eds) *Gender in Amazonia and Melanesia: An Exploration of the Comparative Method*, pp. 309–36. Berkeley: University of California Press.

Harrison, Simon J. 1985. Ritual Hierarchy and Secular Equality in a Sepik River Village. *American Ethnologist* 12:413–26.

Hays, Terrence 1988. 'Myths of Matriarchy' and the Sacred Flute Complex of the Papua New Guinea Highlands. In Deborah Gwertz (ed.) *Myths of Matriarchy Reconsidered*, pp. 98–120. Oceania Monograph 33. Sydney: University of Sydney Press.

Herdt, Gilbert 1981a. *The Sambia: Ritual and Gender in New Guinea*. New York: Holt, Rinehart & Winston.

Herdt, Gilbert 1981b. *Guardians of the Flutes: Idioms of Masculinity*. New York: McGraw-Hill.

Herdt, Gilbert 1982. Sambia Nosebleeding Rites and Male Proximity to Women. *Ethos* 10:189–231.

Herdt, Gilbert 2003. *Secrecy and Cultural Reality: Utopian Ideologies of the New Guinea Men's House*. Ann Arbor, Mich.: University of Michigan Press.

Hiatt, L. R. 1971. Secret Pseudo-Procreation Rites Among the Arunta Aborigines. In L. Hiatt and C. Jayawardena (eds) *Anthropology in Oceania: Essays Presented to Ian Hogbin*, pp. 77–88. Sydney: Angus & Robertson.

Keesing, Roger M. 1982. Introduction. In Gilbert H. Herdt (ed.) *Rituals of Manhood: Male Initiation in Papua New Guinea*, pp. 1–43. Berkeley: University of California Press.

Knauft, Bruce M. 1993. *South Coast New Guinea Cultures: History, Comparison, Dialectic*. Cambridge: Cambridge University Press.

Lindenbaum, Shirley 1987. The Mystification of Female Labors. In J. Collier and S. J. Yanagisako (eds) *Gender and Kinship: Essays Towards a Unified Analysis*, pp. 221–43. Stanford, Calif.: Stanford University Press.

Morinis, Alan 1985. The Ritual Experience: Pain and the Transformation of Consciousness in Ordeals of Initiation. *Ethos* 13:150–74.

Newman, Philip L. and David J. Boyd 1982. The Making of Men: Ritual and Meaning in Awa Male Initiation. In Gilbert H. Herdt (ed.) *Rituals of Manhood: Male Initiation in Papua New Guinea*, pp. 239–85. Berkeley: University of California Press.

Read, Kenneth E. 1954. Cultures of the Central Highlands. *Southwestern Journal of Anthropology* 10:1–43.Read, Kenneth E.

Read, Kenneth E 1965. *The High Valley*. New York: Charles Scribners and Sons.

Tuzin, Donald F. 1980. *The Voice of the Tambaran: Truth and Illusion in Ilahita Arapesh Religion*. Berkeley: University of California Press.

Tuzin, Donald F. 1982. Ritual Violence Among the Arapesh: The Dynamics of Moral and Religious Uncertainty. In Gilbert H. Herdt (ed.) *Rituals of Manhood: Male Initiation in Papua New Guinea*, pp. 321–55. Berkeley: University of California Press.

Tuzin, Donald F. 1997. *The Cassowary's Revenge: The Life and Death of Masculinity in a New Guinea Society*. Chicago: University of Chicago Press.

Whitehouse, Harvey 1996. Rites of Terror: Emotion, Metaphor and Memory in Melanesian Initiation. *The Journal of the Royal Anthropological Institute* 2:703–15.

12. Talking About Sex: On the relationship between discourse, secrecy and sexual subjectivity in Melanesia

Gilbert Herdt

All human societies are concerned with the regulation of sexuality—a truism of anthropology. And all of them, past and present, exert cultural, political, economic and even psychological controls over how people talk about sex: when, where, with whom and why—not why they are motivated, but why they must be stopped from sexual discourse. These barriers to sexual communication are created for a variety of reasons—notably, gender power, the strictures on childhood sexual and gender development, the regulation of the development of pleasure, the social control of adult morality and the inhibition of sexual behaviour that violates norms in such fundamental areas as premarital and extramarital sex and same-sex relationships. The form that sexual objectification takes in a particular society reflects, refracts and reproduces these conditions of discursive control.

Of especial interest to this comparative essay on the Sambia of Papua New Guinea is the fundamental issue: who is sexually objectified in the course of development and why? Among the Sambia, it was the male body that was objectified, and ritual secrecy was critical to its success. These are the issues that inform this chapter, which I offer in honour of the late Don Tuzin, friend and colleague for more than three decades and someone from whom I learned much about these issues in regard to masculinity, male cults and the utopian aspiration of men to seek what he called a 'safe haven' in their dealings with the world. Don was long interested in the scope and meaning of sexuality in Melanesia, and his great ethnography *The Voice of the Tambaran* (1980), as I have suggested elsewhere (Herdt 2003), was both an inspiration and a source of puzzlement in elucidating these issues. In Don's subsequent work *The Cassowary's Revenge* (1997), I believe that he found a partial solution to the question of the social regulation of sexuality and discourse, and I will return to this point at the end of this chapter.

Pre-colonial Melanesian societies influenced sexual talk in myriad ways that suggest desires are socially constructed at most times, for most people, in all of these societies. Ironically, I was reminded of this still-radical claim when reading Michael Young's (2004) brilliant biography *Malinowski: Odyssey of An*

Anthropologist, wherein we find a young Omarakana-resident Malinowski, horny, a hypochondriac and a linguistic genius, describing how Trobriand Islanders inserted sexual discourse into their everyday lives such that he could blush (see, for example, Young 2004:404–5). Ironic because, of course, the Trobriand Islanders were matrilineal in ideology and companionate in their attitudes towards women, creating high-status female roles unknown to Highlands Papua New Guinea. Trobriand sexual desires were commonly folded into social relations, and their expression, while carefully metered by custom, ritual and taboo, was more permissive and fluid than in middle-class American mores even today, especially as pertains to childhood sexual development (Herdt 2009a). I think Margaret Mead (1928) made a similar point about Samoa.

The Sambia people of Papua New Guinea, with whom I have lived and worked since 1974, were traditionally much more restricted in their sexuality.[1] Their culture, however, structured these tendencies into sexuality, social organisation and speech through the mechanism of ritual secrecy—a high form of utopian male culture that produced sexual hierarchy and exaggerated gender differences. War and what I shall variously refer to as conditional masculinity as well as the sexual politics of marriage were root causes. Day in and day out, Sambia were compelled to talk about their sexual roles and fears; but by doing so, they created a language of desire and transgression hidden from the public. They did this through the institution of boy-inseminating rituals—their way of avoiding the intimacy of male and female interaction—but especially through the exquisite secrecy that could screen, hide and manipulate even raw sexuality in the presence of children and women. The emotionality of these actions suggests that they were not simply political tactics but rather deeply motivated subjectivities.

These dynamics among the Sambia created a lifelong hidden discourse of repression and sexual objectification, and I shall try to reveal them through conversation with the two greatest theorists of sexuality in the twentieth century: Freud and Foucault. *Contra* Freud (1904), who believed that sexual repression was a universal developmental pattern, and *contra* Foucault (1980), who argued that sexual discourse was inherently a historical reality of state control over individuals in the transition to a modern sense of selfhood, I will argue that among the Sambia the implementation of ritual secrecy actually created the sexual objectification of the male body. Among the Sambia and their Anga neighbours, the social practice of ritual homosexuality or boy-insemination was the means to this form of male objectification, whereas elsewhere in Melanesia

---

1   The focus of this chapter is ethnographic research up to 1993; subsequent fieldwork reports on the conditions of radical change.

ritual secrecy resulted in myriad forms of homo-sociality that were not explicitly homoerotic (Herdt 1993). In both cases, however, ritual secrecy ensured a form of male agency that would not otherwise have prevailed.

Why did the Sambia—and, by implication, a variety of other Melanesian peoples like and unlike them in the practice and meaning systems of their sexual cultures—take such great pains to regulate, manipulate and otherwise inhibit talk about sex? So desperate were they to control sexual speech, they actually created a world of secrecy and hidden desires that sometimes foiled their own designs.

Like many Melanesian sexual cultures, the Sambia institutionalised a rare and fragile mechanism of social regulation of thought, speech and action unknown to modern society: secrecy—that is, ritual secrecy to be precise—implemented through the embodiment of ritual initiation, the modus operandi for psycho-cultural regulation in their society. How can we understand the impact of this set of complex, situated, discursive and power relationships on the development of sexual subjectivity for individuals? These are questions explored in my 2003 book, *Secrecy and Cultural Reality*, but here I shall attempt to go a bit further in contrasting why neither Freud nor Foucault is adequate in explaining the phenomena.

While not exactly Foucaultian inspired, my interrogation of sexual control, power and the harnessing of sexual speech on behalf of the reproduction of total systems does engage the way in which the French thinker Michel Foucault (1980) worried over the means and ends of power, state manipulation of bodies and minds, and the creation of what has come to be known as 'bioforce', which might transcend these constraints. Foucault's perspective on these issues suggested that discursive state control of sexuality in the modern period became the primary means of how societies imposed new norms of intimate relationships, identities and citizenship more broadly.

In fact, Foucault's *Discipline and Punish* (1995), as is well known, took as its brief the notion that the advance of modernity in the regulation of individuals was made possible in part by the creation of the 'norm' as a fundamental category in human development and social life. Ritual secrecy is to the norm what Westerners today experience as self-censorship.

Beginning in the 1960s, and terminating with his death in 1981, and most importantly, with the publication of *The History of Sexuality*, Foucault built a compelling and powerful counter-hegemonic discourse following upon nearly a century of sexology and the domination of Freud over the central question: why do we talk about sex? Note, however, what a curious thing it is that Foucault's book really is not about history at all; it tells very little about sexual subjectivity, it virtually ignores gender, it defuses the study of power relations, and it invents and then rejects what Foucault calls the 'repressive hypothesis' of Freud. To paraphrase him, not only was 'sexual repression' assumed by Freud to be a universal psychic reality, but the more the individual, innate dispositions were studied, the less were power and society even considered relevant to understanding the nature of sexual repression. The doctor could diagnose what was wrong with the patient but ignore the social reality of the person's real-world frustrations and social life. Freud's model suggests an individual process impervious to social change, making the changing meanings of sexuality impossible or at least irrelevant. Never mind that *The History of Sexuality*—so much based upon bourgeois nineteenth-century France—is no better informed by anthropology than was Freud's *Totem and Taboo*, from 1913.

Nevertheless, just as everyone of my generation had to confront the genius of Freud and many of us were psychoanalysed, for better or worse, Freud's too-mentalist, patriarchal legacy strongly influenced anthropological and sociological studies of sexuality for decades. Indeed, in the field of sexuality today, it is hard to imagine the counter-discourse without Foucaultian theory, with its concerns about sexuality and the reproduction of social inequalities—both at home and in the colonies—of a society. Foucault's critique of the 'repressive hypothesis'— that is, Freud's assertion that sexual wishes and conflict, often over oedipal strivings, understood by the triangulated drama of father/son/mother—lay at the heart of the developmental story of the child about age five, and his final subjectivity.

It was stupendously wrong as a theory, Foucault claimed; for what Freud had taken to be a psychical reality—sexual drives to compete with the father in order to possess the mother and destroy the rival—was not contingent upon person, time, culture or conduct. But how could that be so, Foucault asked? History had determined this repression and its contents—in fact, very recent history: the kind that was closely tied to the schizophrenia of Victorian gender and sexual politics in Freud's patients, as well as moral panics about masturbation, social movements that promoted the creation of the new identity of homosexuality about 1870, and a concomitant range of social things we anthropologists would call 'local culture' (Herdt 2009a).

And I would like to add that 'sexuality'—while being an umbrella term that conveniently covers such divergent areas of subjectivity as love, desire, sexual orientation, relationships and communities—seldom is defined in everyday discourse; and rarely does it communicate precision of meaning in general. It is far more effectively described and interpreted locally, in terms of the moral conventional system of particular beliefs, rules and meanings, also known as culture. This is especially true of sexual pleasure. Or, to paraphrase the immortal Tip O'Neil, all sexuality is local, none more localised than the actual meanings and expressions of pleasure.

Of course, much like Freud, Foucault did not have a burning interest in local culture, regarding 'civilization' as a means to an end (individual repression or freedom). Where he fell short was in his emphasis—some might say his obsession—on a rarefied sense of sexuality as discourse (Herdt 1999). The sense of agency, of individual subjectivity, is largely missing from Foucault's work; but that of course is not what the French scholar was primarily concerned about (Halperin 1995). Here, Freud is more firmly grounded, as he understood that the sexual was but one manifestation of a deeper set of embodied meanings, which discourse could disguise, transpose and hide. Was it not Freud who famously concluded *Totem and Taboo* with these lines: 'For the neurotic, as for the primitive, *inthe beginning was the deed, not the word*' (1955:164)—actions, not talk.

Thus, sexuality for peoples such as the Sambia, in Freud's grand theory, revealed a counter-tendency to act out passion, rather than to repress it, prior to the historical paradigm of Judaeo-Christian codes that narrated how, in the beginning, through God, was the Word, the Old Testament, breathing life into human existence, differentiating animal from the human; and how, with this creation, came the invention of sin, morality and the Oedipus complex. Culture from nature, Lévi-Strauss has said. In other words: a sexuality suited to civilization *is one rooted in words*.

I am reminded of a colleague from Thailand who once impatiently argued against American and Australian researchers—in a conference on HIV now 15 years ago: 'You Westerners only talk about sex—we do it! But we never talk about it—it's too embarrassing; and what's the point?' It is the gap between these two civilizations—between the talking versus the action of sex—that creates differential power relations, pleasures and risk. I will argue that this is part of the problem: in this void, we far too easily imagine that society is stable and cultural reality a given.

Nothing could be further from the truth for the Sambia. The harsh political facts of war and its destabilising effects upon their social organisation impinged upon them and made the mediation of ritual secrecy a tool in stabilising relationships, including the dangers of sexuality; secrecy was essential to the active and wilful creation of cultural reality. And with it came an intentional creation of sexuality—one that was not natural or normal at all in the modern sense of these terms. The Sambia thus were driven to repress some desires while producing and expressing others. Yet unlike Freud's prediction, Sambia sexual development continued the repression and the expression of what we would consider forbidden desires long past the age of five, and not within the oedipal triangle as Freud imagined it. Moreover, the Sambia did this through a system of power relations that made ritual its own engine for the production of desire and pleasure. Men were as much its victims as its victors on the level of discourse, though they had the upper hand with women and children, and the degradation of women, including the terrible manifestations of this in terms of wife-beating and other real-world violence, was cold and cruelly present in everyday life (Herdt 2006; Stolpe 2003).

The Sambia required married men and women to live together in small, round huts, internally divided into male and female spaces, as was common in New Guinea. Men, however, slept for long stretches in the men's house away from their families during wartime and ritual initiations (Herdt 1989). Strategically centred in the village were men's houses where initiated boys and older bachelors lived, while on the periphery and just below the village were menstrual huts. Secrecy surrounded two of the three abodes; only the married couple's house was a public space. And there, as Foucault might have predicted, the regulation of sexual talk was intense.

Traditionally, there were three different types of Sambia discourse: public talk (*iyun-gacheru yungalu*, lit. 'free talk'), secret talk (*ioolu yungalu*, lit. 'hidden talk'), and private talk (no marked category). Public discourse defined daily village gab and was associated with domestic situations in women's houses and casual gatherings on the plaza of a hamlet. Local meetings shaped how Sambia now used the Pidgin concepts *tok publik* (public talk) and *tok hait* (secret talk), because all ritual is *tok hait*. It caused them to refrain from talking about men's-house activities and especially homoerotic relations between younger and older boys, as well as the most secret of rituals, such as the nose-bleeding instrumentalities. In contrast, a married couple's own erotic relations were taboo but private, not secret, always to be hidden from children. Heterosexual coitus was a thing of the deep night, whenever everyone else was asleep; better yet, it belonged to the garden periphery, away from prying eyes. But all the adults knew of it and imagined its effects, always.

In the men's house, secrecy was instilled and reached its apex through six age-graded initiations that created among males the ritual status distinction between younger and older, between the ritual elders at the top and the young adepts, aged seven or eight, at the bottom. The degrees of knowledge, regulation of transmission of secrets to the next grade, hiding of sexual relations with women from younger boys, and shame that younger boys felt and were made to feel in the presence of their fathers, elders and male kin were emotionally intense—a broader oedipal circle. Beginning at an early age, then, boys were not to know of their parents' sexual lives, had hidden from them until initiation the homoerotic relations between older and younger initiates, and graduated into the status of hegemonic adult only after successive initiations during a 15-year period that brought them to marriage and fatherhood. Sexual feelings among boys and girls were strongly inhibited through a traditional culture as prudish as it was preoccupied with war. Thereafter, the nature of oedipal strivings went in different directions for the genders, as they do for us; but here, to engage Don Tuzin's theoretical interests, I shall discuss only the development of male sexual subjectivity through ritual.

A boy's development begins with subordination and repression but then transitions to a cultural reality that allows the creation of desires and their expression secretly. A youth must give up the receptor role and become the dominant player who bestows the gift of semen to younger initiates. But does the youth have enough semen and is his phallus sufficiently close to the image of being a warrior that he will not be silently mocked by the younger initiate who will drink his semen?

This question hangs in the transitional space from being the subject who desires penetration by the older male to becoming the bachelor who desires to inseminate a younger boy. The older youth also begins to anticipate sexual and marriage arrangements. A key informant, the youth Moondi, for instance, once told me how he began to fantasise about inseminating a favoured younger initiate soon after his third-stage bachelor ceremony. Until that time he had perceived himself primarily as an object, not as much as a subject, in the mythopoeic and secret practice of being male. He began to have wet dreams—first of inseminating boys and then of girls. Within the year, though, he began for the first time to consciously desire women, specifically a younger woman betrothed to him, whom he eventually married.

Thus is duty transformed into pleasure. Secret obligation assumes the intimacy of a community of believers who yearn for support from each other and a mode of self-rationalisation in all of the meanings of their public actions. Where the boys begin actively resisting separation from their mothers' bodies and yearn to return to their fold, years of living in the men's house and learning ritual teachings of women's pollution actively transform the boys' desires for renunciation into active fear of menstrual blood, with its traces on the female body. Merely to think of menstrual blood, or the public metaphor for it, is to produce compulsive spitting by a man, since he has taken the thing (menstrual blood) in his mind and mouth and must eliminate it (Herdt 1982). Beginning at puberty for boys, and at first rather awkwardly performed, this spitting has become by the time the agent is an adult an experience, if not in fact a desire, that contains the pleasure of taking in and eliminating that which is so dangerous.

Underlying the ritual teachings is a sexual subjectivity that becomes explicit with development. For example, the growth of the penis, in the men's ritual pedagogy and practice, suggests the notion that the inseminations result in an elongation of the phallus as a 'pure product' of semen. The sense of this 'growth' is forever constitutive of a man's subjectivity of virility and masculinity as he approaches sexual relations with boys and then later contemplates the dangers of sex with women. This sense of timelessness pervades the formation of male subject/object desires and subjectivity in the lifelong practice of ritual secrecy. Adult men cannot do without the barrier of ritual secrecy that separates them and enables their agency in sometimes tense and challenging situations, requiring deceit and manipulation on a personal level. In short, the subjectivity of secret maleness calls to mind the ideology of Maurice Godelier's Great Man, instilled through a split image, the public adult warrior's mature phallic body on the one hand, and the secret subjective body that is still 'growing' as if he were a boy, on the other. This is how the Sambia embodied the objectification of the male body.

As I have often written, there is a sexual paradox in Sambia society. The men have the semen, they are the warriors, they hold the power, and they are the stakeholders in a patriarchal society where descent and property flow down the male line. And yet in Sambia sexual scripts, males are the objects of sexual attraction—that is, they lack agency and are objectified. How is it possible, in such a highly male-dominated, patriarchal culture, that men would be treated as the poster objects? Why would they want to be the desired sexual objects anyway?

As Godelier (1986) has remarked in discussing the neighbouring Baruya, the idealised and preferred sexual object and the object of beauty and attraction in many Melanesian cultures are not the female but the male. Not only is the male the most sexy and ornamented person, but also to desire him is normal and natural—for both genders. The Sambia Great Man is a warrior-hunter—strong, potent and powerfully erotic. He can take many wives and kill many men—a prominent theme in male folklore. It is a kind of glamour that is prestigious, intentional and performative; if you can do it, you are rewarded with sex and power. To bluff, to intimidate, to aggress and to attract are all linked.

The sexual objectification of Sambia males thus arises from two fundamental sources: 1) being more marginal, being subalterns, boys, not women, are the ones truly lacking a voice in their society until they are grown up—women are more powerful then men actually grant; and 2) men's power—that is, masculinity— is conditional and highly permeable, beginning with the awkward and very cumbersome creation of a secret form of masculinity through insemination. It is this permeability of male power that ritual secrecy protects. What is hidden from public discourse is the secret ritual understanding that, to become potent and masculine, an adult man has to be inseminated by many men as he grows up. 'Desire' in this sexual culture is thus the product of, and is dependent upon, ritual secrecy and the cultural control of masculinity in the men's house.

Of course, it will easily be seen that public discussion of this idea would subject the men to scepticism and a variety of forms of accusation of exploitation and manipulation of women and younger boys. Men themselves acknowledge this when they say that they are '*bomwalyu*' men—middle men—situated halfway between sex with the boys and sex with women, a reality they must hide from both sides. Ritual secrecy obviously protects this bisexuality from interrogation all around. But we should not doubt for one moment that the men are genuine, not cynical, in the belief that their inseminations make the boys into strong warriors, since they explain their own personal development in this same way. Cynicism is a luxury of the modern period that a people at war can ill afford.

What men are reproducing is their own (hegemonic) reality, a script that includes repackaging the desires and fears of the subaltern boys. The control of sexuality discourse was absolutely essential to this production. Secrecy was fragile; the material means of social regulation were limited; social arrangements were easily destabilised. Ritual secrecy within the institution of initiation was profound, but it required a violence and necessary brutality to create the desires and controls men needed. The terrible weakness in this system was that boys could not be trusted actually to accept or hold onto the secrecy, the rituals or the cultural reality that depended on it. And that worried the men, always.

The new initiate—before he has been socialised into the men's beliefs and practices—is not trusted and is to be feared because he might be an unwitting agent of destruction. He might unintentionally transmit pollution from his mother into the men's house. Likewise, he might unwittingly spill secrets and give away the military plans of his men's house should he enter into intimate relations with children or his mother. The anxiety of trust becomes part of all male development and all subsequent sexual subjectivity in adult men; no doubt this early trauma is reflected in the fear of men and fathers alike when they ponder the question: can we trust this boy?

Here again, the boy-initiate's compliance with the demands of the men's society to be inseminated by older adolescent bachelors serves as a general proxy for how the men assess their ability to trust a particular boy. One who agrees, who is objectified, who is thought to obey but also to intentionally follow the necessary taboos and ritual rules—such a boy is on his way to having authority in public affairs. The men gradually gain in their confidence of him, and his status rises. Perhaps he will become a Great Man, perhaps not. Thus, the rise in male agency is a direct expression of the boys' agreement with the men to be entrusted by them with their secret reality.

Among the Sambia, the excitement of homo-sociality and boy-insemination drew upon both its fragile secrecy and the devotion to such privilege. Thus, the exclusion of women creates an idealised and fetishised Woman/Other, whose nature precludes understanding the ontology of being objectified in the homoerotic development of the male (Strathern 1988). Surely, we might think of this as a permanent misogyny, concomitant to conditional masculinity, which stems from too much liminality and too much gender segregation via permanent armed camps—harmful effects of a world at war. Sambia women are therefore sexual objects in a way very different than are the boys; they are denied sexual subjectivity and the status of equal social agents, for their role is but to reproduce a system that remains beyond their discursive control. Even more so, they could never understand its male purity and its male pleasures.

I have attempted in this chapter to reconsider our view of pleasure and sexual objectification, remembering the critical voices of Freud and Foucault, in the evolving understanding of sexuality, desire and social action in our society. If sexual repression and frustration, as Freud argued, include both fears and fantasies then the Sambia were right up there, with their institutionalised nose-bleeding that imitated women's periods, homoerotic fellatio that symbolised breast feeding, and semen that was equated with mother's milk. These symbolic equations on the level of individual subjectivity enact a kind of sexual desire and expression unknown to our culture, while on the collective level these same ritual practices, in the logic of sexuality discourse, represent a deeper set of contradictions in the power system that cannot be named. In this cultural logic, boys were sexually objectified—meaning that a boy was developmentally obliged to hold in, to suppress feelings and probably wishes as well—that is, he was repressed. And it was ritual secrecy that institutionalised these controls, built up through ritual measures of power—a kind of domination control. The subaltern in this view was granted, by ritual, private experiences and secret relationships formative of a new self—not the selfhood of American middle-class society, with its constant talking about sex, but an incipient ritual agent increasingly empowered by an erotics of expression, and an expression of erotics, talked about in secret.

And these sexual dialectics were a package of ritual pleasures, both social and erotic, that Freud could never understand, as is clear from his remarks about the ancient Greeks. Pleasure can be a product of cultural things, of social arrangements meant to control sexuality, and even power relations that are not as hegemonic as Foucault imagined. After all these centuries, do any of us truly understand what happened in the formation of the cultural genius and the polymorphous, perverse erotics of Attic-culture Greece (Halperin 1990)?

I think it has always been difficult, in the history of culture and science, and lately in the social sciences in particular, to describe pleasure. We stand in awe of Freud that he took the project on in his *Three Essays on the Theory of Sexuality* (1904). His questions still intrigue us: are men bisexual? Can women fall in love with other women and still be heterosexual? Can children experiment sexually with masturbation or the same sex and still be normal? Today, however, we must insert our own Euro-American questions: can we allow discussion openly and frankly about what *pleasure* is without feeling the fear, shame and silence that surrounds the topic in so many communities? And why *does* the P-word (pleasure) remain so threatening, not just to male authority but to the middle class in general? These are questions of a postmodern society in transition, Internet savvy and no longer as sure a territory for discursive control as was nineteenth-century bourgeois France in Foucault's project.

A recent survey study of more than 11 000 people in 29 countries by renowned sociologist Ed Laumann and colleagues (2003) from the University of Chicago has a surprising and counterintuitive finding, though it probably would not have surprised Freud: sexual satisfaction is inversely correlated with social power. The more patriarchal a country, the more controlling men are in a culture, the less sexual satisfaction men *and* women experience. And men in such controlling societies have *much lower sexual satisfaction* than their peers in more egalitarian societies. Shades of the Trobriand Islanders in the time of Malinowski! Power does not always breed pleasure, and powerful discursive controls over sexuality provide the least pleasure for men and women alike. I wonder what Foucault would have said to that?

In *Secrecy and Cultural Reality*, I suggested that anthropologists avoided taking seriously the power of ritual secrecy in its culture-building and developmental sexual effects, as per Freud, and its discursive effects in regulating social power, as per Foucault. I have posited that there was not only a colonising tendency to treat Melanesian ritual systems as 'child's play'—silly, unreal or symbolic, in the metaphor of the late Ian Hogbin (Herdt 2003). Concomitantly, there was another, more deeply avoidant tendency in the heterosexist and masculinist positionality of white male ethnographers to feel uncomfortable with these male Melanesian secrets. They were uncomfortable with male intimacy and homo-sociality in general and might have avoided anything that smacked of homoerotic events or settings (Herdt 2003:230–1). It sounds like an accusation, but it is meant to be more of an observation that situates each of us in our own time and place (Hammar 2010).

I believe that Don Tuzin's last book on the Ilahita men's society, *The Cassowary's Revenge* (1997), did respond to this implicit concern, when he suggested that Ilahita men were aware of their problematic position of both loving and fearing/ hating women. He went on to say that they needed a psychological outlet for their fears, which they found in the 'safe haven' of the men's cult house and its masculine sociality. Ilahita initiation allowed an objectification of males that substituted ritual scarification and fetishisation of female roles and tasks in secret settings, but without ritual homosexuality (Tuzin 1980). This last was seemingly a violation of masculine standards in Western society at the time and is notable in its own right.

By sexual and gender standards right up to the end of the 1980s, the period when Tuzin was writing, there was a terribly powerful and stigmatising attribution of disease, immaturity, sin, marginality and effeminacy to our cultural conceptions of homosexuality. Anthropology did not escape this medicalising tendency in the analogies, discursive metaphors and models that were selected for representation of same-sex relationships in the non-Western world (Herdt 1999). Freud was responsible for some of this pathologising, and Foucault was the reactor to it. All of us—male and female ethnographers alike—feared being identified with pariah states and categories; and male ethnographers could not quite see that our masculinity, as much as our friends, in New Guinea, was conditional and required the rejection of all things un-masculine: being dependent upon another man, being attracted to him, being in love with him (Herdt 2003). These discourses are experiences of anthropological unreality because there were no words, and no identity categories, to capture these personal meanings until very recently. It is too easy to retroactively make such interpretations from the perspective of the twenty-first century, though we can see how far the field has come in the kinds of ethnographies and the greater understanding of sexual diversity that they represent across cultures (Herdt 2006).

Let me close by returning to make a fundamental point about the relationship between the description of sexuality in our ethnographies and the understanding of how sexual discourse is regulated, even by the ethnographer. The self censors itself in modern society; in pre-colonial times among the Sambia, the self was symbolically censored by ritual secrecy. Contemporary sexuality remains censored and regulated, even in a society such as ours that is saturated with sex—that is, packaged sex—all the time. It seems impossible that it could be, but that part of Foucault's thesis was correct. The trouble we experience with this cultural barrier to free expression is different from what was imagined in Freud's time, when society and sociality were more stable, if less enlightened. And it is even different than in Foucault's time, since his tragic death from AIDS signified a new risk to sexual freedom unimagined before. Sexuality continues to test society, and probably always will, because it contains the possibility of the greatest liberation and the greatest oppression for the individual in the social contract that is culture. But I think that Freud and Foucault, while disagreeing on many things, were at least in agreement about that potential in sexuality for human development.

When societies such as the Sambia and kindred others in Melanesia placed so much social and psychological investment in secrecy, they were signalling their supreme discomfort with allowing individual choice in matters of desire, sex, love and marriage. The comparison with our own recent history—with its stigma and moralising and secrecy surrounding homosexuality, not to mention current controversy over same-sex marriage—is in the same league, though at a different level (Herdt 2009b). As our own society becomes more comfortable with these issues, we might expect the controversy to subside, with the resulting deregulation of sexuality, at least in certain domains. Secrecy, in this way, was never a friend of humanity, being the mother of invention in politically unstable societies, and ritual secrecy was a tremendously powerful albeit primitive way to thwart freedom in human development.

Acknowledgments

This chapter was originally delivered as the ASAO annual distinguished lecture in San Diego, California, in February 2006. I am grateful to the selection committee for the invitation and to the late Don Tuzin for his feedback on it.

References

Foucault, Michel 1980. *The History of Sexuality. Volume 1: An Introduction.* Robert Hurley (trans.). New York: Vintage Books.

Foucault, Michel 1995. *Discipline and Punish: The Birth of the Prison.* New York: Vintage.

Foucault, Michel 1997. *Ethics: Subjectivity and Truth (Essential Works of Foucault, 1954–1984).* New York: New Press.

Freud, Sigmund 1904. *Three Essays on the Theory of Sexuality.* New York: Basic Books.

Freud, Sigmund 1955 [1913]. *Totem and Taboo. The Standard Edition. Volume 13.* J. Strachey (ed. and trans.), pp. 1–164. London: Hogarth.

Godelier, Maurice 1982. Social Hierarchies Among the Baruya of New Guinea. In Andrew Strathern (ed.) *Inequality in New Guinea Highlands Societies*, pp. 3–34. New York: Cambridge University Press.

Godelier, Maurice 1986. *The Making of Great Men: Male Domination and Power Among the New Guinea Baruya.* Rupert Swyer (trans.). New York: Cambridge University Press.

Halperin, David 1995. *One Hundred Years of Homosexuality and Other Essays on Greek Love*. New York: Routledge.

Hammar, Lawrence 2010. 'I Am An "MSM"!...I think': Melanesian Perspectives on Self, Risk, and Other in HIV Prevention. Paper presented to the Annual Meetings of the American Anthropological Association, New Orleans.

Herdt, Gilbert 1981. *Guardians of the Flutes: Idioms of Masculinity*. Chicago: University of Chicago Press.

Herdt, Gilbert 1982. Sambia Nose-bleeding Rites and Male Proximity to Women. *Ethos* 10:189–231.

Herdt, Gilbert 1984. Ritualized Homosexual Behavior in the Male Cults of Melanesia, 1862–1983: An Introduction. In Gilbert H. Herdt (ed.) *Ritualized Homosexuality in Melanesia*, pp. 1–82. Berkeley: University of California Press.

Herdt, Gilbert 1989. Father Presence and Masculine Development: The Case of Paternal Deprivation and Ritual Homosexuality Reconsidered. *Ethos* 18:326–70.

Herdt, Gilbert 1993. Introduction. In Gilbert H. Herdt (ed.) *Ritualized Homosexuality in Melanesia*, pp. vii–xliv. Berkeley: University of California Press.

Herdt, Gilbert 1999. Introduction: Sexual Cultures, Strange and Familiar. In Gilbert H. Herdt (ed.) *Sambia Sexual Culture: Essays from the Field*, pp. 1–28. Chicago: University of Chicago Press.

Herdt, Gilbert 2003. *Secrecy and Cultural Reality*. Ann Arbor, Mich.: University of Michigan Press.

Herdt, Gilbert 2006. *The Sambia: Ritual, Sexuality, and Change in Papua New Guinea*. New York: Thompson/Wadsworth.

Herdt, Gilbert 2009a. Introduction: Moral Panics, Sexual Rights, and Cultural Anger. In Gilbert Herdt (ed.) *Moral Panics, Sex Panics: Fear and the Fight Over Sexual Rights*, pp. 1–46. New York: New York University Press.

Herdt, Gilbert 2009b. Gay Marriage: The Panic and the Right. In Gilbert Herdt (ed.) *Moral Panics, Sex Panics: Fear and the Fight Over Sexual Rights*, pp. 157–204. New York: New York University Press.

Herdt, Gilbert and Robert J. Stoller 1990. *Intimate Communications: Erotics and the Study of Culture*. New York: Columbia University Press.

Laumann E. O., A. Nicolosi, D. B. Glasser, A. Paik, C. Gingell, E. Moreira and T. Wang 2003. Sexual Problems Among Women and Men Aged 40–80 y.: Prevalence and Correlates Identified in the Global Study of Sexual Attitudes and Behaviors. *International Journal of Impotence Research* 17:39–57.

Mead, Margaret 1928. *Coming of Age in Samoa: A Psychological Study of Primitive Youth for Western Civilization*. New York: Morrow.

Stolpe, Birgitta 2003. Cultural Endocrinology: Menarche, Modernity, and the Transformative Power of Social Reconfigurations. PhD Dissertation, Committee on Human Development, Department of Psychology, University of Chicago.

Strathern, Marilyn 1988. *The Gender of the Gift*. Berkeley: University of California Press.

Tuzin, Donald F. 1980. *The Voice of the Tambaran: Truth and Illusion in Ilahita Arapesh Religion*. Berkeley: University of California Press.

Tuzin, Donald F. 1997. *The Cassowary's Revenge: The Life and Death of Masculinity in a New Guinea Society*. Chicago: University of Chicago Press.

Young, Michael 2004. *Malinowski: Odyssey of An Anthropologist*. New Haven, Conn.: Yale University Press.

Section Four: Style

13. Courtesy and Method in Ethnography[1]

Alexander H. Bolyanatz

> Although I did not 'believe' the story, courtesy and method naturally obliged me not to try to disabuse them of their belief. (Tuzin 1997:96)

Don Tuzin was, among his many other virtues, unerringly gracious and polished. Those fortunate enough to have known him will have their favourite anecdotes about how he gently corrected those in error or deflected indignity from a deserving target. The denizens of Ilahita village were no strangers to Tuzin's magnanimity. This is evidenced over and over in *The Cassowary's Revenge* (1997), his poignant memoir of his return to Ilahita in 1985 after a 13-year absence.

In this book, Tuzin weaves a remarkable account that begins in 1969 when he first arrived at Ilahita, moves through an interlude in (mostly) the United States, and concludes back at Ilahita in the mid-1980s. Perhaps 'conclude' is not the right word here. If *Revenge* teaches anything, it holds the lesson that sometimes stories, and their mythopoeic meanings, are amenable to continuous revision—what Tuzin refers to as 'the fluid nature of living myth' (1997:131). When I first met Don Tuzin a few months after his final return from Ilahita, it was certainly true that the meaning(s) of his fieldwork in Ilahita—both instances—was consistently analysed and plumbed for deeper and more meaningful insights. So 'conclude' is a rather inadequate—if not downright inaccurate—way of describing the extensive Tuzin–Ilahita association as represented through the final page of *Revenge*. Like the 'unfinished' (Tuzin 1997:96) story of Nambweapa'w, told and retold, interpreted and reinterpreted, *The Cassowary's Revenge* does not really end. Like the story of Nambweapa'w, in which new elements were added to fit contemporary realities, so *The Cassowary's Revenge* has a reality beyond its last page—a reality that is relevant for anyone engaged in the ethnographic endeavour.

I should explain myself. I conducted doctoral research under Don's auspices among Sursurunga speakers at Tekedan village in New Ireland Province, Papua New Guinea, from late 1989 until early 1992. I returned six years later for several weeks during the summer of 1998. My reading during that stint of fieldwork included the then-recently published *The Cassowary's Revenge*. In

---

1   This chapter has benefited greatly from the comments of Kevin Birth, Mardelle Fortier, David Goldberg and Marie Tenzinger and two anonymous reviewers. Remaining shortcomings can be traced to me.

many respects, in the same way that Nambweapa'w shaped Don's experiences in Ilahita and beyond, *The Cassowary's Revenge* has affected the way I understood (and continue to re-understand) myself in relation to the Sursurunga-speaking folks on southern New Ireland and the ethnographic endeavour during that 1998 field trip and the six field sessions I have conducted since then. Don's notion of prophecy as 'insight' (1997:99 ff.) in relation to the Nambweapa'w story has never really been absent as I think about how I relate to the Sursurunga, and they to me.

Before moving on, I should ensure that my references to the story of Nambweapa'w and *The Cassowary's Revenge* are meaningful to the reader. My recap begins with the story of Nambweapa'w[2] and its cultural counterpoint: the secret men's cult known as the *Tambaran*.[3]

Nambweapa'w was a cassowary who was tricked into living as a human female—wife of the first man, and mother of all humanity. Years later, she discovered that she had been duped and, in an act of vengeance, murdered her husband, the first man. The youngest child of their union—a son—was believed to have been the only one not to have squandered the good life that Nambweapa'w had created for her offspring. He came to be understood as the font of the United States ('America') and all its wealth. The Ilahita *Tambaran* men's cult (like the myth of Nambweapa'w, a nineteenth-century import into the area) was something of an ideological antithesis to Nambweapa'w. The *Tambaran* manifested male dominion over women that was rooted in women's not knowing (ostensibly) that the eerie sounds—and the concomitant legitimacy of male hegemony—coming from the spirit house were in fact merely man-made.

As the influence of the *Tambaran* waned in the face of Western education and the influx of cash after World War II, power and prestige hierarchies were scrambled. Exogenous social movements came and went, some finding the soil of Ilahita too parched or filled with weeds to take root. One movement that did take root was a form of charismatic Christianity—led primarily by women and known as the Revival—prior to Tuzin's second stint at Ilahita. Months before his return, a number of men caught up in the Revival 'spilled their guts' about the *Tambaran* (conceptually reconstituted as the work of Satan), effectively killing the *Tambaran*—an act mythopoeically foreshadowed by Nambweapa'w's act of homicide. The end of one secret resulted in Nambweapa'w's husband's death; the end of another constituted the death of the *Tambaran*. The twin male defeats were noteworthy.

---

2 The complete version of the story can be found in Tuzin (1980:1–8). A synopsis can be found in Tuzin (1997:69–71). My account here is thus a synopsis of a synopsis.

3 Following Tuzin's convention, I capitalise *Tambaran* throughout.

Don's reappearance just months after the Great Disclosure was laden with local meaning(s) tied to the now-emasculated *Tambaran*. For one thing, his return had been the subject of a deathbed prediction on the part of an Ilahita villager named Gidion *three weeks before* the arrival at Ilahita in 1984 of a letter Don had sent informing everyone of his intention to return in 1985. For another thing, his interest in and appreciation of the *Tambaran* had been unmistakable 13 years earlier. And was he not the scion of Nambweapa'w removed to America, finally come to take all of his distant cousins who were stuck in exile at Ilahita into a New World? In his words, the peculiar combination of events included

> the suspicious coincidence of [my return] with the collapse of the Tambaran, the supercharging of Ilahita's atmosphere with millenarian expectations, the death of Gidion, and the coming to life of Nambweapa'w's old tale of retribution and masculine woe. It was not so much my original arrival in Ilahita that had stirred apocalyptic thoughts (at least not for long); it was my *return from America*…amid the agitated conditions of the moment, that created all of the commotion. (Tuzin 1977:132, emphasis in original)

The commotion Don refers to is one that any ethnographer would just as soon avoid if given the choice. After all, the point of ethnography is to report salient cultural events, not create them, let alone star in them—again, if given the choice. The besetting quandary of ethnographic fieldwork is that such a choice is rarely, if ever, offered. Tuzin summarises:

> With each retelling, Nambweapa'w's story remolds itself to changing circumstances, churning itself into a remarkably coherent jumble of older and newer meanings. The detail of the youngest brother's departure 'for America', with its millenarian overtones, dates from the period of World War II. But it was apparently not until my first arrival in 1969 that the significance of a mythic connection with America began to be realized. And it was not until the announcement in 1984 of my return, that the significance of the original visit was realized. Prophecy works that way—by remembrance and revisitation. Today's events fold back upon memories of yesterday and, by a Proustian alchemy, transfigure them. Isolated fragments from the past become realized as significant objects of intentional meaning, animated and integrated with the present. At the core of this process of remembering is an aesthetic illusion: both for individuals in their ways and cultures in theirs, it is the illusion of the self finding itself in memory. (Tuzin 1997:156)

'The illusion of the self finding itself in memory' is a provocative turn of phrase. I take it to mean (not that this is its only meaning) that one's sense of continuity—the connection between the past and the present—is the fabrication of the selective use of memory. In other words, one's selective, filtered, contingent memory of yesterday gives the impression that there is a permanent link between those memories and one's experience of today. And, it goes without saying, the memories are not necessarily shared by others. This generates a matched set of questions: who am I to others; and who are others to me? For a cultural anthropologist, these are important considerations, since interaction with people who are profoundly 'Other' approaches a *sine qua non*. Clearly, Don's new insights about his recollected experiences at Ilahita fit these questions, as do the local understandings of the events surrounding Don's return.

This seems like a good place for a short hiatus in which to examine Don's sense of his own significance vis-a-vis the collapse of the *Tambaran*. In some respects, there is little reason to doubt Don's overall sense of things as reported in *Revenge*, since those who knew him would find a concocted narcissistic fantasy to be simply unimaginable. But there is another reason to assume that Don's portrayal of his own centrality is not inaccurate: a tendency (not unique to Melanesia, but certainly well represented there) to explain phenomena in terms of the unusual, the atypical and the anomalous. Examples are easy to find. In the early 1990s, a trio of Australians was sea kayaking just a bit offshore from Tekedan. After they had departed, I was asked if I thought war was imminent. Stunned by the non sequitur, I asked my aged interlocutor about the source of his question. He told me that just prior to the Japanese invasion in 1942, three boats appeared briefly offshore, heading in the same direction as the kayaks had. An ethnographer in a Melanesian community is an anomaly if there ever was one, so it should be no surprise to read Joel Robbins' account (this volume) of an incident in which a pair of new gloves found in the forest was assumed either to be his (they were not) or to portend a bright new future. Given the import of the *Tambaran*—we are way beyond the scale of a pair of gloves here—in Ilahita life, it is not outrageous, to me at any rate, to imagine that Tuzin's report of his own salience is not exaggerated.

So, when it came to understanding that confluence of events in 1985 Ilahita, local eschatologies varied, and different people drew different conclusions, but the upshot is unmistakable: ethnographers, whether they know it or not, and in ways they cannot predict or control, become part of local lore. And now, finally, I can point to the epigraph for this chapter. It was the story of Nambweapa'w that Tuzin did not 'believe', and it was his own decency, along with his anthropological instincts—'courtesy' and 'method', respectively—by which he explains his letting pass the opportunity for refutation.

Since I am going to allude to courtesy and method often in this chapter, it is worth taking a moment to look more closely at them. 'Courtesy' here is really just a kind of civility, which is to say a reticence to draw attention to another's deficiency. This is not quite the same as the philosophical notion of 'charity', since that stance requires one to assume truth and rationality on the part of the other and Don is clear that he does not assume this for Nambweapa'w. Indeed, he notes that he 'would have to be crazy, credulous, or exorbitantly relativistic' (1997:100) to presume a face-value truth and rationality when it came to the Nambweapa'w account.

By 'method' here, I refer to the ability to gather data—to have access to people and to events—and to the openness of people when talking to the anthropologist. Together, the two constitute a significant segment of that slippery notion: rapport. Clearly, Don was mindful of the fieldworker's awareness that 'how much, or how little, to disclose…affects relationships with informants, especially in cases where full disclosure would expose a clash of values' (Ranson 2005:110).

A closer reading of the phrase might almost make courtesy and method seem joined, as in *'courtesy-and-method* obliged me not to disabuse them of their belief'. Such a usage implies that the boundary between the two is indistinguishable or at least irrelevant. Indeed, that is how I first read them: politeness creates or allows opportunities for gathering information. Likewise, a lack of politeness is almost certain to limit opportunities for gathering information. The strong positive correlation between the two, and the intuitive causal connection, certainly makes them seem, as far as how they operate in the field, fundamentally the same, and this conflation of the two was how I used to think about my own fieldwork in 1989–92 and then again in 1998. I no longer, however, see these two—courtesy and method—as inextricably linked.

Courtesy and method have become detached for me as the answers to the questions 'who am I to the Sursurunga people?' and 'who are the Sursurunga people to me?' have changed. Here is how I used to think about it: when an anthropologist is civil and polite to people at her or his field site (even to the point of not wanting to disabuse people of their beliefs) then one is truly an ethnographer. This is because in order to be an ethnographer, one has to be civil and polite—to my mind. It is almost as if I signal that I am in a data-gathering mode when I exercise courtesy; or that by exercising courtesy, I maintain the possibility of data gathering in the future. When I am short-tempered and rude, or, less extremely, when I speak my mind, even if it rejects what a local person thinks, what am I then—a poor ethnographer or not an ethnographer at all? And if not an ethnographer at all, how then should I see myself when I am on New Ireland? More to the point, how do they see me? From both perspectives, when courtesy—in the form of not wanting to disabuse others of their beliefs—is in short supply, the question is: what have I become? Since first reading *The Cassowary's Revenge*, I have come to recognise that my answer to that question has changed since I first set foot on New Ireland in 1989.

A significant chunk of *Revenge* is Don answering the what-have-I-become question. What he had become, of course, was the result of what courtesy and method had inadvertently and serendipitously set in motion—or at the very least, failed to eradicate: the besetting 'commotion' that struck Ilahita in the mid-1980s. And what he had become had spun wildly out of control, at least from his own perspective.

There is no blame here. This sort of thing happens when and where cultural anthropologists work—very much an occupational hazard. The irony is, of course, cloying; courtesy and method—which in Tuzin's case meant being a decent chap and a crackerjack anthropologist—generated a seriously sticky situation. Imagine for a moment if Don had said, immediately upon hearing the tale of Nambweapa'w, 'Folks, that is just the silliest thing I have ever heard. Only a nitwit would believe such nonsense.' There would, of course, have been no perfect eschatological storm years later. And there probably would have been no Ilahita in the ethnological consciousness of anthropology either. We go, we work, we interact. And we are incorporated—that is, memories selected from the past create an anthropologist in the minds of members of the local community that might not, in fact probably cannot, be the anthropologist's own sense of self in relation to that community. The opposite is also true: the returning anthropologist's selective memories of people and events shape how subsequent fieldwork unfolds. It goes without saying that the anthropologist who does not return never has to deal with these issues. In the context that we are discussing here, making no attempt to debunk other people's beliefs is good fieldwork and virtuous humanity. But upon returning, the consequences of this omission when it comes to the questions of 'who am I to them?' and 'who are they to me?' can be profoundly unpredictable, as *Revenge* chronicles.

I left New Ireland in March 1992 in order to write and defend my doctoral dissertation (Bolyanatz 1994). At that time, I expected to return; I was not sure when, but I did not want my relationships with many of the Sursurunga speakers I had come to know to be terminated. As evidence to others—and myself—that I did expect to return, I purchased a piglet and asked Towor (like most of the names in this chapter, a pseudonym) to raise the pig for me. I gave him some money for expenses and told him that I would compensate him later for any other costs, and he agreed. My plan was to use the pig as a springboard to become involved in the exchanges that culminated in the sequence of mortuary feasts (see Bolyanatz 2000). I imagined that I would visit New Ireland many times over the rest of my life, and I hoped that my involvement in the network of pig exchanges would compensate for the infrequency of my visits.

Towor had become a neighbour over the final year or so of my initial (1989–92) fieldwork, having moved from his natal village, 15 minutes or so away, to mine. Married to a woman of the matriclan into which I had become 'adopted', he was my 'father' and I his 'son'. He became one of my primary sources of information as I delved more deeply into the sequence of feasts in honour of the deceased. More than most people, Towor made frequent requests (for matches, soap, tobacco, kerosene), which, while mildly annoying, seemed not unreasonable to me given the fact that I relied on him more than I did most people.

When I returned in 1998, I discovered that Towor had returned to his natal village. 'He stole your pig', I was told shortly after my return by Tohom, who was, in many ways, my closest friend on New Ireland. Tohom was Towor's wife's sister's son, my Tokbol matriclan 'brother'. When I asked Tohom for elaboration, he told me that Towor had—following local convention—sold the pig for cash to a group that needed one in order to sponsor a mortuary feast. Tohom reported that he had reproached Towor, reminding him that he (Towor) had been serving as the pig's custodian on my behalf. But Towor had a reputation as something of a sorcerer, so Tohom felt that he could not push my case very far, knowing that I—as a *waitskin* ('European') and therefore virtually impervious to sorcery—could escalate the protest if I wanted to.

Towor's penchant for sorcery was something of a revelation to me. When the subject had come up, he had named others as sorcery adepts, and I had no record of others naming him in the early 1990s. But I cannot say that I was shocked upon hearing of his reputation in 1998. Six years' worth of perspective had made me realise that Towor was not, in spite of his helpfulness to me, what anyone would call a 'nice guy'. He had at times been, in fact, a rather nasty sort. This realisation—crystallised for me as Tohom reported Towor's malfeasance—generated a number of questions about my final months those half-dozen years earlier. Why had no-one ever mentioned Towor's reputation to me? How could I not have known this before? (What kind of ethnographer was I, anyway?) Or was this just Tohom's convenient way of dodging an uncomfortable confrontation? At the time the questions that I did not ask (the reading of *Revenge* being perhaps too proximate to glean important lessons) were 'who has Towor become to me?' and 'who have I become to Towor?'. Memory was re-filtered and revision took place. I probably understood him and his fundamental meanness better in 1998, but I needed to understand him as benevolent in 1991–92.

I stopped by Towor's house within a couple of days of getting back. We caught up with each other; I showed him pictures of my family—everyone six years older than when he had last seen them—and he commented on how the kids had changed. I had a feeling that he was not going to bring up the pig. And I knew that it would be rude for me to mention it directly. Courtesy and method, I guess. I waited for the conversation to move towards a related subject but it never did. Thus ended my reunion with Towor.

In the ensuing days and weeks, I proceeded with my work. I wanted to revise my dissertation into a publishable monograph on mortuary feasting and there were some gaps to fill and some clarifications to make that could only be done on site. And there were the usual happenings that will be no surprise to any fieldworker. Topakta, an influential leader, had died several weeks before my arrival; the feud over where he was to be buried was still echoing, and I found myself caught up in that. I discovered and explored a new (to me) means of resolving disputes by means of an extravagant offer of food that, in principle, compels an antagonist to abandon her or his quarrel. I passed through Towor's village now and then, managing to avoid his house for some time.

After nearly three weeks, I had a chance conversation with one of Towor's sons, and he mentioned that Towor wanted to see me. Even though Towor's house was only 15 minutes away, it was another couple of days before I found the time to walk over for a visit. I was not necessarily proud of myself for engaging in that sort of gamesmanship, but who was he to summon me? He could wait until I got around to it. Then again, my debt to him was surely incalculable? With significant help from his insights, I had been able to later write and defend a doctoral dissertation. I had a comfortable academic job. Why was I being so difficult? Courtesy and method, indeed. Was he going to mention the pig? Was an apology forthcoming? Had gathering data somehow become secondary to another agenda? And had I so marked that change by a decline in courtesy? What had I become: a poor ethnographer or not an ethnographer at all?

When I arrived, we sat outside the house and chatted briefly before he told me that since he did not know how long I was going to stay, he wanted to make sure that he saw me before I left so that he could give me what amounted to a shopping list: reading glasses, a shirt, and a pipe. I said that I would see what I could do, mentioned that I was not sure of exactly when I would be back, and that my suitcases were usually overfull anyway. He said he understood and mentioned, as I stood up to leave, that his matrilineage was sponsoring a small mortuary feast the day after next, and that I should be sure to come and bring my video camera.

As I walked back to Tekedan village, I realised that this was about as close as I was going to get to compensation for my pig. At significant cost to him, I was going to be able to participate in another feast and get some footage of it.[4] I discovered afterwards from others that the planning for this feast had occurred in a rush, and it became clear that the situation between us had accelerated the timing of this feast. I also realised that his request for reading glasses, a shirt and a pipe was not just a shopping list; he did want to know when I was going to leave, but only in order to make sure that I would still be there on Saturday and

---

4 In fact, I had trouble with the microphones and ended up with soundless footage, to my great frustration.

that he should go ahead with the feast. He had orchestrated a return to a better time for us by precipitating a feast while I was still there. Memories of those halcyon days of 1991–92 rushed back—for both of us, I daresay. Courtesy and method? I was not as courteous as I might have been, but I had not pushed on the matter of the pig, so I was, I suppose, courteous enough, and courtesy and method were certainly at the core of the adjustment of memory for both of us. I was still an ethnographer. I was still gathering data.

It was five years before I made it back to New Ireland again—this time, in 2002. Although they had been a year earlier, the attacks of 11 September were on the minds of many people when they saw me, and it was often the first thing people wanted to talk about. Was I near any of the destruction? (No.) Did I know anyone who had been hurt or killed? (No.) Had America captured Osama bin Laden yet? (No.) Did I know any Muslims? (Yes.) Was I afraid of them? (No.)

The primary purpose of this field trip was to procure data that were part of an explicitly comparative project—on perceptions of physical attractiveness (Fessler et al. 2005). It was the first of a series of large-scale comparative research efforts that I have joined in which Sursurunga speakers of New Ireland constitute but one of many data sets. More salient in some ways, however, were the conversations I had with Tohom, who was becoming very sick.

Just a couple of years older than me, Tohom had lost a lot of weight and looked terrible. He said that he had seen many doctors, and no-one seemed to be able to help. He wondered aloud whether he had been ensorcelled by Towor, his 'father'. Indeed, Tohom said that he no longer slept in the same place on consecutive nights so that Towor's supernatural powers could not find him. I nodded sympathetically. Courtesy and method? Not really.

It was here where I began to see courtesy and method become decoupled. I said nothing to Tohom about the rationality of his fears (courtesy) but not because I necessarily wanted any information from him (method). Indeed, I found myself *not* wanting to gather data on this case; it was hard to hear about Towor's malevolence as well as about Tohom's anxiety—not to mention Tohom's debilitating illness. I had been courteous but not for the sake of method; and clearly, in my reticence when it came to gathering data, I was being a poor ethnographer in this case.

I did not see Towor in 2002; he was engaged in wage labour at a plantation elsewhere in the province. But I found that some ambivalence towards him resurfaced as memories filtered back and I reconstituted him in my mind yet again. Tohom would suspect him as the source of his illness only if there were some sort of problem between the two of them—real or imagined. And because I liked Tohom, I mentally defaulted to his side of whatever conflict there might be. I asked him what he might have done to provoke Towor's antipathy and he responded that he was innocent of any wrongdoing when it came to Towor. Towor was, after all, his 'father'; therefore, he could only do such a thing because he (Towor) was, at his core, a bad guy.[5] I could not, of course, disagree, and my concurrence had little to do with either courtesy or method.

In 2003, I returned to New Ireland as part of another project, in which economic experimental games were played cross-culturally (see Barr et al. 2009; Berbesque et al. In press; Bolyanatz 2010; Henrich et al. 2006, 2010; Marlowe et al. 2008). Tohom was not any better, but he was no worse, so at least the downward trajectory of his health had been mitigated. Towor was back from the plantation, but I did not have much reason to see him. In the middle of 2003, the ubiquitous topic of conversation around the area was vanilla. Vanilla was going to be the cash crop to put the area on a solid economic footing. Copra was always going to be there, even if prices were down. And coffee had failed.[6] Cacao was currently king, but most people did not have the kind of extensive cacao holdings that would bring in a significant amount of cash. Besides, smallholders had to compete with large plantations just to the north, so cacao was not going to be the long-term answer.

Vanilla, however, was to be the way out of economic stagnation. Apparently, in early 2003, an agricultural expert had visited the region, taken soil samples and proclaimed that southern New Ireland was ideally suited for producing commercial-grade vanilla. Consumer concerns in industrialised countries over cholesterol had significantly affected copra prices a generation earlier, leaving copra with its depressed prices and cacao as the best—really only—ready sources of income. Vanilla stems, though, could be purchased for next to nothing, and vanilla orchards began to spring up. Vanilla vines require some shade and trees to climb, and they have to be watered regularly, especially when young. My 2003 survey showed that nearly two-thirds (16 of 25) of the households at Tekedan village had planted at least some vanilla. The median number of vanilla plantings for all households—including the nine that had not jumped onto the vanilla bandwagon—was 10. Of those households that did begin to cultivate vanilla, the mean number of plants was 164. Vanilla prices had soared just recently, and the passion was palpable.

The enthusiasm over vanilla seems to have engendered other enthusiasms. The expected economic boom made some folks look at the big picture. New Ireland,

---

5   Grammatically, Sursurunga has three noun classes, each of which takes different kinds of possessives. A person's character or true being is one's *ninsán* (the á in Sursurunga is the schwa sound), and is in the same noun class as consanguineous kin, body parts and intrinsic features such as shadows. Nouns in this class are immutable. So when Tohom refers to Towor's *ninsán* as bad, he implies that he always was and always will be bad.

6   See Bolyanatz (1998) for a history of cash cropping in the Sursurunga region.

relative to other provinces in Papua New Guinea, was not poor, and was going to get richer. New Irelanders held important posts in other parts of Papua New Guinea, which was taken as evidence of a burgeoning elite. Indeed, a former Prime Minister, Sir Julius Chan, hailed from Huris village, just a 45-minute walk from Tekedan. And yet, people said, New Ireland's wealth was being squandered on the rest of Papua New Guinea: more money, people and resources such as gold from the mine at Lihir were going out than were coming in. Perhaps it was time for New Ireland's independence. At first, I did not take the secessionist talk seriously, thinking that this was just one more men's house conversation that drifted off into hyperbole as it wound down. But by the third time the topic came up, it was quite clear that, as unrealistic as it might be, there were some people who imagined a nation-state comprising the Bismarck Archipelago. The relative merits of including Manus and/or Bougainville were debated. The transition of the local constabulary into an army was discussed. At some level, I realised that my presence in a conversation like this might make it difficult for the National Government to feel comfortable issuing me another visa. Ever. But that was crazy; nobody was going to report this conversation to anyone in the National Government, least of all me. Method. Courtesy?

I could not help myself. Fellas, I said, the Government of Papua New Guinea is not going to let New Ireland go just because a majority of people vote to leave, even if it ever got to a vote. The mine at Lihir alone is worth an awful lot to them; they are not going to just abandon all claims to it. 'Armed rebellion, then', one man countered. I shook my head. So much for courtesy. What about method? Who were they to me now? Tough economic times (the value of the kina was about one-third in 2003 of what it had been in 1992) and the prospects of vanilla had made for radical, high-risk/high-reward thinking—or if not thinking, then reflexes. Who was I to them now? Well, when it came to conversations in the same secessionist vein, it was clear who I was to them: party pooper. And what had I become? Could I, in that moment, have been considered any kind of ethnographer by anyone?

In 2005, I returned to find out that the Great Vanilla Project had not turned out well at all. Apparently, buyers had little interest in the first vanilla harvests— something about the soil's acidity. Vanilla vines still received some attention, but the thrill was gone. I was disappointed, too. What little I knew about vanilla was consistent with the idea that it would be a successful cash crop on New Ireland, and I had been excited about the possibilities. As I mentioned above, this was not the first local cash-crop expectation that had gone bad, so the local response was fatalistic acceptance.

Reports of the disappointment with vanilla were immediately followed with hope for the next venture: soya beans. At a men's house at nearby Nokon village, one man carefully unwrapped a soya pod from a dirty handkerchief and proudly showed me his ticket to economic freedom. It had cost him K5 (about US$2), but it was a small price to pay, he said, given what the eventual pay-off would be. I was able to stifle a laugh—courtesy (barely), but method? My amusement at this man's gullibility quickly gave way to irritation. Who had exploited this poor guy's naivety? Probably some other unlucky schnook, I imagined.[7] Others agreed that the future, with soya, was bright, and that they planned on planting some seeds—once the price of seeds went down.

That is a bad idea, I said. I told them that I had seen extensive soya bean fields in the United States and that farmers in the United States grew far more soya beans than they could ever sell in their own country and that they exported them all over the world. No way, I said, could New Ireland soya beans compete in such a global market. Perhaps in someone's lexicon somewhere, my efforts to warn people away from cultivating soya beans as a cash crop could be construed as an instance of courtesy, but that is a stretch. Reading disappointment on some faces, I did hurry to add that as far as I knew, soya beans were very nutritious and that, if they were able to flourish in the local soils and climate, they should make a very nice contribution to the daily diet.

Another significant moment of the 2005 field trip took place en route to Tekedan. Riding in the back of a truck with my wife, Pam, who was able to join me for this trip, I was told that my friend Topiknat (not a pseudonym) had died a few months earlier. While he was clearing trees for a new swidden, there was an accident in which a tree trunk had somehow kicked back and struck him in the chest, killing him instantly, according to his widow.

Topiknat was a weekend neighbour at Tekedan village in 1989–92 and 1998. He worked as a tradesman for the Department of Public Works at the town of Namatanai, a couple of hours' drive north. At that time, he stayed in town during the working week, but retired in 2000 and returned to village life, and we enjoyed many pleasant conversations in 2002 and 2003. Affable, smart, well-educated and universally well-liked, he had begun to fill the leadership vacuum caused by the deaths of the two most respected male leaders in 1998 (Topakta, mentioned above) and 1999. His death was a profound setback to his family as well as to Tekedan village—and to me. In 2003, at a farewell gathering on the evening before my departure, he gave a short speech that was something of a

---

7   I do not want to give the impression that the folks on New Ireland are simpletons. In 1991, a men's house discussion at Tekedan about the dramatic political and economic changes occurring in Eastern Europe took place. The conversation was centred on whether, and the degree to which, the change to capitalist economies would eventually result in greater amounts of disposable income for the citizens of those countries. Increased disposable income would almost certainly be used to purchase more chocolate, the argument proceeded, which would increase cacao prices. The question was how many more cacao trees should be planted tomorrow and next week in order to have an increased number of bearing trees a few years from now when these economies hit their stride, Notice that the 'chocolate futures' conversation took place a decade before the K5 soya bean purchase, so one cannot conclude a greater economic expertise over time.

tribute to me—I was one of Tekedan's own he had said, like a kinsman who lived in Port Moresby and whose return trips to the village were all too infrequent but always sure and welcomed. I was flattered and carefully inspected the tops of my own feet as he spoke. I could not know, of course, that it was the last time I would ever see Topiknat.

Protocol in the wake of someone's death required a gift of food to Topiknat's widow, Eriel. We walked to the house and Pam, long since assigned to Topiknat's matrimoiety, sat with Eriel and the two keened as they would have had we been present for the funeral months earlier. My role as a male was to sit nearby and look sad—simple enough; courtesy and method were together again, but not in the usual way. Here, method had provided, over the years, a familiarity with what was expected of me. This led to an easy-to-follow set of expectations for what constituted courtesy in that situation. Who was I to Eriel? Who was she to me? What had I become? Was I an ethnographer in that moment? Clearly, having been an ethnographer there made my expressions of grief locally appropriate. Method had contributed to courtesy rather than, as I had often imagined it previously—and as Don meant it?—the causal arrow pointing the other way. Either way, courtesy and method were becoming more and more unrelated the more time I spent on New Ireland. I could identify times in which I found myself courteous but devoid of method, while at other times engaging in ethnography but with a brusque frankness never far from the surface. I do not remember myself having been that way in 1990. Did they?

Tohom died in December 2008. I am sure that he died believing that Towor was behind his illness. I had hoped to be in the field for a mortuary feast in his honour, but I was not able to make it back until after the second and largest feast in the sequence had taken place. As his 'brother', I would have been expected to contribute to the cost of that feast. This would probably have cost me at least a couple of hundred dollars, but I would have wanted to do it. Courtesy and method were irrelevant as I contemplated the activities surrounding that feast, and the concerns of who I was to them and who they were to me were blunted by grief over the loss of my friend. That loss was felt ever so much more profoundly when I was there in 2009.

In 2009, I arrived back on New Ireland a month after Towor and his wife died—on the same day. This coincidence was quite salient locally and people talked with me as if it had happened just days earlier. In a world where there are perceived to be very few coincidences, these twin deaths were considered to have significant meaning. What that meaning might have been was still being discussed. Towor's reputation as a sorcerer was, naturally, central to many of the interpretations, but now Towor's wife, my 'mother', was also indicted posthumously as someone who used this sort of knowledge for ill. I felt obliged to defend Towor out of some sort of respect-for-the-dead protocol, but I knew that my protestations would ring hollow. After all, *waitskins* do not really understand how sorcery works, so what I said did not matter much. Although I was motivated to say only positive things about Towor, I cannot say that that motivation had much to do with concerns of either courtesy or method. Even as I write this, I wonder about who I had become to Towor in our estrangement. And in a final irony, one of the last things I did during my 2009 field trip was attend the mortuary feast for Towor.

One New Ireland morning in January 2010, I was greeted by Tinkai, who, with her husband, often brought me a kettle of heated water so that we could sit and drink coffee. 'You don't sleep with your windows open, do you?' she asked. When I said that I do, she then asked if I had seen the *sirmát* the previous night. It took me a moment or two to remember that a *sirmát* is a long-haired female forest spirit that sneaks into villages at night. She is not dangerous, but she does things such as seduce men and put her own infant next to a nursing mother in order to have her child fed well. Tinkai related how her twenty-five-year-old son, Tohol, spent half the night chasing a *sirmát* through Tekedan village. As if on cue, Tohol stopped by and regaled me with the account of how he went, flashlight in hand, from this house to that, occasionally catching a fleeting glimpse of her.

Now, Tohol has completed Grade 10 and has worked at the Lihir mine, so he is not a rube. I had already started thinking about and writing this chapter and it was no great epiphany to wonder if this was my Nambweapa'w. While a *sirmát* is no Nambweapa'w in terms of cultural salience, here was my chance to be courteous and not disabuse, as well as to utilise the opportunity to learn more about *sirmáts*. Instead, I sceptically grilled Tohol on whether he had actually seen anything, whether the moon had set by the time he began conducting his search, and if anyone else had seen anything. He was unaffected by my doubt—indeed, he might not have even noticed. In the aftermath of that conversation, I felt a sadness. Who was I to Tohol and his family? And what kind of anthropologist actively works to undermine a belief in *sirmáts*? This kind of wistfulness is different, however, from the grief that 20 years of acquaintance with the Sursurunga people has engendered.

I grieve about the leadership vacuum at Tekedan caused by Topiknat's death. I fret about what will take the place of soya beans in the latest get-rich-quick scheme. I worry about the implications of the talk of secession. I think about my friend Tohom's debilitating illness and death, as well as Towor and our estrangement. I reflect on who else's death I will hear about when I arrive.

I puzzle over why I feel more free to give my views about things nowadays—that is, why, in some respects, I seem to exercise less courtesy than I did in the past on New Ireland. Perhaps it is one of the signs of the onset of a cantankerous dotage.

Clearly, I am not the rookie ethnographer of 1989 with his young family in tow, and I wonder whether all fieldworkers experience the life cycle in the same way that I have vis-a-vis a community in another part of the world. It is obvious that the demographic profile of an anthropologist in the field affects the nature of her or his experience—and therefore of the results, but this is a different question. Things have changed between them and me, and I know that it is not only the perception of things, but also the memories—mine as well as theirs—of what has transpired between us. James Clifford might have captured it when he writes that '[i]n ethnography, what was previously understood in terms of *rapport*—a kind of achieved friendship, kinship, empathy—now appears as something closer to *alliance building*. The relevant question is less: "What fundamentally unites or separates us?" and more: "What can we do for one another in the present conjuncture?"' (1997:87, emphases in original). While this represents Clifford's understanding of the historical change in the epistemological stance of the fieldworking anthropologist that occurred during the second half of the twentieth century, it also captures the ontogenetic alteration in the character of my relationship with the Sursurunga people of southern New Ireland. Perhaps the former question had been wordlessly, implicitly answered and on both sides the relationship had moved to being characterised by the latter question. Certainly, this goes a long way towards describing the difference, but it does not explain how it happened, nor does it shed any light on whether the movement from one question to the other occurred simultaneously on both sides. Tuzin's phrase 'the self finding itself in memory' captures the phenomenon as well as any other, with the reminder that memories are contingent and continuously reformulated. The people of the area on New Ireland where I work first became acquainted with me before I became middle-aged, which is how they know me now. Who have they become to me? The answer is many things, but one thing that can be said is that they are no longer players in a civility-for-data exchange. Who have I become to them? That is impossible to say, but I do know that to myself, I have become someone for whom courtesy and method are no longer linked. Or at least no longer linked in the way they used to be.

There is something else to courtesy, method and the ever-shifting understanding of an anthropologist on the part of a community and vice versa. Perhaps it is the kind of thing people say that determines an appropriate (lack of) response. In 1969, Tuzin's response to the Nambweapa'w tale was to say nothing, as was mine many times, including to Tohom when he told me of his fear of Towor's prowess when it came to sorcery, and how he never slept in the same place on consecutive nights. Local ideas of political or economic content, on the other hand, seem to invite, perhaps by their very nature, an interlocutor's engagement in a way that local ideas about the unseen world do not. Just maybe, my input on secession was desired, and my advice on soya beans was wanted. But did my misgivings about the *sirmát* cross an invisible line? Or does that line exist only in my head because of what I take to be *le pensée sauvage*, and distinguish between that and those matters in which I believe myself more experienced?

There are, certainly, other features of a long-term relationship between an ethnographer and the community to which she or he returns that I have not attended to. And the metamorphosis in courtesy and method that I have described in the relationship between myself and the people in and around Tekedan village must necessarily depend on many factors including changes in the answers to 'who am I to them?' and 'who are they to me?'. But Don Tuzin's experience as described in *The Cassowary's Revenge* represents just how enmeshed—Herzfeld uses the more morally charged term 'complicit' (2001:25)—an anthropologist can become in local affairs.

Don's entanglement in Ilahita's events can, in some respects, be viewed as utterly inadvertent, and yet it is clearly his show of uncritical acceptance of the Nambweapa'w account back in 1969 that set in motion—or maybe better said kept from being stillborn—the events of 1984–86. It was his attention to and concern for courtesy and method that made him responsible for the eventual denouement of the *Tambaran*. He could have done nothing else, of course. And he was no more 'complicit'—although in some ways, yes, ultimately responsible—than were Wilbur and Orville Wright for 11 September.

When I think about my next departure for New Ireland, I think about these changes in courtesy and method as well as the way in which the folks on New Ireland are continuously reinvented in my mind, just as I am certain that I am reinvented in theirs—if not right now then surely when I arrive. Throughout this essay, I have signalled, with Tuzin's phrase, my sense of what I have become to—or, perhaps better, how I fit into—the people and events of New Ireland. At times in the course of my fieldwork, I left things unsaid, feeling now and then mildly thwarted because I wanted to say something but knew that probably I should not. At other times, though, I was glad to have the twin excuses of courtesy and method to keep my thoughts to myself since I was not sure what was appropriate anyway. And of course there were times when attention to courtesy and method—at least that kind demonstrated by Don upon first hearing the tale of Nambweapa'w—was in short supply, as with *sirmáts*. Through all of this, I have been inadvertently constructing a set of memories of me on New Ireland, sometimes quiet and acquiescing to what is being said while at other times— more and more, seemingly—serving as a wet blanket to hopes and dreams, and as a purveyor of heterodoxy.

Consideration for courtesy and method certainly facilitates the ethnographic endeavour—perhaps almost by definition, at least at the outset. But with time and repeated interactions and the reconstruction of memories, this can also move the ethnographer towards a category that is different from the one occupied upon first arrival. Examples of this movement—and it will not be inaccurate to refer to them as method—are that talk of soya beans and talk of secession were not data—nor was *sirmát* scepticism. To me, these conversations were not ethnographic moments, and I did not treat them as such. I cannot say (but wonder) if local people saw me in a profoundly different way, as having become someone or something else—not as an ethnographer—and whether they have meaningful memories of me as someone who has forsaken courtesy and method.

To be sure, courtesy and method are not what they once were for me. When I am on New Ireland, I speak my mind more than I used to, but I do not think I have been rude. And I have conversations that are not ethnographic, yet they appear here in this chapter as evidence used to corroborate points I try to make. Kevin Birth (Personal communication) suggests that another way to express the transformation experienced by ethnographers who keep going back is to paraphrase Tuzin's concept of 'self finding itself in memory' by noting that an ethnographer returning to the same community over a long period is a matter of 'the self finding itself in relationship to methodology'.

Perhaps this is the best way to say it. An anthropologist who keeps returning to the same group of people (although, like Heraclitus's river, it cannot ever really be the same) becomes something very much more than a mere ethnographer. Tuzin's experience in Ilahita is an extreme case, but it is no different in kind from what anyone experiences in returning. What an anthropologist eventually becomes vis-a-vis a community is the result of a negotiation with method. How one conducts oneself in the course of ethnographic fieldwork produces—in ways that are unpredictable and often unknowable—who one becomes.

References

Barr, Abigail Margaret (Corresponding Author), Jean Ensminger, Joe Henrich, Chris Wallace, H. Clark Barrette, Juan-Camilo Cárdenas, Michael Gurven, Edwins Gwako, Carolyn Lesorogol, Frank Marlowe, Richard McElreath, David Tracer and John Ziker 2009. *Homo Æqualis: A Cross-Society Experimental Analysis of Three Bargaining Games*. Documento CEDE No. 2009-09, <http://ssrn.com/abstract=1485862>

Berbesque, Collette, Frank Marlowe, Clark Barrett, Alexander Bolyanatz, Michael Gurvin and David Tracer (in press). The 'Spiteful' Origins of Human Cooperation. *Proceedings of the Royal Society B.*

Bolyanatz, Alexander H. 1994. Matriliny and Mortuary Feasting among the Sursurunga of New Ireland, Papua New Guinea. Unpublished PhD Dissertation. University of California, San Diego.

Bolyanatz, Alexander H. 1998. Economic Cooperatives, Development, and Matriliny in Papua New Guinea. *Notes on Anthropology* 2:31–49.

Bolyanatz, Alexander H. 2000. *Mortuary Feasting on New Ireland: The Activation of Matriliny among the Sursurunga*. Westport, Conn.: Bergin & Garvey.

Bolyanatz, Alexander H. 2010. Does the Use of Money Affect Results in Experimental Games?: Comparing Cash and Betel Nut in Dictator and Ultimatum Games on New Ireland. In J. Franklin, K. A. McElhanon and G. Reesink (eds), *A Mosaic of Languages and Cultures: Studies Celebrating the Career of Karl J. Franklin*, pp. 327–50. Dallas: SIL International.

Clifford, James 1997. *Routes: Travel and Translation in the Late Twentieth Century*. Cambridge, Mass.: Harvard University Press.

Fessler, Daniel M. T., D. Nettle, Y. Afshar, I. de Andrade Pinheiro, A. Bolyanatz, M. Borgerhoff Mulder, M. Cravalho, T. Delgado, B. Gruzd, M. Oliveira Correia, D. Khaltourina, A. Korotayev, J. Marrow, L. Santiago de Souza and A. Zbarauskaite 2005. A Cross-Cultural Investigation of the Role of Foot Size in Physical Attractiveness. *Archives of Sexual Behavior* 34:267–76.

Henrich, Joseph, Richard McElreath, Abigail Barr, Jean Ensminger, Clark Barrett, Alexander Bolyanatz, Juan Camilo Cardenas, Michael Gurven, Edwins Gwako, Natalie Henrich, Carolyn Lesorogol, Frank Marlowe, David Tracer and John Ziker 2006. Costly Punishment across Human Societies. *Science* 213(5781):1767–70.

Henrich, Joseph, Richard McElreath, Abigail Barr, Jean Ensminger, Clark Barrett, Alexander Bolyanatz, Juan Camilo Cardenas, Michael Gurven, Edwins Gwako, Natalie Henrich, Carolyn Lesorogol, Frank Marlowe, David Tracer and John Ziker 2010. Markets, Religion, Community Size and the Evolution of Fairness and Punishment. *Science* 327:1480–4.

Herzfeld, Michael 2001. *Anthropology: Theoretical Practice in Culture and Society*. Malden, Mass.: Blackwell.

Marlowe, Frank W., J. Colette Berbesque, Abigail Barr, Clark Barrett, Juan Camilo Cardenas, Jean Ensminger, Michael Gurven, Edwins Gwako, Joseph Henrich, Natalie Henrich, Carolyn Lesorogol, Richard McElreath and David Tracer 2008. More 'Altruistic' Punishment in Larger Societies. *Proceedings of the Royal Society B* 275:587–90.

Ranson, Gillian 2005. 'I'm Looking Forward to Hearing What You Found Out': Reflections on a Critical Perspective and Some of its Consequences. In D. Pawluch, W. Shaffir and C. Miall (eds), *Doing Ethnography: Studying Everyday Life*, pp. 96–125. Toronto: Canadian Scholars' Press.

Tuzin, Donald F. 1980. *The Voice of the Tambaran: Truth and Illusion in Ilahita Arapesh Religion*. Berkeley: University of California Press.

Tuzin, Donald F. 1997. *The Cassowary's Revenge: The Life and Death of Masculinity in a Papua New Guinea Society*. Chicago: University of Chicago Press.

14. The Anthropologist's Voice: Margaret Mead and Donald Tuzin

Diane Losche

This chapter is dedicated, as is this book, to the memory of Don Tuzin, a great anthropologist who studied the Arapesh-speaking village of Ilahita in the Sepik region of Papua New Guinea. If I seem, at times, to be a wayward admirer, critiquing as well as giving homage, I hope that this will be taken in the spirit meant—as an essay presented in the absence of a great talk with Don, usually a brief time out from the chatter of professional meetings when, for a few moments, two voices might be heard speaking animatedly, sometimes hesitantly, grasping for the right word, seeking meaning, striving to comprehend a point, a parrying engagement of two individuals who have something to say and much in common—a dialogue. I did fieldwork only a few miles from Ilahita in the Abelam-speaking village of Apangai. This proximity meant that I engaged with Don's work in a terrain where similarities and differences in cultural forms could be, at times, closely compared. I, and the rest of us in this volume, will not have that conversational dialogue again; the text might remain, but the voice disappears, except in fragile memory—much to my great sadness.

The work of Don Tuzin (1976), as well as that of Anthony Forge (1966, 1970), cast a long shadow over my own fieldwork and subsequent writing (Losche 1989, 1997, 2001) about Abelam ethnography, not very far from where both men had carried out research before me. My own sense of the field varied so much from the canonical, magisterial textual accounts such as those of Tuzin (1976) that I faltered in confidence. I embodied, when I went to the village of Apangai in 1976 to do PhD research, a zeitgeist of doubt—almost entirely self-doubt. Having read the texts of those who had preceded me—great names of ethnography such as Gregory Bateson (1936) and Margaret Mead (1935, 1938, 1940), as well as Phyllis Kaberry (1941), Anthony Forge (1966, 1970) and Donald Tuzin (1976)—I was rendered almost paralytic with anxiety that the place in which I found myself seemed, as I phenomenologically experienced it, completely different, indeed almost estranged from, in no way commensurate with, the texts I read. So that those reading do not jump to the conclusion that I was entirely witless, I should mention that I was aware, even in my paralysing doubt, that the distance between the field as experienced and the text was great. The memories of those early moments have never left me, because I simply did not realise how remarkably long, arduous, and destructive as well as constructive was the transformation from field to text. The devil is in the details as we all know, and in many cases it takes months, sometimes years—I now know through my own experience—to transform these experiences into written texts called ethnography.

The authors of these memorable ethnographies about the Sepik are not to blame for my uncertainties, for in the beginning I made a basic methodological error: comparing my experience with these polished, finished works. I learned the error of my ways only painfully, slowly, by my own experience of transforming field experiences to text, realising only then the enormous distance between the one and the other. Once, as I lamented the slow pace of my transformative efforts, a great teacher of mine, Robert Murphy, made the observation that the process of going from fieldwork to text took much effort and time because the process involved a form of 'forgetting'—enough forgetting (perhaps the word would be better framed as synthesis) to see, as he put it, the forest for the trees, the form in the huge mass of detail. As the field of anthropology developed through the twentieth century, the emphasis put on the brilliance of the analytical framework grew and the conceptual distance between field and ethnography grew proportionately.

The narrative known as ethnology is at the core of anthropological activity, as any undergraduate major can tell you; it is that from which many other interpretations derive. It has also long been known to be fraught with interpretative problems. There are two moments of interpretative angst in anthropology, from both of which I want to distance my concerns—not so much because they were not useful debates in their time but rather because they have tended to involve the repetitive recitation of now banal insights, which, if they were once fresh and useful, are, by now, trite and clichéd. The first was of the sort embodied by the almost mutually contradictory descriptions of a Mexican village in the ethnographic work of Oscar Lewis (1960, 1963) and Robert Redfield (1930) and the far better-known imbroglio of the so-called Mead–Freeman (Freeman 1983) debate. If one has done fieldwork, one quickly tires of the simplifications to which the debates about these opposing pictures of a place, people and time descend. In this first moment, the question was not of the type of interpretation; rather the ethnography was subjected to a pseudo-scientific notion of a transparent reality, which must be found because it is there to be found. Here it is assumed that whatever the descriptive style of the author, somehow core truths of the social should emerge from the reality of the situation, and if one ethnographer challenges another then it is a matter of a truth versus a falsehood, as was belaboured *ad infinitum* in Freeman's critique of Mead's work in Samoa. Is ethnography description or interpretation? Patently it is both.

I also want to distance the concerns in this chapter from a second, more contemporary moment—that of the interpretative turn in anthropology, embodied in essays looking at the rhetoric of ethnographic description laid out in volumes such as *Writing Culture* (Clifford and Marcus 1986). This particular phase of rhetorical investigation has a gladiatorial edge, and I am thinking here very much of Vincent Crapanzano's text 'Hermes' Dilemma: The Masking of Subversion in Ethnographic Description' in *Writing Culture* (1986). Here, the analyst seems to cling to some ideal of description that is never spelled out, and the analysis of allegorical moves in texts is seen as somehow undermining some utopian, but undeclared, transparently descriptive model. Identification of the gaps in the texts of other ethnographers seems to be a eureka moment for the rhetorical analyst, as if, using Occam's razor, one could not as easily subject their own text to the same form of destructive interrogation.

Both these moments have limitations imposed by the particular methods used to interpret the texts. In many of these analyses, a particular ethnographic text is lifted from a whole set of texts written by an ethnographer and dissected. Although lip-service might be paid to the fact that most ethnographers realise that many of their descriptions are somewhat provisional, nevertheless, each ethnographic description is simultaneously treated as a stand-alone project. In all of this contestation over the truth value of texts, nuances of interpretation are absent, and in this chapter I try to get at one such. I call it the voice of the anthropologist and suggest that we can look at texts as if they contain voices, which are like one particular tone that can suffuse a painting, adding a certain unifying hue to all of the many colours that make up the painting's palette. In the same way, I suggest that a certain voice can permeate entire sections of material, colouring, with one tone of voice, the many different types of cultural forms that an ethnographic work describes.

The characterisation of individual style has long been recognised, and some anthropologists, such as Clifford Geertz (1988) and Margaret Mead (1935), are well known for their brilliant individual styles. At the same time, this style is often greeted with some ambivalence, and brilliant stylists often attract particular attention, critical as well as admiring—as seen, for example, in critiques of Mead and Geertz (Crapanzano 1986; Lutkehaus 1995; Worsley 1957). The point is that style rests ambivalently in the anthropological endeavour, with its roots in the urge to be a science rather than humanity. There is little training in the writing of ethnography as writing *per se* in anthropological education, while there is much emphasis on the analytic frameworks needed to synthesise the vast quantities of material spewed forth in everyday life (for example, the structural analysis of ritual and myth). The problem with this lacuna is that there seems to be little understanding of the complex relationship between the field experience and the final texts produced by an ethnographer.

In this chapter, I want to complicate the notion of style and suggest that style is not simply a mode of writing across a range of texts that identifies an individual author but that different moods or tones can occur in different texts of the same author. These moods often vary according to the circumstances and contexts in which the work is produced. I characterise this as a type of voice, and just as the voice of a person varies with context, so too can the mood of different ethnographic texts by the same author. I chose the term voice, as slightly different from style, to 'open up' the notion of textual stylistics, to allow for variability of tone in the texts of the ethnographer and to allow me, at least in this chapter, to move away from the analysis of ethnographic style as necessarily entwined with truth value and often at odds with it, as has often been done before. Here I want to liken the stylistic tone of texts to the voice of the anthropologist, as I remember the voice of Don Tuzin, in dialogue, as perhaps an unfinished conversation. As in conversation, the voice of the anthropologist is not the same in all texts, and it changes according to many circumstances including new knowledge, who is speaking, to whom one is speaking and a variety of other circumstances. Identifying voice allows new characteristics of texts to emerge and avoids the false idealism of some objectivity embedded in the distinction between description versus interpretation, literature versus science, and it will, hopefully, allow space for ethnographic writing to emerge as a genre separate from other written forms, with its own distinct characteristics.

In this chapter, I am seeking a particular kind of voice, one in which the author opens up his or her text and reveals doubt and uncertainty about the nature of the fieldwork that the author has already carried out. I sought out these texts not for the sake of critique itself but rather because such texts are extremely valuable, for they bear traces of that remarkable but usually suppressed process by which fieldwork becomes ethnography. This search is motivated certainly by my initial shock at the extreme distance between the experience of fieldwork—with its chaos, anxiety and uncertainty—and the finished text. I often wondered if there was any way to write so as to simultaneously present a powerful synthetic analysis and reveal traces of the process of transformation. At the same time, I sought these traces in the texts produced by others working in the same field. I have chosen to examine texts by Donald Tuzin (1980, 1997) and Margaret Mead (1935, 1938, 1940). Both were compelling writers, with extensive works about the Arapesh language group of the Sepik region.

Mead's style has often been commented upon (for example, Geertz 1988; Lutkehaus 1995; Worsley 1957), including by Tuzin himself (Tuzin and Schwartz 1980), in a somewhat awkward obituary piece attempting to characterise her work on the Sepik as a whole, and I am aware that Mead's celebrity/notoriety as well as her voluminous output can swamp other materials. Tuzin's work on the Arapesh is itself voluminous, however, and the juxtaposition of these two very different writers illuminates characteristics of what I call the 'voice' of the text. In this case, I want to compare Mead's much less known and cited work on the

Arapesh in 'The Mountain Arapesh' (1938, 1940) with her description of the Arapesh published in *Sex and Temperament in Three Primitive Societies* (1935). Donald Tuzin's tone in *The Voice of the Tambaran* (1980) is compared with that of *The Cassowary's Revenge* (1997).

Mead described *Sex and Temperament* as 'her most misunderstood book' (Mead 1950:Preface) and, like *Coming of Age in Samoa* (Mead 1961), it has been subject to scrutiny, criticism and doubt (Lutkehaus 1995). Critics have suggested that her description of three Sepik groups was 'subjective' and exaggerated certain features of the three—the Arapesh, the Tchambuli and the Mundugamor—specifically to illustrate elegantly her thesis that what she called 'sexual temperament', as differentiated from sex roles, varied in spectacularly different ways in the small but linguistically diverse region. In *Sex and Temperament*, Mead describes Arapesh culture in global, holistic terms, as the following quote from the beginning of Chapter 2, 'A Cooperative Society', demonstrates:

> Arapesh life is organised about this central plot of the way men and women, physiologically different and possessed of different potencies, unite in a common adventure that is primarily maternal, cherishing and oriented away from the self towards the needs of the next generation. It is a culture in which men and women do different things for the same reasons. (Mead 1935:15)

And this is how she describes their political organisation: 'There are no political units. Clusters of villages are grouped into localities and each locality and its inhabitants have names' (Mead 1935:16).

Mead—once again glossing the Arapesh as a culture—goes on to suggest that one factor in the lack of political organisation is the Arapesh temperament: 'The whole emphasis of their economic lives is that of participation in activities others have initiated, and only rarely and shyly does anyone tentatively suggest a plan of his own...This emphasis is one factor in the lack of political organization' (1935:22).

As the above quote illustrates, Mead's voice is a very authoritative one in this work. Her descriptions of landscape are vivid and her portraits of individuals compelling. There is also a decisive clarity to her description and analysis; indeed, one of the strengths of the work is that the description itself embodies her interpretation so that every environmental, social and cultural feature is described in a way that adds to the cogency of her overarching theme about variations in sex and temperament. So vivid is her picture of place and people that the descriptive passages add to the convincing nature of her premises. This method is familiar in literature, especially fiction. This brilliant, unforgettable description is achieved, however, not only *via* precise descriptions of individuals and the environment but also by broad glosses of large amounts of complex materials into succinct sentences, which by their very nature can only be broad generalities such as 'a lack of political organization'.

Sex and Temperament is not the only text in which Mead describes the Arapesh. Her more voluminous 'The Mountain Arapesh' was published in 1938, three years after *Sex and Temperament in Three Primitive Societies*. What is striking about 'The Mountain Arapesh' text in contrast with *Sex and Temperament* is the scrupulosity of Mead's statements and the care she takes in revealing the limitations of her research, text and methods. The volume opens with a section titled 'Method of Presentation' in which she sets out the limiting conditions of her text: 'The arrangement of any monograph is in itself a statement of method, but may be influenced by a large number of conditions extraneous to the author's methodological intentions' (Mead 1938:148).

She suggests that there were three such limits. The first was that this was part of a joint expedition with Reo Fortune, her former husband. What follows from this is that she will not be including material on issues such as men's initiation or language, both of which were covered by Fortune. A second limitation was the previous publication of *Sex and Temperament*, and she suggests she will be leaving materials covered there out of the Arapesh monograph (Mead 1938:149). Most interesting is Mead's caveat in her regional discussion about the influence her subsequent fieldwork among the Tchambuli and the Mundugamor had on her comparisons: 'The intra area comparisons are drawn, not from those cultures where they would be most illuminating but from those for which some details are at present available. This is a very important distinction in all comparative work, often ignored by advocates of the historical method' (1938:149).

Mead characterises the disproportionate amounts of material she has about the Arapesh compared with the Tchambuli and Mundugamor as a 'disharmony' and suggests that because of this, 'I have frequently overstepped the strict methodological requirements of the historical method' (1938:149).

In her introduction, Mead once again clarifies the necessary limitations of her discussion:

> In cultures in which there is some correspondence between political and cultural boundaries and a degree of interchange within the area, permitting some degree of standardization, it is possible to write about their characteristics as if the observer stood outside and looked down upon a well-defined social system. Among the Arapesh, as among so many New Guinea peoples, this condition does not obtain. The individual Arapesh does not see his culture as a whole, nor does he distinguish the customs of his linguistic group from those of the adjacent

language group, if indeed he clearly notes his linguistic boundaries. Each local community, sometimes only a hamlet, sometimes several hamlets, occasionally three or four villages, presents an aggregation of widely diffused traits peculiar to it. From this narrow vantage ground each individual sees the behavior of members of neighboring communities as becoming steadily more diversified from his own as the distance increases between the communities involved. The ethnographer...who gathers every object found in an area and records the series of non-material traits observed among a people who speak the same language, and publishes these results as the 'culture' of the people who speak such and such a language, is doing great violence to the actual conditions. (Mead 1938:151)

Mead's text here—in contrast with *Sex and Temperament*—has a very careful voice, one that expresses doubt, hesitation and awareness of how her circumstances and methods affected her knowledge. Furthermore, she takes great pains to alert the reader to these limitations. Throughout this text comes a most refreshing sense of a person who is somewhat unsure of her ground, with as many questions as answers, trying to present answers but hedging these with questions. This exploratory and somewhat hesitant text is one that summons far more those doubts, hesitations and uncertainties that characterise the 'field' and those processes that are involved in the transformation to text.

In many of her other texts—both before and after this great work of Sepik ethnography—Mead seems to ignore her painstaking caveats about the difficulties of making generalisations about the area. Many of them fashion materials that, as she cautions against in *The Mountain Arapesh*, do seem to stand outside and look down on the system. Indeed, Mead herself had done this three years before *The Mountain Arapesh*, in *Sex and Temperament*, where, as we have seen, she glossed Arapesh culture with seemingly no concern for those important characteristics that make it so very difficult to gloss Arapesh culture.

We would be in a large company if we, like so many others, critiqued Mead for these apparent contradictions between one kind of text and the other, both based on the same field materials. There is no doubt, however, that Mead was quite aware of the very great differences in her two portraits. As Nancy Lutkehaus (1995:189–90) points out, Mead was one of the most self-aware of writers, one who paid careful attention to the differences that she felt were required in writing texts for different audiences. Mead herself would undoubtedly have pointed out that one text, *Sex and Temperament*, published in the United States by William Morrow, a major publisher of fiction and non-fiction for a large and so-called general audience, was a different proposition than writing a text published by the American Museum of Natural History, a small press that published monographs by scientific staff of the museum aimed at a small, professional audience. What strikes me is how easy it still is to find *Sex and Temperament* in libraries and bookstores while *The Mountain Arapesh* has almost disappeared, even from academic libraries. Perhaps what ought to give us pause for thought is that, even in academic circles, Mead's *The Mountain Arapesh* is seldom referred to, analysed or quoted, while *Sex and Temperament* is often cited and critiqued. It has become part of her infamous celebrity-like profile, her signature and style, while her other texts about the Arapesh, which would challenge this view, are largely ignored. My point here is that not only authors create texts that establish the author's authority and command via cultural glosses and the suppression of all sorts of uncertainties; academia also institutionally privileges, especially via citation and critique, canonical texts. It was not Margaret Mead who turned *Sex and Temperament* into a canonical text but rather the volume's reception and institutionalisation.

Nor was it only Mead who ignored her own caveats about the Sepik area; so too did most subsequent anthropology of the area. By 1941, Phyllis Kaberry's early descriptions of the area around Maprik (a subdistrict headquarters of the Sepik region) glossed the area as home to the Abelam tribe with little caveat (Kaberry 1941). By the 1960s and 1970s, ethnographies such as those produced by Forge (1970) and Tuzin (1976) would routinely gloss certain areas as Arapesh and Abelam with little attention to variations within, or boundaries between, these groupings. I am not so much criticising this move as pointing out that it is the common ground from which texts arise. Indeed this crucial glossing of an area into 'cultures' defined according to linguistic criteria was, and remains, a crucial step in allowing communication between anthropologists—that is, the transformation of the inchoate into objects or units for comparison, study and analysis. That this involves seldom examined and intuitive transformations from field experience to text is an outcome, I suggest, of the peculiar conditions of ethnographic practice in the twentieth century, at least in the Sepik region. Ethnographers had to try to make sense of quantities of material gathered from particular, small populations against a backdrop of the relatively few comparative studies of the region that appeared sporadically and irregularly, in different languages and frameworks, and with almost no systematicity. Indeed, any apparent systematicity only grew out of the articulation of units, such as Abelam and Arapesh, which allowed anthropologists to speak to one another. Much of Donald Tuzin's work, like most ethnography of the Sepik, including my own, thus ignored Mead's caveat against standing outside, and looking down on, the system—but for very compelling reasons!

Thus, by the 1970s, when Don Tuzin began producing his major ethnographic texts on the Ilahita Arapesh (1976), the practice of glossing one's field experience into a unit was already well established. Tuzin's ethnographic writing glossed his experience, which was based in one uniquely large village of some 1500 people called Ilahita, as a text about the 'Ilahita Arapesh' or 'Arapesh', and most of his writing stands outside and surveys this unit, little troubled by the doubts about method that Mead had voiced in her *The Mountain Arapesh* material. Tuzin was a writer who could equal Mead in creating a compelling text, although his 'voice' is very different than either her careful, almost uncertain voice in *The Mountain Arapesh* or her more seamless texts such as *Sex and Temperament*. Tuzin's textual voice is often magisterial, authoritative and very dramatic, creating a sense that we are in a grand narrative of great historical moment. With one exception, his texts seldom introduce caveats, unanswered questions or doubt. These absences, as well as the magisterial tone, create a canonical text about a cultural system. Here as elsewhere, Tuzin writes with a compelling narrative urgency that, as much more commonly in fiction, leads the reader to want to find out what happens next.

In *The Voice of the Tambaran* (Tuzin 1980), his second full-length ethnographic work, which describes the Ilahita Arapesh initiation structure, Tuzin begins each chapter with a myth—a device that operates as a code or key to understanding aspects of the initiation system discussed in the chapter. The opening chapter begins with the famous myth of Nambweapa'w. It takes up eight pages, and Tuzin provides two alternative endings. He does not explain the reason for including these alternative endings, nor does he specify who provided the particular version included in the book. In a footnote, he refers to 'The story teller', as if the storyteller were a single person, but this is not elaborated on (Tuzin 1980:7). Having conducted fieldwork in a nearby but different language, and having gathered a similar though truncated story, I have methodological questions that are seldom answered in Tuzin's book. How many people tell this exact version of the story? How widespread is the knowledge of this particular story? Is this a gloss of many versions or one of the longest versions?

Following the myth of Nambweapa'w, Tuzin continues to create a seamless cultural gloss and to make broad generalisations about the Ilahita Arapesh:

> Nambweapa'w crystallizes for the Arapesh a sense of themselves in relation to (and in mythic priority over) a larger humanity. The Tambaran, largely by virtue of its participation in the same array of existential themes, likewise serves as a summary symbol of Arapesh cultural identity. When the two images are brought together under ritual auspices, the complex wedding of male and female, past and present, creation and destruction—all raised to mythic proportions—yields a transcendent meaning of supreme cultural value. (Tuzin 1980:10–11)

This characterisation of Tuzin's technique of broad glossing is not intended as critique, for indeed I have done the same myself and not as well as he did. Indeed, his text is an extremely good example of the type of ethnographic text exciting to other anthropologists, as was Mead's *Sex and Temperament*, because of an elegant aesthetic, compelling narrative structure and bold synthesis. It might not address questions that would be raised in postmodern discussions of ethnographic texts (Clifford and Marcus 1986), but *Writing Culture* was published six years after *The Voice of the Tambaran* (Tuzin 1980). My point is that Tuzin's is an outstanding and inspiring example of an ethnographic text of its time, as brilliant in its style as was Mead's, and like that volume it ignored, for purposes of the aesthetics of exposition, issues that would obscure what the author considered his most important points. Like *Sex and Temperament*, Tuzin's texts create a powerful synthesis from the motley assembly of field experience, deliberately putting aside some of the fascinating questions raised by Mead in *The Mountain Arapesh*. Many of Tuzin's texts on the Arapesh reflect this seamless quality, where the singular eye of the anthropologist sweeps up irregularities, limitations and variations into summary statements. There are many who would claim that such synthesising activity is the most important aim of ethnography. It was only in the 1980s that some of the concerns voiced by Mead in the 1930s began again to be aired in anthropology. As Lutkehaus (1995:190) has pointed out, Mead's concern with writing led her to observations about narrative styles and audience reception that predate recent critiques of ethnographic texts.

Like Mead before him, Tuzin, in one of his ethnographies, has a voice strikingly different than that in the others. This is his final book-length ethnography of the Ilahita Arapesh: *The Cassowary's Revenge* (1997). This volume, like his earlier Ilahita Arapesh work, is also a compulsively readable narrative with an extremely dramatic tone. The Preface introduces the drama:

> This book is about something that happened in Ilahita, a village in the interior lowland of northeastern New Guinea. The year was 1984. The event was a murder, not a senseless anonymous killing, but a conspiratorial act carried out by men with a purpose. The assailants had known their victim all their lives and most of the time regarded him with profound respect, possibly even love.
>
> The shocking truth is the killing was a parricide. (Tuzin 1997:ix)

In the book, Freud and the Old Testament are summoned as interlocutors, and Greek models, such as Oedipus, hover over this story of the destruction of the men's cult by Ilahita villagers, adding to the drama and sense of the historical importance of the events being described.

Tuzin, however, enters this ethnography as a character, as he finds his own, very personal fate has become entwined with the story of the destruction of the cult of the *Tambaran* in Ilahita. In his Preface, Tuzin not only opens up for the reader a gap created by his own involvement but also frames this involvement as necessitating a structure of multiple narratives:

> The third narrative is awkward to tell, for it is about my return to Ilahita after an eventful absence of thirteen years and my disturbing, uncanny involvement with the recent collapse of the men's cult. Swept into the current of events and fantasies, this return encounter rewrote the significance of my original visit, merging it into a stream of prophecy to which the ethnographer was now a reluctant, hapless contributor... The telling of what happened in Ilahita requires then, three different arguments, three different voices, three different domains. (Tuzin 1997:x)

The Cassowary's Revenge makes for compelling reading particularly because of the shock with which Tuzin recounts how his earlier fieldwork had been incorporated, very prominently, into the history that led to the downfall of the men's cult. He confesses to his own stake in the men's cult during 13 years' absence from the village, during which his own professional activities were heavily invested in describing and analysing it, with his volume *The Voice of the Tambaran* entirely given over to it: 'The intervening thirteen years of writing, lecturing and nostalgizing added up to an emotional investment in all that the villagers were seeking to destroy' (Tuzin 1997:5).

Much of Chapter 1, titled 'Going Home', describes the circumstances of this unwitting involvement in the demise of Ilahita's *Tambaran* cult. This is a complex story in which Tuzin's own cancer (Hodgkin's disease)—diagnosed while preparing his PhD subsequent to his first period of fieldwork (Lipset and Roscoe, this volume)—became known to villagers through letters, and along with the later death of a close informant also from cancer became entwined with the demise of the *Tambaran*. In describing these events, Tuzin broaches the complexities of ethnographic fieldwork in terms much more familiar to contemporary anthropologists than Mead's earlier angst over the limitations of her observations, trying to conceptualise his particular difficulties about the ethnographer's involvement in a particular place and to make important points regarding the nature of the ethnographic enterprise:

> In all the recent attacks on ethnographic objectivity, no one as far as I know has remarked on the difference between going to the field for the first time and returning there after a lengthy absence...Both situations may involve observer bias, but returning to the field entails a larger, more complex hazard because it means tampering with a relationship that already exists laden with emotion, personal history and moral ambiguity. (Tuzin 1997:5)

Tuzin not only narrates the story of his role in the events he describes, he also conceptualises and comments on the processes involved in the rethinking necessary when the unexpected causes one to reframe earlier work, producing a meta-theory about the processes of long-term fieldwork in an area:

> Rediscovering, restarting, revisiting, reconsidering, folding back—these are the convolutions of symbolic process, and therefore these must be the apparatus of understanding. Ethnographers return to the field and modify the meanings of previous facts in the light of intervening events; cultures return to their mythic charter and unwittingly edit it to accord with historical experience; individuals return to places of precious memory, thinking to capture some fragment of the experience—never to succeed. (Tuzin 1997:xi)

The lodestone that Tuzin suggests for conceptualising the problems of his own experiences is memory—a recent and powerful entry to the arsenal of analytic frameworks used to conceptualise historical change at an institutional and individual level. He suggests that memory will be the touchstone that unites his three narratives—personal and collective—and that will provide the framework for analysing the problems made evident in his earlier understandings of Ilahita, made evident only on his return after 13 years:

> Always one must go back, searching for what things of the past 'really' meant as a clue to present realities. Going is never the same as going back. Going is mundane, going back is mythic, because it confronts the self in memory. Indeed, in a curious way that poets understand, it is through memory that past and present are finally reconciled, finally realized, and the future is made possible. Individuals relate to themselves in this way, and so do cultures. (Tuzin 1997:xi)

Here, in a most poetic voice, Tuzin is suggesting a methodological solution to the problem of the very disparate pictures that emerge when one does long-term research in an area.

In *The Cassowary's Revenge*, Tuzin returns to the story of Nambweapa'w, the cassowary myth that occupied such a central role as a charter for the *Tambaran* in his earlier volume. He acknowledges some of the difficulties (not explored in the earlier text) he had with conceptualising the role of the Nambweapa'w story in *The Voice of the Tambaran*: 'The truth was that I did not know what to say that would do justice to the story's intuitive importance. Additional years and events have clarified and, in curious ways that this book tries to explain, realized and fulfilled those intuitions' (Tuzin 1997:71).

Three chapters of *The Cassowary's Revenge* are devoted to the Cassowary myth, and in these Tuzin is far more meticulous in outlining the questions of variation that the myth, as deployed in *The Voice of the Tambaran*, had raised for me. I suggest that the involvement of his personal narrative in the events described in *The Cassowary's Revenge* also sensitised him to give greater attention to issues of irregularity, variation and uncertainty in a variety of the cultural phenomena found in Ilahita.

The point of this chapter has been to suggest that, rather than lifting particular texts out of an entire body of work and arguing the validity of a particular ethnographic point vis-a-vis the facts of a particular field site, we look across the entire body of work of an ethnographer, giving attention to a variety of circumstances surrounding the production of different kinds of texts, which, as I have tried to demonstrate here, vary in mood, tone and voice. These tones cast particular cultural phenomena into remarkably different kinds of forms, from the nature of the social units under discussion and how broadly the anthropologist can generalise from a very small sample, which troubled Margaret Mead, to the variations in myth that Tuzin took as a central issue in *The Cassowary's Revenge*.

In the introduction to this chapter, I mentioned two modes of analysis from which I distanced the concerns of this chapter: the critique that privileges de-contextualised social fact, and the interpretative turn, which ignores the issue of the truth value of social facts but critiques the rhetorical narrative modes by which the author of a text constitutes him or herself as an 'authority'. Both these forms of critique, I have suggested here, ignore the complexities of both fieldwork and ethnography, including the many 'moments' of this arduous and often lifetime venture. As Donald Tuzin suggested, going back is quite different from going. I suggest that in 'going back' to the texts of anthropologists who have gone before us we listen to the questions they raised in their own 'going back'. The insights that both Mead and Tuzin gained from their own revisions are some of the most valuable of their contributions to the ethnography of this area, and they provide glimpses of that arduous process by which the 'field' becomes the 'text'. This chapter has examined two authors who produced texts that bear the marks of uncertainty and hesitation—characteristics that, under a variety of compelling professional forces, are often lost. It is intended as homage to those works, with all their caveats and hesitations, for they bear the trace of the anthropologists' voices, which I imagine I still hear.

References

Bateson, Gregory 1958 [1936]. *Naven: A Survey of the Problems Suggested by a Composite Picture of the Culture of a New Guinea Tribe Drawn from Three Points of View*. Stanford, Calif.: Stanford University Press.

Clifford, James and George Marcus (eds) 1986. *Writing Culture: The Poetics and Politics of Ethnography*. Berkeley: University of California Press.

Crapanzano, Vincent 1986. Hermes' Dilemma: The Masking of Subversion in Ethnographic Description. In James Clifford and George Marcus (eds) *Writing Culture: The Poetics and Politics of Ethnography*, pp. 51–77. Berkeley: University of California Press.

Forge, Anthony 1966. Art and Environment in the Sepik. *Proceedings of the Royal Anthropological Institute* 1965:23–31.

Forge, Anthony 1970. Learning to See in New Guinea. In Philip Mayer (ed.) *Socialization: The Approach from Social Anthropology*, pp. 269–91. London: Tavistock.

Freeman, Derek 1983. *Margaret Mead and Samoa: The Making and Unmaking of an Anthropological Myth*. Cambridge, Mass.: Harvard University Press.

Geertz, Clifford 1988. *Works and Lives: The Anthropologist As Author*. Cambridge: Polity Press.

Kaberry, Phyllis M. 1941. The Abelam Tribe, Sepik District, New Guinea: A Preliminary Report. *Oceania* 11(3):233–58; 11(4):345–67.

Lewis, Oscar 1960. *Tepotzlan: Village in Mexico*. New York: Holt, Rinehart & Winston.

Lewis, Oscar 1963. *Life in a Mexican Village: Tepotzlan Restudied*. Urbana, Ill.: Illinois University Press.

Losche, Diane 1989. Frankenstein Stalks the Coral Gardens: The Cult of Secrecy in the Abelam. *Australian Journal of Art* viii:7–19.

Losche, Diane 1997. What Do Abelam Images Want from Us?: Plato's Cave and Kwatbil's Belly. *The Australian Journal of Anthropology* 8:35–50.

Losche, Diane 2001. Anthony's Feast: The Gift in Abelam Aesthetics. *The Australian Journal of Anthropology* 12:155–66.

Lutkehaus, Nancy 1995. Margaret Mead and the 'Rustling-of-the-Wind-In-The-Palm-Trees School' of Ethnographic Writing. In Ruth Behar and Deborah Gordon (eds) *Women Writing Culture*, pp. 186–207. Berkeley: University of California Press.

Mead, Margaret 1935. *Sex and Temperament in Three Primitive Societies*. New York: William Morrow.

Mead, Margaret 1938. *The Mountain Arapesh, I: An Importing Culture. Anthropological Papers of the American Museum of Natural History* 36(3):139–49.

Mead, Margaret 1940. *The Mountain Arapesh, II. Supernaturalism. Anthropological Papers of the American Museum of Natural History* 37(3):317–451.

Mead, Margaret 1950 [1935]. *Sex and Temperament in Three Primitive Societies*. New York: New American Library.

Mead, Margaret 1961 [1928]. *Coming of Age in Samoa*. New York: William Morrow.

Redfield, Robert 1930. *Tepotzlan, A Mexican Village: A Study of Folk Life*. Chicago: University of Chicago Press.

Tuzin, Donald F. 1976. *The Ilahita Arapesh: Dimensions of Unity*. Berkeley: University of California Press.

Tuzin, Donald F. 1980. *The Voice of the Tambaran: Truth and Illusion in Ilahita Arapesh Religion*. Berkeley: University of California Press.

Tuzin, Donald F. 1997. *The Cassowary's Revenge: The Life and Death of Masculinity in a New Guinea Society*. Chicago: University of Chicago Press.

Tuzin, Donald F. and Theodore Schwartz 1980. Margaret Mead in New Guinea: An Appreciation. *Oceania* 50:241–6.

Worsley, Peter 1957. Margaret Mead: Science or Science Fiction? *Science and Society* 21:122–34.

Donald F. Tuzin: A bibliography

Books

1976. *The Ilahita Arapesh: Dimensions of Unity*. Berkeley: University of California Press.

1980. *The Voice of the Tambaran: Truth and Illusion in Ilahita Arapesh Religion*. Berkeley: University of California Press.

1997. *The Cassowary's Revenge: The Life and Death of Masculinity in a New Guinea Society*. Chicago: University of Chicago Press.

2001. *Social Complexity in the Making: A Case Study Among the Arapesh of New Guinea*. London: Routledge.

Edited Volumes

1983. (with Paula Brown) *The Ethnography of Cannibalism*. Society for Psychological Anthropology, Special Publication. Washington, DC: Society for Psychological Anthropology.

2001. (with Thomas Gregor) *Gender in Amazonia and Melanesia: An Exploration of the Comparative Method*. Berkeley: University of California Press.

Journal Articles

1972. Yam Symbolism in the Sepik: An Interpretative Account. *Southwestern Journal of Anthropology* 28:230–54.

1975. The Breath of a Ghost: Dreams and the Fear of the Dead. *Ethos* 3:555–78.

1977. Reflections of Being in Arapesh Water Symbolism. *Ethos* 5:195–223.

1978. Politics, Power and Divine Artistry in Ilahita. *Anthropological Quarterly* 51:60–7.

1978. Sex and Meat-Eating in Ilahita: A Symbolic Study. *Canberra Anthropology* 1:82–93.

1980. (with Theodore Schwartz) Margaret Mead in New Guinea: An Appreciation. *Oceania* 50:241–7.

1984. Miraculous Voices: The Auditory Experience of Numinous Objects. *Current Anthropology* 25:579–89, 593–6. [Abridged and reprinted in 1995 in *Amok Journal: Sensurround Edition: A Compendium of Psycho-Physiological Investigations.* Stuart Swezey (ed.), pp. 427–36. Los Angeles: Amok Books.]

1988. Prospects of Village Death in Ilahita. *Oceania* 59:81–104.

1991. Sex, Culture, and the Anthropologist. *Social Science and Medicine* 33:867–74.

1992. Sago Subsistence and Symbolism Among the Ilahita Arapesh. *Ethnology* 31:103–14.

1992. (with Richard C. Atkinson) Equilibrium in the Research University. *Change* 24(3):20–31.

1994. The Forgotten Passion: Sexuality and Anthropology in the Ages of Victoria and Bronislaw. *Journal of the History of the Behavioral Sciences* 30:114–37.

1995. Art and Procreative Illusion in the Sepik: Comparing the Abelam and the Arapesh. *Oceania* 65:289–303.

1998. (with Thomas Gregor) Amazonia and Melanesia: Gender and Anthropological Comparison. Conference Report. *Current Anthropology* 39:274–77.

2002. Art, Ritual, and the Crafting of Illusion: The Anthony Forge Memorial Lecture, 2001. *Asia Pacific Journal of Anthropology* 3:1–23.

Chapters in Edited Volumes

1974. Social Control and the Tambaran in the Sepik. In A. L. Epstein (ed.), *Contention and Dispute: Aspects of Law and Social Control in Melanesia*, pp. 317–44. Canberra: Australian National University Press.

1977. Kinship Terminology in a Linguistic Setting. In S. A. Wurm (ed.) *New GuineaArea Languages and Language Study.Volume 3: Language, Culture, Society, and the Modern World*, pp. 101–29. Pacific Linguistics, Series C, No. 40. Canberra: Department of Linguistics, The Australian National University.

1982. Ritual Violence Among the Ilahita Arapesh: The Dynamics of Moral and Religious Uncertainty. In Gilbert H. Herdt (ed.) *Rituals of Manhood: Male Initiation in Melanesia*, pp. 321–55. Berkeley: University of California Press.

1983. (with Paula Brown) Introduction. In Paula Brown and Donald Tuzin (eds) *The Ethnography of Cannibalism*, pp. 1–5. Society for Psychological Anthropology, Special Publication. Washington, DC: Society for Psychological Anthropology.

1983. Cannibalism and Arapesh Cosmology: A War-Time Incident with the Japanese. In Paula Brown and Donald Tuzin (eds) *The Ethnography of Cannibalism*, pp. 61–71. Society for Psychological Anthropology, Special Publication. Washington, DC: Society for Psychological Anthropology.

1983. Circumcision. *Funk & Wagnalls New Encyclopedia*, pp. 298–9. New York: Funk & Wagnalls.

1983. Rites of Passage. *Funk & Wagnalls New Encyclopedia*, pp. 291–2. New York: Funk & Wagnalls.

1989. The Organization of Action, Identity, and Experience in Arapesh Dualism. In David Maybury-Lewis and Uri Almagor (eds) *The Attraction of Opposites: Thought and Society in the Dualistic Mode*, pp. 277–96. Ann Arbor, Mich.: University of Michigan Press.

1989. Visions, Prophecies, and the Rise of Christian Consciousness: A Case of Religious Imagination. In Michele Stephen and Gilbert H. Herdt (eds) *The Religious Imagination in New Guinea*, pp. 187–208. New Brunswick, NJ: Rutgers University Press.

1990. Of the Resemblance of Fathers to Their Children: The Roots of Primitivism in Middle-Childhood Enculturation. In L. Bryce Boyer and Simon Grolnick (eds) *The Psychoanalytic Study of Society. Volume 15: Essays in Honor of Paul Parin*, pp. 69–103. Hillsdale, NJ: Analytic Press.

1990. Fighting for Their Lives: The Problem of Cultural Authenticity in Today's Sepik Region. In Nancy Lutkehaus, Christian Kaufmann, William E. Mitchell, Douglas Newton, Lita Osmundsen and Meinhard Schuster (eds) *Sepik Heritage: Tradition and Change in Papua New Guinea*, pp. 364–9. Durham, NC: Carolina Academic Press.

1991. The Cryptic Brotherhood of Big Men and Great Men in Ilahita. In Marilyn Strathern and Maurice Godelier (eds) *Big Men and Great Men: Personifications of Power in Melanesia*, pp. 115–29. Cambridge: Cambridge University Press.

1992. Revelation and Concealment in the Cultural Organization of Meaning: A Methodological Note. In Bernard Juillerat (ed.) *Shooting the Sun: Ritual and Meaning in the West Sepik, Ida Revisited*, pp. 251–9. Washington, DC: Smithsonian Institution Press.

1992. The Melanesian Archive. In Sydel Silverman and Nancy J. Parezo (eds) *Preserving the Anthropological Record*, pp. 31–42. New York: Wenner-Gren Foundation for Anthropological Research. [Reprinted in the second edition, 1995, pp. 23–34.]

1994. (with David Western, Shirley C. Strum, K. Sayre and R. Michael Wright) A Few Big Challenges. In David Western and R. Michael Wright (eds) *Natural Connections: Perspectives in Community-Based Conservation*, pp. 536–47. Washington, DC: Island Press.

1995. Discourse, Intercourse, and the Excluded Middle: Anthropology and the Problem of Sexual Experience. In Paul R. Abramson and Stephen D. Pinkerton (eds) *Sexual Nature/Sexual Culture*, pp. 257–75. Chicago: University of Chicago Press.

1996. The Spectre of Peace in Unlikely Places: Concept and Paradox in the Anthropology of Peace. In Thomas A. Gregor (ed.) *A Natural History of Peace*, pp. 3–33. Nashville: Vanderbilt University Press.

2001. (with Thomas A. Gregor) Comparing Gender in Amazonia and Melanesia: A Theoretical Orientation. In Thomas A. Gregor and Donald Tuzin (eds) *Gender in Amazonia and Melanesia: An Exploration of the Comparative Method*, pp. 1–16. Berkeley: University of California Press.

2001. (with Thomas A. Gregor) The Anguish of Gender: Men's Cults and Moral Contradiction in Amazonia and Melanesia. In Thomas A. Gregor and Donald Tuzin (eds) *Gender in Amazonia and Melanesia: An Exploration of the Comparative Method*, pp. 309–36. Berkeley: University of California Press.

2001. (with Thomas A. Gregor) Reflections on the Land of Melazonia. In Thomas A. Gregor and Donald Tuzin (eds) *Gender in Amazonia and Melanesia: An Exploration of the Comparative Method*, pp. 337–43. Berkeley: University of California Press.

2001. Cannibalism. *International Encyclopedia of the Social and Behavioral Sciences. Volume 3*. Neil J. Smelser and Paul B. Baltes (eds), pp. 1452–4. Amsterdam: Elsevier Science Limited.

2001. Research Ethics, Cross-Cultural Dimensions of. *International Encyclopedia of the Social and Behavioral Sciences. Volume 19*. Neil J. Smelser and Paul B. Baltes (eds), pp. 13 231–5. Amsterdam: Elsevier Science Limited.

2004. Male Bonding. *The Encyclopedia of Men and Masculinities.* Amy Aronson and Michael S. Kimmel (eds), pp. 488–9. Santa Barbara, Calif.: ABC-CLIO.

2006. Cults, Shrines and the Emergence of Regional Ritual Centers: The View from New Guinea. In David Alon and Thomas E. Levy (eds) *Archaeology, Anthropology and Cult. Volume 2: The Sanctuary of Gilat (Israel)*, pp. 34–53. London: Equinox.

2006. Base Notes: Odor, Breath, and Moral Contagion in Ilahita. In James Drobnick (ed.) *The Smell Culture Reader*, pp. 59–67. Oxford: Berg.

Other

1998. Comment on Michael F. Brown's 'Can Culture Be Copyrighted?'. *Current Anthropology* 39(2):217–18.

2001. In Memoriam: Derek Freeman, 1916–2001. Association for Social Anthropology in Oceania. *Newsletter* (110):17–18.

2001. Death Notice: Derek Freeman. *Anthropology News* 42(8):26.

2002. Derek Freeman (1916–2001). *American Anthropologist* 104:1013–15.

2002. Derek Freeman Remembrance. *Borneo Research Bulletin* 33:12–13.

www.ingramcontent.com/pod-product-compliance
Lightning Source LLC
Chambersburg PA
CBHW061242270326
41928CB00041B/3374